Mallarmé in the Twentieth Century

Mallarmé in the Twentieth Century

Edited by
Robert Greer Cohn

Associate Editor
Gerald Gillespie

Madison • Teaneck
Fairleigh Dickinson University Press
London: Associated University Presses

© 1998 by Associated University Presses, Inc.

All rights reserved. Authorization to photocopy items for internal or personal use, or the internal or personal use of specific clients, is granted by the copyright owner, provided that a base fee of $10.00, plus eight cents per page, per copy is paid directly to the Copyright Clearance Center, 222 Rosewood Drive, Danvers, Massachusetts 01923. [0-8386-3795-7/98 $10.00+8¢ pp, pc.]

Associated University Presses
440 Forsgate Drive
Cranbury, NJ 08512

Associated University Presses
16 Barter Street
London WC1A 2AH, England

Associated University Presses
P.O. Box 338, Port Credit
Mississauga, Ontario
Canada L5G 4L8

The paper used in this publication meets the requirements of the American National Standard for Permanence of Paper for Printed Library Materials Z39.48-1984.

Library of Congress Cataloging-in-Publication Data

Mallarmé in the twentieth century / edited by Robert Greer Cohn ; associate editor, Gerald Gillespie.
    p.   cm.
  Includes bibliographical references.
  ISBN 0-8386-3795-7 (alk. paper)
  1. Mallarmé, Stéphane, 1842–1898—Criticism and interpretation. I. Cohn, Robert Greer. II. Gillespie, Gerald Ernest Paul, 1933–
PQ2344.Z5M264 1998
841'.8—dc21   98-2933
                                                                                        CIP

PRINTED IN THE UNITED STATES OF AMERICA

Contents

Translated by RICHARD WILBUR
   Sea Breeze   7
Editor's Preface   9

Part I: Primary Aspects of Mallarmé

MICHEL DEGUY
   The Energy of Despair   19
JULIA KRISTEVA
   The Revolt of Mallarmé   31
ALBERT COOK
   "Etendre, simplifier le monde": The Philosophical
   Purchase of Mallarmé   53
MARY ANN CAWS
   Mallarmé's Progeny   86
CHARLES R. LYONS
   Mallarmé and Representation in the Theater   92
ALBERT SONNENFELD
   Mallarmé and His Musicians Webern and Boulez   104

Part II: On His Texts

OCTAVIO PAZ
   Commentary on the "Sonnet in IX" of Mallarmé   119
ANNA BALAKIAN
   Hérodiade and Virtual Reality   131
TAKEO KAWASE
   A Crisis before "the Crisis": On Mallarmé's "Les
   Fenêtres"   143

Part III: On Translating Mallarmé

JUDD D. HUBERT
   Mallarmé and Critic-Friendly Translators   159

KENNETH FIELDS
  Mallarmé's Humility: "Quelle soie aux baumes de
  temps..."   167
WALTER MARTIN
  Scratching the Adamant   176

Part IV: On the Poet's Influence
WILLIAM CARPENTER
  "Le Livre" of Mallarmé and James Joyce's *Ulysses*   187
JOHN FELSTINER
  "Here we go round the prickly pear" or "Your song,
  what does it know?" Celan vis-à-vis Mallarmé   203
GERALD GILLESPIE
  Mallarmé and Germany   212
MICHAEL P. PREDMORE
  Mallarmé's Hispanic Heirs   221

Part V: On an Affinity and an Indigestion
ROMAN DOUBROVKINE
  Leo Tolstoy, Mallarmé, and "The Sickness of Our
  Time"   235
PATRICIA TERRY
  Mallarmé and Basho   264

Part VI: On the Whole
ROBERT GREER COHN
  Mallarmé's Wake   277

Contributors   296

Sea Breeze

RICHARD WILBUR'S TRANSLATION OF "BRISE MARINE,"
WRITTEN FOR THE CENTENARY OF STÉPHANE MALLARMÉ

The flesh grows weary. And books, I've read them all.
Off, then, to where I glimpse through spray and squall
Strange birds delighting in their unknown skies!
No antique gardens mirrored in my eyes
Can stay my sea-changed spirit, nor the light
Of my abstracted lamp which shines (O Night!)
On the guardian whiteness of the empty sheet,
Nor the young wife who gives the babe her teat.
Come, ship, whose masts now gently rock and sway,
Raise anchor for a stranger world! Away!

Now strange that Boredom, all its hopes run dry,
Still dreams of handkerchiefs that wave goodbye!
Those gale-inviting masts might creak and bend
In seas where many a craft has met its end,
Dismasted, lost, with no green island near it . . .
But hear the sailors singing, O my spirit!

Editor's Preface

Who seeks, in the dying days of the twentieth century, one hundred years after his own departure, Mallarmé?

Qui cherche . . . / Verlaine? Il est caché parmi l'herbe, Verlaine . . .
("Tombeau")[1]

[Who seeks . . . / Verlaine? He's hidden amid the grass, Verlaine . . .]
(Tomb)

Herbe et verbe. The green and the wooly whiteness in his name are intimately bound up with the grass, the sheep in a meadow, and the clouds of a summer day, as in "L'Echelonnement des haies" (set by Debussy):

> Des arbres et des moulins
> Sont légers sur le vert tendre . . .
> Dans ce vague d'un Dimanche
> Voici se jouer aussi
> De grandes brebis aussi
> Douces que leur laine blanche . . .
>
> [Some trees and mills
> Are light on the tender green . . .
> In this vagueness of a Sunday
> One sees also playing
> Big sheep just as
> Gentle as their white wool . . .]

Mallarmé was in this mood when he wrote:

> Simple, tendre, aux prés se mêlant
> Ce que tout buisson a de laine
> Quand a passé le troupeau blanc
> Semble l'âme de Madeleine
>
> [Simple, tender, mingling in the meadows
> What every bush has of wool

> When the white flock has passed
> Seems the soul of Madeleine.]

"This divine name, *Hérodiade*. The little inspiration I had I owe to this name . . ."[2]

"The Word remains more massively bound to nature" (522).

"To be really man or nature when thinking, one must think with one's whole body."[3]

Geneviève, his daughter, said that nature was what he loved most. Yes, the nature of a poet.

In this humble-as-a-lamb, much-abused, "referent," at the core of existence, we seek and find the Mallarmé we *know* and cherish: the poet of "simplement la vie, vierge" ("Sur Poe," 872).

Marcel Proust later spoke of *la vraie vie* as his artistic aim: In the wasting years of his middle age, as youth disappeared, he heard a train whistle in the night that pierced through to his soul—recorded in the first pages of *A la recherche du temps perdu*—and his vanishing world sprang afresh with the incipient meaning and shape of his Work.

Later, as he lay daydreaming he remembered the buttercups in the meadows along the way to Guermantes, their childish wholesomeness—*boutons d'or*—telling us something essential about what Scott Moncrieff missed in his style. They are tiny bubbles of life's fountain, microcosms of his ambitious totality, monumentally saved from the death of all he cared about most. Mallarmé's "gem intact from the disaster" (*Hamlet*).

> At the source of the longest river
> The voice of the hidden waterfall
> And the children in the apple-tree.
> (T. S. Eliot, "Little Gidding")

At this juncture one thinks, too, of Charles Baudelaire, whose poignant imagery surely got through Mallarmé's defenses. At a crucial inner crossroads between a nostalgic old Paris and a modern one a-borning and, in another direction, between gravity and grace, in "Le Cygne," he came alive with the expansiveness of his vision, in his crystallizing midriff where his "chers souvenirs sont plus lourds que des rocs"—pregnant with a world.

In his deeply commemorative sonnet on him, again Mallarmé took his cue from the dead poet's name: eighteen b's bubble forth: "B . . . sens, divers et cependant liés secrètement tous, de production ou enfantement, de fécondité, d'amplitude, de bouffissure et de courbure" (*Les Mots anglais*, 928–29) [B. . . diverse senses, but all secretly joined, of production, childbearing, fecundity, of amplitude, of puffing out and of curvedness] (English words).

Most readers know of Mallarmé as the leader of the Symbolist movement and the author of *L'Après-midi d'un Faune* (The Afternoon of a Faun), which powerfully influenced modern music through Debussy. They may be aware of his friendship and kinship with major Impressionists—like them, he eliminated all but light, essential touches, vibrant "suggestions," from his pure white pages—and of his influence on all sorts of moderns, from Proust and Valéry to Yeats, Eliot, Joyce, Faulkner, Picasso, Apollinaire, Matisse, and Boulez.

The public is less likely to know that practically all the major critics of our time have assigned him a central role in the formation of the twentieth-century mindset altogether. Edmund Wilson and Hugh Kenner compared him to Einstein in this sense; George Steiner sees him as sharing the pivotal spotlight with Heidegger and Rilke; Sartre, Blanchot, Barthes, Foucault, Bachelard, and Richard essentially concur in this exuberant assessment.

How can we explain this elite magnification along with widespread indifference or ignorance on the part of the literate masses? Easily. His mature work, like that of Joyce (who was deeply influenced by him), is very intricate and difficult. And there is another subtler aspect of the problem: few are equipped to appreciate the plenitude of his vision, which seems to follow Pascal's prescription for genius: "Touch both extremes simultaneously" and involves a globe-shaped ("multipolar") nexus of polarity dimensions crisscrossing in every direction, that is, complex and simple, totally lucid and naive, transcendent and volcanically sensual (like his Faun); free and obedient (in the Nietzsche sense); sacred and profane (echoing Leonardo), male and female, right brain and left (artistic-intuitive and rational—"scientific," à la Dante, Donne, Goethe), deeply and demonically late-Romantic and still sanely classic, dark and light, warm and cold, mobile and static, continuous and discontinuous, tragic and comic, musical and literary ("La Musique et les Lettres").

What makes this soul-stretching generosity of spirit especially more problematic for many is that all the opposing poles not only tend to converge in a union of opposites, but they also startlingly change places at times, as in real hidden life: pain from pleasure, motion from rest, male from female, and so on. His "Supreme Game" is sparklingly alive, vibrant, rife with paradox and ambivalence. And, yet, as we approach with him—at whatever varying distance in varying readers—a certain magnetic zone and sense, however waveringly, that we are "on to something," "latch on" to an Edenic vision, a lodestar—"vers/UNE CONSTELLATION" (*Un Coup de Dés*, 477)—way out there in space-time, if we are lucky, the inkling of a cosmic faith mercifully takes over and begins to resolve the diverse splits in being, offering the "promise of wholeness" that Flannery O'Connor glimpsed in her favorite art.

We know that in music or painting, like Mozart's or Vermeer's, an awe-struck admirer may not be able to parse a single note or stroke, yet a sense of the "real thing" may seize that person unawares. Like Einstein, somehow Mallarmé gets through in glimpses of exquisite light that are apt to cause "conversions," or at least a certain marveling respect such as Valéry's, who saw him as the "purest writer who ever held a pen." Indeed, there are now, at the different levels of consciousness—more or less intuitive—thousands of sophisticated and/or naive readers around the world—throughout the Americas, Europe, Japan—who acknowledge that powerful presence and its durability.

Among those readers, a number of the most distinguished and *literary* were invited to participate in this volume honoring the centenary of Mallarmé's death. They illustrate the universality and interdisciplinary impact of Mallarmé's influence as groundbreaking poet and thinker.

The *fons et origo* of the project was the Mallarmé Festival held at Stanford University, from 27 to 29 October 1996—proposed by the eminent comparatist Ricardo Quinones and organized and hosted by Robert Greer Cohn, author of various books on Mallarmé and editor of the present one.

Professor Gerald Gillespie, president of the International Association of Comparative Literature and professor of German Studies and Comparative Literature at Stanford, is the associate editor.

The Editorial Advisory Board is made up of Professor Mary Ann Caws, Chair of the CUNY Graduate Center French Department, Gerald Gillespie, and Judd Hubert, Professor Emeritus of French, University of California, Irvine.

Warm thanks are offered here to our sponsors, Professor Quinones and Professor Ralph Hester, chairman of the Department of French and Italian at Stanford, and Emmanuel Delloye, French cultural attaché at San Francisco, who has offered generous support, financial and personal. Katarina Kivel is immensely responsible for the proper presentation of the publication. It is hard to imagine its existence without her judgment and varied skills.

Professor Akitoshi Nagahata, Nagoya University, Japan, was extremely helpful in locating and translating the unpublished article of Takeo Kawase.

Joy Conlon translated Octavio Paz's essay. The Spanish version is in his *Obras completas* (Barcelona, Spain: Circolo de lectores, 1994), volume 2, pages 100–114.

The German language translation of the poem "Rondel" by Mallarmé, is that of Paul Celan in *Gesammelte Werke* (©Suhrkamp Verlag, Frankfurt am Main, 1983) and is published with the permission of the publisher in the article by John Felstiner.

An excerpt from Stéphane Mallarmé, *Collected Poems*, translation and commentary by Henry Weinfield (© 1994 The Regents of the University of California) is published with the permission of the publisher in the article by Judd Hubert.

"Mallarmés Wake" appeared in a slightly different version in *New Literary History*, volume 26, number 4. It sums up my overview of Mallarmé at the end of my career. I am grateful to the editor for permission to reprint it here.

Notes

1. Stéphane Mallarmé, *Oeuvres complètes*, ed. Henri Mondor and G. Jean-Aubry (Paris: Gallimard-Pléiade, 1945), 71. (Subsequent references indicated within parentheses.)
2. Stéphane Mallarmé, *Correspondance, 1862–1871*, ed. Henri Mondor and Lloyd James Austin (Paris: Gallimard, 1959), 154. (Hereafter cited as *Corr.*)
3. *Corr.*, 353.

Mallarmé
in the
Twentieth Century

I
Primary Aspects of Mallarmé

The Energy of Despair
Michel Deguy

FRENCH criticism of recent years has scarcely let go of Mallarmé. Since the decisive work of J. P. Richard and J. Derrida, a good number of essays have been devoted to him: from J. L. Backès to A. Badiou, P. Bénichou, J. Rancière, Y. Bonnefoy—not to mention much university research upon which these renewed readings rely (in particular "Anglo-Saxon" research, as we call it, which I salute in passing).

My intention is not to add something new to all this (could I, even if I really wanted to?), and if I first considered presenting the exercise of analyzing *one* poem, a sort of "lesson," I quickly gave up that project. Instead I decided to present *myself* as a French fin de siècle poet (and why not *fin de millénaire*, while I am about it?)—a French fin de siècle or *fin de millénaire* poet who asks himself what he has learned, received, and integrated from Stéphane Mallarmé through his own poetic art.

Quite likely there will always be room for augmenting and refining analytical readings, paraphrasing and glossing Mallarmé's poems, and I will give a small example below. But since I have just used the term "paraphrase," I am going to pause for a moment, just long enough to venture an axiom that runs counter to the *doxa:* the poem *is* paraphrasable, or "translatable," to stay with today's contemporary corpus—J. Rancière or Y. Bonnefoy—defying, dilating, and undoing Mallarmé's extreme condensation, Mallarmé's work of which the possible commentary is indefinitely open. There is no reading of the poem without the mediation of interminable paraphrase, linking this or that obscurely finite syntagm with the text that surrounds it, linking it to its library and to the Library of Babel that it augments. There is no *immediate* relation to poetry. No more than there is one between poetry and "things"— and one is always astonished at the illusion of popular belief in the "immediate."

My (small) addition to the commentaries, very simply and free of any polemic because the reading of Mallarmé will never be finished, is the following: Recently, having picked up P. Bénichou's *Selon Mallarmé*[1] once again, and considering a given page, for example the 277th, which offers a commentary on the 1887 sonnet "Tout orgueil fume-t'il du soir," I noticed that the attention Bénichou pays to "console" (the last word of the poem) applied to describing the small piece of furniture with its marble, brought with it no development on the seme of *consolation*. Yet, the grammar is not opposed to the last word of the poem having the value of a verb in the third-person indicative present, with the "fulgurante" as subject (even if, of course, this semantic trail offers little sense or interest). But even if this reading were impossible (in the sense of a mediocre impasse in the labyrinth), it responds to the undeniable fact that the francophone reader hears and understands consolation in "console," particularly when it is a matter of a poem on death and grieving. The absence of consolation resonates around the term of "console," preceded thirteen syllables earlier by a negation ("ne . . . console"). Many words hold in reserve an effect of allegory in the depth and texture of such homonymy, if I may say, which their etymology contains, saying in effect something else (allegory) at the same time as what they seem to be saying uniquely. This will be R. Roussel's procedure, but it is first and foremost the proceeding/process of the poem or rhyme. And perhaps we might speak of an oxymoronic effect if the same (*le même*) in words comes to be rescinded in new readings until the antonymical idea can be brought into play: its underside, its other. Here, in my example, the inconsolable beneath the console. The verse is the preterition of an underside, of the other side.

Having opened up the 1995 Bénichou volume again—such a useful book for teaching, which lives on paraphrases, useful because of its minutiae and its very deliberate platitude (and my object here is neither to correct it nor to speak ill of it)— I might take up his conclusion for debate. Or, at the very least, I might indicate that for me "the lesson" of Mallarmé ("mes bouquins refermés sur le nom de Stéphane") is found in a direction and a vanishing point for which Bénichou's "conclusions" ring too negatively, in a too-simple sense of "negation," precisely that from which Mallarmé taught us to disengage ourselves. There is no failure of Mallarmé. There is only a general failure, that of all, which this word assigns with its broad gesture, which subsumes and subjugates any relative opposition between "success" and "failure," that of the Mallarméan sentence: "Ratés nous le sommes, tous"; or that of a definitively antinomical formula, intrinsically thwarted, tied up, blocked, but *not prevented,* which I might risk as follows: Poetry is a check to the victory of death.

But Bénichou speaks of "untenable extremity," of "violent contradiction," of an "impasse where poetry exhausts itself," of "a logical development of Romantic disenchantment" (382 et seq.), formulae with which I would be inclined to agree if they allowed that the impasse is our passing and our sojourn, our dwelling. And to say it all, Bénichou is just too keen to keep Mallarmé in the age of romanticism. Yet I share Bénichou's thought as he completes his book (*Selon Mallarmé*) by writing that we have today reached the point where no one knows what humanity will become, and even less so, what will become of poetry. But I do not think for a moment that hope ("the hope of a harmonious unity of humankind" [389]) would be an issue "opening a new horizon to poetry." Mallarmé did not think that. And the development of telecommunications or technologies of image synthesis does not render Mallarmé's thought obsolete and should not authorize us to begin again with utopian ideology. What he calls impasse is the issue; the summit is the exit for a climber and what is particular to the summit is that it is the whole of the impasse.

I would speak rather of the "energy of despair."

And just what is this energy of despair in poetry and in the poem, in language, as we say? To be "in poetry" means to be more deeply within language, to be more closely bound up in language, more immanent to language, to that language of language in which the poem consists, more bound up in the procedures, the turnings ("les tournures"), which characterize and fashion its proceeding, if you will. This is not at all a "formalist" way of seeing and saying things, for the things of poetry depend precisely on the recognition that in poetry form and content do not fall away from each other, but rather their tenor consists in a *contenance*— a containing and a disposition. Language with poetry does not lose, but rather gains, a countenance.

And Mallarmé is a model of this. A model, then, of manner that produces in the poem "the energy of this despair," which culminates in the book. I cannot leave him alone now. Let us start with some broad generalities. To begin with, Mallarmé operates a tightening up, a bringing together or a *rapprochement* —a term that will acquire a central importance for the next generation (Saint-Pol Roux, Reverdy), that of the presurrealists—of things that were altogether too separated before him, things such as "form" and "content," still so distant from one another, or, to take up another mode of separation once again, that between prose and poem. These are modalities of the general Mallarméan rapprochement that I am looking at: a tightening-up that brings poetry into the syntactical and terminological workings of language. He adds a tightening, he infinitizes the transition, the "in-between" between these two (prose and poem), like a microscopy in physics, always more discriminating, picking out, inventing finite species between too separate genres, a work of fine discrimination carried out right up to today by optical instruments, picking out or inventing "missing links."

And we must first apply to him and to his entire work this tightening-up that I am invoking. That is to say, we should follow Yves Bonnefoy's current rereading,[2] which consists of reattributing Mallarmé's minor works to him and reintegrating the poems of circumstance to the grand oeuvre. And not only would I willingly insist upon this more strongly than does Bénichou, who only tends toward it, but I would argue that perhaps even Bonnefoy himself still maintains (as is my hypothesis) too much distance, too much reserve between the major poems and the so-called "frivolous pieces" (cf. his preface to the 1995 volume).

If Mallarmé reduces separation (or brings closer), do we not find in this an incitation, first of all, in our own readings, not to separate too absolutely this or that small piece (addresses that found their destination thanks to the post), this or that compliment or dedication, and this or that versification, which has its place in the principal volume? (I must confess that I have found more pleasure and profit among the envelopes and albums than among the piles of so-called youthful alexandrines.) And what difference can subsist between a certain *petit air,* or an *éventail* with its proper names and its punning, its "prosaisms," and its virtuosities, and a given "poème de circonstance," galet or chocolat, where the poetic correspondences become part of the correspondence of the poet?

Any poem is a poem of circumstance (circumstances are eternal, says the *Coup de Dés*). What happens in the workshop of the poem of circumstance? The proper name becomes more common there; the common name becomes proper (and *bracelet* becomes more proper, if I may say so, for rhyming with *ce l'est*). The significations become more intense and, through them, meaning. According to the Saussurean lexicon that is current, the signifier and the signified live more intimately their *indivision*. The phonematic and the semantic dimensions multiply their value through the paranomasis. A "name" (Vasco or Degas, Paphos or Puvis) becomes the augury of its meaning. We might say that the demands and the effects of rhyme are communicated to the whole verse: the obsession of its "holorhyme" in absentia doubles up the line, a broad hypogram searches itself out, disseminated throughout the stanza, the poem mints a cryptogram, "mot de l'énigme."

To this example of the proper name becoming an "allegory of itself" (and we recall that this expression comes to subtitle the "Sonnet en YX"), an allegorizing dynamic is added (if I take allegory as the saying-something-else of a given utterance), and this gets communicated to literality: There is allegory everywhere that there is a signifier. It results from this general meaning, and the (various) significations are less disjointed: There is "sense" because the meanings get played out more intensely in and through the poem. So it is that the counter-sense, the antonym, may rhyme mutely with the sense. The same is divided within itself, or, if you prefer, and to make an allusion to Freud reading Abel, the intimate contrariety of a "word" potentially unfolds itself. "Its" oxymoron, if I may say, comes to haunt it. An air of reenchantment of the world comes into play again, locally. Hail to the good enchanter!

Now I will come back to the general motif of a tightening-up, or rapprochement, by transporting and transposing it very broadly into the following two perspectives: prose and poetry, and *le rien* (nothingness)

Prose and Poetry

The prose—the phrase—of Mallarmé is transformed by the verse, that is, by the poetics of the poem. Not that it consists, we know this, in some kind of prosody made up of "feet," of rhythmic cells reiterated without rhyme, but rather because the turns, tropes, and turns of phrase, or however we might put it, of condensation or of "tmesis" (of conjunction and of disjunction in general), all that the term of "obscurity" that we employ to designate the regime of acceleration and of slowing-down, of nomination and of periphrase, of "thunder" and of leap of Mallarmé's poem (cf. Bénichou) is at work in his "prose"—including the play of all registers of punctuation, with the white of the page: the same obscurity as in that which is given as "poetries" and as "proses." The poem is "in prose." The most famous example is *Un Coup de Dés*. Symmetrically, we might say, and as a necessary counterpart, prosaism invades the poem in a familiar tone or through humor such as the smoke of a cigar invades the room. For example, a miniscule sample, which bears on the lexicon: "mes *bouquins* refermés sur le nom de Paphos" (my books closed on the name of Paphos); or the procedure of making an enclave in the stanza for this or that padding of a ready-made locution or expression familiar to ordinary exchange: "sans se faire autrement de bile" / "s'il survenait par le couloir" / "m'introduire dans ton histoire" (without getting worked up otherwise / if he dropped in through the corridor / to get myself into your story). And this goes for the precious turn of phrase that Molière mocked—as in *Un Coup de Dés:* "le papier blême de tant d'audace" (the paper blanched from such audacity)—which was and may still be made fun of in schools, only making a return, a comeback, in the ironized prose poem, in a wink risked with a smile through the mouth of a recitant.

Mallarmé invents a text, a textual space "between" the "on the one hand" of the poem disposed (justified) as a poem (be it in regular or in free verse) and the "on the other hand" of ordinary prose where phrases with indeterminate syllabic counts get strung together. This intermediate space, or text, is directed by the two fundamental procedures of the poem: that of the multiplication of the "isotopy" or multivocity (I will explain) and that of the indented.

1. The reader opens *Un Coup de Dés* and reads, for example, on the third page, the line, "et couvrant les jaillissements" (and covering the spurtings). Can one couvrir des jaillissements (cover spurtings) the ordinary francophone user of the Larousse wonders. And is that not just the ordinary reproach made to poetry and to its obscurity (even if the example that I have chosen is relatively simple). As though the ordinary register of a term, of a "verb," for example, limited it to the restricted entourage of its habitual complements: We cover silence or the roof, for example, and after enumerating a few items, we have made a list of what we can (and therefore *may only*) cover. The poetic usage consists then in an "abstraction." I mean it consists in the elevation of the word to its "notion," the most generous or general seme, in such a way as to spread out, augment its regime, its suzerainty, the court of its complements, if you wish, expanding throughout the dictionary. And so it is now that we can cover up spurtings, "couvrir des jaillissements." This is what I am calling the multiplication of the isotopy. The "action restreinte" of the poem (its restricted or restrained action), is *illimiting*.

2. Lower down on the same page of *Un Coup de Dés*, we read this line: "d'un bâtiment." Why is it isolated? And we have, first of all, as an incipit in very bold characters, JAMAIS. What commands the relative autarchy of this or that line, the arbitrariness of its isolation?

As we know, *Un Coup de Dés* gets banalized: A few years later, dedramatized by Cendrars, it comes to give the scalar dimension of the prosaic until (this is today) any sentence in ordinary prose, cut up, "à la ligne" according to (for example) "logical analysis" obtains a place in the whiteness of the page. And to finish, it is the syntax that gets entrusted to the blankness, frequently by authors who "cover" their ignorance that way, through the mute emphasis of silence! The posterity of *Un Coup de Dés* is journalistic publicity.

Le rien—Nothings and Nothingness (From Nothingness to Nothings or of the Everyday Whole)

Rien, cette écume, vierge vers

Mallarmé introduces zero into the poetic calculus. The Mallarméan toast, in just the same way as the equation equals a polynomial to zero, turns and turns over things through their names to nothingness. Haunted by "elevation," which in the Catholic rite turns the offering toward the Absent, the operation implies a bringing-together (composing, with a bouquet-gesture that discerns and gathers); a bringing-to-glory (exalting, elevating); an offering, a returning to nothing; for nothing. It absents in order to render unto Absence. We may understand the program in this passage from the "Nénuphar blanc":

> Résumer d'un regard la vierge absence éparse en cette solitude, et, comme on cueille en mémoire d'un site, l'un de ces magiques nénuphars clos qui y surgissent tout à coup, enveloppant de leur creuse blancheur un rien, fait de songes intacts, du bonheur qui n'aura pas lieu et de mon souffle ici retenu dans la peur d'une apparition / . . . /.

> [Summing up with one look the sparse virgin absence in this solitude, and as one might gather in the memory of a site, one of these magic closed water lilies which surge up there all of a sudden, enveloping with their hollow whiteness a nothing, made of intact dreams, of the happiness that will not have been and of my breath here held in fear of an apparition / . . . /]

"Nothingness," with Mallarmé, oscillates between Nothing and something-which-is-nothing, "a nothing." It is nothing, we say in order to say *something*: "Rien, cette écume." So, it is a matter of *proportioning one's life to nothingness, by means of the work*, a

Mallarméan task (this is one of the propositions that might be drawn from the famous statement, "Destruction was my Beatrice"), so I will say that Nothingness, which is one of the names of the Whole (All, or Nothing), passes better through small nothings, sweet nothings, the nothings of life or "circumstances" in the equation of the thought that "annuls" them—than through anyTHING else.

Let us continue. The "whole," that correlate of thought, which thought cannot "totalize," that is to say, cannot grasp "itself," only allows itself to be taken in a relation (taking place in some way) through nothingness. *Pars pro toto* is the formula, the "totum" being "the whole" of a thing (e.g. a "vessel," where "sail" can be put *for* the vessel); or this *whole* for the big *Whole* that Baudelaire calls an "infinite diminutive" (e.g., the immensity of the ocean with the fold of sky at the horizon); or the whole *through* nothingness. It is only insofar as the part (*pars*) is intimately linked up with nothingness (in the risk of annihilation, that "as nothing" it will disappear) that it is so-related to the whole (*pro toto*). "The whole," *All* can only enter into the real by means of calculation with the "or-nothing" into which it can change itself. We are the relation with the whole in the part when it is nothing that is at stake. *Partout—par tout*. It is all for nothing, "pour un rien."

The question is that of disappearing. It is not a matter of making disappear, purely and simply, but of making-disappear-in-order-to-reappear-as-or-in-something else. My breath is held, says the poet, in fear of an apparition. This is the strict signaling of his rigorously "phenomeno-logical" posture. Because no word is for Mallarmé simply "negative," *fear* is here the name of the attention of the word ("breath") turned toward things ("apparition"). From the "Apparition" of 1864 (a poem that was published only in 1883), which says "Tu m'es en riant apparue" (You appeared to me laughing) in the twelfth verse, to that "fear" in which inspiration (the poem) is held back, Mallarmé's "art poétique" hollows itself out (the hollow making a place for emptiness, which is one of the names of the "sensation" of nothingness): from a certain belief in the possibility of simple astonishment, the possibility of the positivity of an "apparition," like that of a desired woman who may be present "herself," right up to and including the negative formula for the dancer, "extatique impuissance à disparaître" (ecstatic impotence to disappear), who is not a woman, and who does not dance (no more than the Demoiselles d'Avignon are women and are prostituting themselves).

From description to definition, the paradoxical double negation inserts disappearance between simple apparition and reappearance-*as* (as a Néréide, for example, in the case, if I can put it that way, of Madame de Guermantes by Marcel).

"Avec *comme* pour langage / Rien (qu'un battement aux cieux)" (With *as* for language / Nothing but a beating in the skies)—I take pleasure in reading the *Eventail* of 1891 as a monostiche, as an *art poétique* that would propose the "langage du comme" or Nothingness. What is this "logis très précieux"? The intimacy of Madame's little world? The sojourn offered by her apartment? Or is this the whole earthly world that Corneille called "cet amas de merveilles" (this heaping of marvels)? The Mallarméan poem causes, for example, the dancer to disappear for its reapparition as "metaphor" (in a figure), that is to say, as itself with others, with its others ("glaive, coupe, oiseau," etc.)—a sort of return to the same through negation of the dancer or a return to the figure of the dance through the abstraction of its property (properties). This changes everything, while changing nothing. In its "autrement dit" (otherwise said) or "allegory" it causes disappearance, and the oxymoron is like the short-cut (the condensed version) of a metamorphosis in its course, a reversible metamorphosis from one extreme to the other, between the names of those extremes.

A thing disappears as it has appeared, or appears as it disappeared. The appearing depends on, or is contained in, this vibration disappearing/appearing on the flail of the *comme* (like-or-as) of comparison. The appearing as a *trans-appearance* (the French verb *transparaître* suggests this) takes and loses countenance, consistence, and measure in an oscillation/vibration where appearing and disappearing, apparition and disappearance, are laced together around the like-or-as of comparison. This is clear whether I follow the formula, "He disappears as he appeared" (which, again, is reversible), or another formula, "disparaître par où il est apparu" (he disappeared from whence he came), and again, this is reversible. Would disappearing in appearing (Baudelaire's *beauté fugitive*) and the apparition in the disappearance (Emmaüs), be reversible, equivalent formulations of the "phenomenon"? This would have to be analyzed very painstakingly, with multiple examples, taken from many poems.

And what would the operation reveal for us today, and what about in a century? This means that the palinody, in its change of tone, does not lose, at least not purely and simply, that which it reverses. The song draws the superstition of incantation right along to its loss. After having done this to all the diverse beliefs and illusions, which the chant included, it accompanies their swing toward? Doesn't conducting opinions to their perishing, drowning them in song, imply that we take them with us, that we make them dance until they drop, turning them over, but as what?

Mallarmé has become legendary. A poet becomes, through the "legend," the poet that he does not appear to be. Quite a number of French poets of the preceding fin de siècle have passed into legend. What is Mallarmé's legend? For us, his figure is an extraordinarily moving one. From Tournon to Valvins, it is enough to "make us cry," thanks to Henri Mondor (thanks are due to Henri Mondor and to the tomes of correspondence)—cry with admiration and respect and sympathy before the rigor, the fidelity, the insomniac elaboration of the great poetic calculus, the sweet and implacable energy of despair, in friendship, love, before human fraternity, the lucidity without the slightest resentment, the devotion (to choose a word from Rimbaud, not from Tartuffe)—the devotion to the idea of poetry. In conclusion, I would like to make an allusion to all of this from a single angle: that which coalesces in Mallarmé's "self-portrait as Edgar Poe," if I dare put it that way. And if we are increasing our efforts and the attention given to the famous "donner un sens plus pur aux mots de la tribu" (giving a purer sense to the words of the tribe)—these are not *other* words, not *other* phrases, not another *speech,* there is no need for another "linguistics" to approach them; nothing more, really, than our idiom and definitely not a "special language"— it is because today an unprecedented threat is pressing down on our "s'entre-parler" our speaking-among,-amidst,-between. To *resist,* following one of today's most insistent motifs, is to construct something that resists, in order that it should resist. It is making a work, and a well-worked, well-constructed work, thinking of the work as an ark—if we follow the Baudelairean parable of the deluge—an ark capable of transport, able to transport "things" in a transportable artifact. A painter never ceases depicting: He has to make the visible pass *as* and, certainly, pass into and through himself by means of idiosyncracy and manner; but his aim is not that everything should resemble him. Think of Picasso.

Art is this shipyard, art this ark-yard. There is no final promised land, unless it exists as an illusion of the accessible aim, but there is the measureless ocean, the voyage, the transport. So we construct the drunken boat, "le bateau ivre," to transport that which we desire to pass (on).

With Mallarmé, there is the drawing or *design* ("la destruction fut ma Béatrice"), and there is the beautiful piece of work. How is its sense held together? How is it turned and tightened up, and by what sort of knots is this operation achieved? Put in other terms, an object (Ponge's *objeu*) "Bibelot d'inanité sonore" (trinket of sonorous inanity), no matter what, was worth the blank concern of our canvas. But what is an object today? Is the poem-object still worth it, worth the effort, worth the trouble? How can it be constructed?

Let us take a look at this console, this fan, this wall, this stairway, this chapel, this "diamond." Those who constructed it are dead and forgotten, and NOTHING of their subjectivity has remained. Beauty is the tomb, the common grave, of their "lives." Nothing of it has entered into the constitution of the object; between this angle of marble and their melancholy, there was no direct link. The beautiful object *for others* abolishes all of that. It is the opposite of "memory," the opposite of the souvenir, with its suggestion of the personal and the idiosyncratic, of "miserable secrets."

Are poetic imaginations "maîtresses d'erreur et de fausseté" (mistresses of error and of falsehood?), as our classic writers say? We must begin everything again, with the exception of hope. Revisit, disabuse. Now we must invent poetic arts without ideology, without adolescent utopias, adjust them better to what poetry can (and must?) do. "La poésie doit avoir pour but la vérité pratique" (poetry must have as its aim practical truth), as we like to quote from Ducasse. Perhaps, but we need to ask ourselves again, then (with new philosophical contributions), what practical means here and now? Poetry is neither morality nor politics.

It is likely that poetry does not just make poems. This is no reason for it to become intoxicated at ethnic festivals and international banquets. It is likely that the enigma is still, and always will be, that of fraternity and reciprocity ("hypocrite lecteur"). But today it is the energy of despair that must be exchanged for paradoxes, impossibilities, in playful sobriety. Poetry will be neither formalist nor hollow if it desires or aspires to contain everything.

When the loss of all (false) hope is resolved, the question becomes "into what can this loss be transformed?"—for someone who at the bifurcation takes no active part in the management of social transformation. The sequence would then be the following: loss; abandonment of utopia as an avatar of hope; transposition (translation) of loss into a rebound or a ricochet toward an "impossibility" of another type.

Poetry cannot be substituted for revolution. (Political) revolution is necessary to make poetry desired, desirable, to make poetry, and, reciprocally, one cannot take charge of the hopes of the other. They must not deceive each other mutually, nor serve as alibis for one another. Nonetheless, they do hold together, they can transport one another mutually, and one often takes refuge in the other, sometimes in a clandestine manner. They exchange with one another, feed one another, transpose one another. What we call life comes out of a number of hopes, said multiply, rival claims in the good sense of that term. And perhaps we now need a fecund misunderstanding in order that one of the pair might believe that it is making the other, and this, reciprocally.

What is needed is a nonradical conversion, one that can be shared and communicated—a weak conversion, a minimal conversion, within reach of "inauthentic existence," feeling the threat of the worst, similar to what nonviolence was—a conversion that would begin by attaching the coeffcent NO to a certain number of intolerable things: a certain change, and would propose putting on the brakes, blocking, conservation, resistance. But how do we resist the irresistible?

Translated by Christopher Bryan Elson

Notes

1. P. Bénichou, *Selon Mallarmé* (Paris: Gallimard, 1995), 277.
2. Yves Bonnevoy, *Vers de circonstance* (Paris: Gallimard-Poésie, 1995); and *Poésies*, ed. de Bertrand Maréchal (Paris: Gallimard-Poésie, 1992).

The Revolt of Mallarmé
Julia Kristeva

ALREADY more than twenty years have passed since I first scandalized connoisseurs of Symbolist mysteries and Mallarméan ellipses by claiming that the exquisite master of the Rue de Rome had wrought a revolution in poetic language. I fully intend to aggravate my case here, and thereby attempt to justify the scandal, by insisting once again upon the meaning of the Mallarméan revolt. In other words, I have not at all relinquished my former position, and indeed I have recently had the occasion to restate it in the context of my seminar at the University of Paris 7, which has just been published under the title *Sens et non-sens de la révolte.*[1] The analyses of this seminar, while focusing first of all on Freud, then go on to consider three other figures of paradoxical revolt, namely, Aragon, Sartre, and Barthes.

As in *Revolution in Poetic Language,* here I also use the word "revolt" in accordance with its etymological, and Proustian, sense of "return," "displacement," "unveiling," and "change." (I am thinking particularly of the Sanskrit forms in +wel, and of words or expressions such as "volte-face," "the earth's revolution around the sun," "volume" [from "volvere": to roll or to roll up], but also of "vaudeville," with its reference to repetition and to a turning upon itself, and of "omelette," with its reference to turning over.)

From Socrates-Plato to St. Augustine, Western thought affirms that the truth of (the form of) Being preceding human existence can be attained by a movement of retrospection: "se quaerere," "quaesto mihi factus sum." This common destiny of truth, memory, and speech has, after Augustine, found its affirmation in the interior experience that—from prayer to Georges Bataille—never ceases to reveal the scandalous effects of what I mean precisely by a "re-volt." However, this fundamental questioning, this "remembrance of things past," was to lose momentum and, indeed, come to a halt when the re-volt assumed the fixed form of political revolt. To put it succinctly, it would seem that from at least the French revolution on, and under the pressure of technical evolution, revolt has come to mean the substitution of "new values" for old, in such a way that these new values cease to be subjected, in their turn, to a continued questioning. These values come, therefore, to be erected as dogma; indeed, the suspension of revolt—in the sense I define it—constitutes the very logic underlying dogmatism and totalitarianism.

However, the salutary retrospective questioning that I am referring to by the term "revolt" finds an expression in two adventures of the modern era: the Freudian exploration of the unconscious, on the one hand, and certain experiences of poetic language, on the other. Freudian anamnesis is not only a reconstitution of a preexisting truth, but re-creates the mutually incompatible truths of a plural and fragmented subject who no longer seeks a hypothetical unity (in contrast to the believer, for whom such a unity is as though the mirror-image of the God he or she searches: "coram Deo"). In a parallel manner, poetic language, as I understand it, unfolds the apparent meaning of sign and syntax, and, under a provisional and fragile serenity, gives expression to the permanent conflict of psychic life. The notion of the "semiotic" or of a "semiotic modality"[2] was an attempt to elucidate this conflict which is a condition of all psychic life, and finds its laboratory in poetry—again, in the sense I give to this—with its confrontation of different registers: signification/music, paternal/maternal, masculine/feminine, and so on.

Mallarmé was one of those—and, in my mind, the first—who not only practiced poetry as a revolt, but who formulated the stakes of this practice. In this way, he participates in a phenomenon that has profoundly marked European literary experience from German romanticism on, and which I have termed the encounter of modern poetry (and more broadly, literature) with the "impossible." To explain what I mean by this, it is first necessary to specify that, while marked by the Schlegel brothers, Schelling, Hegel, Schopenhauer, and Nietzsche, indeed even by the dramatic lucidity of Hölderlin, and while clearly heralded by the journal *Athenäum* (Berlin, 1798), this encounter nevertheless received its most radical form in French language texts. Here, literature renounces its role of quintessentially beautiful language, or, let us say, as religion's seductive sister, to take up the exploration of the underlying resources of the "word": What to say? How to say it? What is the meaning of "to say"? Of the making and unraveling of sense? From the outset, literature engages in a radical debate, or confrontation (similarity and, then, dissociation), with religion and philosophy, exploring in this way the blockages of consciousness, and allying itself with madness. Additionally, it comes up against the resistance of social reality: not because it disavows this reality but, rather, because in refusing to continue to play the role of reality's reflection, it finally opts for social reality at the expense of the imaginary and, therefore, of literature. We are all familiar with the singular destinies of the poet turned businessman or of the "poète engagé."

In France, this encounter between literature and the impossible has known three moments: the first is that of Rimbaud, Lautréamont, and Mallarmé; the second that of surrealism; and the third, that of "Tel Quel."

As regards Mallarmé, it is in a more meditative, less destructive, manner than Lautréamont, and in a more elliptical manner than Rimbaud, without pathos, on the brink of silence and of depression—his "Beatrice," as he puts it—that he enacts in his texts the "questioning" of which we are speaking. Simultaneously operating both upon memory (his personal as much as the national past) and meaning (the layer of sign and syntax), this questioning extends as far as, and brings into play, the drives' oscillation, preverbal, or transverbal, music, and those limits of nonsense that are *silence* and its paradoxical double, *polysemy*.

The fragmentation of word and syntax, the elimination of their boundaries, and the semanticizing of "insignificant" elements in a new rhythmic and semantic whole: These are the traits that I chose to emphasize in the reading of Mallarmé that I presented in *Revolution in Poetic Language,* following in this respect, in my own fashion, the admirable, and seminal, analyses of Robert Greer Cohn. I would immediately like to underline that it is precisely this process, of the pulverization and the reconstruction of meaning, which constitutes the veritable retrospective return—revolt—by which meaning is opened to its genealogy and rebirth. What Mallarmé invokes under the term of "mystery," or under that of "sacred," is indeed nothing other than this internal re-volt, that can equally be characterized as the gestation of psychic space. This genealogical or gestatory movement is so radical that it exceeds the subject as such; this latter is thereby opened up to an extra-psychical realm and immersed in the very palpitation of Being. Sadly, the psychologizing reader construes this as indifference, coldness, or esotericism.

Formal Re-volt

Let us now review some of Mallarmé's positions concerning this formal revolt and its targets: the unity of the speaking subject, of the referent, and of meaning itself. Previously, I furnished the demonstration of these aspects in analyzing *Prose* and *Un Coup de Dés*. Here, I wish merely to recall the fundamental principles of Mallarmé's operation.

The phonic rhythmicity apparent in Mallarmé's texts—which is simultaneously a semantic rhythmicity, acts primarily to dissolve the univocity of signification and the *position of the denoted object,* in favor of a generalized series of relays and relations that indeed encapsulates language's fundamental specificity.

> Mais la littérature a quelque chose de plus intellectuel que cela; les choses existent, nous n'avons pas à les créer; nous n'avons qu'à en saisir les rapports; et ce sont les fils de ces rapports qui forment les vers et les orchestres.[3]

> [But literature is more of an intellectual thing than that. Things already exist, we don't have to create them; we simply have to see their relationships. It is the threads of those relationships which go to make up poetry and music.]

> Evoquer, dans une ombre exprès, l'objet tu, par des mots allusifs, jamais directs, se réduisant à du silence égal, comporte tentative proche de créer.[4]

> [To evoke, in an intended shadow, the tacit object, by allusive words, never direct, reducing themselves to an equivalent silence, constitutes an attempt near creation.]

> A l'égal de créer: la notion d'un objet, échappant, qui fait défaut.[5]

> [Equal to creating: the notion of an object, escaping, that fails to appear.]

> ... peindre non la chose, mais l'effet qu'elle produit.[6]

> [... paint not the object, but the effect it produces.]

Consequently, the meaning produced by rhythm is necessarily imprecise: "Le sens trop précis rature / Ta vague littérature"[7] (The overly precise meaning crosses out / Your vague literature). This rhythmic division of the object of signification is determined by the *subject's impossibility to position him/herself*:

> Le point de vue où l'on se place, tout en dépend; or, il est multiple et c'est même une succession de points de vue, se reliant entre eux, qui peut, seul, vous faire une conviction à cet égard.[8]

> [Everything depends on the point of view that is adopted. This, however, is not only multiple, but indeed, it is only through the succession

of different points of view, linked one to the other, that any conviction can take form.]

Mallarmé describes the poet as "voué à un travail de mosaïque point rectiligne. Trop de régularité nuit"[9] (devoted to a work of mosaic not at all rectilinear. Too much regularity does harm). The text is therefore likened by Mallarmé to a mosaic, which would be harmed by too much regularity and where "Les mots [...] prompts tous, avant extinction, à une réciprocité de feux distante ou présentée de biais comme contingence"[10] (words are all quick, before dying away, to an exchange of fires that is distant, or obliquely presented as contingency). Each and every signified is split up, even if a general orientation, endowed with verisimilitude, remains intact:

> ... subdivisions prismatiques de l'Idée, l'instant de paraître et que dure leur concours, dans quelque mise en scène spirituelle exacte, c'est à des places variables, près ou loin du fil conducteur latent, en raison de la vraisemblance, que s'impose le texte.[11]

> [... prismatic subdivisions of the idea, the instant when they appear and during which their cooperation lasts, in some exact mental setting. The text imposes itself in various places, near or far from the latent guiding thread, according to what seems to be the probable sense.]

If this rhythm is what Mallarmé calls "mystery," it is no less constitutive of meaning: "Mystère ou n'est-ce pas le contexte évolutif de l'Idée"[12] (Mystery or perhaps the evolutive context of the idea).

> Tout l'acte disponible, à jamais et seulement, reste de saisir les rapports, entre temps, rares ou multipliés; d'après quelque état intérieur et que l'on veuille à son gré étendre, simplifier le monde.[13]

> [The whole available act, forever and only, remains to seize relations, between times, scarce or multiple according to some interior state and, willfully, whimsically, extend, simplify the world.]

Or, in even more explicit terms:

> ... l'ambiguïté de quelques figures belles, aux intersections. *La totale arabesque* qui les *relie,* a de vertigineuses sautes en un effroi que reconnue; et d'anxieux accords. Avertissant par tel écart, au lieu de déconcerter, ou que sa similitude avec elle-même, la soustraie en la confondant. *Chiffration mélodique tue, de ces motifs qui composent*

une logique, avec nos fibres. [. . .] nulle torsion vaincue ne fausse ni ne transgresse l'omniprésente Ligne espacée de tout point a tout autre pour instituer l'idée; sinon sous le visage humain, mystérieuse, en tant qu'une Harmonie est pure.[14]

[. . . the ambiguity of a few fine shapes, at the intersections. *The total arabesque,* that *binds* them, makes vertiginous leaps in a barely recognized fright; and anxious resolutions. Alerting by such variation, rather than disconcerting, to its similarity with itself, withdraws it while confounding it. *Melodic ciphering silenced, with these motifs that constitute a logic, with our fibers.* [. . .] no vanquished inflection can bend or cross the omnipresent Line which runs infinitely from point to point in its creation of idea—unless invisible to human eyes, mysterious, like some Harmony of pure perfection.]

In this way, rhythm transgresses the line of syntax and allows the infinitization of configurations (of applications):

Surprendre habituellement cela, le marquer, me frappe comme une obligation de qui déchaîna l'Infini; dont le rythme, parmi les touches du clavier verbal, se rend, comme sous l'interrogation d'un doigté, à l'emploi des mots, aptes, quotidiens.[15]

[Constantly reveal this, mark it, seems to me as though obligatory for Infinity's unleashing—Whose rhythm, amongst the keys of our verbal instrument, can be rendered, as though by a sure touch, by the fitting words of our daily tongue.]

Univocal signification is, accordingly, pulverized: The *Bedeutung* is still there, but in a multiplied form, and it tends to disappear in the interrelation of differences that produces a "musicalization" of meaning. Nonetheless, this "pluralisation" of the *Bedeutung,* which may equally be characterized as *connotation* or as *mimetic* signification, is not to be construed as some form of free flux, lacking all definition: On the contrary, a new semiotic disposition ("supreme mold"), marked by a specific formal nature, is produced, and this constitutes a new identity taking the place of the multiplied *Bedeutung:*

Signe! au gouffre central d'une spirituelle impossibilité que rien soit exclusivement à tout, le numérateur divin de notre apothéose, *quelque suprême moule qui n'ayant pas lieu en tant que d'aucun objet qui existe:* mais il emprunte, pour y aviver un sceau tous gisements épars, ignorés et flottants selon quelque richesse, et les forger.[16]

[Sign! at the central gulf of a spiritual impossibility that anything be exclusively of all, the divine numerator of our apotheosis, some supreme mold not taking place as being of any existing object: but it borrows, to burnish a seal there, all scattered buried precious minerals, unknown and floating, according to some richness and forge them.]

Political Re-volt

However, Mallarmé was also the first to insist upon the political implications of this re-volt of the subject and of Being. Not, of course, in the sense that he proposed a theory or practice of commitment, as would subsequent avant-gardes, but, rather, inasmuch as he was to take up a strangely oblique political position, between the center and anarchism, from where, while cultivating his complicity with both sides, as well as multiplying his rejections of dehumanization, of capital and of political reductionism, he was ultimately to uphold an analogy that he is the first to have proffered with such a degree of conviction and irony: the book as arm.

Given that I have been accused by some American academics of not taking the historical context in which Mallarmé wrote into account, here let me present and develop a certain number of points related to this subject that are to be found in my *Revolution in Poetic Language*—which, it would seem, these critics have neglected to read.

A famous letter by Mallarmé to Cazalis, written during the war of 1871 while he was teaching at Avignon, shows his disinterest in politics, but also, and above all, the total transference of his revolutionary passions onto the arts and letters, which are themselves certainly not, however, spared a perpetual and corrosive questioning. Indeed, in specifying in this letter that his indifference to the current political events is a reaction as much to what he views as a certain fatalistic blind destructiveness as to the horrifying chain of causality that had led up to this, Mallarmé states clearly that his major concern is his return to Paris and the play he is currently writing and hopes to put on in the capital.

Même réussissant, il ne faut me dissimuler que cela est dur à imposer à une foule qui songe à remuer des pavés.

Mais précisement, il n'y a pas de mal que la politique veuille se passer de la littérature et se règle à coups de fusil. La littérature en est quitte, et en garde ce qu'elle veut; assez, par exemple, pour savoir se conduire vis-à-vis de deux rivaux, l'Art et la Science, qui semblaient la confiner dans des chroniques quotidiennes, Gaulois, etc.—On sera las de se battre.[17]

[Even if I'm successful, I'll have to face the fact that it isn't easy to get the general public—more concerned, these days, with rioting than anything else—to accept a work like this. But, after all, it's probably just as well for politics to get along without Literature and decide its fate with guns. Literature can get along very well on its own, all in keeping enough political sense for its needs, such as knowing what's the best action to take with respect to its two rivals, Art and Science, whose aim would seem to be to confine it to daily chronicles.—One will tire of fighting.]

Social power not only was shown to be so moribund that a foreign war could menace it by a Commune, but the very existence of this power also seemed inseparable from the death that it carried within it. Therefore, it follows that Mallarmé's own experience, which can be characterized as veritably a mortal experience insofar as it constantly confronted death, should prove able to adapt itself to the new social logic, at least on the condition that it implant itself in the weak points, where this logic was most likely to give way. Moreover, it was within such a social system, rendered unstable by war, and undoubtedly because of this very instability, that Mallarmé, in his disabused and ironical manner, was to attack, if not social power as such, at least a certain sovereignty. Right in the middle of the debacle of the Commune, Mallarmé contemplates staging a play in Paris, dealing with science and the arts, to play a joke on the bourgeoisie:

Pour le moment, je prépare un Drame et un Vaudeville, discréditant aux yeux d'un Public attentif l'Art et la Science pour un nombre possible des années. Le tour peut être bien joué. Et je m'empare de la position. (J'ai voulu te faire sourire. De loin, ce sera ainsi.)[18]

[At the moment, I am preparing a play and a vaudeville that should utterly discredit Art and Science in the public's eyes for a good number of years. The manoeuvre has a good chance of being pulled off, allowing me to master the situation. (I'm joking. But from a distance, that's how things shall be.)]

No sooner had he arrived in Paris than he launched a subscription to found a monthly magazine, *L'Art décoratif*. A whole new period now opened up for him, through the salons of the Parisian bohemia (notably that of Nina de Villard) and with the Parnassians, the Symbolists, and the Impressionists, as well as with Valvins and Méry Laurent. In its own way, this entire social network was in tune with the events of the Third Republic; and, although not specifically aligned with any one party, it furnished the neutral territory where the cultural "center-Right" and "center-Left" could meet and part company. Following the constitutional vote of 1875, establishing the presidential and parliamentary Republic, the enterprising Catulle Mendès founded *La République des Lettres* (20 December 1875), to which Mallarmé was to contribute. Although Republican, these intellectual milieux were also attracted by a religious syncretism, and their unity was more ideological in nature than political. Moreover even this ideological coherence was fragile, and what one might call the center-Left—the position of A. France, for example—was not long in distancing itself from the Parnassian and Symbolist citadel because of theoretical and aesthetic differences. Mallarmé himself patronized these various coteries with a discrete irony, as if they were necessary components for the conservation of the "saveur morbide," or, alternatively, as though as many therapeutic devices by which to assure a unity, a structure, a provisional but communicable meaning, and thereby prolong the beneficial period during which" la chose murie, immuable, devient instinctive, presque antérieure et non d'hier"[19] (ideas, in their developed and immuable form, become instinctive and almost as though preexistent, as though they have always been so). This is shown by the ease and lack of fanaticism with which Mallarmé circulates amongst the different groups, while, at the same time, his texts bear no explicit reference to any of them. If the review *Le Troisième Parnasse contemporain* rejects him in 1875, he is adopted by the *La République des Lettres* at the same time. If he acclaims Swinburne and the Pre-Raphaelites, he is no less admiring of Zola's *L'Assommoir* (1877). And, in a like manner, he can dialogue allusively with Verlaine about the value of Catholicism, even while seeking solace, upon the death of Anatole, in his memories, on the one hand, and in the arms of Marie-Rose Laurent, on the other. Simultaneously Republican and supporter of "strikism" ("grévisme"), Mallarmé shows a certain reserve toward Germany after the war (he refuses, for example, to visit the parents of his wife, who was German, after the birth of Anatole, 16 July 1871; although it is probable that he was more anxious to avoid his in-laws than German militarism), while at the same time belonging to the milieu of *La Revue wagnérienne*, which the hard-line Left, headed by Madame Adam, was to combat violently. Equally, he refuses to write on anarchism, but nonetheless leaves the tranquillity of Valvins to go and testify at the trial of Fénéon in 1894. However, this does not prevent him from welcoming Clemenceau to his Tuesday evenings, even though the latter had frankly seized power by toppling Ferry in 1885.

In short, Mallarmé passes from one to the other of these social circles without lingering in any one of them, persuaded as he is of their "inanité sonore." Such groupings serve merely to underpin the ongoing process that sweeps along in its path as much language and the subject as every historical formation. All the small entities under the sway of the bourgeois state, whether the family, the aesthetic and spiritualistic groups, or the salons, are but so many ephemeral expressions of the pervasive nonsense, and can therefore but be a subject of irony, as in the *Vers de circonstance* (witness *Eventails*, for example) or in the *Chansons bas*. However, insofar as such entities not only are useful, but inevitable and necessary for productive activity, they mark the points of stasis that are logically required by the process—the revolt—that we are talking about here, just as they are unable to escape those constraints of the historical era alluded to by Mallarmé in his letter to Cazalis, cited above. Underlying Mallarmé's acceptance of these entities is his recognition, in keeping with the very logic of the process of signifiance,[20] that a *limit* is necessary for this process to take place. In this sense, Mallarmé's attitude is more realist than the relatively negative revolt of Romanticism, and what appears to be social and "mondaine" compromise on his behalf is, in fact, the expression of a logic that he had more comprehensively seized in all its ramifications than any Romantic. Mallarmé not only ensures, in this way, a "medical" balance of his corporeal and signifying functions but, by the same gesture, which ceases thereby to be simply a preventive or protective measure, shows up the inanity of these pockets of stasis and shelter as such, regardless of whether they be of an aesthetic or social nature, or directly related to the State. As much by his irony, as by the skepticism that he constantly displays concerning his own work, even during the period that he is acclaimed as "le Sage de la rue de Rome" and as the "Prince des poètes," and, up to the clause of his will insisting that "Le Livre" be destroyed, Mallarmé rejects the very structures that he himself had put into place to produce. Indicating in this way that it is the process alone that counts and not what it leaves behind, Mallarmé distinguishes himself definitively from the groups that he had created, contributed to, or challenged, from the Parnassians to Symbolism, and positions his practice as pure expenditure ("dépense"), cutting across all social and aesthetic structures.

In a letter to Henri de Régnier, written on 29 September 1891, after the duel between Catulle Mendès et Vielé-Griffin, Mallarmé states:

> La littérature devient trop drôle, et il y a quelque chose d'impudique à paraître y tenir par quelque lien.[21]

[Literature is decidedly becoming a most curious affair, and it takes a certain shamelessness to display any attachment whatsoever to it.]

Anarchism

Anarchism is undoubtedly the political movement that most aptly tallies with this transgressive functioning of the process of signifiance. The principle of protest that it embodies corresponds to the movement of that "sovereign subject" that Georges Bataille would much later conceptualize but that Mallarmé is one of the first to presage, escaping in this way, as we have seen, the confines of the Third Republic. Indeed, Mallarmé was even to refuse all institutionalized forms of anarchism—from political organizations per se to special editions of reviews. Accordingly, it is not all that surprising that Louise Michel, in a lecture she delivered in London, could acclaim Mallarmé to be of like political ilk. Indeed, whether her declaration was founded upon misunderstanding or lucidity, it is undoubtedly much closer to the interpretation that I am proposing here than is the position adopted by John Payne. In relating Michel's comment to Mallarmé, he talks of Michel's confusion of decadents for anarchists, of her having been taken in by Mallarmé's pretending, "out of the pure love of paradox," to be a Republican and "strike-supporter" ("gréviste") and describes Mallarmé as being, in reality, "conservative, refined, indeed aristocratic."[22]

Payne's position in respect of Mallarmé has, as we all know, become a widely accepted view, without any questions being asked, however, as to why one should judge as authentic the aristocratic aspect of Mallarmé rather than his "strikism" ("grévisme"), or, if pretense there be on Mallarmé's behalf, why this might not apply as much to his refinement as to his Republicanism. The fact is that the "decadents" did consider themselves to be anarchists, as is shown by R. de Gourmont, among others, when he writes that insofar as the decadents stem from Hegel, they can "admit of only one type of government, anarchy," for, just as "Schopenhauer's pessimistic idealism leads to despotism," so "Hegel's optimistic idealism' finds its resolution in anarchy."[23] In the same vein, de Gourmont adds that, once Symbolism has been recognized, despite its derivatives, as amounting to a revolution as much against the rules of grammar as against all aesthetic or individual self-satisfaction. Thereby, "purified of the outrageous connotations given to it by short-sighted half-wits," it can then be "translated literally by the word freedom or, for those of a violent bent, by the word Anarchy."[24]

Mallarmé did not, however, identify with this word either.[25] Judging that state institutions, while futile, are nonetheless necessary or at least impossible to do without during the period in which he lived, Mallarmé did not consider that they deserved, any more than did any other institution, moreover, to be combated by means other than the process of signifiance enacted by the text. Adopting a Hegelian perspective, he seemed to consider that if these institutions exist, it is undoubtedly because they are necessary both for social subjects and for industrial development; it is therefore by acting upon the relation of the subject to the process of signifiance and by dissolving one's own blockages, that one can contribute to the putting into question of the existing social divisions. Consequently, when Paterne Berrichon suggests, in 1891, that he contribute to the special edition of *Plume* to be devoted to anarchism, Mallarmé refuses, and similarly, when he appears as a witness for the defense at the trial of F. Fénéon, a regular visitor to the Rue de Rome, it is the sociability of the anarchist that he accentuates. Mallarmé's statement to the court therefore emphasizes Fénéon's "gentle and upright character," his "astute and curious mind," the fact that neither Mallarmé himself nor any other of his guests had "ever heard Fénéon discuss anything which is not concerned with art or literature," and that, in this respect, Mallarmé judged Fénéon to be "one of the most subtle and astute critics that exist."[26]

More than simple camouflage designed for the occasion, this declaration may indeed be construed as legitimate testimony of Mallarmé's attitude toward social protest, which, in the same way as history as a whole, has—in Mallarmé's view—for sole purpose and ultimate end, the impossible, theatrical, "Livre":

Je me figure par un indéracinable sans doute préjugé d'écrivain, que rien ne demeurera sans être proféré; que nous en sommes là, précisément, à rechercher, devant une brisure des grands rythmes littéraires [...] et leur éparpillement en frissons articulés proches de l'instrumentalisation, un art d'achever la transposition, au Livre, de la symphonie ou uniment de reprendre notre bien.[27]

[I imagine with an ineradicable no doubt prejudice of a writer that nothing will remain without being uttered; that that's where we are, precisely, seeking, confronted by the breaking up of the great literary rhythms [...] and their scattering into articulated shivers near to instrumentation, an art of finishing the transposition, into the Book, of the symphony or simply taking back our own.]

It is the common attempt to capture the ephemeral that establishes a parallel between political parties (which aim at translating the process into existing institutional forms), and Impressionism (which strives to reconstitute the enigmatic process on canvas). Undoubtedly, precisely because of this orientation, Impressionism, as well as all avant-garde practice, is allied with the sudden entry onto the political scene (and within its "structures") of that protagonist who constitutes in fact the mobile underpinning of this scene as such, namely, the "people." It is in this sense that Mallarmé compares the Impressionist movement with "the participation of the people, hitherto ignored, in French political life,"[28] even if this comparison may well be "bémolisée d'ironie" (set in an ironic key), to borrow the expression that Goncourt employs in his *Journal* to describe Mallarmé's voice.

The interest of Symbolist authors for the anarchist movement, and indeed even their participation in his movement, has often been viewed, in a somewhat perfunctory and offhand manner, as simple "snobbishness." This was effectively the judgment of the bourgeois press of the time, but it was also expressed by certain socialist journals. However, the notion of snobbishness is totally insufficient to explain the psychic and sociological mechanisms that account for the propagation of a political or intellectual movement. Even though one can remark a genuine infatuation on behalf of some Parisian salons for movements of social protest, a more thorough analysis of the relation between aesthetic subversion and political anarchism remains *indispensable*. I might add that this conviction guided my analyses of Mallarmé and Lautréamont in *Revolution in Poetic Language,* and, accordingly, it is from this perspective that I situate my remarks here.

This stated, let me succinctly recall a number of facts concerning the political position of the so-called "bourgeois avant-garde" writers of Mallarmé's time. The contributors to *La Revue socialiste* (under the editorship of Benoît Malon) and to the anarchist review, *La Révolte,* for the most part were intellectuals from *La Revue moderne.* Mallarmé does not seem to have contributed to *La Révolte,* but he was a subscriber to the review, as were J. Ajalbert, P. Adam, P. Arène, L. Ménard, Aurélien Scholl, A. France, J. K. Huysmans, Leconte de Lisle, and R. de Goncourt. The review *Entretiens littéraires et politiques* (edited by Vielé-Griffin) was, from 1892 onward, marked by distinct anarchist leanings, publishing articles by Bakounine and Kropotkin.[29] At the same time, it not only published reviews and praise of Mallarmé,[30] but texts by Mallarmé himself. *La Revue blanche,* which published the Symbolists, equally had anarchist leanings. In sum, the convergence between anarchistic action and the activity of the Symbolists seemed evident for the participants of the two movements. As J. Maitron writes: "The chronological coincidence of Symbolism and anarchism gave rise to a mutual sympathy. One was Symbolist in literature, anarchist in politics. One needs but think here of the examples of Stuart Merrill, Rémy de Gourmont, Fr. Vielé-Griffin, Pierre Guillard, and Saint-Pol Roux."[31]

It is difficult to have a clear idea of the ideological currents that existed within the anarchist movement of that time, but it seems that at least some currents (notably that of Kropotkin and Louise Michel) joined to their anarchism a spirituality that, while anti-Catholic and antiecclesiastical in nature, was not devoid of a reference to "faith."[32] It would therefore appear that certain currents of anarchism did not confine themselves to opposing existing social and state structures alone, but also propounded the necessity of a profound transformation in the very conception of the speaking-subject. Writers were, evidently, the best placed to support such a demand; and yet, given the lack of adequate means by which it could be realized, this demand was doomed ultimately to lead to a form of religion—however revised or revamped.

The Circumspection of the Anarchist-Writer

No signifying function can bypass the thetic modality, and the text least of all given that, as a new signifying device, it only destroys existing symbolic laws to construct its own. Indeed, the affirmation of an organizational and unifying principle is indispensable for textual practice. It follows, from this point of view, that the correspondence between anarchism and textual practice is necessarily limited, and it is not surprising that Lautréamont rejects anarchism in the name of "immutable values" or "primary principles" that do not allow discussion. Consequently, the practice of both Lautréamont and Mallarmé places them in a position not only to grasp what the anarchist irruption brings with it of value, but also its limitations and, most notably, its lack of positivity. The text compensates for this lack by producing a new signifying disposition for the process.

This is not, however, the only point of difference in relation to anarchism: The linguistic and "instinctual"[33] economy of the subject producing the text distances him or her as much from the everyday concrete social action of anarchists as from their spontaneous, naive, humanist discourse. Admittedly, the ideology of Mallarmé's (and of Lautréamont's) texts shares with the ideology of anarchism that spirituality—which we have just discussed—that characterizes, in fact, all pre-Freudian discourse pertaining to the subject. However, the analysis to which the process of signifiance is submitted in textual practice operates implicitly upon this ideology itself; as a result, this ideology is dismantled in the very sphere of its operation, decentered and exceeded: in short, "disideologized." Subsequently, to state that anarchist spiritualism and Mallarmé's idealism do not speak the same language is to state that there is no dialogue between them, no communication, and that their complicity is restricted to their shared, but distinct, nature as practices in rupture with the sociosymbolic order. It suffices to read the poems of Louise Michel and those of Mallarmé to become aware of the distance that separates the "artistic" avant-garde from political subversion, even if their practical solidarity remains operative.

This stated, the solidarity displayed by avant-garde writers with the anarchist movement underlines their distance from groups involved in "social reformism," such as socialism, and later, communism. Moreover, this distance could only be confirmed, if not directly determined, by the entire history of the Third Republic. For example, the affair of Panama (1888–1889) was, for Mallarmé, yet further evidence of the fragility of social power, and this confirmed his disinterest in current events. The condemnation of the previously revered Ferdinand de Lesseps revealed an abstract social justice that, while waiving all "respect for the individual," proved nonetheless, despite its sacrificing of principles, to be inefficient and fundamentally invalid. For in a society where money alone wields power and therefore is the sole guarantee of truth, a justice that proves incapable of its restitution can but be fictive. In this way, juridical authority becomes "the monster in whose favour the previously human individual gradually abdicates" ("le monstre en faveur de qui peu à peu abdique l'individu jadis humain"), while the "victim of justice"—noble and suffering—becomes identified as the "hero" that capitalism produces. Indeed, henceforth, the tragic protagonist takes the form of the individual who, engaged in the process of production and obeying, without fully being aware of it, the logic of this process, comes to bear the responsibility when this logic fails.

In other words, a new truth comes into being, one consisting in the fragmentation of unity, of power, as of truth itself, into the series of hazardous operations that are nothing other than the laws of the capitalist market. In the face of this logic, the logic of capital, "the previously human individual" no longer has any place. But nor is there any longer a place for a moral authority, of whatever kind: no form of justice (itself a remnant of a precapitalist era) can effectively condemn the individual in the name of financial logic, for it lacks the means to redress the reality of capital. This being the case, Mallarmé considers but one possible conclusion, such as, that it is necessary, despite all, to defend the individual—that "previously human individual"—as much against the implacable modern configuration, epitomized by capital, as against the archaic state, and ideological, apparatuses. In this sense, the text devoted by Mallarmé to this affair constitutes a plea for the humanist spirit that he believes to be embedded as much in the unconscious[34] as in the French tradition ("a cette acuité dans le goût et l'émotion, qui fut son passé français"), or, again, in the elite. He summarizes this spirit as an anarchistic attitude that, in opposing authority and the state, rejects categorically all condemnations pronounced in the name of a fictive law: "Tant de mains, en quelque sorte, *anarchistes* [. . .] qui serrent dignement, spontanément, gravement, la main des condamnés . . ."[35] (So many outstretched, in a certain sense *anarchistic,* hands [. . .] that spontaneously shake, with solemn dignity, the hands of those condemned by law).

The Book as Arm

It is precisely this ambiguous status of power and justice in the bourgeois state that conditions Mallarmé's conception of the role of the writer. Insofar as the social fabric shows itself to have become, as it were, both necessary and without cohesion, constraining and evanescent, it can only be represented by that which

THE REVOLT OF MALLARMÉ 47

is itself signification and music, law and transgression, namely, a book. Moreover, such a book is all the more necessary in this context to make conscious this character of the social relation that would otherwise remain invisible:

> A savoir que le rapport social et sa mesure momentanée qu'on la serre ou l'allonge, en vue de gouverner, étant une fiction, laquelle relève des belles-lettres—à cause de leur principe mystérieux ou poétique—le devoir de maintenir le livre s'impose dans l'intégrité.[36]

> [Notably that the social relation and its momentary measure, whether one tightens or stretches it out for the sake of governing, being fiction, which has to do with pure literature—because of its mysterious or poetic principle—the duty of maintaining the book is imposed in its integrity.]

Characterized by a structure of ambiguous signification, where oppositions interpenetrate in a constant play of irony, the book defies the law's authority and, in the same way as the "simple individual," is liable to incur the reprimand of the government, or more simply of the Academy. By the same stroke, however, the book uncovers the character of every form of government—be it, literary or political—because no government, or, in other words, power, can tolerate that its law, however allegorical and uncertain, be treated as such, and with irony.

> Imaginez un gouvernement mal instruit se confondant avec l'allégorie, d'ou il vient; et que, concurremment, un Livre parût, relatif à la Société, éprouvantable et délicieux, hors les sentences rendues par "ceci est beau—cela est mauvais," quelconque, inhumain, étranger, dont l'extase ou la colère que les choses simplement soient ce qu'elles sont, avec tant de stridence absolue montât: qu'on faillirait, souvent, prendre ire et joie l'une pour l'autre et les deux, incontestablement, pour de l'ironie. L'auteur est saisi, non, M.M., je parle aux Académiciens, pas même son oeuvre [. . .]. Loyal, il se présente—point au tribunal courant, nulle tête à choir effectivement, plutôt défendre une pensée, aussi la comparution, devant ses pairs. Tout récusé sauf vous. Il attend le jugement que, pour ma part, j'aimerais à voir libellé.[37]

> [Imagine a badly informed government confusing itself with the allegory whence it comes; and imagine that, concurrently, a Book should appear relative to Society, horrible and delightful, beyond the judgment of "this is beautiful—that is bad," indifferent, inhuman, strange, where the ecstasy or the anger that things should be simply what they are, with so much absolute stridency would arise: that one would often

almost take ire and joy one for the other or the two, incontestably, for irony. The author, called to account—no, Messieurs, I'm addressing the Academicians—not even his work [. . .]. Loyal, he presents himself—not to the current tribunal, no head to fall in fact, rather to defend a thought, hence the appearance before his peers. All is rejected except you. He awaits the judgment which, for my part, I'd like to see written up.]

Literary activity is likened by Mallarmé to the explosion of a bomb, to a sort of anarchist assault that is followed through right to the end, until the uprooting of that most tenacious of dogmas and sociality's ultimate guarantee: codified language. Accordingly, in 1894, during his conference in England on "La Musique et les Lettres," Mallarmé emphasizes:

Les gouvernements changent: toujours la prosodie reste intacte : soit que, dans les révolutions, elle passe inaperçue ou que l'*attentat* ne s'impose pas avec l'opinion que ce dogme dernier puisse varier.[38]

[Though governments change, prosody remains untouched; for either, when revolutions occur, prosody goes unnoticed, either, the opinion that it is possible to change this ultimate dogma fails to launch the assault].

Equally, in the same text, Mallarmé talks of the poet as source of the explosive force that accrues to the overpure concept: "Lui, ce l'est, tout de même, à qui on fait remonter la représentation, en tant qu'*explosif*, d'un concept trop vierge, à la Société,"[39] just as he alludes to literary life, to its conflicts and its innovations (the invention of free verse, for example), as the transposition, in language, of the political terrorism that, although deplorable as regards its violence, is nevertheless the only means by which one can shed light on the "definitive incomprehension" displayed by the law:

Les *engins,* dont le bris illumine les parlements d'une lueur sommaire, mais estropient, aussi à faire grand'pitié, des badauds, *je m'y intéresserais,* en raison de la lueur—sans la brièveté de son enseignement qui permet au *législateur d'alléguer une définitive incompréhension;* mais j'y récuse l'adjonction de balles à tir et de clous.[40]

[The *devices,* whose breaking illuminates parliaments with a summary light, but cripples onlookers piteously, *I'd be interested in them* in proportion to the light—without the brevity of its teaching which allows *the legislator to allege a definitive incomprehension;* but I reject the adjuncture of shot and nails.]

It would seem that, for Mallarmé, true literary subversion consists not in the allegiance to any particular literary innovation, but in the assertion of the rights due to the "exception," to the "minority," to "rare connoisseurs." Without such a minority, the battle of free verse is interesting solely by virtue of its "ingenuousness," and its effect is more one of casting "disrepute, than of a bomb." The conclusion of this paragraph would seem a particularly strong statement of Mallarmé's belief that, if acts of political or literary violence assure *the very life of society,* they nonetheless have but a relative impact, inasmuch as they are controlled by the sovereign legality of the bourgeois state ("whatever divergence the furious conflict of citizens creates, all under the *sovereign gaze* make a *unanimity*"). Mallarmé here contends that it is necessary to set worthwhile objectives for these healthy, if peripheral, contradictions ("were, at least, that what people devour each other for something that counts"), and that true subversion consists in a pure expenditure ("dépense"), outside all institutions and outside of the race for profits that characterizes society ("in any concurrence of the multitude somewhere toward interest, amusement or convenience"). Recognizing collective needs, but turning away from them, such an expenditure may be described as gratuitous, unidentifiable, futile perhaps, or, let us say, as literary:

> Il importe que dans tout concours de la multitude quelque part vers l'intérêt, l'amusement ou la commodité, de rares amateurs, respectueux du motif commun en tant que façon d'y montrer de l'indifférence, instituent par cet air à côté, une minorité : attendu, quelle divergence que creuse le conflit furieux des citoyens, tous, sous l'oeil souverain, font une unanimité—d'accord, au moins, que ce à propos de quoi on s'entre-dévore, compte : or, posé le besoin d'exception, comme de sel! la vraie qui, indéfectiblement fonctionne, gît dans ce séjour de quelques esprits, je ne sais, à leur éloge, comment les désigner, gratuits, étrangers, peut-être vains—ou littéraires.[41]

[It's important that in any concurrence of the multitude somewhere toward interest, amusement or convenience, a few rare connoisseurs, respectful of the common purpose in a way that shows indifference to it, set up through that aloof attitude a minority: given, whatever divergence the furious conflict of citizens creates, all under the sovereign gaze make a unanimity—were, at least, that what people devour each other for something that counts: well, given the need for exception, as of salt! the true one which, ineluctably, functions, lies in this sojourn of certain minds, I don't know—this is to their credit—how to designate them, gratuitous, unidentifiable, futile perhaps,—or literary.]

Gratuitous, unidentifiable, or literary: the Mallarméan revolt is of a most peculiar kind.

Translated by Louise Burchill

Notes

1. Julia Kristeva, *Sens et non-sens de la révolte* (Paris: Fayard, 1996).
2. (Julia Kristeva is referring here to one of the major concepts developed in her *Revolution in Poetic Language,* trans. M. Waller (New York: Columbia University Press, 1984). *Trans.*)
3. "Sur l'évolution littéraire," in Stéphane Mallarmé, *Oeuvres complètes,* ed. H. Mondor and G. Jean-Aubry (Paris: Gallimard-Pléiade, 1945), 871. (Hereafter cited as *OC.*) The English translation of this passage is by B. Cook, *Mallarmé: Selected Prose Poems, Essays and Letters* (Baltimore: The Johns Hopkins University Press, 1956).
4. "Magie," *OC,* 400. The English translation of this passage is by R. G. Cohn, *Mallarmé's Divagations. A Guide and Commentary* (New York: Peter Lang, 1990), 350.
5. "La Musique et les Lettres," *OC,* 647. The English translation of this passage is by P. Barnard with D. Hayman, in *Modern Critical Views: Stéphane Mallarmé,* H. Bloom, ed. (New York: Chelsea House, 1987), 49.
6. Stéphane Mallarmé, *Correspondance, 1862–1871,* I, ed. H. Mondor and Lloyd James Austin (Paris: Gallimard, 1959), 137. (Herafter cited as *Corr.*)
7. "Hommage," *OC,* 73.
8. In *Les Mots anglais, OC,* 1047.
9. Ibid., 1026.
10. *Le Mystère dans les lettres, OC,* 1026. The English translation of this passage is by P. Barnard with D. Hayman, in H. Bloom, ed., *Modern Critical Views,* 105–106.
11. Preface to *Un Coup de Dés, OC,* 455. The English translation of this passage is by M. A. Caws, in *Stéphane Mallarmé: Selected Poetry and Prose,* ed. M.S. Caws (New York: New Directions, 1982), 105.
12. "La Musique et les Lettres," *OC,* 653. The English translation is by B. Cook, *Mallarmé,* 55.
13. Ibid., 647. The English translation is by P. Barnard with D. Hayman in H. Bloom, ed., *Modern Critical Views,* 48–49.
14. Ibid., 647–48, emphasis added. The first part of the translation presented (up to "fibers") is by P. Barnard with D. Hayman; the remainder is, with modifications, by B. Cook.
15. Ibid., 648.
16. "Solennité," *OC,* 333, emphasis added. The English translation of this passage is by R.G. Cohn, *Mallarmé's* Divagations, 219.
17. Letter to Cazalis, 23 April 1871, in *Corr.,* 1:351. (The first two sentences of the translation in the body of the text have, with the exception of the interpolated clause, been taken from the translation proffered by B. Cook in the selection

of Mallarmé's prose and poetry, 98–99. The rest of the translation of this passage [and its continuation further below—see the following note] is our own. *Trans.*)

18. Ibid.

19. Ibid

20. ("Signifiance" is the term by which Kristeva refers to language understood as a heterogeneous practice, formed of both the semiotic modality [dealing with the psychosomatic underpinning of the subject and of language] and the symbolic modality [which has to do with signification, syntax, and predication]. See her *Revolution in Poetic Language*, 17. *Trans.*)

21. *Corr.*, 4:315.

22. Payne's comments, which were made in a letter that he sent to Mallarmé along with a cutting from *The Globe,* reviewing Louise Michel's London conference, are cited by H. Mondor, *La Vie de Mallarmé* (Paris: Gallimard, 1941), 492.

23. See R. de Gourmont, "L'Idéalisme," *Mercure de France,* 1893, 14–15.

24. Ibid., 23.

25. After a riot in Paris' Latin Quarter, anarchism makes its literary debut with the novel *Le Soleil des morts* by Camille Mauclair (Ollendorff, 1898). Mauclair's novel depicts an aristocratic anarchism on the side of the people; its main character, Calixte Armel, the master and leader of the anarchists, is portrayed as an aloof but nevertheless active figure, and is based on none other than Mallarmé himself. It is not, however, this type of "evidence" that proves that Symbolism and Mallarmé share an affinity with anarchism. Mauclair himself, who was to judge the *Internationale* ""inept," will later speak of such an affinity with disdain (see *Solitude et grandeur littéraire* [Ollendorff, 1932], 121). Indeed, far from imagining any logical relation to exist between the two movements, taken up in the process affecting a common social-economic formation, Mauclair deems that whatever convergence they might display is simply of a superficial and ultimately fashionable nature.

26. Mallarmé's testimony is reported in the *Gazette des Tribunaux,* 9 August 1894, 780.

27. "Crise de vers," *OC,* 367. The English translation of this passage is by R.G. Cohn, *Mallarmé's* Divagations, 249–50.

28. In his article, "The Impressionists and Edouard Manet," published in *The Art Monthly Review,* 30 September 1876; see *OC,* 1624.

29. See Bakounine,"La Commune de Paris et la notion d'Etat," 29 (August 1892): 59–70.

30. See 42 (May 1893), Vielé-Griffin, 535.

31. J. Maitron, *Histoire du mouvement anarchiste en France (1880–1914)* (Société universitaire de l'édition et de la littérature, 1951).

32. Paul Adam describes the anarchist as someone interested in Marx, political economy, the Church Fathers, and rare editions of the Revelation of St. John the Divine. See "Le Nouvel Anarchiste" in *Critique des moeurs* (E. Kolle, 1893), 255–60.

33. (We have translated "pulsionnelle" as "instinctual" to comply with the terminology adopted by the translator of *Revolution in Poetic Language*. However, it should be signaled that "pulsion" is, in our view, more correctly translated as "drive." Accordingly, our preferred translation of "une économie pulsionnelle" would be "an economy of the drives." *Trans.*)

34. For example, in writing of hands held out in solidarity to those condemned by law, he states that "elles ont signifié quelque chose d'inconscient" (they had a certain unconscious signification).

35. "Faits-divers," *OC*, 1579.
36. "Sauvegarde" (May 1895), in *Grands Faits divers*, *OC*, 420. The English translation of this passage is by R. G. Cohn, *Mallarmé's* Divagations, 249–50.
37. Ibid., 419–20. The English translation of this passage is by R. G. Cohn, *Mallarmé's* Divagations, 400–401.
38. "La Musique et les Lettres," *OC*, 643–44.
39. Ibid., 651; emphasis added.
40. Ibid., 652; emphasis added. This sentence is an allusion to the bomb filled with nails that Auguste Vaillant threw into the Chamber of Deputies on 9 December 1893 to protest against the Panama scandal. The evening of the explosion Mallarmé had dined with Rodin, Zola, Verlaine, and Tailhade. The latter, when asked by a journalist to give his first reaction to the event, replied: "What does the death of humanist masses matter, if by that death, an individual can affirm his existence? Who cares about the victims if the gesture is a beautiful one?" Tailhade was later to lose an eye in another bomb explosion, alluded to by Mallarmé in his text "Laurent Tailhade, frontispice" (*OC*, 526–27). In the period between the incident occasioning Tailhade's injury and the publication of Mallarmé's text, the assassination of president Carnot took place in Lyon, on 24 June 1891.
41. Ibid., 652. The English translation (modified) is by R. G. Cohn, *Mallarmé's* Divagations, 339.

"Etendre, simplifier le monde": The Philosophical Purchase of Mallarmé

ALBERT COOK

> Je crois qu'il y a tout un immense travail d'idées à l'ombre de son oeuvre, qui est ignoré de la plupart de ses meilleurs lecteurs.
> —PAUL VALÉRY to MADAME MALLARMÉ
> 15 September 1898

VALÉRY, well placed to observe it, noticed "an immense work of ideas" in the shadow of Mallarmé's work. This philosophical substratum in Mallarmé surfaces in his hauntingly prismatic aphorisms, and also at the heart of the poetic enterprise of which the poems are the dazzling center. This impulse, speculative and abstract, is formulated in "La Musique et les Lettres," as well as constantly elsewhere. As he says in that late and nearly valedictory essay,

> Tout l'acte disponible, à jamais et seulement, reste de saisir les rapports, entre temps, rares ou multipliés; d'après quelque état intérieur et que l'on veuille à son gré étendre, simplifier le monde.[1]

[The whole available act, forever and only, remains to grasp the relations between times, rare or multiple, after some interior state and that one would wish to extend at will, to simplify the world.]

Simplifying the world does not mean simplifying poetry, and Mallarmé was also often at pains to justify—clearly, he gloried the difficulty-producing condensations in his expression. Simplifying means reducing to essentials, getting to bedrock. And to do that involves, he says here, an activity that would seem to contradict it. For how can "extend"—to extend an inner state—mean "simplify"? As often, his comma between the two words "étendre, simplifier" arrests the voice and alerts the thought to make the connection between the two, which is also a break, because in the main syntax it is an interior state that is extended, the world that is simplified. In the most rudimentary sense, any verbal expression whatever adds to the world, and can be said to extend it. But "simplify"? For an act of expression to simplify the world at the same stroke that it extends the world calls for considerable tact and attention, the tact and attention we have come to expect from the philosopher, or even the scientist, for whom simplicity or economy is a feature of elegance.

Such an act of expression calls for an underlying logic, and Mallarmé goes on to make that point:

> La totale arabesque, qui les relie, a de vertigineuses sautes en un effroi que reconnue; et d'anxieux accords. Avertissant par tel écart, au lieu de déconcerter, ou que sa similitude avec elle-même, la soustraie en la confondant. Chiffration mélodique tue, de ces motifs qui composent une logique, avec nos fibres. (648)

[The total arabesque that joins them has vertiginous leaps in a fright as recognized, and anxious accords. Warning by such a gap, instead of disconcerting, or that its similarity to itself withdraws it in confounding it. A melodic figuring silenced, of those motifs that compose a logic, with our fibres.]

The "accords" involve at once sound and sense; they are musical accords, and they are also accords within a proposition. This "chiffration," in being "mélodique," composes not just a logic, but a logic that reverberates inwardly, "avec nos fibres." The process happens not just "in" our fibers but "with" them. It must happen in accord with an inward state, "d'après quelque état intérieur." They are called into play, the fibres, for the logical operation, with the accompaniment of vertiginous leaps and fright. So, seen in this simplified and extended poetry, the language of the tribe is purified enough to bring small evanescent acts like those coded into *Igitur* and *Hérodiade* under the trembling inspection, with the trembling built essentially into the inspection, a trembling Mallarmé called a vibration; it was "vibratoire."

"Les mots" are a "centre de suspens vibratoire" (386), center of vibratory suspense. But for the vibration to be of any use it must reach the pure notion; in philosophical terms it must get down to the bare bones of a proposition: "A quoi bon la merveille de transposer un fait de nature en sa presque disparition vibratoire selon le jeu de la parole, cependant; si ce n'est pour qu'en émane, sans la gêne d'un proche ou concret rappel, la notion pure" (368),

(What good is the marvel of transposing a fact of nature into its nearly total vibratory disappearance according to the play of the word, however, if it were not that there emanates therefrom, without the hindrance of a near or concrete recall, the pure notion). "Disparition vibratoire" is a near oxymoron flagged and qualified by the "presque" preceding it.[2] The "presque," "nearly," is a crack through which the proposition can enter. This significance-in-vibration is, of course, not easy to achieve; he racks his brain and his "nerves" to attain the vibration while retaining the thought:

> J'essayai de ne plus penser de la tête et, par un effort désespéré, je roidis tous mes nerfs (en pectus) de façon de produire une vibration en gardant la pensée à laquelle je travaillais alors, qui devient le sujet de cette vibration, ou une impression—et j'ébauchai tout un poème longtemps rêvé, de cette façon.[3]

> [I tried to think no more with the head, and, by a desperate effort, I stiffened my nerves (in my breast) so as to produce a vibration, retaining the thought I was then working on, which becomes the subject of that vibration, or an impression—and I drafted a whole poem long dreamed about, in that manner.]

This is, so to speak, a constantly engaged and engaging crisis, a "crise de vers" (368), which raises the question of how and in what the crisis comes about. It is at once broached and solved when a sequence gets going in which the poet can "se livrer ensuite à la seule dialectique du vers" (332). The expression cuts two ways: "la seule dialectique du vers" can mean "no other dialectic but that in verse." And it can also mean "only that in verse which is a dialectic." As Valéry says of this poet, "La Syntaxe, qui est calcul, reprenait rang de Muse"[4] (Syntaxe, which is arithmetic, resumed the rank of Muse).

Mallarmé's is a syntax loaded with propositional values: "vu que les mots sont la substance même employée ici à l'oeuvre d'art, en dire l'argument" (334) (seeing that words are the very substance used here for the work of art, that is to say, the argument). As Michel Deguy puts it, "Mallarmé introduces zero into the poetic calculation."[5] As Jacques Derrida points out, "Les langues, nous le savons maintenant, sont des réalités *diacritiques;* l'élément est en elles moins important que *l'écart* qui le sépare des autres éléments"[6] (Languages, we now know, are *diacritical* realities; the element in them is less important than the *gap* that separates it from other elements). The diacritical realities are those brought forth here, which lie latent in the possibility of language generally when the proposition leaps the *écart,* the gap of distance that separates one element from another. The gap for Mallarmé's late critical prose is figured in his abundant supernumerary commas.

The commas, which are notably present as reinforcing the suspensions in Mallarmé's prose, are notably absent in highlighting the suspensive leaps of his verse. There in the verse his hyperbaton enlivens the vibrations in a way that confers predicative power on his suspensions.

> Le livre, expansion totale de la lettre, doit d'elle tirer, directement, une mobilité et spacieux, par correspondances, instituer un jeu, on ne sait, qui confirme la fiction.
> Rien de fortuit, là, où semble un hasard capter l'idée. (380)

> [The book, total expansion of the letter, must draw, directly, a mobility and spacious, in its correspondences, institute a play, as it were, which confirms the fiction.
> Nothing fortuitous, there, where a chance seems to capture the idea.]

The process gets stepped up when the late sonnets shorten their lines and thereby intensify their syntax; and then the intense process is further dimensionalized in the *Coup de Dés*. The lines of "A la nue accablante tu," for example, present a predicative reductum of syntax, while intensifying the multidimensionality of reference to key notions such as white, and siren and possibly subliminal ones to seed, flight, and loss, as Cohn and Derrida maintain:[7]

> A la nue accablante tu
> Basse de basalte et de laves
> A même les échos esclaves
> Par une trompe sans vertu
>
> Quel sépulcral naufrage (tu
> Le sais, écume, mais y baves)
> Suprême une entre les épaves
> Abolit le mât dévêtu
>
> Ou cela qui furibond faute
> De quelque perdition haute
> Tout l'abîme vain éployé
>
> Dans le si blanc cheveu qui traîne
> Avarement aura noyé
> Le flanc enfant d'une sirène.

[To the overwhelming cloud hushed
Base of basalt and of lava
To even the echoes slaves
For a trump without virtue

What sepulchral wreck (you
Know it, foam, but drool there)
Supreme one among the hulls
Abolished the stripped mast

Or that which furious fault
Of some high perdition
The whole vain abyss spread out

In the so white hair that trails
Avariciously will have drowned
The infant flank of a siren.]

The singleness of this scene is enforced by repetitions of near-identity that verge on tautology—"naufrage" and "épaves," "perdition" and "Abolit," which are all versions of each other, and draw the other terms into the whirlpool of the initial adjective, "accablante." At the same time, there is a predicative contradiction: a cloud is on the face of it too vague to be overwhelming, and the vagueness is continued in the puzzle about whether "tu" at the end of the first line is the past passive participle of "taire"—as it turns out to be, or the second-person single pronoun, which the same vocable repeated turns out to be in the identically rhymed symmetrical beginning of the second quatrain. The puzzle about "tu" is not solved until that very fifth line, with the word "naufrage," which precedes the parenthesized second "tu." Along with contradictions there remain the persistent near-identities: Basalt and lava are different shades of blackish gray. And they are also forms of one another, because lava comes from a volcano and basalt is volcanic rock. However, this near-identity, too, nests a contradiction: Basalt is solid, as the term "basse" also suggests. But how can a cloud be a base? Only in a logical sense that raises this very puzzle, if one takes "basse" in apposition to "nue," though in the combinatory possibilities offered by the suspension here, it could alternatively be the grayish stormy sea below the cloud. Lava, in any case, contradicts both cloud and base, and it is a more ominous, thicker alternative to water. Lava is at first liquid, but then a former liquid arrested in too friable a condition to be a base.

In this poetry, the mental action scripted into the syntax that it stirs up corresponds to the turmoil it describes, while displacing it by foregrounding both the verbal connections and concurrently the psychic excitation of the experienced-experiencing poem.

Perdition, abyss, blackness, volcanoes, shipwrecks—these terms graze the tautology of identity as their referentiality hovers toward metaphoricity. This significative process comes off, because there is the possibility of a literal reference to marine disaster. The underlying near-tautologies of predication both insist on the disaster and overcome it by foregrounding the act of verbal attention. The alternative formulation between octave and sestet, the "or," is also a submerged predication of near-identity. What happens is "naufrage," a "wreck" or else it is "perdition." Against the grays and blacks of the first quatrain is the white of the last tercet that resembles them in being equally portentous, the "blanc cheveu" that is merely a trace. It is trailing—and in a further puzzling predication it involves "avariciousness." Commentators agree that the white hair is a metaphor for a slip of foam in the water. But, in a final puzzle, what is the siren? Why is she drowned? This climax is at once capital and gratuitous, making the voyager an absent Odysseus, who is replaced by the legendary temptress, singular here rather than in the legendary plural, who herself is drowned rather than tempting him to drowning, though he has never since been brought forward, he cannot be thought of as either escaped or caught by the "furibond faute." That term, itself, like all, nests a predication, one that connects fault and fury. The siren herself is childlike or a child; given the characterization of "enfant" on her flank, she combines, at least in lexical association, the innocence of the nymphs of *L'Après-midi d'un Faune* and the potential for a murderous seductiveness that is actualized in the language of *Hérodiade*. Sirens come up in "Salut," too, with an explicit twist in their declared function ("à l'envers"), and again in comparison with a cup that is compared with a "vierge vers," "Telle loin se noie une troupe / De sirènes mainte à l'envers" (Such far there drowns a troop / Of sirens numerous in reverse).

Hyperbaton, the juxtaposition of words out of normal syntactic order, has served as a device of poetic intensification since Horace and before. The wrenching of the hyperbaton, notably in this poem but generally in Mallarmé, simultaneously mounts and displaces the abstracting array of equivalences and oppositions for which the symbology of this poet, elaborated by Jean-Pierre Richard, is at once source, goal, and a sort of antitype of calm amid the stresses of energetic formulation. The "absente" is an "absente de tous bouquets"; the *néant* is teeming through the ordonnance of the words. Words such as "abolir" and "taire" announce their dissolution along with their moment in the music while each one "musicalement se lève" (musically is raised). Mallarmé's process of handling ordonnance is so thorough that it transcends the merely ornamental use of hyperbaton, which is defined by Quintilian somewhat equivocally as "a word dragged [out of order] at some distance for the sake of grace."[8] Hyperbaton proper is a transposition of a word to a syntactically strained position. For Mallarmé, suspension is added to transposition, as in the first line here, where "à la nue accablante tu" offers only one possible transposition, the deferral of "tu" to final place; and even that is permissible within normal French word order, so that the suspension is paramount—the suspension that holds up and equivocates "tu" to be defined as a past participle only at line five. Though suspensions continue through line eight, the transpositions of a full-fledged hyperbaton do not get under way until line three with "même," picked up suddenly and powerfully by the suspension so complicated at the parenthesis in line five of "Quel sépulcral naufrage (tu)." The suspension is so complicated that it has the feeling of a transposition; the stirring up of the rhythms creates the illusion of a greater stirring up of the syntax than actually occurs.

In the firmness of predication, such divergences get solved and so resolved. In the sonnet "Salut" "le flot de foudres et d'hivers," because it is that which the prow cuts, makes the flood locally literal in the description of a sea voyage but metaphoric overall. Floods have something atmospheric to do with lightnings, but no necessary connection with winters. In that local literalness, the lightnings and winters are subordinately metaphoric, and their contradictions dissolve into a scene. Again, in a suspensive parenthesis within the poem "M'introduire dans ton histoire," the phrase "tonnerre et rubis aux moyeux" sets up a predicative puzzle. "Thunder" at the "axles"? "Rubies" at the axles? Thunder and rubies together? They belong to different domains that are yoked here, their parenthesis resolved in the last phrase of the poem, which draws these subsidiary metaphors into an engulfing metaphor, "la roue / Du seul vespéral de mes chars." And the poetic staple of "the chariot of evening," the conventionality of the metaphor, a topos about twilight, seals the assertion as though it were a single word validated by the lexicon.

The abstractive movement of the poem, stirred by the hyperbaton or near-hyperbaton into multiple verbal association, generates a neutrality of perception, an indifference: "Tout écrit, extérieurement à son trésor, doit, par égard envers ceux dont il emprunte, après tout, pour un objet autre, le langage, présenter, avec les mots, un sens même indifférent" (382) (Everything written, outside of its treasure, must, with respect toward those from which it borrows, after all, for an object that is other, language, present, with the words, a sense even indifferent). However, in "M'introduire dans ton histoire," the philosophical equanimity of the formulation masks the erotic intensity of what is being evoked, a love passage between the poet and the beloved. "Il doit y avoir quelque chose d'occulte au fond de tous, je crois décidément, à quelque chose d'abscons, signifiant fermé et caché, qui habite le commun" (383) (There must be something occult at the base of all, I believe decidedly, for something hidden, a signifier closed and concealed, which inhabits the common). These abrupt sequencings produce somewhat contradictory effects. On the one hand, "On peut, du reste, commencer d'un éclat triomphal trop brusque pour durer; invitant que se groupe, en retards, libérés par l'écho, la surprise" (One must, besides, begin with a triumphal burst too brusque to last; inviting it to group itself, in delays, liberated by the echo, the surprise). On the other hand, "L'inverse: sont, en un reploiement noir soucieux d'attester l'état d'esprit sur un point, foulés et épaissis des doutes pour que sorte une splendeur définitive simple" (384–85) (The inverse: they are, in a black bending back that is careful toward attesting to the state of spirit on one point, crowded and thickened with doubts so that there may issue a splendor definitive and simple). Surprise and splendor of definition converge. Always there is a prime, or primitive, combinatory attention, a logic, which at its most concentrated or abrupt, produces thunderstrokes: "Les abrupts, hauts jeux d'aile, se mireront, aussi: qui les mène, perçoit une extraordinaire appropriation de la structure, limpide, aux primitives foudres de la logique" (386) (The abruptnesses, high sports of the wing, will be mirrored also; he who leads them perceives an extraordinary appropriation of the structure, limpid, to the primitive thunderbolts of logic). As though in a recapitulation of Aristotle or an anticipation of Heidegger, Mallarmé centered on the fundamental and rudimentary verb of predication, the copula or existential assertion "it is":

> Rien là que je ne me dise moi-même, moins bien, en l'éparse chuchoterie de ma solitude, mais où vous êtes le divinateur, c'est, oui, relativement à ce mot même: *c'est:* notes que j'ai là sous la main, et qui règne au dernier lieu de mon esprit. Tout le mystère est là: établir les

identités secrètes par un deux à deux qui ronge et use les objets, au nom d'une centrale pureté.[9]

[Nothing there that I do not say myself, less well, in the sparse whisperings of my solitude, but in which you are the diviner, that is, yes, relative to this very word: *it is*, notes that I have under my hand, and which reigns in the last corner of my spirit. The whole mystery is there: to establish the secret identities that in a two-by-two which gnaws and wears down the objects, in the name of a central purity.]

The force of the philosophical gesture marks the difference between hyperbaton in Mallarmé's poetry and the hyperbaton in other poets such as Gongora and Hopkins. Mallarmé's ordonnance, in its hyperbaton, forces a philosophical reflection on the sequentialized word; coupled with his frequent meditation on actual or threatened death, the hyperbaton turns the predications toward a memento mori. The predications intensify starkly in the face of death. "Tel qu'en lui-même enfin l'Eternité le change" is the first line of the "Tombeau d'Edgar Poe," where the suspensions are strong enough to dispense with actual hyperbaton, to induce, from this first line on, the sense both of propositional nesting and propositional solution. So, too, the "Toast Funèbre" for Gautier, where the inclusion of common humanity in mortality sets something like the *Sorge* of Heidegger into a nesting proposition too complex to be the aphorism it strives to become: "Nous sommes / La triste opacité de nos spectres futurs."

Mallarmé wrote, as René Daumal says, a "Poème pour désosser les philosophes"[10] (a Poem to de-bone the philosophers). And, as Daumal specifies,

Ce mouvement de retour, laissé d'ordinaire à l'initiative du lecteur, Stéphane Mallarmé l'introduit dans le corps même du poème, effectuant, pour telle image évoquée d'abord, l'ascèse négatrice qui miraculeusement rend visible d'une chose son néant essentiel. Les mots "aboli bibelot" imposent par le terme "bibelot" une image concrète qui est d'avance niée par le terme "aboli", si bien que la représentation suggérée n'est pas celle d'un néant quelconque, mais du néant d'un bibelot.[11]

[This backward movement, left ordinarily to the initiative of the reader, Stéphane Mallarmé introduces into the very body of the poem, effectuating, for a given image first evoked, the negational askesis that miraculously renders the essential nothingness of a thing. The words "aboli bibelot" impose with the term "bibelot" (trinket) a concrete image that is negated in advance by the term "aboli" (abolished), so well that the representation suggested is not that of just any nothingness but of the nothingness of a bibelot.]

The ideational fluency in Mallarmé's prose offers a version of the permeability between philosophical theory and artistic practice characteristic of French cultural life since Diderot and noteworthy for the extensibility into profound domains of abstraction found in Baudelaire's art criticism. Such a function of thought empowers Mallarmé's poetry, even though Mallarmé operated in a tension of distance from the philosophers of his day, while very much in the swim, like Baudelaire, when it not only came to comment upon the arts but to responses to their ultimate ideational thrust, built into his poetry as commentary.

The aesthetic process is philosophized in these poems by the same stroke that the philosophical process is aestheticized. The suspensive movement of the hyperbaton, in a poem such as "A la nue accablante tu," matches and keeps rising to the generality of a theme, stormy weather and shipwreck, that itself hovers and operates suspensively between the description of an actual landscape or marine scene and the evocation of internal properties that would find their embodiment therein. However, the logical suspension between description and metaphor, reinforced by the grammatical suspension, prohibits a locking of the poem into a mere *paysage moralisé*. In this particular poem, the suspension is shadowed, and also intensified in a foreclosed possibility, by the grace note of a false lead, the reading of "la nue" as "the nude" instead of "the cloud." This possible reading, while false, is furthered by the associations in Mallarmé's symbology that would make a nude more accablante, more overwhelming, than a cloud. This reading is suspended and not foreclosed fully until "une" in line seven, although the foreclosure begins in the second line, which offers a concrete apposition, "basse de basalte et de laves." The expression would be strange if attributed to a nude, though, in fact, it is only slightly less strange applied to a cloud. But the shadow-reading of "nude" attains a quasi-thematic closure in the last line of the poem, which introduces an otherwise unnamed and unsuggested figure, "Le flanc enfant d'une sirène." A siren, indeed, is a nude that is "accablante," except that this siren retreats somewhat into infancy through the adjective applied to her flank. And she, too, retreats into a different sort of contingency than the false nude of the first line, because her appearance-in-disappearance, her drowning, is only an alternative happening or reading of the scene, introduced by the "or" of the sestet and further qualified into contingency by the future-perfect that indicates her drowning, "aura noyé."

The parenthesis in the fourth and fifth lines, "(tu / Le sais, écume, mais y baves)," cancels, but then furthers, a predicative strength by absurdity: foam cannot know anything; cognition is not a property of water. Construing this parenthesis forces a metaphorical reading either of "écume," as the words of the poem or of "sais" in a sense of "act in accord with your known properties." This action is a kind of drooling, metaphorically, because drool is liquid like the water of the ocean, but lexically it is a bodily function of a mammal's mouth, metaphorized if it be extended from an involuntary bodily function to an involuntary mental one.[12] All this predicative action puts considerable pressure on "y," a word of location, which offers in this context a specificity that turns out to be quite general, at this moment, as in the poem as a whole, not to be confined either to a physical place or a logical position. The identical rhyme of "tu" and "tu" breaks, but also reinforces, the "hushed" of the first "tu" with the intimate second person of the second "tu," the reference of which is then generalized to be either the water or the speaker of the poem speaking to himself. The consequent inescapable identification of these two activates a proprioceptive act of quasi–identification between self and nature, which itself does not enter into easy merging but only participates energetically in the possibility. This process moves us toward the Heideggerian function of poetry as a realization of the human implication in an awareness of its own mortality by forcing an engagement with absences at the heart of being, with the "trompe sans vertu" of this poem and its questioned "sépulchral naufrage." So, in the words of Gérard Bucher, "le langage (la poésie) pourrait enfin assumer le rôle tiers, hyperbolique, *entre* la pensée et l'être, *entre* l'homme et le divin qui jamais ne lui fut concédé"[13] (Language [poetry] could at last assume the third role, a hyperbolic one, *between* thought and being, *between* man and the divine, which had never been conceded to it). The process of countering being with nonbeing through an enacted becoming is analogous to the philosophy of Hegel, who early interested Mallarmé.[14]

The diction of these poems tends to implode locally on itself, as here in "naufrage," "écume," "baves," and even "y." The words rise quickly to the thematic, and for the thematic in Mallarmé, as Richard says,

> Comprendre un thème, c'est encore "déployer (ses) multiples valences"; . . . la rêverie mallarméenne du *blanc* peut incarner tantôt la

jouissance du vierge, tantôt la douleur de l'obstacle et de la frigidité, tantôt le bonheur d'une ouverture, d'une liberté, d'une médiation, et c'est mettre en rapport en un même complexe ces diverses nuances de sens.[15]

[To understand a theme, is already to "deploy its multiple valences"; ... the Mallarméan dream of *white* can incarnate now the enjoyment of the virgin, now the sorrow of obstacle and frigidity, now the happiness of an opening, of a liberty, of a mediation, and it acts to put into relation in a single complex these diverse nuances of signification.]

In other words, the individual term, in itself, nests both metaphor and predications that enlist and reassign metaphor. Even in the prose discourse a term such as *idée* in "idée même et suave" can neither be referred to the Platonic system—"suave" lightly displaces it therefrom—nor can it be divorced from that origin. Mallarmé has digested as well as appropriated and reangled the term, toward a usage so melded it cannot effectually be either deconstructed or unpacked into a systematic set of meanings: "Je dis: une fleur! et, hors de l'oubli où ma voix relège aucun contour, en tant que quelque chose d'autre que les calices sus, musicalement se lève, idée même et suave, l'absente de tous bouquets" (368) (I say: a flower! and, aside from the oblivion into which my voice relegates any contour, insofar as anything other than the known petals, musically there arises, the very idea and suave, the absent one of all bouquets). He here activates what he characterizes as "un trépignant vis-à-vis avec l'idée" (369), a thumping dance facing the idea; or else as "preuves nuptiales de l'Idée" (387) (nuptial proofs of the idea), effective linkages of the Idea that constitute not one proof but several.

The disappearance of the flower that erects it to a higher plane not only out-sublates the *eidos* of Plato. It also, by anticipation, sets up the complex antinomy that engages the modern consciousness between word cutting back inescapably to the referentiality of the sign and word designating the referendum, a topic that Charles Sanders Peirce had already addressed with a far greater complexity than the Saussure who set it up in a correct, but oversimple, fashion. In the *Cours de linguistique générale,* arbitrary letters designate an idea in the mind about the tree out there in the world. Mallarmé's "hors de l'oubli" bypasses at one stroke the Saussurian formulation and accepts, while celebrating it, what amounts to the Peircian complexity. The voice relegates the utterance of a single word "flower" into oblivion, because the inescapable temporality of language in an utterance makes it disappear when uttered. But aside from the forgetting or oblivion, "hors de l'oubli," there arises a very absence or silence, an afterecho that makes the word not just a designation, a *Bedeutung* and not just a sense, a *Sinn,* but, linking these terms of Frege, an "idée." "The absent one of all bouquets" thus becomes the Platonic pure notion of what internalizes presence. Again, the constant inversions and suspensions of the hyperbaton in Mallarmé's hands force a consideration of predication, and simultaneously of the relation of reference and sense. Thus, the theory of Mallarmé's "je dis: une fleur!" already envisages what his poems act out, a referential complexity here, as it were, heralded in the exclamation point after "une fleur," a complexity that was being discussed at this very time by his philosophical contemporaries Peirce and Gottlob Frege. It is at all times, however, not the process of ratiocination alone, but verse, that serves as the binder both for these conjunctions and for the aerations and powerful indirections that their word linkages unleash. Verse becomes, in the hands of his manipulation, the supreme mold, the "suprême moule," that effectuates these conjunctions:

> Ainsi lancé de soi le principe qui n'est—que le Vers! attire non moins que dégage pour son épanouissement (l'instant qu'ils y brillent et meurent dans une fleur rapide, sur quelque transparence comme d'éther) les mille éléments de beauté pressés d'accourir et de s'ordonner dans leur valeur essentielle. Signe! au gouffre central d'une spirituelle impossibilité que rien soit exclusivement à tout, le numérateur divin de notre apothéose, quelque suprême moule qui n'ayant pas lieu en tant que d'aucun objet qui existe: mais il emprunte, pour y aviver un sceau tous gisements épars, ignorés et flottants selon quelque richesse, et les forger. (333)

> [Thus launched by itself the principle which is only—-Verse! attracts no less than it disengages for its blooming (the instant that they shine and die there in a rapid flowering, on some transparence like ether) the thousand elements of beauty pressed to rush there and organize themselves in their essential value. Sign! In the central gulf of a spiritual impossiblity that anything be exclusively to everything, the divine numerator of our apotheosis, some supreme mould which not taking place in so far as any object that exists: but it borrows, to vivify in it a seal, all locations dispersed, ignored, and floating according to some richness, and to forge them.]

All these considerations serve as a deep current for the flow of such a poem as, for example, the "Prose (pour des Esseintes)," where the structuring of the flowers in the theory of "Crise de vers" comes into poetic expression:

> Oui, dans une île que l'air charge
> De vue, et non de visions
> Toute fleur s'étalait plus large
> Sans que nous en devisions.
>
> Telles, immenses, que chacune
> Ordinairement se para
> D'un lucide contour, lacune,
> Qui des jardins la sépara.
>
> Gloire du long désir, Idées
> Tout en moi s'exaltait de voir
> La famille des iridées
> Surgir à ce nouveau devoir. (56)
>
> [Yes, in an isle the air charges
> With view and not with visions
> Every flower spread out more large
> Without our devising from it.
>
> Such, immense, that each one
> Ordinarily decked itself
> With a lucid contour, lacuna
> That severed it from the gardens.
>
> Glory of long desire, Ideas
> All in me was exalting itself to see
> The family of irises
> Rise up to this new duty.]

The island referred to here is a logical or virtual, not an actual, island, and so the focusing of attention in "vue, et non de visions," on the visible flowers nevertheless anchors that attention in a theoretical recapitulation that allows the actual flower, the present of all bouquets so to speak, to take on the propositional extensibility of the act of poetic saying and also become, in the poem according to the notion of "Crise de vers," the "absente de tous bouquets." These flowers, liberated in theory from our theory ("Sans que nous en devisions"), every one of them, is remembered in the near past—the shift of tense from present to past reminds us—as having spread out more broadly. The spreading involves a focusing that shifts tense once again, now not an imperfect but a

"ETENDRE, SIMPLIFIER LE MONDE"

past definite, "se para," which mimes the act of focusing from the indefiniteness of the imperfect. The shift of tenses here activates, as does the indirectness of naming ("not a thing but the effect it produces"), a powerful vagueness that gains by evading sharp definition: "Le sens trop précis rature / Ta vague littérature" (73) (A sense too precise erases / your vague literature). These flowers are such that each one decked itself with a lucid contour, and it did so "ordinarily." At the same time, each one posits an absence: It is a "lacune." All this action, hyperbolic in its formulation as the first word of this poem tells us, "Hyperbole," is a glory of the long desire. "Gloire du long désir," as an expression, compresses the stretch of desire with the splendor of fulfillment, with "Gloire."

The whole process, which began with a view and not with visions, results in a plenitude of multiple conceptions that might in one sense become visions: with "Idées." This contemplation of flowers fully organizes the perceptions and the psyche of the speaking poet into exaltation—"Tout en moi s'exaltait" (all in me was exalting itself), and this, the returned imperfect reminds us, is an ongoing process. The family of irises, endowed by the poet's formulation and viewing, makes the viewing see it rise to something new—and this something new bears not the signature of pleasure, though that too, but the signature of what on the face of it would seem a wholly different area, "devoir," ethics not aesthetics. It bears the signature of a duty that in this context has then provided the implicit philosophical proposition that the highest duty is pleasure: a higher utilitarianism in its calculus of pleasures than that envisaged by the Utilitarian John Stuart Mill who was Mallarmé's contemporary.

Mallarmé famously recommended that the poet "Peindre, non la chose, mais l'effet qu'elle produit"[16] (To paint, not the thing, but the effect it produces). And in answer to an interview question, "pour la forme. Et le fond?" (for the form. And the base?), he declared expansively,

> au fond, les jeunes sont plus près de l'idéal poétique que les Parnassiens qui traitent encore leurs sujets à la façon des vieux philosophes et des vieux rhéteurs, en présentant les objets directement . . . par là ils manquent de mystère; . . . *Nommer* un objet, c'est supprimer les trois quarts de la jouissance du poëme, qui est faite de deviner peu à peu: le *suggérer*, voilà le rêve. C'est le parfait usage de ce mystère qui constitue le symbole: évoquer petit à petit un objet pour montrer un état d'âme, ou, inversement, choisir un objet et en dégager un état d'âme, par une série de déchiffrements. (868–69)

> [basically the young are nearer the poetic ideal than the Parnassians are, who still treat their subjects in the fashion of the old philosophers

and the old rhetoricians, presenting objects directly . . . by which they lack mystery . . . *To name* an object is to suppress three quarters of the enjoyment of the poem, which is made to be divined bit by bit: to *suggest* it, that is the dream. It is the perfect usage of this mystery which constitutes the symbol: to evoke little by little an object to show a state of soul, or, inversely, to choose an object and disengage a state of soul from it by a series of decipherments.]

The "déchiffrements" involve a suggestiveness; bare naming must fall into the background as it enters the combinatory poetic process. In such decipherments, as he says of Poe (curiously seeming for the moment to overlook Poe's philosophical treatise, *Eureka*), he reveres him because the philosophy, while included, remains latent: "Je révère l'opinion de Poe, nul vestige d'une philosophie, l'éthique ou la métaphysique ne transparaîtra; j'ajoute qu'il la faut, incluse et latente" (872) (I revere the opinion of Poe, no vestige of a philosophy, ethics or metaphysics will show through; I add that it must be there, included and latent).

This force in Mallarmé's individual terms, and his combinatory suspensions, differentiates his hyperbaton from that of, say, his almost exact contemporary Gerard Manley Hopkins. As in Hopkins, the disjunction of the word in its ordonnance, the hyperbaton, produces a fetishization of the word, but for Mallarmé the suspensions, enlisted for predication, push the predication(s), so to speak, inside the word, which does not happen in Hopkins:

> I think; where from and bound, I wonder, where,
> With, all down darkness wide, his wading light?

These forceful lines from Hopkins's poem "The Lantern out of Doors," as the explicitly designative title can be taken to imply, employ their hyperbaton in the service of "inscape," the verbal reproduction of the mental apperception of a physical process.

Gongora attains elevation for his rhetoric but not a logical complication through his own hyperbaton:

> Menos solicitó veloz saeta
> destinada señal, que mordió aguda;
> agonal carro por la arena muda
> no coronó con más silencio meta
>
> que presurosa corre, que secreta
> a su fin nuestra edad.

> [Less eagerly the swift arrow
> its set target, which it sharply bit;
> the agon-chariot on the mute sand
> crowned not with more silence the goal post
>
> Than promptly runs, than secretly
> to its end our age.]

This poem is an expansion on an aphorism or proverb about the brevity, swiftness, and unexpected end of human life. The hyperbaton mimes these features, but with it Gongora does not set up any Mallarmé-like propositional interaction, and the metaphors themselves of arrow and chariot are relatively straightforward and simple. Neither Hopkins nor Gongora, then, approaches the predications of Mallarmé, for which his own term—a term that will comprise both predication and hyperbaton—is "transposition."

Transposition implies both a reordering of words out of their normal order that is effectuated in hyperbaton and the manipulation of relatable terms through series of propositions. For the poet, all this happens by a kind a self-revising instinct, and some such process is implied in the obscure doubling referred to by the "Prose (pour des Esseintes)," "Notre double / Inconscience approfondit" (Our double unconsciousness deepens). The terms themselves, thus juxtaposed, constitute another act of predication, which can only have taken place through a prior transposition, that of setting the word "double" with its powerful philosophical implications, up against the term "inconscience," in all its psychological evasiveness and obscurity. At the time, Hartmann had begun to write about the unconscious, and he was taken up by Laforgue. Again, the poem is contemporary with the young Freud, but, of course, it cannot be pushed much in that direction, which would clarify it. In Freud's sense, the unconscious does deepen, but how this "inconscience" of Mallarmé's does so involves an unnamed and flatly declared doubling. As so often with Mallarmé, juxtaposition brings us back to transposition.[17]

Words, in a related conception, involve a scale and the transitions through it—on the analogy of a musical scale. These transitions can be defined as transpositions:

> et ce à quoi nous devons surtout est que, dans le poème, les mots—qui déjà sont assez eux pour ne plus recevoir d'impression du dehors—se reflètent les uns sur les autres jusqu'à paraître ne plus avoir leur couleur propre, mais n'être lue les transitions d'une gamme.[18]

[And that to which we are above all obliged is that, in the poem, the words—which are already enough themselves no longer to receive an impression from outside—reflect one another to the point of appearing to have no longer their own color, but to be read as the transitions of a scale].

This "scale" is something like what governs the words as they enter into an intellectual music, through the doubling of an "inconscience." Coming at the intersection of such purposes, Mallarmé empowers their convergence by forcing a structure upon the divergence of words in such a way that every pause underscores both the divergence and the structure.

The term "transposition" comes up with a capital in "Crise de vers": "Cette visée, je la dis Transposition—Structure, une autre. L'oeuvre pure implique la disparition élocutoire du poète, qui cède l'initiative aux mots, par le heurt de leur inégalité mobilisés; ils s'allument de reflets réciproques." (366) (This focus, I call it Transposition—Structure, something else. The pure work implies the elocutionary disappearance of the poet, who cedes the initiative to the words, mobilised by the shock of their inequality; they illuminate each other by reciprocal reflections.) And the word is repeated on the next page, in apposition to "instrumentation," "un art d'achever la transposition, au Livre, de la symphonie" (the art of achieving the transposition, in the Book, of the symphony).[19] As Mallarmé says, writing about Banville,

> Une ligne, quelque vibration, sommaires et tout s'indique. Contrairement à l'art lyrique comme il fut, élocutoire, en raison du besoin, strict, de signification.—Quoiqu'y confine une suprématie, ou déchirement de voile et lucidité, le Verbe, reste, de sujets, de moyens, plus massivement lié à la nature.
>
> *La divine transposition,* pour l'accomplissement de quoi existe l'homme, *va du fait à l'idéal.* (522–23)

> [A line, some vibration, summaries and all is indicated. Contrary to the lyric art as it was, elocutionary, by reason of the need, strict, for signification.—Although it confines there a supremacy, or rending of the veil and lucidity, the Word, a remainder, of subjects, of means more massively linked to nature.
>
> *The divine transposion,* for the accomplishment of which man exists, *goes from the fact to the ideal.*]

And again, "A savoir que n'existe à l'esprit de quiconque a rêvé les humains jusqu'à soi rien qu'un compte exact de purs motifs rythmiques de l'être qui en sont les reconnaissables signes: il me plaît de les partout déchiffrer." (345) (To know that there exists in the spirit of whoever has dreamed of humans just to oneself nothing but an exact count of pure rhythmic motifs of being, of which they are the recognizable signs: it pleases me to decipher them everywhere.) These "purs motifs rythmiques de l'être" nest propositions that conflate music, ontology, and poetic composition in a combinatory reach for identities. Mallarmé's own work offers what he attributes to the theater of Villiers, "motifs brefs de vaste portée" (506) (brief motifs of vast import).

Here, too, as at the end of "Crise de vers," which preoccupies itself with rhythm, Mallarmé at the same time insists on getting beyond mere rhythm. Immediately following the "fleur... absente de tous bouquets" passage, in the last two paragraphs of this (composite, recomposed) essay, he asserts a control through verse of "le hasard," the very principle that can in no way be abolished by a throw of the die, according to the rib statement of that last poem:

Le vers qui de plusieurs vocables refait un mot total, neuf, étranger à la langue et comme incantatoire, achève cet isolement de la parole: niant d'un trait souverain, le hasard, demeuré aux termes malgré l'artifice de leur retrempe alternée en le sens et la sonorité, et vous cause cette surprise de n'avoir ouï jamais tel fragment ordinaire d'élocution, en même temps que la réminiscence de l'objet nommé baigne dans une neuve atmosphère. (368)

[Verse which with several vocables remakes a word, that is total, new, a stranger to the language and as though incantatory, achieves this isolation of speech: denying, in a sovereign stroke, chance, remaining in the terms in spite of the artifice of their tempering alternated between sense and sonority, and causes you this surprise of never having heard some ordinary fragment of elocution, at the same time that the remembrance of the object named bathes in a new atmosphere.]

What this "neuve atmosphère" may imply in its full dimensions calls for amplification, in its connection with "la réminiscence de l'objet." But the new atmosphere is only created if sufficient conditions have been satisfied for the words that are both multiple (*plusieurs vocables*) and single (*un mot*). The word must be total: It must comprise the converged references that the symbology of Richard has traced. If it is so total, it will have purified the language of the tribe, and so it will meet the second condition; it will be "neuf." If it achieves this, it will automatically have met the third condition; it will be "étrange." And this, in turn, will release it to join other words and meet the fourth condition, to become "incantatoire." The logic of transpositions will have brought about a music—but all not without "le hasard," Mallarmé's quasi-mathematical version of the principle of chaos. And the last statement of the *Coup de Dés* centers on intellection as at least the efficient cause of the die, "Toute Pensée émet un Coup de Dés" (Every thought emits a throw of the die). The risk, at an extreme, is expressed in the single enigmatic proposition of "Le Démon de l'Analogie," "La Pénultième est morte," a phrase that could be taken generally as a metaphor for the structure of predicates, as its formulation within the poem reverberates with the poet's consistent theorizing:

>   *La Pénultième*
>   finit le vers et
>   *Est morte*
>   se détacha de la sus-
>   pension fatidique plus inutilement en le vide de signification.
>   (272)

>   [The Penultimate
>   finishes the verse and
>   is dead
>   detaches itself from the
>   fateful suspension more uselessly in the void of meaning.]

Mathematics has the clarity to which poetry aspires, and music, has the supreme identity of sound with sense. The term "number" covers both mathematics and music; and the thought of Mallarmé aspires to both, while engaging what neither need find as a limit, namely, "le hasard." It is only poetry that need undertake that risk while formulating propositions or projecting sounds; for it, as for the game of thinking, "Toute Pensée émet un Coup de Dés." So, although "Le Hasard" is a key category both of Mallarmé's thinking and of the text of the *Coup de Dés,* the term "number" comes up, as does the figure who cannot be identified with the prince, the "maître":

>   C'ÉTAIT   LE NOMBRE
>   *issu stellaire*
>   (472–73)
>   LE MAÎTRE   hors d'anciens calculs
>   où la maneuvre avec l'âge oubliée
>   (462–63)

"ETENDRE, SIMPLIFIER LE MONDE" 73

(IT WAS   THE NUMBER
stellar issue

THE MASTER   beyond former calculations
                             or the maneuver forgotten with age)

These statements make the die urgent as well as playful, and comprehensive as well as singular—much like the relation between deixis and syntax that the poem itself deliberately shuffles and throws into relief.

Nevertheless, as Derrida says, "Cet espacement et cette répercussion, Mallarmé les affirme à la fois comme contingence ('réciprocité de feux distante et présentée de biais comme contingence') et comme 'hasard vaincu,' entrelacs, dans le vers, du nécessaire et de l'arbitraire"[20] (This spacing and this repercussion, Mallarmé affirms at once as a contingency ["a reciprocity of fires distant and presented on the bias as contingency"] and like a 'chance overcome,' an interlacing, in the verse, of the necessary and the arbitrary). The implicitly contradictory categories of hazard and mastery, and consequently of chaos and order, are being yoked not propositionally but in a set of spacings and supreme hyperbatons that try to escape the proposition as they try to aerate syntax. In this segment "number" is linked paratactically, appositionally, but not quite propositionally, with "stellar issue" and "master," while at the same time it is qualified as being "out of ancient calculations, in which the manoeuver is forgotten with age," when it would have seemed that number would be timeless and at the same time always subject to "anciens calculs."

When the "absente de tous bouquets" is articulated, the function of number becomes at once primary and hazardous. This "number" is not just supplementary to normal "chiffrations"; it is contrary to them: "Au contraire d'une fonction de numéraire facile et représentatif, comme le traite d'abord la foule, le dire, avant tout, rêve et chant, retrouve chez le Poëte, par nécessité constitutive d'un art consacré aux fictions, sa virtualité" (368) (As opposed to a coin's easy and representative function, as the crowd treats it initially, the statement, above all, dream and song, rediscovers in the Poet its virtuality, necessarily constitutive of an art devoted to fictions). The supreme act of saying "le dire" does not just purify the language of the tribe. By consecrating it to fictions, to virtuality, it reverses an easy and representative numeration. It does so not only by singing but by dreaming, "rêve et chant." This act doubles the ordinary language, which normally does not dream or sing. Thus, this speaking deepens ordinary language. And this is a social retrieval. In the "Prose (pour des Esseintes)," it is "*notre double inconscience*" that "*approfondit.*" "The unconscious is structured like a language," Lacan demonstrates, and Mallarmé's centrality consists in his structuring the language as though it were the unconscious not by a protosurrealism but by attending precisely to the moments of its structuration.[21] This act of social retrieval is double in the sense that there is a dialectic between conscious and "inconscience," and also in the sense that the dialectic thus achieved in this poetry becomes double or dialogic in its social context, however other and resistant the crowd may be to it.

Thus, there is an achieved link between these propositionally mounted images and the common life. The fusions between social and literary destinies become emblematized in Mallarmé's recursion to the meditation on common mortality in all the *Tombeaux*. To a circularized periodical questionnaire, "Définissez la poésie," Mallarmé replied in 1886, "Je balbutie, meurtrie: La Poésie est l'expression, par le langage humain ramené à son rythme essentiel, du sens mystérieux des aspects de l'existence: elle doue ainsi d'authenticité notre séjour et constitue la seule tâche spirituelle."[22] (I stammer, wounded: Poetry is the expression in human language brought back to its essential rhythm, of the mysterious sense of aspects of existence: it thus endows our sojourn with authenticity and constitutes the sole spiritual task.)

The execution of mystery and authenticity in the spiritual task strengthens the "Tombeau d'Edgar Poe":

>Tel qu'en Lui-même enfin l'éternité le change
>Le Poëte suscite avec un glaive nu
>Son siècle épouvanté de n'avoir pas connu
>Que la mort triomphait dans cette voix étrange!
>
>Eux, comme un vil sursaut d'hydre oyant jadis l'ange
>Donner un sens plus pur aux mots de la tribu
>Proclamèrent très haut le sortilège bu
>Dans le flot sans honneur de quelque noir mélange.
>
>Du sol et de la nue hostiles, ô grief!
>Si notre idée avec ne sculpte un bas-relief
>Dont la tombe de Poe éblouissante s'orne,
>
>Calme bloc ici-bas chu d'un désastre obscur,
>Que ce granit du moins montre à jamais sa borne
>Aux noirs vols du Blasphème épars dans le futur.

[As into Himself finally eternity changes him,
The Poet rouses with a naked sword
His age, horrified at not having known
That death was triumphing in this strange voice!

They, startled like a vile hydra of old,
When the angel purified human words,
Loudling proclaimed his magic had been drunk
In the base flood of some sinister brew.

From the ground and the cloud hostile, o struggle!
If our idea with it sculpt not a bas-relief
With which the dazzling tomb of Poe is decked,

Calm block fallen down here from an obscure disaster,
May this granite at least show forever the boundary
To the dark flights of Blasphemy scattered in the future.]

The hyperbole of this poem returns us to an honorific but ordinary meditation on last things. It is the language of the tribe to which it gives a purer sense. The first line broaches and leaves undefined the religious context of "eternity," which here means at once the life and the achievement of the poet that are seen "sub specie aeternitatis." In death his identity becomes capitalized as "Lui-même," and that identity of the self takes on apocalyptic functions. For, as Robert Greer Cohn reminds us here, the angel holding a sword against the hydra that listens to him and fails to honor him evokes Mallarmé's own conception of the substratum of myth: "There is also a vague feeling of reference to some myth, such as Perseus and the Gorgon, Oedipus and the Sphinx. According the the *Dieux antiques*, every myth is based on a combat of the angelic or heroic sun and the clouds that obscure it at sunset."[23] The poet is gathered, while the blasphemy, frozen into the abstraction of a capitalization, is neverthless scattered in the future of the poet's self and work. These are "at last" changed by eternity, a calm block, like the monument this poet has sculpted for him, fallen down from a disaster that has become from this point of view obscure in all its connections, though the disaster that ended Poe's life, and the disaster of the failure of communication, are both all too clear. The graveyard, which is the underlying metaphor of the last lines of this poem, has become a sort of road, which has a milestone on it, a "borne." This borne, for an English teacher preoccupied with Hamlet, perhaps echoes Hamlet's "the undiscovered country from whose bourne / No traveller returns." It is also a boundary stone setting down, as these words do in their hyperbolic afflatus, a limit to detractions against the poet that now take on a religious cast: they are technically to be defined as blasphemy.[24]

The hyperbole of the "Prose (pour des Esseintes)" is hyperbolic in the first place because of the title, which funnels the whole poem off into the fictive and into the sociologized dialogic, both set up and closed out in its initial conception, because des Esseintes is not a person at all but a character in a novel, the protagonist in *A Rebours* by Mallarmé's friend Joris Karl Huysmans, a novel in which Mallarmé's poetry is highly praised. The hyperbole goes against the grain, *à rebours*, by providing a verse described as prose, forcing us to take the term "prose" in an archaic and descriptive sense, as a "religious litany." The title, thus highlighted, fictively and ironically returns des Esseintes to a whole religious culture that he takes seriously enough to set himself against its grain, the way Huysmans himself finally did when he converted later in life.

It is a hyperbole of the memory of the writer who crosses the line between fictive and real by asking a fictive person to react to his real self:

> Hyperbole! de ma mémoire
> Triomphalement ne sais-tu
> Te lever, aujourd'hui grimoire
> Dans un livre de fer vêtu
>
> [Hyperbolic! from my memory
> Triumphally do you not know
> How to rise, today a magic book
> In a book of iron clothed]

It is a hyperbole of his own memory: the psychological process is undercut by being discredited at the outset as a sort of exaggeration. What would be a nonexaggeration, what sort of *Wahrheit* might underlie this *Dichtung,* is a consideration that is at no point allowed purchase. The question cannot even be asked because it is submerged in the other more insistent, more trivial, and at the same time more unreal question framed into this first stanza by a person who can by definition not answer because he is confined to the pages of a book as though in iron, "un livre de fer vêtu." And the book is not just a book, "un livre" rather than "Le Livre" of Mallarmé's constant, lifelong meditation, but a religious book, a "grimoire" whose very name announces its superannuation into the antique, though it derives from a culture of the Book with a capital "B" for which "Le Livre" would have been a secular equivalent.

A meditation on flowers, through the poet's "antique soin," touches on a "désir" allowed an erotic dimension through the impenetrably generalized term "soeur" that the literalist would want to confine either to Méry Laurent or to the sister Maria whose death, when Mallarmé was fifteen, affected him so profoundly:[25]

> L'ère d'autorité se trouble
> Lorsque, sans nul motif, on dit
> De ce midi que notre double
> Inconscience approfondit.
>
> Oui, dans une île que l'air charge
> De vue, et non de visions
> ———
>
> Mais cette soeur sensée et tendre
> Ne porta son regard plus loin
> Que sourire et, comme à l'entendre
> J'occupe mon antique soin
>
> [Authority's era is troubled
> When, with no motive, it is said
> Of this noon that our double
> Non-consciousness deepens.
>
> Yes in an isle the air charges
> With view and not with visions . . .
> ———
>
> But this sister, sensible and tender,
> Did not carry her look further
> Than smiling and, as if to understand her
> I attend to my ancient care]

The "Oui" has to be a pseudodialogic answer to the self, because the person who is being addressed, to repeat, is in a book, and therefore only obliquely to be taken—though surely thus—for the book's author.

The poem recounts another muted dialogue, that between the sister whose look carried not into words but no further than a smile, and the answer of the speaking poet who rose in this account also not to speech but "as though to hear her" (or "it," the elision allowing the antecedent of "l'" to be either *la soeur* or *le regard*).

A smile is not heard, of course, and in this semisubmerged synesthesia, the speaker is either hearing what he sees (her look, her smile) or hearing a silence that carries a message not risen to words, when the family of irises also mute, has risen to this new duty, *à ce nouveau devoir* —a duty to have the pleasure of an idea, which carries with it an intimation of erotic pleasure.

Eroticism, in any case, plays through Mallarmé's poetry generally. "Le Phénomène futur" presents at twilight the image of an unattainable beauty. This is Baudelaire on the way to becoming *Hérodiade*. In "Mes bouquins refermés sur le nom de Paphos," under this distracting preoccupation with Venus he evokes on the one hand the "chair humain et parfumant," and on the other the "sein brûlé d'une antique amazone."

The centrality of Mallarmé, here as throughout his best work, is to fuse all these possibilities whose intensity derives precisely from their nonactualization. In his most persistently meditated work, Mallarmé's expression involves the erotic, and the erotic in an extreme form. In the "Faune," the erotic is identified with the "flute" of the pastoralizing poet. It begins, "Ces nymphes, je veux les perpétuer" (These nymphs, I want to perpetuate them), and the pluralization of the nymphs siphons them off from any actual embrace to the idealization that "perpétuer" implies. *Hérodiade*,[26] the poem of his longest meditation, staying on his desk for over thirty years, involves complicated erotic withdrawals, substitutions of murder for consummation, and postponements of union through a constantly displayed narcissism.

The "incantation" of the Nourrice in *Hérodiade* is simply descriptive of the scene and recursive to her own voice, "Est-ce la mienne prête à l'incantation?" This preoccupation dominates the second part, too, in Hérodiade's command to the nurse to withdraw, and she (an anti-Phèdre) describes not her passion but her hair and her situation. She calls for the nurse to comb her hair, refusing the essence of rose balm. She asks for her mirror. The poem envisages a monumental indirection, haunted by the severed head of John the Baptist on a platter, which is finally in Mallarmé's composition brought forward to sing in the third part, the "Cantique de Saint Jean."

The eroticism of *L'Après-midi d'un Faune* and of *Hérodiade* becomes after the fact legendary. It is also philosophically oriented, in what was to become the era of Wilde and Sacher-Masoch.

Both show traces of and transform the Parnasse in a Baudelairian direction that Baudelaire himself did not take. *Hérodiade* reflects, and redirects by heavily aestheticizing and eroticizing it, the milieu of Renan.[27] The two dramatic poems parallel the concerns of Renan both in intellectualizing his material and sublating the opposition between pagan (Faune) and Christian (Hérodiade). *Hérodiade* combines perverse eroticism and exhibitionism with the displacement into the Bible of the algolagnia absent from the sonnets of "jubilation nue" that derive from his relationship with Méry.

At another extreme of his contemplation, Mallarmé envisages a silent theater, the mime, that involves, in his illustration, an erotic extreme, the murder of Columbine by her betrayed love Pierrot. She is murdered in her bed by the outrageous and extreme torture of tickling. Mallarmé withdrew somewhat from his youthful preoccupation with the theater[28] to replace it by the stasis of *L'Après-midi d'un Faune* and *Hérodiade*, so that the dynamics within the phrasal conjunctions can be energized, as it were dramatically. For the difference between these finally late works and works contemporary with their initial conception like "L'Azur" or "Las de l'amer repos" surfaces in the dynamic interaction of the late poems, justifying the notion that it was the idea of drama rather than drama itself that energized Mallarmé.[29]

Cast originally as dramas, the *Faune* and *Hérodiade* do not lose that form. Tinkering with them, Mallarmé abandons the form—to set the interaction of the words on the page as an analogue to the dramatic encounter. As Peter Dayan says, "Thus the theatre provides Mallarmé with the archetypal image of both the distinguishing formal feature of ideal patterns—they are artificial figures, knot-like, with an inward-looking logic—and the basic movement by which the ideal pattern is rendered sensible—projection. The audience looks out; whereas the performance itself is inward-looking, folded, suspended or knot-like, like the ideal figure. In consequence, Mallarmé often indicates the ideal nature of non-theatrical ideal experiences by hinting that those experiences are theatrical in form."[30] This conception redounds in his chacterization of mime in "Le Mimique":

> Voici—"La scène n'illustre que l'idée, pas un action effective, dans un hymen (d'où procède le Rêve), vicieux mais sacré, entre le désir et l'accomplissment, la perpétration et son souvenir: ici devançant, là remémorant, au futur, au passé *sous une apparence fausse de présent*.

Tel opère le Mime, dont le jeu se borne à une allusion perpétuelle sans briser la glace: il installe, ainsi, un milieu, pur, de fiction." (310)

[Here it is:—"The scene illustrates only the idea, not an effective action, in a hymen (from which the Dream proceeds), vicious but sacred, between desire and accomplishment, the perpetration and its memory: here progressing, there reminding, to the future, to the past, *without a false appearance of a present.* So does Mime operate, of which the play limits itself to a perpetual illusion without breaking the mirror: it installs, thus, a milieu, pure, of fiction."]

He casts "le Livre" as a teacher to a "théâter borné" (319).

Hyperbaton mounts the dialogue between the words, and the syntactic tension that here effectually substitutes for that on stage. The interaction of the words, livened, mimes the process of thought. This counters the syntactic movement and then repeats it by a Hamlet-like suicide (*Igitur*) and a Hamlet-like vanishing prince (*Coup de Dés*), a prince d'Aquitaine who is *aboli* not *à la tour* but in the whirlwind/whirlpool of a hazarded ship. Hamlet remains here a vestige and reprojection of Mallarmé's lifelong preoccupation with that figure, as also with the drama.

A large share of the *Poèmes en Prose* recount some version of dramatic performances. This is so of "La Déclaration foraine," which quotes the imagined recitation of Mallarmé's sonnet, "La Chevelure." In his text, he places this sonnet immediately after *Hérodiade* and separate from the other sonnets.[31]

Close to the end of his life, the villagers come to his summer theater in Valvins. And for it he wrote a Preface to the medieval play *Maître Patelin* (1512). "Crayonné au théâtre" manifests the engagement and pressure of thinking about theater (dance and melodrama are here two illustrations) when the writer goes "presque jamais" to the theater. "Hamlet" begins with the trope that autumn is the theater of nature, an untheatrical application of a theatrical type. Mallarmé projected a one-man drama, "Hamlet ou le vent."[32] One can treat this intention, communicated to George Moore, possibly as part of the project that became the *Coup de Dés*.

As a counter to his preoccupation with a wordless theater—mime, ballet, dance—is his fascination with the opera of Wagner, and the question of how verse can rival opera:

Oui, en tant qu'un opéra sans accompagnement ni chant, mais parlé; maintenant le livre essaiera de suffire, pour entr'ouvrir la scène intérieure et en chuchoter les échos. Un ensemble versifié convie à une idéale représentation: des motifs d'exaltation ou de songe s'y nouent entre eux et se détachent, par une ordonnance et leur individualité. (328)

[Yes, and an opera without accompaniment or singing, but spoken, now the book will try to suffice, to half-open the interior scene and whisper the echoes. A versified ensemble leads to an ideal representation; motifs of exaltation and dream intricate among themselves and separate by an ordering and their individuality.]

But then the wordless dance can rival opera, "La Danse seule capable, par son écriture sommaire, de traduire le fugace et le soudain jusqu'à l'Idée—pareille vision comprend tout, absolument tout le Spectacle futur" (541) (Danse alone capable, by its summary writing, to translate the fugitive and the sudden as far as the Idea—an equal vision comprises all, absolutely all of the future Spectacle). But, at the same time, the myth has a capital importance, "le siècle ou notre pays, qui l'exalte, ont dissous par la pensée les Mythes, pour en refaire!" (545) (the century or our country, which exalts it, have dissolved by thought the Myths, to remake them). This defines Wagner much as the contemporary Nietzsche was defining him (not to speak of the essays of Wagner himself).[33] Mallarmé's exclamation point underscores the capital force of the imaginative act. For, of the myths, as he continues, "Le Théâtre les appelle, non: pas de fixes, ni de séculaires et de notoires, mais un, dégagé de personalité, car il compose notre aspect multiple. . . . Type sans dénomination possible, pour qu'émane la surprise" (545) (The Theater calls them, no: nothing fixed, secular, notorious, but single, disengaged from personality, for it composes our multiple aspect. . . . Type without possible denomination, so that surprise may emanate).

But the tragic, too, is a final category—for drama, and also for the poem: "Voilà une théorie tragique actuelle ou, pour mieux dire, la dernière: le drame, latent, ne se manifeste que par une déchirure affirmant l'irréductibilité de nos instincts" (321) (Here is a present tragic theory, or, to speak more precisely, the last one: the drama, latent, only is manifested in a rending that affirms the irreducibility of our instincts). The theater of these wrought poems does affirm "the irreducibility of our instincts" by forcing them to seem to undergo the reductions of the transposed words that set them up into such striking conjunctions that they push back, thereby manifesting and defining their evoked power.

Finally, in the *Coup de Dés,* the process of predicative connection is stretched even further, the white spaces between words and phrases foregrounding the distance between the words that the process of thought and rhythm must bridge by stepping forth on the stage of the mind. A hieratic dramatic figure, the "prince" who is hypostatized from the conventional Hamlet deprived of the contours of his specifying name, occupies the center of this stage where center and margin have been shuffled.

In the *Coup de Dés,* there are three areas: (A) shipwreck, (B) Hamlet, (C) Abyss and constellation.[34] Each of these areas is governed by a large-type group of the rib statement, (a) Un Coup de Dés Jamais, (b) N'Abolira, (c) Le Hasard—the last having a whole page to itself. The correspondences A-a, B-b, C-c are not, however, symmetrical. Shipwreck is a deducible instance of the throw of the die, "N'abolira" is a temporalized angle on Hamlet. Le Hasard is set into an antithesis between abyss (full chaos) and constellation (order)—potential predications never actualized until the final sentence.

Further, there are three, not two, sizes of type (at least) in the poem, and these propose different interlocking relations, especially as the second-order type takes over for a run at the very beginning of the poem for concession, or for framing ("Maître," "Si . . . Si," "Comme si . . . comme si"). All these, as concrete poems, interact with the down-spiral of the third-order type, in which the narrative is carried forward, as well as in the intervention of white spaces, which Mallarmé tabs in his introduction as semiotic. That black-and-white effectually advances beyond his previous poems, as the Richard intensive symbology, and the Cohn fetished Rimbaud-like letters (both emphasized by Derrida) do not. The distinctness of the poem, then, cannot lie in the concretely varied word-clusters by themselves, but in them as they interact with the white spaces.

Derrida's inflection of Richard's symbology, the abstractable character of the symbology itself, and its extrapolability up to the macrolevel of R. G. Cohn's tetrapolar system on the one hand and the microlevel of his significant phonetic constituents on the other, all testify to the charged philosophical air that this poetry carries. It does so under the additional tension that both the prose and the poetry are more often than not rhetorically occasional: They respond to an occasion, an assignment, or an event. And they are poised upon the occasion.[35] So, congruently, Mallarmé's philosophizing is built into his literary practice and the unusually coordinate, poetically succinct, literary statements, so that he could serve as a model for the lifelong philosopher of the *Cahiers*, Valéry.

Notes

1. Stéphane Mallarmé, *Oeuvres complètes*, ed. Henri Mondor and G. Jean-Aubry (Paris: Gallimard-Pléiade, 1945), 647. Further page references to this edition will be given in parentheses.

2. Akin to "vibration" is the "flottaison" that Jacques Derrida notices as revelatory and typical for Mallarmé (*La Dissémination* [Paris: Seuil, 1972], 269): "Chaque fois qu'il apparaît, le mot *flottaison* suggère la suggestion mallarméenne, dévoile à peine, tout près de disparaître, l'indécision de ce qui reste suspendu, ni ceci ni cela, entre ici et là, *donc* entre ce texte et un autre" (Each time it appears, the word *flottaison* suggests the Mallarméan suggestion, unveils, scarcely, on the brink of disappearing, the indecision of that which remains suspended, neither this nor that, between here and there, *hence* between this text and another. *Trans. Ed.*)

3. Vibration letter, 17 May 1867 (Mauron associates this letter with Yoga or yogalike practices, *Mallarmé par lui-même*, 56).

4. Paul Valéry, *Oeuvres* (Paris: Gallimard, 1957), 1: 646.

5. Michel Deguy, "The Energy of Despair." Paper given at the Stanford Mallarmé Festival, 26 October 1996 (this volume).

6. Derrida, 281.

7. Ibid., 298; Robert Greer Cohn, *Toward the Poems of Mallarmé* (Berkeley: University of California Press, 1980), 229–36.

8. "At cum decoris gratia tracitur longius verbum, propie hyperbaton tenet nomen" (8.6.65). And again, simply translating the Greek "hyperbaton" or "overstepping" Quintilian says "hyperbaton, that is transgression of the word" (hyperbaton, id est verbi transgressionem, 8.6.62).

9. Letter to Vielé-Griffin, 8 August 1891; quoted by Maurice Blanchot, *L'Espace littéraire* (Paris: Gallimard, 1955), 35.

10. René Daumal, *Le Contre-ciel* (Paris: Gallimard, 1970), 103.

11. Daumal, 25, 37–38.

12. However, in *Les Mots anglais*, Mallarmé renders "baver" by a more intensive and pejorative English word, "slaver" (944).

13. Gérard Bucher, *Le Testament poétique* (Paris: Belin, 1994), 10.

14. See Charles Mauron, *Mallarmé par lui-même* (Paris: Seuil, 1964), 52–55. See also Jean-Pierre Richard, *L'Univers imaginaire de Mallarmé* (Paris: Seuil, 1961), 185. Sartre found in Mallarmé "le rythme hégélien" and spoke of him as the "héros d'un drame ontologique" (Jean-Paul Sartre, "L'engagement de Mallarmé," *Obliques* [1979]: 192), as cited by Henri Meschonnic, *Stéphane Mallarmé: Ecrits sur le Livre* (Paris: L'Eclat, 1985), 37–38. Derrida subtly discriminates the closeness, and the distance, between Mallarmé and Hegel, and also Plato in "La Double Séance" (235).

15. Richard, 27–28.

16. Letter, October 1864.

17. Rebecca Saunders deduces from what amounts to Mallarmé's deeply ingrained hyperbaton a double movement toward both the expression of the anthropological contamination linked to lamentation and the antithetical purification "of the words of the tribe" thus imposed. "Mallarmé's crisis of verse thus mimes

the moment and the language of lamentation and in so doing appropriates a language that is at once a sign of defilement and an instrument of purity" ("Shaking Down the Pillars: Lamentation, Purity, and Mallarmé's 'Homage to Wagner'" *PMLA* 111, no. 5 [October 1996]: 1106–20 [1117]).

18. Letter to François Coppée, 1866. Stéphane Mallarmé, *Correspondance, 1862–1871,* ed. Lloyd James Austin and Henri Mondor (Paris: Gallimard, 1959), 234. (Hereafter cited as *Corr.,* followed by page number.)

19. See Peter Dayan, *Mallarmé's Divine Transposition* (Oxford: Clarendon Press, 1986). Dayan (44) emphasizes Mallarmé's use of this term as Mallarmé defines it in "Averses ou Critiques," *Revue Blanche* (September 1895): 228–31 (in a paragraph omitted from the Pléiade edition).

20. Derrida, 310.

21. Lacan's own prose style finds perhaps its closest analogue for suspensions and condensations in the prose of Mallarmé.

22. Lettre à Léo d'Orfer, 27 June 1884, in *Corr.* 2:266.

23. Cohn, 155.

24. Mallarmé uses religious terms constantly while avoiding doctrinal identifications. J. H. Rosny asks Mallarmé near the end of his life (Mauron, 57) if he believes in immortality, and he replies "Je ne sais . . . j'espère peu, mais je fais comme si j'étais immortel, puisque, en toute chose, je cherche une synthèse, puisque je poursuis quelques symboles qui expliqueraient l'infini." Here the Hegelian language (*synthèse*) merges into the theological (infinite = immortality) and the literary (*symboles*).

Religion is often reduced or confined to art in his statements.

On the other hand, the expression emphasized by R. G. Cohn, "On ne peut se passer d'Eden," implies a centrality and finality for what amounts to a religious definition (402–3).

25. Mauron links this death psychologically to the early death of the poet's mother (*Mallarmé par lui-même,* passim). This, and other possibilities for specifying readings in the poem, are discussed by Lloyd James Austin, *Essais sur Mallarmé* (Manchester: Manchester University Press, 1995), 92–150. See also Cohn, 240–60. For convergent multiple readings as forging a degree of generality in a poetic utterance, see Albert Cook, "Generality," in *Prisms* (Bloomington: Indiana University Press, 1967), 25–73, especially for Mallarmé (41–46).

26. Letter to Cazalis, November 1865 , "Non plus tragédie mais poème." In 1896, he still (*OC*, 1465) writes that he is to complete it.

27. Ernest Renan (1823–92) was an older contemporary of Mallarmé whose best-known book, *La Vie de Jésus,* was published in 1863, a peak year of intellectual development in Mallarmé's early manhood.

28. This is exemplified in some of the essays of the *Proses de jeunesse,* 249–69.

29. As Derrida says (264), "Que pour Mallarmé le monde théâtral soit un monde mental, qui pourrait en nier l'évidence? Encore faut-il la lire sous verre. Mallarmé dit bien 'le milieu mental identifiant la scène et la salle' [298]. Le livre n'est-il pas en effet l'intériorité du théâtre, la scène du dedans?" (That for Mallarmé the theatrical world is a mental world, who could deny the evidence? But it has to be read under a magnifying lens. Mallarmé well says "the mental milieu identifying the stage and the hall" [298]. Isn't the book indeed the interiority of the theater, the inner scene? Trans. Ed.).

30. Dayan, 64.

31. Surely meter alone would not account for this, Cohn's reason; though the two reasons, poetic form and dramatic situation, could go together. The Shakespearean sonnet is histrionic.

32. Richard, 159.

33. See especially Richard Wagner, *Hauptschriften* (Stuttgart: Kröner, 1956), 116–50.

34. I am here following Charles Mauron, "Commentaries," in *Mallarmé: Poems,* trans. Roger Fry (New York: New Directions, 1951), 181–303.

35. See Albert Cook, "Mallarmé: The Deepening Occasion," in *Thresholds: Studies in the Romantic Experience* (Madison: University of Wisconsin Press, 1985), 162–78.

Mallarmé's Progeny

Mary Ann Caws

What was it about Mallarmé that we still find so riveting? No one else has lasted this well in French literature, it seems to me, except Montaigne, Rousseau, Diderot, and Proust. Mallarmé feels modern beyond our wildest imagination; what he gives us is everything that comes after him. This is more or less what I want to show: what he gives us—from his time to ours. I want to look at what Mallarmé meant to some others and, by extension, what he has meant to us.

Part of the enduring excitement is over loss. We know that Mallarmé's great piece on the impressionists and Manet was lost in the original French. But there are currently at least two translations back into French, wildly different, multiplying possibilities of speculation. In some implausible Derridian move of great chance and good fortune, we got back doubly what we had singly lost. In any case, we know how Mallarmé cared about the major impressionists, how he said of himself that he was "happy to live in the same epoch as Monet,"[1] how he loved Redon and frequently took him out boating, how he defended Manet and went to his studio every day for ten years.[2]

But my interest in Mallarmé goes around the house where we keep seeing him in conversation with Manet and Méry, or Berthe Morisot, around to find him in his long, close, and surprisingly affectionate association with that other early symbolist, the impossibly arrogant, touching, impossible Scottish American genius James Abbott McNeill Whistler, whose most famous portrait is heard to murmur: you know, my son Jimmie, the painter. About his superb artistry, even the difficult Degas concurred. After some especially outlandish stunt on Whistler's part, Degas exclaims: "You'd be impossible, Whistler, if only you weren't a genius." Mallarmé sponsored, cared about, nurtured, corresponded with, flattered, and loved this unlikely friend—not just this genius, but this man.

It is surely one of the great friendships and correspondences of the art world, and brought out the best in both creators as they, in a sense, translated and influenced each other. Mallarmé translated Whistler's lecture called the "Ten O'Clock" (because of the evening hour at which it was held, Whistler insisting that the audience would be in a better mood and more elegantly dressed, having already dined), with the help of Vielé-Griffin and George Moore.[3] He also admired Whistler's work, wrote for him and on him, got him the Legion of Honor, and arose from his sick bed to give him the news, and saw to it that his mother's portrait was purchased by the French government. And Whistler loved Mallarmé above everyone except his beloved Trixie.

Now I cherish obsessions and obsessiveness—and for me, the Mallarmé-Whistler combination leads straight into my present obsession with both artists as seen from the perspective of Bloomsbury. From the beginning, Vanessa Bell loved Whistler's work; Roger Fry loved Vanessa and, finally, also Whistler's work, although he began by Cézanne-worship; more importantly, he translated Mallarmé, over and over, for far longer than twenty years.

And then, like the loss of the Mallarmé-Manet manuscript, Roger Fry's translations were lost to a thief in the St. Lazare station, and he had to wait for them to rise from the dead, as he thought of it: destruction turned out to be his Beatrice, too. For rise they did, and as Julian Bell rather elliptically describes it, one piece came in from here, one from there ... so Fry picked up the pieces, he enlisted, as you probably know, the commentaries of the founder of psychocriticism, Charles Mauron, the ex-chemist and translator of Forster, T. E. Lawrence, Virginia Woolf, and Henry James.[4] What Roger Fry had cared about so much was finished, at his death, by Mauron with Julian Bell before the latter went off to get himself killed in the Spanish Civil war, against the advice of Mauron, whom he trusted, and the wishes of Vanessa— another loss.

But what we have, besides the rather literalizing translations, is the elaborate correspondence around the layers of Mallarmé's possible meanings and their truly obsessive hold on Fry as on Mauron. Nothing had held Fry like this: we have tale after tale of his cycling off to sketch some cathedral in the early morning, guiding the others through obscure byways later in the day to see some little-known piece of art, wearing everyone out until midnight, and then exclaiming how he and Julian had just enough time to play a game of chess and translate another sonnet. Then he would lie on his camp bed, reading for hours until he sprang up before breakfast to bike off to some other church. "He put me to shame," said Clive Bell, far younger. "Look at him!"

Roger Fry's immense generosity of spirit meant he had everything to give to what he loved, and you can feel that in his own poems, in his translations of Rimbaud, Baudelaire, and particularly Mallarmé. I have been poring over the manuscripts of those, and marveling now at their precision. I used to reject their literality, preferring suggestion to statement as I thought Mallarmé would. Yet, now I see Fry's mind at work, seeing just how the same sorts of things we lament, and he sometimes lamented, in his art—the static quality, the lack of emotion—show through in his translations, even as his musical ear is just.[5] Let me give an example of that precision, that *justness* from *Hérodiade:* trying out equivalents for "seul," he tries solitary, then lonely, and ends up with "lone." That seems to me just right, like fierceness chosen over ferocity; for decrease, he tried "ungrow," then opts for "grow less," tries out "aether" before settling on "azure." If God is anywhere in the details, it is certainly in such translations.

As for Fry's remarks on Mallarmé's style, among the more useful seem to me his distinction between the poetical and the witty effects of language: that in wit, the vibrations come to a stop, whereas in poetry like that of Mallarmé, the vibrations continue, as in the Chinese sense of "stop-short"—unlike an epigram, in poetry the words stop short, but the sense goes on. In our age, still so influenced by Benjamin's analysis of the "aura" of the object, Fry's study of just how Mallarmé uses the cumulative effect of the auras of words is all the more striking. What Fry did for Mallarmé, Mallarmé did for those who came after him: He gave. And it is just what he saw that he gave to those who see after him. I'll just refer briefly to the major lesson as I see it here.

It was always a labor of self-abnegation, for he knew how to listen: "The poet's voice must be stilled and the initiative taken by the words themselves . . . as they meet in unequal collision." Now I want to latch on to that last phrase, which sticks in my mind: unequal. Thinking of that inequality, I think also of his celebrated statement: "I think that once we have perfectly defined poetic form, our principal aim should be to make the words of a poem self-mirroring (since they are sufficiently autonomous to begin with and need no outside impression) to such an extent that no one of them will seem to have a color of its own, but only the transitions of a scale,"[6] in which the word "self-mirroring" is crucial to the undoing of exterior reference. Putting those two key words together, I think we can see that Mallarmé's emphasis on reciprocal relations within the text is a complicated one, not just for interior referentiality but for a definite one-sided stress.

And in that mode, Mallarméan, and about difference, we can celebrate both Matisse and his illustrations for Mallarmé's poems, remembering how Matisse said of himself, in the *Notes of a Painter:* "I don't paint things, I paint only differences between things."[7] In painter as in poet, the elements, words, ideas, whatever, are self-reciprocating, differentiating, and productive of a sparkle unlike any other.

But the crucial part is, or so it seems to me now, what has been left out. Something there suggests *ellipsis*—the idea of coming up short on one side, long on another, in that "unequally" with which he comes up twenty years later, in his "Crise de vers" of 1886: "If a poem is to be pure, the poet's voice must be stilled and the initiative taken by the words themselves, which will be set in motion as they meet unequally in collision" (366).[8] Again like Mallarmé, it is like looking at the other side of the thing: He, like Antonin Artaud, was, in the words of Breton, always passing to the other side of the mirror. If destruction was Mallarmé's Beatrice, and the abyss his at least partial destination, ellipsis was usually his method, being the means under the suggestive end.

As for his influence on the visual artists who came after him, thus, his progeny, my examples, after Whistler, come from five of our own century's artists and writers. The names are emblematic, representative of many others: René Char, from Mauron's Provence and Nicolas de Stael, from Russia and Provence; Robert Motherwell, from California and New York; Joseph Cornell, from Utopia Parkway, Queens, part of the New York he treated like the quintessence of Europe; and Yves Bonnefoy, from Mallarmé's Paris, who has become contemporary poetry's old master spokesman for the Mallarmé heritage, writing the prefaces for all three of Gallimard's volumes of Mallarmé in paperback editions.

What Mallarmé gave Char was a sense of the interior lighting, the interior theater and model, and the inviolable mystery of it all. Char's own talismans against his night's work, like his poems, move toward a symbolism as deep and dark as that of the hero of the night of Idumée. "Whatever is sacred, whatever is to remain sacred, must be clothed in mystery," comes the voice of Mallarmé's "Artistic Heresy: Art for All."[9] We see that everywhere in Char, and I will discuss these visual reactions in more detail below. Char used to say of Arthur Rimbaud, if we knew what he was, we would know what the future held: he knew what Mallarmé held out, in the mystery of his being, and never forgot him. Mallarmé was the great ancestor for Char, sometimes unspoken but always present as long as I knew him. There was absolutely no question in Char's mind or mine: there was Hölderlin, there was Mallarmé, and there was Rilke—and the greatest of these was the other Frenchman. As for the artists, his haunting by Mallarmé was echoed by the way Mallarmé haunted, in particular, Nicolas de Stael. You can see it, you can hear it, this protest that is also a prose poem: "Yes, yes, I know: we are all empty forms of matter—empty and yet sublime, because we have invented God and our own souls. So sublime, indeed, that my ambition is to show forth this matter as it becomes conscious of its own being and plunges nonetheless desperately into dreams, which (it well knows), are nonexistent."[10]

Robert Motherwell, who loved Baudelaire and Bach, explicitly dedicates one of his greatest canvases to the French poet he admired above all others. It might seem, I suppose, that a man whose great series were the *Elegies* and the *Opens* would scarcely be as close as he proved to be to the poet of mystery, but take a look. This is a symbol of a swan, a poet, two artists, and a memory. For this is the story Motherwell told me: Joseph Cornell, a lover of Mallarmé, thought of this canvas, where the boat is forever setting out, like some sail for some shipwreck unnamed but felt like Mallarmé's Swan, because he, Cornell, was close to that celebrated sonnet about the swan in the ice, that sign in the page. And Motherwell, who had called this painting Mallarmé's Dream, changed the title, to accord with what, as he said, Joseph had thought.[11] The more I think of this anecdote, the more profound it seems to me.

And Joseph Cornell, that American genius who never forgot Mallarmé and whose memory looms always larger for many of us, made of his shadow boxes the sort of interior mental theater that Mallarmé made of his *Igitur,* and Proust of his cork-lined room. There is no closer equivalent in all of art or literature, as I have known them at least. Such reciprocal reflection passes both understanding and commentary. Mallarmé was, without any doubt at all, Cornell's Beatrice.

Lastly, the poet Yves Bonnefoy, translator of Shakespeare and Yeats, and the great commentator on Mallarmé, is as haunted by Mallarmé as the latter was by all the hosts inhabiting his mind. Bonnefoy describes Mallarmé's goal as that of rendering "transparents l'un à l'autre, dans chaque mot, le dedans et le dehors de la chose" (transparent to each other, within each word, the inside and outside of the thing). And when Bonnefoy shows Mallarmé becoming conscious of the failure of his poetry, as he puts it, to "'creuser' dans la langue moderne de l'extériorité une issue vers une authentique présence de ce qu'il appelle l'Idée" (to hollow out in our modern language of exteriority a way towards an authentic presence of what he calls the Idea),[12] you sense Bonnefoy's own struggle with just that. You would never understand Bonnefoy had you not started with some other poet, and this would be the one. Here, I am thinking, for instance, of his remarkable small prose poem called "L'Anti-Platon." We American professors of American poetry continually hark back to Wallace Stevens, of course, that French-American poet par excellence—our equivalent of both those other Frenchmen. And still, Mallarmé, before his shipwreck, steers a course straight through our poetry and our art up to the present moment.

Notes

1. Quoted by Dore Ashton, in her article for Christopher Wilmarth's book featuring his artistic impressions of Mallarmé: *Breath*, published by the author (New York, 1982). She uses Stéphane Mallarmé, *Oeuvres complètes*, ed. Henri Mondor and G. Jean-Aubry (Paris: Gallimard, 1945) (cited below as *OC*), and also Bradford Cook, *Selected Prose Poems, Essays and Letters* (Baltimore: The Johns Hopkins University Press, 1956).

2. All information in this sentence is from Ashton.

3. See my "Translation and the Art of Friendship: Signed Mallarmé and Whistler," *Yearbook of Comparative and General Literature* 42 (1994): 109–26.

4. Mauron, losing his eyesight, was urged by Fry to take on the task of commenting Mallarmé in Fry's translations, and was repeatedly suggested by Fry, sometimes with success, as a translator of works from English, which he knew perfectly. Thus it is that he translated a chapter of *Orlando*, two stories of Henry James, and the novels of Forster.

5. He wrote at least two chapters of a manuscript on music, which I hope to publish shortly.

6. Letter to François Coppée, 5 December 1866 in Stéphane Mallarmé, *Correspondance, 1862–1871*, ed. Henri Mondor and Lloyd James Austin (Paris: Gallimard, 1959), 1:234.

7. Quoted in Ashton, 16.

8. "Crise de vers" (1886) in *OC*, 366.

9. Ashton's commentary. See above.

10. Letter to Théodore Aubanel, 16 July 1866. Quoted in Ashton.

11. For Cornell, see my edition of *Joseph Cornell's Theater of a Mind: Selected Diaries, Letters, and Source Files* (New York: Thames and Hudson, 1994).

12. Yves Bonnefoy, Preface to Stéphane Mallarmé, *Poésies* (Paris: Gallimard, 1992).

Mallarmé and Representation in the Theater

Charles R. Lyons

Mallarmé began the writing of the poetic dialogue between a young woman and her nurse, titled simply, *Scène,* in 1864. After composing this section, he wrote a monologue for the nurse, and eventually he wrote a third section, the *Cantique de Saint Jean.*[1] Mallarmé self-consciously framed the composition of the introductory monologue as the mark of a generic metamorphosis: "Je commence *Hérodiade,* non plus tragédie, mais poème"[2] (I begin *Hérodiade,* no longer tragedy, but poem). Possibly this statement means that the piece began tentatively as a work of theater and then was detheatricalized, first conceptualized as speech embodied in the physical presence of actors in space and then dematerialized becoming as evanescent, in the imagination of readers, as the psychic transformations for which its language calls. The first published version, "Fragment d'une ancienne étude scénique d'Hérodiade," in *Le Parnasse contemporain,* differs from an earlier unpublished version principally in that it deletes stage directions that would prescribe the actor's emotion: anger, imperiousness, dreaming.[3]

I do not want to participate in the debate over the stage worthiness of this dialogue, a debate that has an interesting history of its own. I would say, however, that I find Peter Szondi's claim that *Hérodiade* violates key principles of the stage to be insupportable. Mallarmé's aesthetic transgressions, according to Szondi, include the fragmentation of character, the substitution of narration for action, and Mallarmé's propensity toward processes of dematerialization. Scholars such as Szondi have been relentless in ignoring that much of drama is the staging of narration and that plays from Sophocles to Ibsen use theatrical space as the pretext for narration which is, indeed, a form of action. The late plays of Samuel Beckett that suppress plot and explore the equivocal relation between narration and subjectivity espouse the rigid conventionality of

Szondi's judgment.[4] Ironically, Szondi's argument repeats some of the objections voiced by Banville and Coquelin of the Comédie Française when Mallarmé read to them from a draft of *L'Après-midi d'un Faune*.[5] However, I would like to concentrate here upon Mallarmé's statement of a particular aesthetic/critical crux that was, perhaps, impelled by the criticism of Banville and Coquelin and that relates obliquely to Szondi's argument. I refer to Mallarmé's now well-known claim that this poem is "non possible au théâtre mais exigeant le théâtre"[6] (impossible in the theater but calling for the theater).—It may be, as Evlyn Gould argues, the idea of a theater becoming a kind of imaginative conceptual space within which the texts perform themselves in the act of reading. Gould puts forward this argument as she defines her notion of *virtual theater*.[7] It may also be, however, that Mallarmé's claim of the requisite, but impossible, theatricality of his writing acts out an aesthetic problem within the theater itself that came to a crisis two decades later, an aesthetic dilemma that remains unresolved. That is, the poet's rejection of the theater, his claim of its impossibility, may respond to the relentlessly mimetic movement in which modernist theater began. Also, Mallarmé's invocation of the theater as a space that frames, or encloses, or facilitates an imaginative experience may anticipate the nonmimetic movement of theatrical modernism that attempted to transform theatrical experience from the objective witnessing of the mundane to a subjectively grounded spectacle of acoustic and visual imagery. In the new symbolist theater, the functions of subjectivity and objectivity merge, divide, and reconfigure themselves, complicating the conventional theatrical division between the subjectivity of beholding and the objectivity of the performing figure.

One of the most interesting phenomena in the history of the theater, in my opinion, is the rapidity with which the avant-garde in the last decades of the nineteenth century, particularly the Parisian avant-garde, embraced the highly specific, novelistic referentiality of dramatic realism and then repudiated it. That attraction toward the referential and its rapid rejection in favor of the symbolic acted itself out in the struggle between Antoine and Lugné-Poe as producers of the plays of Ibsen, the writer whose performances in Paris played most fully into this aesthetic dispute. The critical transition I am discussing was marked in Paris by the movement of Lugné-Poe from Antoine's theater of realism at the Théâtre d'Art and eventually to the founding of the Théâtre de l'Oeuvre. We have a similar defection, but not a precise analogy, in England, where the referential conventions of realism dominated the experimental theater more vigorously. Edward Gordon Craig withdrew to Florence to found his own experimental theater program at the Arena Goldoni based on the rejection of referential mimetics and serious experimentation with the symbolic. At the Moscow Art Theater, of course, the more literal-minded Stanislavski faced the analogous defection of Meyerhold who abandoned the realist strain of modernism for the kind of theater suggested by the plays of Maeterlinck and others.

In the center of this transition, of course, we find Anton Chekhov, strongly influenced by Maeterlinck, whose plays he urged upon the Moscow Art Theater. Chekhov's aesthetic sympathies were with Meyerhold but he did not live long enough to be able to follow Meyerhold's direction. In 1897, Tolstoy's *What Is Art?* signaled this significant division between old and new forms, and Chekhov's tact, perhaps, explains why his argument with Tolstoy was not more public. Tolstoy's essay, as is well known, vehemently attacked Mallarmé, Maeterlinck, and the exhibitions in Paris in 1894 of Manet and the Impressionists. Although Anton Chekhov venerated Tolstoy, his correspondence reveals that he rejected the fundamental premises of *What Is Art?* even before he read the published essay on the basis of his conversations with its author. Tolstoy's objections to symbolist art based themselves on his demand that all art should be immediately accessible to a naive sensibility and that the production of the deliberately obscure and complex was decadent. Tolstoy praised Chekhov's prose fiction and encouraged the oral reading of his stories in his own household, but categorized the plays, to the playwright himself, as inferior. Simon Karlinsky notes that after a performance of *Uncle Vanya*, the novelist confronted the playwright with the statement: "You know I can't stand Shakespeare, but your plays are worse than his."[8] The radical simplicity of plotted narrative and the oblique revelation of incident in apparently random conversation perhaps exposed Chekhov's debt to Maeterlinck—himself indebted to Mallarmé—too clearly for Tolstoy to appreciate Chekhovian drama.

In each of these transitional documents, the definition of a new form of performance, positively or negatively described, recognized that the new drama rejected the use of the speaking actor as a concrete, specific embodiment of behavior that demanded to be interpreted on the basis of its correspondence to the psychological, sociological, biological, economic, and social systems with which the moment configured real experience. In other words, Mallarmé, Maeterlinck, Meyerhold, Lugné-Poe, and Craig each, in different but related forms of aesthetic and theoretical writing and practice, demanded a reconceptualization of the actor's body as the principal medium of theatrical performance. I have argued elsewhere that since Fifth-Century Athens, Western theater has embodied a tension between the concrete referentiality of the human body and the fluidity, equivocation, and multivalence of dramatic language. In other words, the text, with its almost infinite capacity to open reference, has always functioned as an attempt to transcend the more limited and precise signifying function of the body that grounds the complexity of language in a necessarily stable image of physical presence. This claim, of course, is not a particularly popular one to make at this moment of theory when the *performing body is seen to be an agent of subversion, working against the logocentric authoritarianism of the text.* I would argue, instead, that the operative and often coercive cultural regulations of the body inform our perceptions of the materiality of the actor and that it is language that subverts and complicates these naturalized assumptions. My anti-Bakhtinian claim needs, surely, to be modified or qualified with an awareness of the degree to which language—in various forms of discourse—determines the ways in which we experience and perceive the body, as Judith Butler reminds us energetically.[9]

To speak plainly to the point of the obvious, I would say that our experience trains us to read the language voiced by the actor as speech. That speech, which we assume expresses character, informs the representation of behavior, that we then interpret and judge on the basis of whatever systems of analysis we implement in the evaluation of the human actions and reactions we encounter in our day-by-day experience. Despite the gaps, anachronisms, and rhetorical conventions, the conventional reception of a performed text includes an oscillation between the data of performance and some sense of how human behavior operates. Emphasizing the function of dramatic language as speech, Tolstoy, in 1898, criticized Shakespeare on the basis that his language remained consistent from character to character and was not individualized to differentiate the specific speakers—in any of the four languages in which the Russian novelist read the plays. Surely we respond to Tolstoy's judgment of the consistency of Shakespeare's language as an idiosyncratic critical response, but the principle from which he writes is important to my argument: the requirement of the theater to render an acceptable and accessible replication of the world of our experience. In this notion of the theater, the body of the actor, as a signifying image, loses its appearance as aesthetic figure, as image, and becomes transparent, the medium through which we see and hear the body of the fictive character who is physically present to us, moving and speaking within the range of our perception. That is, we see and hear the body of actor as the body of the character. The virtuality of the character, the aesthetic function of her or his speech, which may be accessible to us in reading, merges with the materiality of the actor in the performance so that it becomes difficult to see the difference between character and actor. Housing the virtuality of speech or text within the materiality of the body of the actor may confine the text, delimiting the range of its reference as the words immediately disappear into acoustical memory and are not immediately retrievable as they are in reading. But, in performance, the indeterminacy of language contends with the determinate body of the actor.

Clearly, the particular aesthetic crux that I am attempting to discuss here—the attempted transition from a mimetic to a nonmimetic theater—is confounded by the fixed materiality of the actor, the presence that the human body assumes when it occupies a theatrical space, the power of the body of actor to ground itself in a representation of a fictional character whose stance, dress, demeanor, gesture, and speech make concise reference to categories of gender, race, class, and psychological condition. The commercial subversion of the referential materiality of the actor's body in plays such as *Madame Butterfly* and films such as *The Crying Game* only documents the power of the convention in their use of nudity to correct an illusory reading of gender, the imposition of "false" signs on the body of the actor and the power of the "natural" to reimpose itself. In more simple terms, I am trying to contrast the stability of the material presence of the actor with the instability or transformations demanded by nonmimetic forms of performance, by language. Dance is able, occasionally, to suppress reference to behavior sufficiently to turn the body into a nonmimetic medium; but it is far more difficult to dissolve the referentiality of the body when it speaks.[10]

Gordon Craig's hypothesized solution to the concrete materiality of the actor was his demand to replace the human actor with the Übermarionette. Maeterlinck's preference for puppets over living actors predates Craig's polemic.[11] Long ago I argued that Craig's shocking and controversial mandate actually argued for a highly disciplined human actor whose body and voice would respond unquestioningly to the vision of a strong director.[12] Meyerhold's solution was the development of his system of biomechanics. Many in the theater, from Craig, to Yeats, Brecht, and others attempted to appropriate the conventions of the Oriental theater, as the Impressionists appropriated the flatness of the Japanese wood block print to shift the balance from the dimensional object to the processes of seeing the object, foregrounding the experience of viewing the subject as surface.

The dominance of the text in the theatricalized poem of Mallarmé that we shall see below is not antithetical, I think, to symbolist drama's emphasis on the visual. In a clear sense, the language of this piece is emphatically visual, moving from image to image as the body of Hérodiade herself becomes a dazzling scene within her imagination. To continue a complication, I would resist claiming that the equivocal resistance to theatrical performance contained in the paradox, impossible for the theater but demanding the theater, does not find its source in a desire for the dematerialization of the actor, but, on the contrary, for a materiality that can transform itself beyond the limits of the living actor.

George Fuchs's polemic text *Revolution in the Theater,* published in 1909, participated in the denigration of the practices of dramatic naturalism and realism, and this document plays into the theories of Appia and Craig, theorizing the new theater of the early twentieth century. Fuchs claims that the three-dimensional *mise en scène* of realism draws the actor into the depth of the stage and counters the instinctive movement of the actor to thrust himself forward toward the audience in an overt theatricality. The drama that he promotes is a performance of surface, the stage becoming rather like a bas relief, an aesthetic realized in the Munich Kunsttheater. Fuchs is also working in a discourse that would counter the emphasis upon complex acoustic imagery in much of symbolistic drama, because he also claims that the dominance of the text in realistic drama restricts the work of the actor. Realism holds the actor captive in the stage space, whereas the *new drama* allows the performer to break loose and confront the space of the audience. In general, the symbolist drama—even Maeterlinck— works to suppress the acoustic in favor of the visual. The reconfiguration of the *mise en scène*—in most instances clearing the stage of the proliferating details of the realistic environment and sculpting the whole space as an overpowering symbol, primarily with the new technology of light—proves easier than repressing the referentiality of the speaking human body. The dominance of the text in the theatricalized poem of Mallarmé, *Hérodiade,* is not antithetical, I think, to symbolist drama's emphasis on the visual. In a clear sense, the language of this piece is emphatically visual, moving from image to image as the body of Hérodiade herself becomes a dazzling scene within her imagination. To continue a complication, I would claim that the equivocal resistance to theatrical performance contained in the paradox, *impossible for the theater but demanding the theater*, does not find its source in a desire for the dematerialization of the actor but, on the contrary, for a materiality that can transform itself beyond the limits of the living actor.

I have tried here to offer some kind of brief summary of the theoretical dialogue that was acting itself out in writing and aesthetic practice at this moment in which the antirealistic was supplanting realism in the work of the avant-garde. My argument has focused on the problem that the mimetic referentiality of the body provided for writers and artists within the theater who wished to break loose of the concrete behaviorism of the program of dramatic realism. I would continue my argument by making the claim that in this staged dialogue we will discover Mallarmé using acoustic imagery and subtle narrative reference to destabilize the material presence of the actor and to open up the signifying potentiality of the actor's voice by not limiting speech to the expression of a single, unified subjectivity. Despite Szondi's claim that nothing really occurs during this dialogue, the scene seems framed as a specific moment in a narrative sequence: the young woman's preparation of her body for the loss of her virginity, the movement from childhood to adulthood; and, in anticipation of the violating gaze of John the Baptist, the scene performs itself in front of the mirror in which the young woman gazes at her image, perhaps anticipating the fatal gaze. The figure of the young woman—I refrain from saying character—conflates the biblical image of the mother, Herodias, and the daughter, later identified as Salomé. Recall that John offends Herod by questioning the legality of his marriage to Herodias who had been his brother's wife. The daughter of Herodias dances for the king at his birthday celebration and pleases Herod who offers to fulfill any wish she makes. At her mother's instigation, she asks for the head of John the Baptist on a charger. We can think of this conflation as a disturbing puzzle, as a deliberate obscuring in Tolstoy's sense. We can also think of this conflation as a fascinating condensation, as an effort to reduce narrative to the essentials, siting within a single transformative figure the political and familial hierarchy, cruelty, obedience, fear, erotic desire, the narcissistic pleasure of the eroticism of the body, the fulfillment of erotic desire in violence, the equivocal identification of the self as subject and object, the compression of the masculine and the feminine. By positioning the figure of the young woman before the nurse who holds the mirror, and by limiting her consideration of her reflected image as the principal act of perception dramatized (with the nurse sharing the physically limited space and mediating our perception of the young woman at the mirror), the text refuses the full depth of a realistic *mise en scène* for a shallow presentational space, not quite the flatness of a painted surface but closer to the bas-relief of Fuch's aesthetic. If the nurse, holding the mirror, does mediate the perception of the audience, it would be possible to position the speech of the young woman as the direct address to the audience, emphasizing an overt theatricality.

Mallarmé's rejection of the theatrical leads me to reject this connection. For example, one of the points of Mallarmé's analysis of the work of his friend Manet was the justification of the Impressionist practice of painting in the open air, outside of the studio, in natural light. Mallarmé writes:

> Woman is by our civilisation consecrated to night, unless she escape from it sometimes to those open air afternoons by the seaside or in an arbour, affectionated by moderns. Yet I think the artist would be wrong to represent her among the artificial glories of candle-light or gas, as at that time the only object of art would be the woman herself, set off by the immediate atmosphere, theatrical and active, even beautiful, but utterly inartistic. Those persons much accustomed, whether from the habit of their calling or purely from taste, to fix on a mental canvass the beautiful remembrance of woman, even when thus seen amid the glare of the night in the world or at the theater, must have remarked that some mysterious process despoils the noble phantom of the artificial prestige cast by candelabra or footlights, before she is admitted fresh and simple to the number of everyday haunters of the imagination. ... The complexion, the special beauty which springs from the very source of life, changes with artificial lights, and it is probably from the desire to preserve this grace in all its integrity that painting—which concerns itself more about this flesh-pollen than any other human attraction—insists on the mental operation to which I have lately alluded, and demands daylight—that is space with the transparence of air alone.

Mallarmé continues his discussion in a reference to Manet's *Le Linge:* "The natural light of day penetrating into and influencing all things, though itself invisible, reigns also on this typical picture."[13] Although this is a digression, think of the image fleshpollen to refer to the skin of the woman's face. As Michael Fried notes, this peculiar gender conflates the male act of pollination with the radiant receiving surface. This ambivalence seems related to the language of the *Hérodiade*. To return to my argument: One of the ways in which Michael Fried configures the work of the painter Manet in relationship to the aesthetic discourse of the moment and the course that modernism would take is to apply his differentiation between absorption and theatricality that he appropriates from Diderot.[14] The impetus toward realism displays human figures absorbed in their activity, and their action and language is confined to the space represented. Their behavior suppresses their awareness of the presence of the viewer. The impetus toward theatricality brings the aesthetic construction of the work of art to the foreground, self-consciously identifying itself as a work to be perceived. In the theatrical painting, the subject of the painting—like Fuch's actor—directs her or his gaze out to the spectator. I suggest that Mallarmé's celebration of the Impressionist practice of painting in the open air derives from his preference for painting in which people are sited in activities that absorb them and suppress their awareness of being subjects for viewing. The painting of women, lit by artificial light—as in a theater—would configure them as subjects principally for viewing. The irony here is that Mallarmé does not seem to celebrate what we would find the most aesthetically progressive aspect of Manet's painting, the exploration of what Clement Greenberg has called "optical experience." We would expect, I think, that Mallarmé's response to the paintings of Manet would perform the concept he borrowed from Edgar Allan Poe of moving deliberately from effect to effect. Remember that Mallarmé and Manet collaborated on an edition of *The Raven*, in which Mallarmé translated the poem and Manet provided illustrations.

Let me return to Mallarmé's preference for Manet's more Impressionist paintings that display the subject, preferably women, in sunlight—figures sited, unself-consciously, in a "natural" environment," so that their faces are not artificially or theatrically illuminated masks overlayered by paint and light. Mallarmé's objection to the theatrically painted woman may relate, to some degree, to the obscurity of his poetic language. That is, the theatrical display of the woman's skin is a mediated image, almost fully processed by the painter, leaving no gaps between aesthetic object and the spectator before the canvas. The interpretation is complete within the work itself. Several critics have worked with Mallarmé's claim—impossible for the theater but demanding theater—from the idea that the appropriate reading of the poem is not an interpretation but, rather, a staging of the imagery within the mind. That is, the poem demands that images be placed within a space to play and disport themselves—and witnessing the dynamics of these visual images displayed on that stage of the mind *is* the reading. In *plein air* painting, figures disposed in the sunlight allow us to access their images with the least mediation and construct our own reading of the painting. This point is consistent with Mallarmé's emphasis on the role of the viewer in determining what is and what is not a proper tableau for exhibition.

Mallarmé's dialogue demands not a dematerialization of the body but an imaginative series of rematerializations as the containing subjectivity of Hérodiade goes through a series of permutations that I marked earlier. Those permutations—crossing boundaries of character and even gender—have never been more clearly and provocatively charted than in Robert Greer Cohn's detailed study published thirty-one years ago.[15] The point that I have wanted to make in these remarks is that Mallarmé's theatricalized poetry plays a significant role in the theoretical discourse and theatrical practice at an important point in the history of modernism in the theater. That significance derives, I think, from the demand to abandon the mimesis of behavior and to explode the signifying potential of an imaginative body—if not the body of a real actor. I wish to emphasize that this amplification of the possibilities of the body as a transforming visual image within a dynamic *mise en scène* —in the extremity of its radical stand— cleared some of the way for theater practitioners such as Meyerhold, Lugné-Poe, Fuchs, and Gordon Craig, and eventually for the later work of Samuel Beckett.

The concept—impossible for theater but requiring theater— marks a particular aesthetic controversy in the theater today. Once again, the theater is taking radical steps to question the authority of the actor's material presence. The interaction of live performers and their own video images is rapidly becoming a staple of theatrical experimentation; the concrete materiality of the living actor is challenged by the transformations and rematerializations of her or his mediatized images, images that may speak and question the authenticity or aura of the actor physically present to us. One of the consequences of the shared presence between actor and a media counterpart is our recognition that the actor herself or himself, placed in the scenic environment, is nothing more—nor less—than image, an aesthetic construct that uses the materiality of the actor as medium. If the living actor is the medium of an image construction, does the actor physically present to us have any more authority—any more complexity, any more presence— than the image produced by technology? This is the question we might ask Benjamin today. To continue: Is there a substantial difference between the actor as an aesthetic technology for image construction and the technology of film and video when these media invade the stage space of live performance? The aesthetically enabling resources of technology at this moment provide us with the means to readdress the issues that voiced themselves, partly through Mallarmé, in the division between realism and symbolism, in the theater at the end of the nineteenth century. Mallarmé may help us to see the way, once again, to displace the imitation of behavior that continues to hold both the commercial theater and much of the experimental in its grasp, with the staging of plays that do not find their source in the mimesis of behavior but rather in the serious play of provocative images.

Notes

1. Gardner Davies, *Les Noces d'Hérodiade* (Paris: Gallimard, 1959).
2. Stéphane Mallarmé, *Correspondance, 1862–1871,* ed. Henri Mondor and Lloyd James Austin (Paris: Gallimard, 1959), 174. (Hereafter cited as *Corr.*)
3. See Frantisek Deak, *Symbolist Theater: The Formation of an Avant-Garde* (Baltimore: The Johns Hopkins University Press, 1993), 271 n. 5.
4. Szondi's argument may be found in *Poésies et poétique de la modernité* (Lille: Presses universitaires de Lille), 73–141.
5. Théodore de Banville was himself one of the major advocates of the new drama, documented by his essays in the National from 1869–81. His writing de-emphasizes the power of the actor and brings to the foreground the work of the poet.
6. *Corr.*, 166.
7. Evyln Gould, *Virtual Theater from Diderot to Mallarmé* (Baltimore: The Johns Hopkins University Press, 1989).
8. Simon Karlinsky, *Letters of Anton Chekhov,* ed. Simon Karlinsky and Michael Henry Heim (New York: Harper and Row, 1973), 375 n. 2.
9. Judith Butler, *Bodies That Matter: On the Discursive Limits of "Sex"* (New York and London: Routledge, 1993), 1–21.
10. We process speech, in part, by framing it within an image of the speaker and we seek clues, sometimes subtly, sometimes not so subtly, to construct an image of the speaking subject that remains sufficiently stable for us to sustain an evaluation of the ongoing speech.
11. See Deak, 174–75, 280–81 n. 70–75.
12. Charles R. Lyons, "Gordon Craig's Concept of the Actor," in *Total Theatre,* ed. E. T. Kirby (New York: E. P. Dutton, 1969).
13. Mallarmé's comments are found in *Art Monthly Review* 1 (30 September 1876) and reprinted in *Documents Stéphane Mallarmé,* ed. Carl Paul Barbier, 7 vols. (Paris: Nizet, 1968–80), 1:59–86. I was directed to Mallarmé's comments by the footnote on pages 408–12 of Michael Fried's recently published *Manet's Modernism or, The Face of Painting in the 1860s* (Chicago: University of Chicago Press, 1996). The original French text of this essay by Mallarmé has been lost, and the English translation is by Arthur O'Shaughnessy. Fried notes that the

essay has been retranslated into French, but lacks the authority of the translation that was approved by Mallarmé himself.

14. In my most recent writing on Ibsen I have, in turn, borrowed this scheme from Fried.

15. Robert Greer Cohn, *Toward the Poems of Mallarmé* (Berkeley: University of California Press, 1965).

Mallarmé and His Musicians Webern and Boulez

ALBERT SONNENFELD

I am offering this essay in a very conflicted mode: On the one hand, I have been commissioned by Robert Greer Cohn, my old friend and "Maître, par un oeil profond," to express some general reflections on Mallarmé and music. On the other hand, my own recent particular ruminations have centered on Pierre Boulez, "Magnifique, total et solitaire," and on his pronouncements and music. The very model of a modern Mallarméen, he is especially as embodied in his Third Piano Sonata and in his espousal of the reading of "Le Livre" (or at least of Jacques Schérer's introduction to it) as in his interest in Mallarmé's notion of the "Opérateur."[1]

At the risk of being "orgueilleux," though never for even a moment "dédaigneux,"[2] I have decided to play both these hands and even to compound my risk of falling "pendant l'éternité" (33) by evoking "Avec, comme pour langage" (37) some Mallarméen musical analogies reflected in the works of Anton Webern and Boulez.

We are faced, in some (too many) American universities today with students, and even colleagues, who, having been raised on reading only fragments (usually during "ordinary evenings in New Haven"), suffer from such extreme anxiety of influence that genuine research would seem to be a threat to their narcissistic claim to an originality that I have come to see as largely attributable to their disinclination to read (or to acknowledge) their critical ancestors. That said, I hasten here to proclaim my own genuine debt to Suzanne Bernard's study of Mallarmé and music;[3] to Robert Greer Cohn's studies of *Igitur* and *Un Coup de Dés* and his whole production on Mallarmé; to Jacques Schérer's *"Le Livre" de Mallarmé;* to Boulez's own voluminous commentaries in *Notes of an Apprenticeship* and in *Orientations (Points de repère);*[4] and, inevitably, to Dominique Jameux's masterly 1984 book-length study of Boulez's *Trajectories,*[5] as well as to a little-known 1974 article by Ivanka Stoianova, "La Troisième Sonate de Boulez et le projet mallarméen du Livre."[6]

The uncial letters must be Valéry's, pernicious though their influence has been on the always elusive topic of Music and Poetry:

> Ce qui fut baptisé le Symbolisme, se résume très simplement dans l'intention commune à plusieurs familles de poètes (d'ailleurs ennemies entre elles) de "reprendre à la Musique leur bien." Le secret de ce mouvement n'est pas autre.[7]

> [What was baptized as Symbolism is very simply summed up in the intention common to several families of poets (besides, enemies among themselves) to "take back their own from Music." The secret of this movement is not to be found elsewhere.]

Pernicious, because, in a Mallarméan perspective, the result is the cult of prettification à la popular view of Verlaine, or of an excess of lexicographical rigor from René Ghil to André Spire, as we apply to Poetry a possibly alien vocabulary: melody, timber, harmony, and so on. In Valéry's definition, the key words ("reprendre à la Musique leur bien") are in quotation marks, for they derive from Mallarmé's refection of Music in "Crise de Vers," written with "un indéracinable sans doute préjugé d'écrivain," proclaiming his mission to be

> un art d'achever la transposition, au Livre, de la symphonie ou uniment de reprendre notre bien: car ce n'est pas de sonorités élémentaires par les cuivres, les cordes, les bois, indéniablement mais de l'intellectuelle parole à son apogée que doit avec plénitude et évidence, résulter, en tant que l'ensemble des rapports existant dans tout, la Musique. (367–69)

> [an art of carrying off the transposition to the Book, of symphony or simply of taking back our own: for it cannot, undeniably, form elementary sonorities through the brasses, strings, woodwinds, but the intellectual word at its apogee that must with plenitude and evidence to result, as the ensemble of relationships existing in all, Music.]

And, in a letter to Rhené Ghil (1885): "Cet acte de juste restitution qui doit être le nôtre, de tout reprendre à la musique"[8] (This act of resolution that must be ours, of taking back everything from Music).

The ultimate enigma, not to say paradox, is that what Mallarmé sought to recapture from Music was not its sonorous expressivity, but its silence, the "sound of silence," if you will, and to this impossible ideal he remained surprisingly faithful. Tragically, or perhaps ironically, the embodiment of the problematic of Music for Mallarmé was Wagner, the inventor of the continuous melody, to whom silence was anathema:

> La grandeur du poète se mesure surtout par ce qu'il s'abstient de dire, afin de nous laisser dire à nous-mêmes, en silence, ce qui est inexprimable; mais c'est le musicien qui fait entendre clairement ce qui n'est pas dit, et la forme infaillible de son silence retentissant est la *mélodie infinie.*[9]

[The greatness of the poet is measured especially by what he abstains from saying, so as to let us tell ourselves, silently, what is inexpressible; but it is the musician who makes clearly heard what is not said, and the infallible form of his resounding silence is the *infinite melody.*]

It is because of Wagner's "trompettes tout haut d'or pâmé sur les vélins" (71) (trumpets aloud with gold fainted on the vellums) that Mallarmé must apostrophize the "Génie" of Bayreuth, reluctantly:

> O Wagner, je souffre et me reproche, aux minutes marquées par la lassitude, de ne pas faire nombre avec ceux qui, ennuyés de tout afin de trouver le salut définitif, vont droit à l'édifice de ton Art, pour eux le terme du chemin. (546)

[O Wagner, I suffer and reproach myself, in minutes marked by lassitude, at not being among those who, bored with everything, in order to find definitive salvation, go straight to the edifice of your Art, for them the end of the path.]

Mallarmé's own "Salut" (originally entitled "Toast" in 1893) contains the expression of his aesthetic of the music of silence: "Rien, cette écume, vierge vers / A ne désigner que la coupe / [. . .] Le blanc souci de notre toile" (27) (nothing, this foam, virgin verse / To designate only the cup / . . . the whole concern of our canvas). The greeting "Salut" becomes salvation; the cup becomes the "coupe" of verse; the white sail becomes the blank canvas. The public *recital* of the sonnet "Toast" at the banquet of *La plume* is transformed into the vast silence of fourteen octosyllabic lines of a *printed page,* a virtually blank canvas.

In his early "Hérésie(s) artistique(s)," *L'Art pour tous* (1862), Mallarmé articulates his musical credo. The sacred implies mystery, and, like religion whose arcana are unveiled only to the predestined elite, Art has its sheltered secrets:

> La musique nous offre un exemple. Ouvrons à la légère Mozart, Beethoven ou Wagner, jetons sur la première page de leur oeuvre un oeil

indifférent, nous sommes pris d'un religieux étonnement à la vue de ces processions macabres de signes sévères, chastes, inconnus. Et nous refermons le missel vierge d'aucune pensée profanatrice. (257)

[Music offers us an example. Open casually Mozart, Beethoven or Wagner, throw on the first page of their work an indifferent eye, one is overcome with a religious astonishment at the sight of those macabre processions of severe, chaste, unknown signs. And we reclose the missil virgin of any profaning thought.]

The mystery is twofold: the unsanctified reader of scores sees only the procession of undecipherable signs on a page minimally darkening the whites between the bar-lines, minute traces of ink. The "seul prédestiné," it is implied though not stated, knows how to read these signs and to transpose them into a silent concert taking place within the sphere of ideality, the mind's ear, as it were; and this "reading" gesture is both horizontal and vertical, as he (Mallarmé) will seek to realize in Un Coup de Dés:

Un solitaire tacite concert se donne, par la lecture, à l'esprit qui regagne, sur une sonorité moindre, la signification: aucun moyen mental exaltant la symphonie ne manquera, raréfié et c'est tout—du fait de la pensée. (380)

[A solitary tacit concert is offered, through reading, to the mind that regains, with a lesser sonority, the meaning: no mental means exalting symphony will be lacking; rarefied and that is all—resulting from thought.]

This is from "Le Livre, instrument spirituel." The book is the "instrument" of the mind or spirit, but the mind is the performing instrument of the score embodied in the book. Far from being merely an *odi profanum vulgus*, these lines seen retrospectively tell us that seeing the incomprehensible procession of musical signs is the very act of perceiving the mystery of the unstated. Deciphering them is the charge of the ideal creator and reader "magiquement produit par certaines dispositions de la parole; où celle-ci ne reste qu'à l'état de moyen de communication matérielle avec le lecteur comme les touches du piano"[10] (magically produced by certain dispositions of language; where it remains only as a means of material communication with the reader like the keys of a piano). We have here what is an aesthetic of reading, interpretation, and creation.

Little wonder, then, that Mallarmé's ideal page resembles that mysterious score:

> Je préfère selon mon goût, sur page blanche, un dessin espacé de virgules ou de points et leurs combinaisons secondaires, imitant, nue, la mélodie—au texte, suggéré avantageusement si, même sublime, il n'était pas ponctué.[11]

> [I prefer according to my taste, on the white page, a scattered design of commas or periods and their secondary combinations, imitating, nakedly, melody—to the text, advantageously suggested, even if sublime, it was not punctuated.]

The use or rejection of these signs is what distinguishes verse from prose, "nommément tout notre art," and the abundant, disconcerting, and perplexing use of these "signes convenus" represent the poet's attempt to make his prose as obscure, mysterious, and syntactically complex as his poetry. In short, Mallarmé's mature prose attains the density and "musicality" of poetry, whether labeled "Poèmes en prose" or "Crayonné au théâtre."

Despite Mallarmé's ballet of commas in his prose, he fails to achieve his purported ideal of expressive punctuation to the same extent as the self-consciously and wilfully simplistic Maeterlinck. In *Pelléas et Mélisande,* the fourth act love scene contains 15 ellipses in eight lines of dialogue (or if one prefers, at 3 dots per ellipsis, 45 dots); it is in these interstices that the true vagueness of the symbolic idea purports to dwell, "le théâtre du silence." Mallarmé, far more genuinely philosophical and in many ways as much aesthetician as poet (despite his avowed disdain for the "professorial"), writes about the ineffable without achieving it in radical form until *Un Coup de Dés* and the fragmentary "Le Livre." He will use minimalization ("Une ligne d'azur mince et pâle serait / Un lac [. . .] Non loin de trois grands cils d'emeraude, roseaux"),[12] (A line of thin and pale azur would be / A lake [. . .] Not far from three great emerald lashes, reeds), much the way he speaks of music:

> Si je recours, en vue d'un éclaircissement ou de généraliser, aux fonctions de l'Orchestre, devant lequel resta candidement, savamment fermé notre musicien de mots, observez que les instruments détachent, selon un sortilège aisé à surprendre, la cime, pour ainsi voir, de naturels paysages; les évapore et les renoue, flottants, dans un état supérieur. Voici qu'à exprimer la forêt [. . .] suffit tel accord dénué

presque d'une réminiscence de chasse [. . .] Une ligne, quelque vibration, sommaire et tout s'indique.[13]

[If I resort, for purposes of clarification or generalization, to the functions of the Orchestra, before which our musician remained candidly, knowingly closed, observed that instruments detach, according to a magic easily seized, the peak, if we see it so, of natural landscapes; evaporates them and reknots them, floating, in a superior state. To express the forest [. . .] suffices a certain chord almost stripped of a reminiscence of chase [. . .] A line, some vibration, summary, and all is indicated.]

The brush stroke of the Chinese painter on the printed page is minimal darkening of the pure ideal of the white page ("le vide papier que la blancheur défend") by the short poem, the sonnet, the "Chansons bas," the "Petit air": "Ce sont les blancs qui me donnent le plus de mal! Ils ont la valeur des silences en musique. Ce sont eux qui créent le rêve, l'ineffable"[14] (It is the white spaces that give me the most trouble! They have the value of silences in music. It is they that create the dream, the ineffable). Or:

Vraiment entre les lignes et au-dessus du regard cela se passe en toute pureté, sans l'entremise des cordes à boyaux et des pistons comme à l'orchestre, qui est déjà industriel; mais c'est la même chose que l'orchestre, sauf que littérairement ou silencieusement.[15]

[Truly between the lines and above the look that happens in all purity, without the interference of gut strings and pistons as in the orchestra, which is somewhat industrial; but it is the same thing as the orchestra, except being so literarily or silently.]

The paradoxes of Mallarmé never cease to amaze: *L'Après-midi d'un Faune,* a loquacious poem of more than one hundred lines, narrates the move toward the silent inner concert of the mind. Repeated attempts to recount the vision of the two nymphs in musical narrative by the musician-faune ("qui cherche le la") fade and fail until they are minimalized into "une sonore, vaine et monotone ligne." But even this is too much "sound of music"; the vision retreats into silence, vision, dream, the ultimate music. As the poet states in "Le Livre, instrument spirituel":

Plus le va-et-vient successif incessant du regard, une ligne finie, à la suivante, pour recommencer: pareille pratique ne représente le délice, ayant immortellement, rompu une heure, avec tout, de traduire sa chimère. Autrement ou sauf exécution, comme de morceaux sur un clavier, active, mesurée par les feuillets—que ne ferme-t-on les yeux à rêver? (380)

[No more incessant coming and going of the look, one line finished, to the next, to start over: such a practice does not represent the delight, having broken with all for an hour, of translating his chimaera. Otherwise or apart from the active execution, as of pieces on a keyboard, measured by the pages—why not close one's eyes and dream?]

The next line begins: "Un tacite concert se donne, par la lecture, à l'esprit." Or, from the essay on Banville: "Une ligne, quelque vibration, sommaires et tout s'indique" (522) (a line, some vibration, summary, and all is indicated); and from "La Musique et les Lettres": "moins le tumulte des sonorités, transfusibles, encore, en du songe" (648) (less the tumult of sonorities, transfusable, still, into dreams).

To approach Mallarmé and music by succumbing to the demon of analogy is a perilous pilgrimage, I admit, but allow me this brief parenthesis. If the intellectual armature of the poem is hidden, to be contained and to live in the very spaces that isolate the stanza and all through the whiteness of the page's "meaningful silence," we could indeed be describing Anton Webern's *Five Pieces for Orchestra*,[16] which represents *his* attempt to undermine the tyranny of Wagnerism. In barely five minutes of music, he "argues" for an economic aesthetic of sighs and whispers rather than the screams and breast-beating of Wagner's "souriant fracas" or "trompettes tout haut d'or" (75). Boulez himself said that Webern "représente le seuil de la musique nouvelle: l'homme indélibile"[17] (represents the threshold of the new music: the indelible man). Arnold Schoenberg prefaced Webern's *Six Bagatelles,* praising their brevity: "To contain an entire novel in a simple gesture, all good fortune in a single breath, one needs a concentration that banishes all sentimentality."[18] These marvelous Webern pieces will be understood only by those who believe that one can express in sounds only what can only be expressed in sounds. Webern's entire *Oeuvre* takes 3 hours; of 31 officially numbered works, only his last cantata lasts longer than 10 minutes, the shortest piece less than 2 minutes. The composer Ernst Krenek evoked the reduction of musical matter into "a few drops of precious essence [. . .] a music so lean and transparent that its single elements seem to float in isolation between airpockets of total silence."[19] The tones vanish into nothingness, taking on an unheard, almost frightening significance. If, in Sartre's words, Giacometti had taken the fat off space to reach the skeleton, Webern and Mallarmé reached the same sublime ascesis in their own art: "Puisse ce silence se faire entendre d'eux" (May this silence be heard by them). Schoenberg wrote of Webern.[20] "Je réclame la restitution au silence, impartial" (I call for the restitution of silence, impartial), wrote Stéphane Mallarmé.

Music, as we have earlier seen, had a profound resonance in Mallarmé's sensibility, though he did not begin to attend concerts until 1885 (according to Geneviève). Reciprocally, Suzanne Bernard's study enables us to take partial measure of Mallarmé's direct impact on musicians. Debussy and Ravel each have produced settings of various Mallarmé poems, to which we must, of course, add such instrumental pieces as *Syrinx* and the *Prélude à l'Après-midi d'un Faune*. There are also settings by Milhaud ("Deux petits airs") and Henri Sauguet ("Renouveau," "Tristesse d'été"), as well as by a host of illustres *inconnus* (mostly *inconnus*). Vellones, Caby, Busser, Cartan, along with others, occupy this micro-Pantheon.

On sheer statistical evidence, Pierre Boulez is Mallarmé's most consistently faithful musical disciple, working and reworking (from 1957 through the late 1970s) a cycle of five poems in his masterful work-in-progress *Pli selon pli:* "Don du Poëme," "Le vierge, le vivace," "Une dentelle s'abolit," "A la nue accablante tu," "Tombeau (de Verlaine)." The liminary "pli selon pli" (taken from the fourth line of the splendidly entitled sonnet "Remémoration") serves as title, therefore epigraph, and is not transposed into music:

> Il indique le sens, la direction de l'oeuvre. Dans ce poème, l'auteur décrit ainsi la manière dont le brouillard, en se dissolvant, laisse progressivement apercevoir les pierres de la cité de Bruges. De même, se découvre, au fur et à mesure du développement des cinq pièces, pli selon pli, un portrait de Mallarmé.[21]

> [He indicates the meaning, the direction of the work. In this poem, the author describes this the way in which the fog, dissolving, allows one to progressively perceive the city of Bruges. Likewise, there is discovered, along with the development of the five pieces, fold according to fold, a portrait of Mallarmé.]

The two outer pieces, "Don du Poëme" and "Tombeau de Verlaine," are instrumental, quoting only the initial verse "Je t'apporte l'enfant d'une nuit d'Idumée!" to inaugurate the cycle, and "Un peu profond ruisseau calomnié la mort" to enunciate a framing enclosure. Boulez's own extensive commentaries must be quoted at length here as by far the most luminous unveiling of the problem of marrying a poetic text to music, varying from "inscription" to the amalgam of a significance within the cycle as a whole, what he calls *direct* and *indirect* understanding:

> l'alliance du poème et de la musique y est certes tentée sur le plan de la signification émotionelle, mais tente d'aller au plus profond de l'invention, à sa structure. On ne peut oublier que Mallarmé était obsédé par la pureté formelle, par la recherche absolue de cette pureté: sa langue en porte témoignage, ainsi que sa métrique. La syntaxe française, il la repense entièrement [...] Quant à l'organisation du vers lui-même [...] elle est dominée par la rigueur du nombre, par le rythme des valeurs sonores implicites dans le mot, pour aboutir à une fusion et du sens et du son, dans une extrême concentration du langage. [...] cette adéquation parfaite du langage à la pensée, n'admettant aucune déperdition d'énergie.[22]

[the alliance of poem and music is certainly attempted there on the plane of emotional meaning, but try to go to the depth of the invention, to its structure. One cannot forget that Mallarmé was obsessed by formal purity, by the absolute search for this purity: his language testifies to that as well as his metrics. He rethinks entirely French syntax [...] As to the organization of the verse itself [...] it is dominated by the rigor of number, by the rhythm of sonorous values in the word, to finish in a fusion of both meaning and sound, in an extreme concentration of the language [...] the perfect adequation of language to thought, admitting no loss of energy.]

For Boulez, musical settings never replace reading the poem *without* music; indeed he builds on prior reading and understanding of the poem ("le meilleur moyen d'*information* sur le contenu d'un poème") by his *hypocrite auditeur,* as Boulez calls him.[23] What the composer performs is a transposition or transmutation of poems: from "des valeurs sonores implicites dans le mot" to, as in Boulez's manifesto demanding for music, "the right to parentheses and italics . . . a notion of discontinuous time . . . a development in which the closed circuit will not be the only solution envisaged."[24] Singing implies a relationship of the poem's sonorities with intervals and rhythms that differ fundamentally from spoken intervals and rhythms . . . a transmutation and a destruction of the poem.

Pli selon pli, even more than the better-known *Le Marteau sans maître* (to texts by René Char), is a countermanifestation to Arnold Schoenberg's purportedly revolutionary *Pierrot lunaire* and its much heralded novelty, *Sprechstimme*. Despite Boulez's categorical assertion that "any musician who has not experienced—I do not say understand, but, in all exactness, experienced—the necessity for the dodecaphonic language is *useless*, for his whole work is irrelevant to the needs of his epoch,[25] despite his admission that "one finds oneself in the presence of a musical fact that is uniquely successful."[26] Boulez proclaims: "Schoenberg est mort!" This was ostensibly because of the aesthetic that was propagated by Pierrot lunaire, thanks to Schoenberg's participation "with all his sensibility in the German postromanticism of the nineteenth century."[27] "La lune, ce fromage!" Boulez writes in *Orientations*. Where does Pierre Boulez turn, in his apprenticeship? Certainly not toward that vestigial romantic, Alban Berg; nor to Webern (a more likely elective affinity), but to Claude Debussy, thanks to whose first measures of *L'Après-midi d'un Faune*, in Boulez's view, awareness of a new poetic direction was established "and all of Wagner's heavy heritage ... liquidated."[28] And, here, the Mallarmé-Boulez connection takes a new turn: "Ought we, he writes, ... to establish a Debussy-Cézanne-Mallarmé reality at the root of all modernity?" he asks; "a luminosity that withstands refraction by any prism of simple analysis? They are 'outside.' What do they show us? Perhaps this: that their revolution must not only be constructed, but also dreamed."[29]

"J'abomine les écoles et tout ce qui est professorial appliqué à la littérature qui, elle, au contraire, est tout à fait individuelle" (969) (I abominate schools and all that is academic applied to literature, which is, on the contrary, entirely individual). These words by Mallarmé could be those of Boulez speaking of Debussy, "that force of refusal opposed to the Schola of the venerated *d'indouilles, indouille-witz, indouilles-mith*."[30] The organization of sounds is a rejection of existing harmonic hierarchies; the rhythmic participates in a will toward variability in metrical conception. Debussy rethought all aspects of musical creation, carrying out a radical revolution. And Boulez concludes with a salute: "dans son expérience ineffable et dans sa somptueuse réserve, cet unique et universel Français maintient un pouvoir hermétique et troublant de séduction"[31] (in his ineffable experience and his sumptuous reserve, this unique and universal Frenchman maintains a hermetic and troubling power of seduction). Is there a better definition of Boulez himself in his seventieth year?

The year 1957 marked a key moment in the Mallarmé-Boulez nexus: Schérer's *"Le Livre" de Mallarmé* was published by Gallimard; Boulez published his essay "Aléa" in the *Nouvelle Revue Française*,[32] and he began *Pli selon pli*.

Like Mallarmé, he concedes that literary inquiry has anticipated much of what Boulez was about to explore. "One may note," he writes in *Sound and Word,* "that poets who worked on language itself are the ones who left the most visible imprint upon the musician; surely there come to mind immediately, he says, the names of Mallarmé rather than Rimbaud; of Joyce rather than Kafka,"[33] Mallarmé through whom "thought becomes an end in itself; its main justification being an essentially poetic quest."[34] What matters to Boulez in Mallarmé's "Le Livre" is reading *as performance*. The Tuesday evenings in the rue de Rome took place in front of an audience of twenty-four, with the reading divided into two parts, separated by an interval. Successive versions of incomplete sections of "Le Livre" were presented two at a time. And Mallarmé was less author than he was officiating priest and "opérateur" of the Scripture. As Schérer puts it, "Le prêtre [...] officie [...] il refigure l'opérateur du théâtre mallarméen" (The priest [...] appreciates [...] he refigures the operator of the Malléan theater). The operator shuffles the "feuillets" of the book, which are "mobiles, différents et pourtant interchangeables" (mobile, different, and nevertheless interchangeable). One reads according to laws of permutation: from death it comes to life.[35] "Tout hasard doit être banni de l'oeuvre moderne et n'y peut être que feint"[36] (All chance must be banished from the modern work and cannot be pretended there). So, too, Pierre Boulez, having read and been spellbound by Schérer's *"Le Livre" de Mallarmé*, moves from separate completed works in, what Jameux calls, "their autonomous and deadly perfection"[37] like ordinary bound books, to a continuing work in progress, forming an open-ended project in *Eclats/Multiples,* The Third Sonata, and the endless revisions of *Pli selon pli.* Boulez rebels against "chance," the aleatory of a John Cage, say, to espouse in reaction an opening-up in which the *performer* (in The Third Sonata), *not the composer,* can vary the sequence of the movements to maintain its status as a work in progress—"controlled chance" as Boulez calls it. In instrumental works, the pianist as operator is replaced by the conductor, in a glorification of the interpreter: "And not at all glorification of an interpreter-robot of bewildered precision but of an involved interpreter freed to make his choices."[38] Boulez calls it an interplay between freedom and discipline, between the conductor's gestures and the printed score: the gestures can be made into the void, signs to an individual player that amount to saying: "over to you." The player can then choose his own tempo. The passages concerned are printed in small notes in his part, in the same way as they used to notate ornaments. The maximum time allowed for these mobile structures is marked by arrows. In support, Boulez cites a lengthy passage from *Igitur*.

Pierre Boulez has now moved on from the open-ended works of the 1957 period, but the shadow of Mallarmé still hovers over the composer-conductor-pedagogue and critic. In this light, let us therefore try to disregard Milton Babbitt's accusation that "some of us composers wrote our music with at least one ear directed toward its susceptibility to public exegesis. That is, we wrote our music so we could talk about it."[39]

Notes

1. Jacques Schérer, ed., *"Le Livre" de Stéphane Mallarmé* (Paris: Gallimard, 1957).
2. Stéphane Mallarmé, *Oeuvres complètes* (Paris: Gallimard-Pléiade, 1979), 260. (References indicated within parentheses refer to this edition.)
3. Suzanne Bernard, *Mallarmé et la musique* (Paris: Nizet, 1957).
4. Pierre Boulez, *Notes of an Apprenticeship* (New York: Knopf, 1968) and *Orientations (Points de repère)* (London: Faber and Faber, 1986).
5. Dominique Jameux, *Pierre Boulez's* Trajectories, tr. Susan Bradshaw (Cambridge, Mass.: Harvard University Press, 1990).
6. Ivanka Stoianova, "La Troisième Sonate de Boulez et le projet mallarméen du Livre," in *Geste, texte, musique* (Paris: Union générale d'édition, 1978).
7. Bernard, 11.
8. Stéphane Mallarmé, *Correspondance* II, ed. Lloyd J. Austin (Paris: Gallimard, 1972), 286.
9. Wagner's letter to Villot, quoted in Bernard, 19.
10. Letter to Edmund Gosse, in Bernard, 75.
11. "Solitude," *OC*, 407.
12. *Las de l'amer repos, OC*, 28.
13. "Théodore de Banville," *OC*, 522.
14. Bernard, 41.
15. Letter to Edmund Gosse, in Bernard, 75.
16. Op. 10.
17. "Homage à Webern," in *Domaine musical* I, 123–24.
18. Arnold Schoenberg, *Essays* (Berkeley: University of California Press, 1966), 113.
19. Quoted by Schoenberg, 221.
20. Jameux, 74.
21. Pierre Boulez, *Nouvelle Revue Française*, 1 November 1957, 341.
22. *NRF*, 347.
23. *NRF*, 322.
24. *Orientations*, 26.
25. *Notes*, 148.
26. *Notes*, 261.
27. *Notes*, 260.
28. *Notes*, 260.

29. *Notes*, 27–28.
30. *Notes*, 29.
31. *Notes*, 33.
32. *Nouvelle Revue Française*, 1 November 1957.
33. Pierre Boulez, *Sound and Word*, 52.
34. *Trajectories*, 95.
35. Schérer, 191.
36. Schérer, 127.
37. Jameux, 231.
38. *Notes*, 50.
39. Milton Babbitt,*Words about Music*, ed. Stephen Dembski and Joseph N. Straus (Madison: University of Wisconsin Press, 1987), 2

II
On His Texts

Commentary on the "Sonnet in IX" of Mallarmé

OCTAVIO PAZ

Ses purs ongles très haut dédiant leur onyx,
L'Angoisse, ce minuit, soutient, lampadophore,
Maint rêve vespéral brûlé par le Phénix
Que ne recueille pas de cinéraire amphore

Sur les crédences, au salon vide: nul ptyx
Aboli bibelot d'inanité sonore,
(Car le Maître est allé puiser des pleurs au Styx
Avec ce seul objet dont le Néant s'honore).

Mais proche la croisée au nord vacante, un or
Agonise selon peut-être le décor
Des licornes ruant du feu contre une nixe,

Elle, défunte nue en le miroir, encor
Que, dans l'oubli fermé par le cadre, se fixe
De scintillations sitôt le septuor.

[Her pure nails very high up dedicating their onyx,
Anguish, this midnight, holds up, lamp-bearing,
Many an evening dream burned up by the Phoenix
That no funeral amphora gathers.

On the buffets, in the empty salon: no ptyx,
Abolished knickknack of sonorous emptiness,
(For the Master has gone to dip tears from the Styx
With this sole object through which the Nothingness honors itself).

But near the vacant casement turned to the north, a gold
Agonizes according perhaps to the decoration
Of unicorns kicking fire against a nixie,

She, defunctive nude [or cloud] in the mirror, while,
In the oblivion bounded by the frame, is fixed
Of scintillations at once the septet.][1]

THERE are two known versions of this sonnet. The first is from 1868 and carries a title that Sister Juana would have envied: "Allegorical Sonnet of Itself"; the second, and definitive one, appeared in *Poésies,* in 1887, untitled. The differences between the two versions are notable, and such an examination would require a separate study. Here, I am content to point out that these changes do not reveal an essential modification of the poetics of Mallarmé but rather a greater exactitude and a more rigorous concentration.

Since its publication, this sonnet caused surprise, irritation, intrigue, and marvel. Apart from the difficulties of syntax and interpretation, the vocabulary presents various enigmas. The most arduous is the significance of "ptyx." In a letter of 3 May 1869, addressed to Eugène Lefébure, the poet confided to his friend: "I have written a sonnet and I only have three rhymes in *ix*. Try to ascertain the real meaning of the word *ptyx*. I assure you that no language has it, which does not stop pleasing me as I would love to have created it through the magic of rhyme."[2] Madame Emilie Noulet, it appears to me, has elucidated the mystery: "il faut remonter à son origine grecque où l'idée de pli est fondamentale... 'ptyx' désigne une conque, un de ces coquillages qui, collé à l'oreille, fait entendre le bruit de la mer" (If we go back to the Greek origin of the word, it would tell us that the idea of fold is fundamental... 'ptyx' denotes a conch, one of those shells from which, when bringing it to our ears, we have the sensation of listening to the sound of the sea).[3] The majority of the critics agree with the Belgian writer's interpretation. Another difficulty: "nixe." It is a Germanism: the poet alludes to the aquatic spirits of Teutonic mythology. The "nixes" are the nymphs and naiads of Latin myths.

Part of the popularity of the sonnet is due to the rhyme. Mallarmé does not follow the traditional rhyme scheme (ABBA:ABBA and CDE:CDE) but rather uses crossed rhymes (ABAB:ABAB/CCD:CDC). In the quartets, the rhymes are in "ix" and in "ore"; in the tercets, in "ixe" and in "or." Extreme economy and no less extreme difficulty. This strict simplicity provokes a muffled and ritual music—cabalistic, the poet would say.

Another peculiarity: the composition is formed only by two phrases, one that comprises the quartets and one the tercets. The dual syntactic structure subdivides, at the same time, into the traditional rhetorical structure: two quartets and two tercets. Mallarmé restores the sonnet to its essential strophic scheme: an octave and a sestet. Or, rather, it regresses to the neoplatonic dualism that, in its origin, is co-substantial to this poetic form. Now, the sonnet adopted, since its introduction in France, the quadripartite syntactic division that the Italian poets, above all Petrarch, had given it: four phrases, one in each one of the quartets and tercets.

The same happened in Spain and Portugal. Even though, of course, this rule is not expressed and inflexible, but rather an implicit tendency, the French poets of the nineteenth century almost always followed the rule, from Nerval to the Parnassians and symbolists, including Rimbaud and Verlaine. The majority of the sonnets are composed, as much in French as in Italian, Spanish, and Portuguese, by four phrases: the first quartet is an exposition, the second its negation or alteration; the first tercet is the crisis, and the last the denouement. The sonnet is a proposition or, better said, four propositions connected by a logic no less rigorous then that which links the members of a syllogism. Without altering this logical-poetical structure, Mallarmé attenuates the opposition between quartet and tercet. The relations among the four parts of a traditional sonnet could be represented as the following (a and a' designate the quartets, and b and b' the tercets):

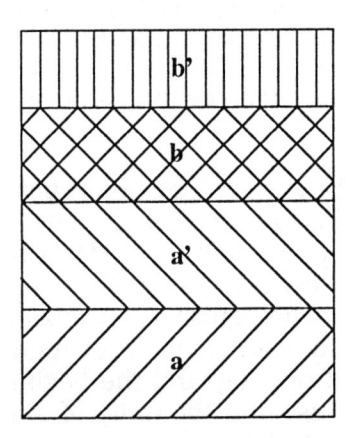

The graphic representation of the "sonnet in ix" would be:

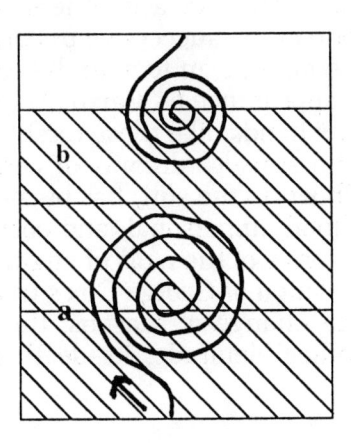

The first phrase wraps itself up like a spiral and coils up until it is canceled out; the second uncoils until it is confused with the universe, and is dissipated.

At the end of 1868, Henri Cazalis (Jean Lahor) asks Mallarmé to collaborate on the book *Sonnets and Etchings* that the editor Lemerre was preparing. The poet sent him the first version of the sonnet and a letter that contained valuable suggestions:

> It is an inverse sonnet. That is, I want to say that the sense, if it has one (I would resign myself painlessly to the fact that it might not have one, thanks to the dose of poetry that, it appears to me, it has), is evoked by the illusion of the words themselves ... It is not a *plastic* art but, at least it is very *black and white,* as you requested. I believe that it could lend itself to a full etching of Sleep and Void. For example, a nocturnal window, the two closed blinds; a room with no one inside, despite the stable air that the closed blinds offer, and in a night made of absence or interrogation, without furniture, other than the plausible sketch of vague consoles, the frame, bellicose and agonizing, of a mirror hung at the end, with the reflection, stellar and incomprehensible, of the Ursa Major, that ties this abandoned room of the world to the lonely sky.[4]

The description of 1868 coincides point by point with the definitive version of 1887. Utilizing these suggestions and the observations of Gardner Davies,[5] I will now try to describe the sonnet as the place (the desert) where the drama (the rite) is represented.

The character of the first quartet is Anguish. In the first version it was Night. Anguish is a metaphor for night, and especially for midnight, the end of one day and the beginning of another. An anguished hour because in it the unity of time and its continuity appear to break down. Will the sun come out again? Will it resuscitate from the ashes and from its "vesperal dream"? Or does the hour point to the beginning of a darkness without shores and without time? In spite of the successive uncertainties that magic, religion, and science have given to man, he repeats this question to himself since his appearance on Earth. Anguish raises its arms and holds between its hands, like those torchbearers of Antiquity, all the dreams of the sunset—dreams of consummation and of resurrection. The Phoenix (the sun) has burned them and no urn holds these ashes. Total, impersonal, and cosmic blackness. The only reflection is the onyx of the nails of anguish, like an offering. In a note to his translation of George Cox's treatise on mythology, Mallarmé says: "The change of seasons, the birth of nature in the spring, its summer plenitude, its death in autumn and its disappearance during winter (phases that correspond to sunrise, noon, sunset, and night), is the great and perpetual theme of Mythology, the double solar, daily and annual evolution . . . *the tragedy of nature.*"[6] Therefore, the first quartet presents an aspect—the final—that of tragedy in its daily phase. The hour is midnight, homologous, in the daily cycle, to the winter solstice in the annual cycle. Midnight, at the same time, is anguish—the indecisive awareness, assaulted by the horror of the unexpected and surrounded by shadows. That awareness is impersonal: it is not the poet who interrogates but rather it is the universe itself that, upon touching the extreme point of its distress, has asked again and awaits. Anguish is not psychological: it is a phase of the solar rite. In the middle of successive analogical reductions, Mallarmé encircles in four lines the nocturnal and negative aspects of the drama of nature: solstice of winter-midnight-anguish.

In the second quartet, the natural world is replaced by the human world. In the dark salon, a double absence—that of the Master (the owner of the house but also the poet, the initiated, the penitent) and that of that enigmatic, although quotidian, object by which the same Nothingness is honored: the *ptyx*, the marine conch. The Master has left to recapture sobs in the River Styx, and this act possesses a triple meaning. It alludes to a daily fact, like when we say: so-and-so isn't at home; it is a descent to the underworld, an initiation that requires the symbolic death of the neophyte and his resurrection; and finally, it is a purging of the I, an *epoché*, that is, the consciousness retires from itself, empties itself, and returns to the impersonal transparency. Realism, myth, and intellectual experience. Tragedy is cosmic and quotidian, it happens in the sky and in the room of a bourgeois. The Master is not the author of the drama: his conscience is the theater, and, even though his life is being played out there, he is more of a reflection than a spectator. The same analogy that links midnight to anguish unites the Master and the empty room. The Master is a metaphor for Nothingness—his awareness of himself, or more precisely, his knowledge that he is only an absence of himself. Analogical transformations: the room = the Master (his empty awareness) = Nothingness.

Something similar occurs with the instrument of the poet. It is an empty and sonorous *bibelot*—and it is the only object in which Nothingness exalts itself. The snail-shell is a structure that coils in on itself. According to Jean-Pierre Richard, the coil is a vital form of reflection: To think, to reflect, "it is to get coiled in oneself."[7] But the coil is also carnal: The sex organ of the woman refolds in on itself and hides beneath a dark fleece. Reflexive and erotic symbol, the snail-shell is also a room, a house—a theme as frequent among the Japanese poets as the carnal symbolism is among those of the West. And there is another meaning that includes all others: the snail-shell contains the sea and as such is an emblem of universal life, of its perpetual death and rebirth. At the same time, the snail-shell contains only air, it is nothingness. This duality (similar to that of the Master as the poet and the absent man of the house) converts it simultaneously into a vessel and into a ritual object. The snail-shell, in its immense smallness, summarizes all of the other images, the metaphor of metaphors: solstice of winter = midnight = anguish (universal) = empty room = Nothingness = Master (bourgeois) = snail-shell (vessel). But the series is reversible if the movement of the coiling is followed by an uncoiling: snail-shell (ritual object) = Music = Hero (poet) = Theater (dialogue, community) = universal consciousness = noon = summer solstice. The snail-shell is the point of intersection of all of the lines of force and the locus of metamorphosis. The snail-shell itself is metamorphosis.

The conclusion of the quartets is negative: darkness, absence. Nevertheless, in the golden frame of the mirror, a light (of gold) agonizes. And the spasms of that agony reproduce the disturbed and violent movements of a mythological scene painted or etched on the frame of the mirror: a group of unicorns zealously attack a *nixe* with flares. A new analogy, now among the death-rattles of the erotic and incendiary death and violence. The "perhaps" of the second line denotes that the darkness of the room does not allow one to affirm with certainty if the frame represents that scene or if it deals with a hallucination. The first tercet repeats on the level of individual fantasy (the adverb of doubt indicates obliquely that perhaps it deals with a visual sensation) and on the level of the mythical imagination (the unicorns and the *nixe*) the theme of the first two quartets—the crime of the night and the death of the sun. The relation of the first tercet with the first quartet is very close: the frame's blade of light and the onyx of the nails of anguish, the fiery death of the vesperal dreams and that of the nymph. The sun, the solar and virile hero, in one case lights himself on fire; he is the Phoenix. In another instance, converted into a unicorn, he lights the desired object, the nymph, on fire. Three representations of what Mallarmé called "the tragedy of nature." The first is cosmic: the death of the sun. The second is spiritual: the disappearance of self-consciousness. The third is erotic: the violation and the death of the nymph.

The first line of the second tercet consummates the action of the first: the nymph sinks into the mirror. In the last two lines, the change is operated: the black wings of the mirror close around the body of the dead nymph, and so, like the sudden sounding of a gong that breaks the silence, the seven luminaries of the constellation appear like a septet. Astronomy and music: transfiguration. In the tercets, the mirror performs the same double function as the snail-shell in the quartets. It is an ornament of the room and the magic locus of metamorphosis. It reflects us, and, when it internalizes us in its tricky surface, it dissolves us. The mirror as instrument of reflection offers us proof of our reality only in order to, an instant later and without even a reflection, betray it; it tells us that we are images: nothing. At the same time, it is the theater of metamorphosis: black in the shadow, it suddenly glitters and reflects the sparkling of the seven stars. The mirror projects in space those luminaries like the snail-shell flings into the air the musical notes of the sea. Adornment hung on a wall and instrument of magicians and sorcerers, symbol of the perdition of man and the origin of the speculation, the mirror receives and buries the winter solstice, midnight, the abandoned room, the dead nymph—all those signs that denoted the empty consciousness—to transform them, by luck of instantaneous reversion, into the sparkling of the Ursa Major. The mirror closes the sonnet and, soon after, opens it, already changed, to the infinite: in it personal consciousness drowns, and in it, it is reborn as pure consciousness, in accord with the essential reality of the world.

Perhaps it is useful to show, in two figures, the double movement of the coiling and uncoiling of the two phrases that comprise the sonnet and the movement of the two we might call snail-phrase and mirror-phrase. The first only describes the interior movement, of concentration (the descendent series of analogies), and from there encloses in parenthesis the distinct moments of the ascending series; in the second, the two phases of rotation—the coiling and uncoiling—appear. (See following page.)

The two series of analogies are fused in one that encompasses them: snail > mirror. This last one receives and buries the negative symbols that coil in the snail to, almost instantaneously, uncoil them like light and music. Those symbols can be reduced to an ancient mythic and poetic pair: water and fire, first in opposition and later fused. In the first quartet, fire is the destructor. The Phoenix burns the vesperal dreams and it is dissolved in shadow and ash. In the second quartet, water, having lost all of its enliv-

First phrase

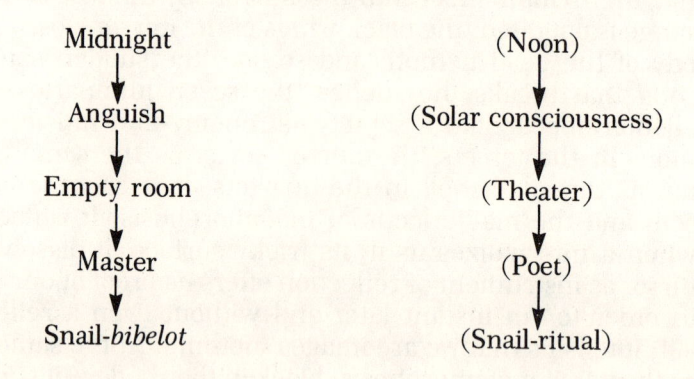

Midnight → Anguish → Empty room → Master → Snail-*bibelot*

(Noon) → (Solar consciousness) → (Theater) → (Poet) → (Snail-ritual)

Second phrase

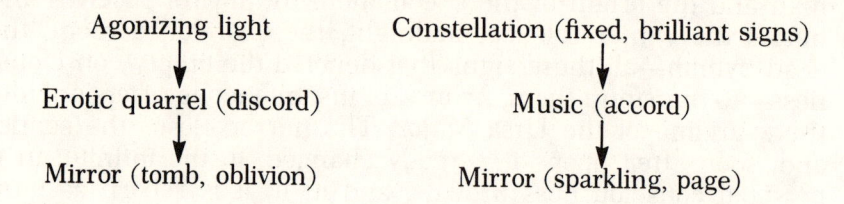

Agonizing light → Erotic quarrel (discord) → Mirror (tomb, oblivion)

Constellation (fixed, brilliant signs) → Music (accord) → Mirror (sparkling, page)

ening powers, is the ashen river of the dead. In the first tercet, the fire reappears, again as destruction: the unicorns attack a nymph (aquatic creature) with flames. Here, as opposed to what occurs in the quartets, fire and water are fused but its embrace is polemical. In the second tercet, the nymph scarcely disappears in the water of the mirror, when luminous and musical signs, the twinkling of the Ursa Major, are inscribed upon this liquid tomb. Like the snail and the mirror, water and fire are dual symbols: creation and destruction. The relation between the first phrase and the second can be reduced to a tripartite outline: solar fire that burns the vesperal dreams = unicorns that attack the nymph with flames; water from the river of the dead = stagnant water of the mirror; (absent term: snail that encloses the music of the sea) = stellar septet. Or, in another mode: solar fire (ash) > water (River Styx) > fire against water (unicorns and nymph) > water (tomb of the nymph) > stellar fire in the water of the mirror.

The above description omits something essential: We have not witnessed the cyclical rite of the resurrection of the sun but rather a transmutation of a different order although of an analogous meaning. The constellation is not the sun but rather its ideal double: its transfiguration in a cluster of signs, its Idea. The sun is a star of movement and the seven stars *are affixed* to the mirror in shadow. The drama of nature is not resolved in the cyclical and natural repetition but rather in a unique and irreproducible act. If the act does not destroy the chance, the sun could not come out; it absorbs and protects it in an immobile form, these seven stars that are the ideogram of poetry and music. The act of transfiguration, in the empty consciousness of the poet, is similar to the act that the sun performs when appearing and disappearing on the horizon, but, even though both are twin forms of chance, its signification is diverse and almost contrary: One is cyclical and fatal, the other is unique and, in a certain way, free. In the natural drama, reality is realized in a process that undoes it and redoes it; in the poetic act, reality is realized as Idea. It stops being a process and becomes a sign. So that, at the two natural moments of coiling and uncoiling, another moment, final and provisionally definitive, occurs: the appearance of those stars that have become writing. The mirror converted into page. The final moment is provisional because Idea, now a sign, should now suffer the test of the act of reading and realize itself, like the sun, in the memory and oblivion of the reader. I return to the succession. In his letter to Cazalis, Mallarmé said: "Negated sonnet that is reflected in itself in every one of its parts."[8] Sonnet-snail-shell, sonnet-mirror: the last line, luminous, is opened to the night and music is dissolved into silence. Sonnet in rotation and allegorical of itself.

All that remains is to position "sonnet in ix" in the work of Mallarmé. Davies underlines that it is one of the most perfect and polished expressions of the theme of night and solar resurrection. At the same time, the critic says, it is a prefiguration (*I would say it is a miniature model*) of his three most ambitious and complex works: *Hérodiade, Igitur,* and *Un Coup de Dés*. Although Mallarmé finished only the last, we can conjecture as to the relationship between these works and the sonnet (thanks to the fragments that he left of the first two) and because of what we know, through his prose texts and his correspondence, about the final form that he dreamed of giving these projects. In *Hérodiade*, Saint John "realizes in death the anonymity that the poet demands; his inclined head corresponds to the image, in *Igitur*, of a character whose thought is not conscious of itself."[9] The analogy with the

Phoenix, the empty room, the nymph and the mirror of the sonnet is evident. The suppression of the I and of personal consciousness—the theme of *Igitur* and *Un Coup de Dés* —appears in the sonnet in an allegorical form: Master and mirror. The negation of itself is the precondition of the work's creation and of the resurrection of the true life, which is not the immortality of the I in the beyond but rather the act through which the infinite absorbs chance and fixes it in a constellation—a figure in rotation, a configuration. In a letter of 1867, Mallarmé confided to Cazalis: "I have just had a dreadful year; my thought has thought itself and has arrived at a pure conception.... Now I am impersonal and no longer the Stéphane that you knew."[10] In another letter to Cazalis, he says that he has finally *felt* the Nothingness of Indian philosophy, "without knowing Buddhism."[11] But Mallarmé is not a nihilist (and neither are the Buddhists) and adds: "After having found vacuity, I found beauty."[12] Nagarjuna would say vacuity is not contrary to the phenomenal world but rather it is its ultimate reality. Mallarmé does not renounce vacuity to the world and to the word, but rather he renounces it as a method of personal liberation and recreation of the world. The death of the sun, the decapitation of Saint John, the night of Igitur in his abandoned castle, the shipwreck of *Un Coup de Dés* and the sudden appearance of Ursa Major that comes in the septentrion as the consequence, the refutation and the rhyme of the dice thrown to the ocean—all of this coils in the "sonnet in ix," like a snail and, like a mirror, uncoils out and twinkles. Everything is fixed, as if on a page.

Conclusion

This attempt at translation confirms to me something that I had already pointed out, in passing, in a text years ago (collected in *Corriente alterna* [Alternate current])—the similarity between Góngora and Mallarmé is tricky. The two are difficult, enigmatic, and luminous but their clarities, even though they may appear blinding, are different. The forte of Góngora is noon: the *Fábula de Polifemo y Galatea* (Fable of Polifemo and Galatea); that of Mallarmé, despite *L'Après-midi d'un Faune,* is midnight: *Igitur, Un Coup de Dés, Hommages et Tombeaux.* Both are painters: the first evokes Caravaggio and Rubens, the second, Monet and Redon. In Góngora, the word is architecture and sculpture; in Mallarmé, music and calligraphy. The point of convergence is the dance, collective in Góngora—the passes and dances of the *Soledades* (Solitudes)—and solitary in Mallarmé—*Hérodiade*. Analogy is the religion of Mallarmé: his vision of the world, his method of knowledge, and his doctrine of redemption. For Góngora analogy, that is, metaphor, is an aesthetic—a method of transfiguring reality, not a way toward truth. Góngora saves the world through the image; he converts it into dazzling appearances that hides nothing. His world does not have depth or weight. Reality loses gravity, it unburdens itself of the guilt of original sin, and the ancient wound closes. All is surface. Góngora, the poet, is not Christian. Neither is Mallarmé, but his poetry saves neither the appearances nor the reality that sustain it; his work is a negation, a criticism of reality. He said: *Destruction was my Beatrice*. In one instance, transfiguration of the world; in the other, transposition. The critical operation does not annihilate the world, but it does reduce it to a few transparent signs.

The aesthetic of Góngora is that of the undeceived; that of Mallarmé is a response to the adversity of present history and a convocation of a time to come that will make a theater out of the hymn. His individualism is a defense, not a negation of the others. The essence of man is a chorus. The Andalusian and the Frenchman passed through some bad times. In opposition to a decadent society, the first positioned the inaudible spectacle of a verbal machine that does not emit a meaning other than that of its perfection. To be is to appear. The sense of meaning does not dissolve in the being; it disintegrates into the appearance. Abolition of history. Everything is present, everything is located in the present. Mallarmé, on the other hand, believes in history, even though he lives it like a lack and an absence: *There is no present, no—a present does not exist*. Nevertheless, he hopes that the poet, in his "recueillement à préparer l'édifice de haut verre essuyé d'un vol de la Justice"[13] (the poet, in his retreat in order to prepare the tall glass building [that will be] wiped clean by a flight of Justice). But perhaps the true difference between them is not in their diverse attitudes toward history and the present (the two were anachronistic in their times and because of this they are our masters) but rather in the following: Góngora shows us to see, Mallarmé shows us that vision is a spiritual experience. For Góngora, the poem is a metaphor for the world; for Mallarmé, the world is a metaphor for the word, for the Idea. This Idea that in *Un Coup de Dés* finally reveals itself as a Maybe. Góngora dissolves the world in the image, just as it is. Mallarmé injects the criticism into the interior of the image, just as it may be.

Notes

1. Translated by Robert Greer Cohn.
2. Stéphane Mallarmé, *Correspondance, 1862–1871,* ed. Henri Mondor and Lloyd James Austing (Paris: Gallimard, 1959), 274. (Hereafter cited as *Corr.*)
3. *Oeuvre poétique de Mallarmé* (Paris: Droz, 1940), 454.
4. *Corr.*, 278–79. (Unless otherwise indicated, all quotations are my translations of Paz's Spanish translations. *Trans.*)
5. Gardner Davies, *Mallarmé et le drame solaire* (Paris: Corti, 1959).
6. *Les Dieux antiques,* in Stéphane Mallarmé, *Oeuvres complètes,* ed. Henri Mondor and G. Jean-Aubry (Paris: Gallimard-Pléiade, 1945), 1169. (Hereafter cited as *OC.*)
7. Jean-Pierre Richard, *L'Univers imaginaire de Mallarmé* (Paris: Seuil, 1961).
8. Letter to Cazalis, *Corr.* 278–79.
9. *Hérodiade* (Davies, 29).
10. Letter to Cazalis, 1867, *Corr.*, 242.
11. Letter to Cazalis, 1866, *Corr.*, 207.
12. Letter to Cazalis, 1866, *Corr.*, 220.
13. "L'Action restrainte," *OC*, 372.

Hérodiade and Virtual Reality
Anna Balakian

It is a miracle that at a time when literary criticism is so charged with political and social overtones, a biographical milestone of Mallarmé—the poet who turned his back on society—can be remembered and celebrated. Of course, I am not ignoring the fact that in recent years he has been interpreted politically and in terms of dialectical materialism, but here in the broader context it can be said that a hundred years after his death Mallarmé is still the most cryptic and yet the most globally comprehensible poet of our time, in both his concern over the loss of anthropocentrism and in his desire to promote concepts of interartifactuality and the shared intricacies of the creative process in the arts.

Many poets since time immemorial have talked *about* relationships among the arts, and the impact of scientific revelations on the arts, but there are very few who have actually staked their reputation on demonstrating in their own writings the possible effects of such awareness.

Two points need clarification before discussion of Mallarmé's anticipatory notion of virtual reality:

> 1. Mallarmé is not an abstract poet, which does not mean to say that he is a materialist in the twentieth-century political meaning of that word. To some of the most astute critics, he has conveyed the impression of being abstract because he manages through his special use of language to move concrete realities surrounding us or recognizable by all of us, and, if rare, explainable by a visit to the dictionary, into his own reorganization of a controlled reality, perhaps best associable by current readers with the term "virtual reality." He used the word "virtual" in this sense about a hundred years before the scientific mind appropriated the term for its own technical manipulation of reality. Let us be reminded of Mallarmé's reference in *Variations sur un sujet*: "Le dire avant tout, rêve et chant, retrouve chez le Poète, par nécessité constitutive d'un art consacré aux fictions, sa virtualité" (368)[1] (The utterance above all, dream and song, rediscovers in the Poet its virtuality, necessarily constitutive of an art devoted to fictions).

2. The second misconception I have observed rises out of a misreading of a much-quoted sentence from "Crise de vers":

> L'oeuvre pure implique la disparition élocutoire du poète, qui cède l'initiative aux mots, par le heurt de leur inegalité mobilisés; ils s'allument de reflets réciproques comme une virtuelle traînée de feux sur des pierreries, remplaçant la respiration perceptible en l'ancien souffle lyrique ou la direction personnelle enthousiaste de la phrase. (366)

[The pure work implies the elocutionary disappearance of the poet, who yields the initiative to the words, mobilized by the clash of their inequality; they light up with reciprocal reflections like a virtual trail of fires on jewels, replacing the respiration perceptible in the old lyric breath or the enthusiastic personal direction of the sentence.]

Mallarmé is telling his fellow poets to get rid of the oral rhetoric that binds the poem to the personality rather than the artistry of the author. Freed of that bond, the poem can function independently of its temporal circumstances, and the interaction of the words and their objects mobilized can *virtually* create their own sparks and ignite the poem into motion.

So much poetry criticism has been catalyzed by one who wrote so few poems! And as I have tried to show lately,[2] so much poetry engendered internationally by Mallarmé in our own century is indeed proof of the semantic and existential fertility of his sparse crop rather than of his magnetic but not so spectacular personality.

Hérodiade and *L'Après-midi d'un Faune* are the works in which Mallarmé best creates his "fiction" or "virtual reality," which at the end of the twentieth century we can identify with what the scientists call cyberspaces. To refer again to his theoretical statement—the verse from which he has tried to banish chance: "et vous cause cette surprise de n'avoir ouï jamais tel fragment ordinaire d'élocution, en même temps que la réminiscence de l'object nommé baigne dans une neuve atmosphère" (368) (gives us the surprise of never having heard such an ordinary fragment of elocution at the very moment that it recalls the object bathed in a new atmosphere).

The irony is that in both these poems Mallarmé is rather unwillingly a poet. He wanted so much to be a dramatist, but the paradox is that drama functioned in his time through elocution, and, in banishing the elocutionary, he was annihilating the dramatic form of artistic communication as practiced in his era. Maeterlinck and his followers were the ones to find a way to create drama through *tension* rather than elocution, and Mallarmé's failure was to be a factor in their success.

If not with drama, Mallarmé was much more successful in associating "fiction" with poetry; he identified with "fiction" by releasing its connection from its conventional connotation, which stipulates narration of invented plot, psychological conflict, and the intrigue related to circumstantial events.

In illustrating Mallarmé's virtual reality, I will dwell primarily on *Hérodiade,* which is to date the least explicated of his repertory.[3] Here he took a known legend and placed it in his contrived virtual reality both by manipulating the objects in it and the established meaning of the words used to distinguish between the living and the inert. In creating Hérodiade, he chose a name that fell between two legendary figures. His Hérodiade is neither the biblical Hérodiade nor her daughter Salome, the latter being a favorite character of the literature, opera, and paintings of his contemporaries. She is simply of the ancestry of Herod, which sends a message of "murder" through the minds of those who know their Bible.[4]

Mallarmé places his fictional character in a castle that constitutes organizationally an *obsolete* site. He constructs his stage for stagnation with objects as concrete as building blocks with the cooperation of physical nature (a warning aurora) and a human artifact—an ancient tapestry that is a part of a family's past encrusted in the structure of the castle and its furnishings along with a moat that separates it from the normal reality of the moment of the writing of the poem. But what makes this artificial world different from a purely aesthetic representation is that the creator of the space will participate in it as will his readers to the extent of their imaginative ability.

Hérodiade becomes part of this virtual reality and is relieved of all elocutionary discourse. Whatever is said to her or of her is in glaring ambiguity in relation to the precision of the language expressing tension and forewarning of impending crisis. We, the readers, are submitted to the working of the heritage of Herod, the collision of exterior perilous stagnation with Hérodiade's inherent potential for violence.

Throughout the three parts that constitute the official version of *Hérodiade,* Mallarmé uses his verbal powers to organize and control his creation without the intrusion of his personal voice, and the participation of the readers in the creative process can be likened to church ritual (his word is "sacre"). It is common knowledge that the three parts were revised many times in the course of his life; there is a record of his working on the Overture as early as 1865, and as late as 1897, a year before his death, he was still working on *Hérodiade*. It is astonishing that the final version, the official one published in the Pleiade edition, achieves such a unity of intention and realization.[5]

What exactly are these powers if the elocutionary has been rejected? Are they musical? Not in the Verlainian or symbolist sense ("Les sanglots longs des violons de l'automne"). He does not pursue the sound of music but the organizational system of music, the calculated positioning of words, the resonances of the chosen code words, their attraction to others as to each other. He does not choose these words for their pleasurable sounds nor for any specific meaning. In fact, he has a nostalgia for that primitive practice of polyvalence, which had been rekindled by the linguistic studies in his time by the German Friederich Dietz and the French Emile Littré. He also chooses his words in their semiotic complexities that produce that other quality of music that he calls "entendement," the same word Baudelaire had used upon hearing the music of Wagner: a vaster comprehension of the dictionary meaning of signification than through verbal communication and that challenges the meaning of meaning.

Mallarmé's poem would have become as static as many a poem of the "art for art's sake" school of aestheticism if it were based merely on the felicities of language. That embellishing power of form, according to Mallarmé, performs a rhetorical function rather than what he considers a poetic one. For language to become a poetic act, it has to be involved in an existential quest, become an act of exploration. With language he has reconstructed a concrete setting to frame a character marked by an ambiguous genetic flaw. The name "Hérodiade" gives the readers of his time a common referential base for the principal question. "What leads to violence? What turns apparent purity into evil?" we may be wondering. But in Mallarmé's nontheological way of thinking, it might be more appropriate to ask "how does the cell containing the genetic flaw placed in a culture (a biological one) convert into an agent of destruction?"

The first actor in this capsuled drama is not a human but an animated aspect of cosmology, the Dawn. We are made to follow it like the eye of a camera into a place full of evidences of devastation.

>Abolie, et son aile affreuse dans les larmes
>Du bassin, aboli, qui mire les alarmes,

Des ors nus fustigeant l'espace cramoisi,
Une Aurore a, plumage heraldique, choisi
Notre tour cinéraire et sacrificatrice,
Lourde tombe qu'a fuie un bel oiseau, caprice
Solitaire d'aurore au vain plumage noir. . . .
Ah! des pays déchus et tristes le manoir!

(41)

[Abolished and her fearful wing in the tears
Of the basin, abolished, which stares at the alarms
Of nude golds flagellating the scarlet-hued space,
A Dawn has, armorial plumage, chosen
This our tower, ash-scattered and sacrificial
Oppressive tomb fled by a beautiful bird, lone
Caprice of dawn with shadowy, black plumage . . .
Ah! of lands fallen and mournful the dwelling place!][6]

Let me note the features of the beginning of this impermeable text. In a self-referential play of imagery, it conveys the notion of decrepitude that unites a failed sunrise with a deteriorating castle. The key word is "abolished" in its feminine ending keeping us in suspense as to its reference to the dawn until four lines later, but in the very next line is repeated in its masculine ending to qualify the dilapidated moat meant to be a protection for the castle from the perils of invasion. The dawn depicted as an incapacitated bird drops its tears into this dried-up moat that no longer serves its function to guard the castle from danger, and the dawn's uncertain rays pass through a red and uncertain morning sky heralding doom and sparking in the crumbling structure gold spots that evoke past glories of the fallen domain. The red sky of morning, a proverbial sailor's warning of impending storm, is the first danger signal. A red, tearful aurora contaminates space and alights on a fortress associated with words signifying destruction and decomposition, such as "tomb," "mausoleum," "cinerary," and "dead star," which presage doom and are arbitrarily ominous, because the choice of aurora is capricious as it seeks a complicity with elements of fire, air, earth, and water in their choice of this particular place to prepare for an imminent sacrifice."Crime! Stake! ancient aurora! punishment" bespeak a drama that normally would take reams of paper to transcribe and, even on stage, an hour or two to represent. For Mallarmé, four words suffice to tell us the story of Hérodiade. The reader is spared the mimetic dimensions necessary to transmit into normal reading time the state imagined by the poet. In the use of "ancienne" in connection with "aurore,"

Mallarmé's support of the initial "abolie" is double-tiered: It contains the mythological context of a legend revisited on us and the perennial character of sunrise that is no longer relevant to his new use of the old phenomenon either in its physical or its mythological functions. By contamination, the sense of crime and punishment must be equally banished or abolished as we enter a psychic space (today it would be called a "tele-experience") whose boundaries have been determined by its legendary and its cosmological filiations.

The ray of crimson—such an obvious word as "red" will not enter Mallarmé's lexicon—has penetrated the chamber, and the reader glides in on its path. The effect of "abolie" is continued through "eteinte" and "neigeux jadis" where the adverb indicating a long forsaken past is used as a noun. (He was to create the same disturbing effect with "aujourd'hui" in "Le Vierge, le vivace et le bel aujourd'hui".) We also know from the first section that autumn's fiery colors had yielded passage to a more fiery conflagration of a burning dawn. So the retreat into abolished time is becoming deeper as we advance into the setting and its artificial climate. The next grimoire/glyphe is woven into tapestry—also an act of abolition, for is there anything more useless than shrouded eyes of sibyls? Their usual function is to look into the future but in this particular situation, they are woven into a future that is long past.

In the next passage, the Nurse seems to absorb the material texture of the tapestry as well as the prophetic function of the sibyls. Whatever meanings the reader's efforts extricate from the sibylic words, by its very nature the discourse prohibits unilateral meaning. The reader is freed of any meanings the author may have had in mind. The morphologically obscure passage belies the contention repeatedly made by critics that *Hérodiade* is a poem of absence; on the contrary, the elements of a vanished past have a functional presence. The topography of the tapestry is transferring the investiture of its qualities into the garment worn by a nurse like the passage of its effects into the room on the wings of an aroma that suggests regret for a time past. The silenced voice (auditory absence) has assumed the communicative power of the olfactory sense that makes its presence felt in its very invisibility. It has the resilience of flowers that refuse to lose their petals with the coming of night. The effect of immanence, prevalence, and resistance is masterfully suggested by the unlikely and unexpected alliance of fragile aroma with that of hard metal, "aroma of cold ores."

In the lines tracing the passage of a historic past into a fictitious present, the readers are put into the process of weaving the tapestry themselves whereby the visionary capacity of a past and buried eye and a past frail finger leave their residual effect on all aspects of the inert present. This is how the absence of a time long past becomes a possible and frightening presence and gives intimations of an equally frightening future. The final concrete presence of an absence is Hérodiade's empty bed, in which she has left the purity of a creaseless sheet.

In all this concrete set of denotations, there is not a single abstract word. There is no rarefaction to suggest ambiguity or generalization. The rest of the Overture prepares the closure of an era—the millennium, the absence of the ruler, the failing power of prophecy of the old finger whose warning goes unheeded. And we are made to realize that the sunrise, which the reader has embraced in its fictitious climate, is semantically a twilight. It is captured in the image of a candle burning out or a star whose present light is the luminous presence of a constellation long dead.

The Overture, like musical overtures, contains the comprehensiveness of motives, elaborated in the next parts of the poem, which were no doubt intended to be much longer and more elaborate than they turned out to be. Ominous in its preliminary signals, did the poem not suggest a climax in brutality and destruction? On another tier, it is also suggestive in terms of the arts of the fin de siècle of what Mallarmé characterized elsewhere as an "interrègne"—a gap in the continuity in the progress of the arts, paralleled in the political emblem of Herod as a break in the command. The perdition of the old ruler and the old rules is to open up space for something radically new. Of course, you might say that Mallarmé was not in a fin de siècle situation when he began working on Hérodiade in 1865, but he could foresee, with that quality of seer/sibyl assumed as the role of the poet, both the end of his century and the eventual end of our millennium.

The second part, "Scène," focuses on the ambiguity of action on the part of the principal persona. The Nurse, in her inquisitiveness, assumes the position of the spectator who enters the space of this succinct and impending drama; she verbalizes the reader's query into the mystery of human behavior. The dialogue involves the dichotomy between the human and the desired nonhuman condition. The central image is *hair*, organically the human element most resilient to putrefaction, and metonymically representative of the beauty of woman (human) and transformed by its possessor into something nonhuman, gold, metal, untouchable, eventually elevated to the level of a meteor. Behind the will to transform the human into something inhuman is the intention of the poet to be other than what he is as he enters the space he has created and carries out the transfer: man into woman, historical situation into legendary, poet into archeologist, the writing into sculpture, the verbal communication into gesture, the stillness of the physical environment into movement, the folio into mirror, the mirror into a deep well. In fact, Mallarmé was reticent about using the word "poet" within his poetry because he wanted to find something other than his self-portrait in his writings. If he were simply retreating into his subconscious, as our Freud-oriented contemporary commentators would have us believe, he would indeed be sinking into the quicksand of the ego. On the contrary, he intended to escape from the human self and, not believing in sainthood, faced the tragic dilemma of the agnostic. Rejecting the human, he made Hérodiade say: "Mais qui me toucherait, des lions respectée? / Du reste, je ne veux rien d'humain et, sculptée" (47) (But who would touch me, respected as I am by the lions / Besides I want nothing human, sculptured as I am)—and yet at the same time he was rejecting the azure and had nothing else to cling to!

The legendary dance of Hérodiade is here transformed into a gradual fixation into immobility; as eyes become jewels, and darkness is willed to be a permanent atmospheric condition, she awaits a metamorphosis that will distance ineffective dreams and turn useless flesh into cold but enduring stone. In Mallarmé's crisis to find a means of expression to present that passage out of the strictly human, without transcendence into theological salvation, *Hérodiade* is the cornerstone. And taken in that light, the severance from life, the closing of the windows and blowing out of the candle, paralleled by the descent into a hinterland between life and nonlife, the recognition of the vanity of "human" mystery, the nudity of flesh without future, all lead here and in subsequent works to the worship of art as the alternative to death. But art must recoil from the human into its virtual reality even as Hérodiade recoils when the Nurse tries to touch her hair; art can survive for Mallarmé to the degree to which it can detach itself from the mimetic and create its own fiction.

Although it is not clear when part 3, the "Cantique de Saint Jean," was actually written in the chronological composition of *Hérodiade,* and although it was not published in Mallarmé's lifetime, the logic of its presentation after the "Scène" is obvious in light of the struggle that the totality of the concept represents. The decapitation of Saint Jean is as normal as the closing of the shutters in "Scène" and the extinguishing of the candle in that other cryptic writing of his youth, *Igitur*. To reach the "Cantique," we pass from intention to premonition, and finally to realization in the most radical rupture with the past. If in "Scène" Hérodiade rejects human procreation, in Saint Jean the rejection extends to the theological. If the movement of decapitation is compared with the movement of the rise and fall of the sun, that may well be its visible pattern. But the saint is fictitious like every other character in Mallarmé's work, be it derived from classical legend or Hebraic theology. If, however, on one level the violent act is the release from the deterioration and the tension of Hérodiade's earlier position, it is also linked to the creative process of the poet. We can view the decapitation not as a death in terms of Mallarmé's artistic life, but as the emancipation of the created work from its creator and its historical tradition. It is a new baptism: "illuminated" qualifies "head" four stanzas earlier as the act is fulfilled according to the principle "which elected me," the severance of the head making a new salvation possible. Of the three parts, the "Cantique" is the least somber, the fall being equated with a triumphant release, the orphic return from darkness into illumination in the kind of relief from frustration that alone saves the artist-persona from suicide. We have, in the case of Mallarmé, the answer to the Nurse's question to Hérodiade: "Madame, allez-vous donc mourir?" The answer is no, for like Orpheus, the poet returns from death to lead an existence better explained in his next and more complete construction of virtual reality in *L'Après-midi d'un Faune*. In fact, if we were to carry the analogy of the virtual reality to his other works, we could see *Hérodiade* as the cyberspace that initiates his severance from both standard reality and fantasy as his first tentative at exploration. *L'Après-midi d'un Faune* then proceeds to the savoring of the self-created "souffle artificiel," or, in current language, the creator's consumption of his creation, and, in that perspective, *Un Coup de Dés jamais n'abolira le hasard* would extend the cyberspace into the cosmos.

Critical references to "Scène" and to "Cantique" have been somewhat more numerous than those to the "Overture," but they also bear the mark of embarrassing and understandable inconclusiveness on the part of the interpreter. Such interpretations of "Scène" lean heavily on the biographical situation related to the text and to references to other writings or, as a last resort, to Freudian interpretations identifying the mystery of Hérodiade with unconscious forces. In a sense "Cantique," which verbally is perhaps the most cryptic of all, gives the reader an easier referential access because of what is *not* in the poem rather than what *is* in it. The beheading of Saint John is such a collective reference that substitutions of the common knowledge to the language of Mallarmé are readily possible, as is the recognition of the parallelism between the rise and fall of the sun and the rise and fall of the head of the saint.

In the Gnostic tradition there are two kinds of hermetic scriptures: the open and the closed. The Open Book is decipherable with zeal. In the case of Mallarmé's cryptography, the intelligent reader is highly tempted to untangle meaning. But his cyberspace poems have the structure and language of The Closed Book, which may well underlie his notion of "Le Livre." Actually, verbal explanations of any part of Mallarmé's cryptic work are counterproductive activities on the part of the reader in view of the basic theory of the poet—his stated desire to find a new language (his purpose was affirmed in a letter to Cazalis as early as 1865) that would imitate the other arts in conveying ambivalent meaning and shrouding the ideological meanings of poetry, so that it becomes no more accessible to conceptual explanation than are music or the visual arts. Instead the reader must assume a world of fiction such as when placed in the presence of a musical composition that evokes imaginative "entendement," or a painting of a landscape that remains ever green, of faces that do not wrinkle, of flowers that never fade.

If reception of Mallarmé's poetry is to be anything other than exegesis or a blanket dismissal as "obscure," then his intentions must be taken into account because they are an integral part of his poetic theory: "Le vers ne doit donc pas, là, se composer de mots, mais d'intentions" (1440) (Verse must thus not be a composition of words, but of intentions). And the intention is to learn from music its power to impress and evoke rather than to transmit thought, from dance the fusion of the creator with the object of the creation, and from painting indisputable transformation of the mimetic into fictional and permanent existence. Mallarmé *intends* to use the qualities of all three of these arts in the writing of his poem, which is conceived in turn as dance, as opera, and as fresco, but always falls back into poetry; it is rejected as poem, edited endlessly, never released as a completed work, the intention never quite fulfilled, the process relentless.

Finally, if Mallarmé would banish the elocutionary character of the poet from his poetry, it was to better focus on the existential anguish that was the motivating dimension of his writing. If the story of *Hérodiade* is fascinating for him, it is not because of a particular predilection for archeology or history, or for biblical studies, or for the relationships between mythology and anthropology. I dare say that he was not even particularly interested in probing the nature of human violence.

His most obsessive and continuing meditation or preoccupation is with the creative process, which gives him his reason for living and which he sees irrevocably linked to the destructive process even as it is in the material world. As a result, the reading of *Hérodiade* is not primarily to savor a pleasurable piece of art or to provoke dreaming as in the case of Flaubert's *Salambô*, nor will it cause a catharsis as might the attendance of a performance of Oscar Wilde's *Salome* or Richard Strauss's opera of the same name.

It presents a vaster import beyond its existence as a single artifact. It is an epistemological phenomenon recurring in Mallarmé's other major poems and reappearing sporadically in the writing of later poets associable with him such as Yeats, Rilke, and Wallace Stevens who wanted to discover the process of becoming a poet as much as of finding subjects for their writing and who wondered how they could create a true bond with the other arts. The major fact is that the unexpected potential of the gestation process of the work of art in any of its branches is unrestrictable to any single product that emerges. It is as powerful as a biological gene and can surface any time to destroy the past and create its own reality. This quiet, nonelocutionary man was an unsuspected subversive and a revolutionary who aimed to modify the very nature of the imaginary by attempting to find a common unifying source for the arts beyond the aegis of a vague spiritual bond, which in his personal life he enjoyed with so many musicians and artists. Outside of the obvious collegiality, he was seeking a fundamental linkage under the sign of universal natural laws in the real universe. His obstinate efforts were only a beginning, and we have not yet envisaged its broader repercussions, although we are on the outermost edge of the millennium that was the target of his speculations.

Notes

1. All quotations from Mallarmé are from the Pléiade edition of his works: Stéphane Mallarmé, *Oeuvres complètes,* ed. Henri Mondor and G. Jean-Aubry (Paris: Gallimard-Pléiade, 1945). (Subsequent page references indicated within parentheses.) All translations of the prose are mine.

2. See Anna Balakian, *The Fiction of the Poet* (Princeton, N.J.: Princeton University Press, 1992) for a detailed study of Mallarmé's virtual reality in the light of its multilingual ramifications.

3. The most comprehensive attempt at exegesis of this work is that of Robert Greer Cohn, which includes a study of themes, images, and associable references to other interpretations, as well as intertextual references within Mallarmé's other writings.

4. Mallarmé developed three methods of deconstructing reality and constructing his own fictitious world: existential, referential, and connotative. Here we are dealing with the referential: he evades the direct identification of the obvious Salome legend popular in his time by his subtle reference to the family, which produced a creature endowed with a potential for violence; and he substantiates his reference with archeological evidence encrusted in stone, tapestry, and furnishings.

5. It is to be noted that reference to *Les Noces d'Hérodiade* is omitted as a matter of principle. Mallarmé has left many drafts and fragments, because he corrected his work endlessly. My respect for his search for perfection makes me loath to evaluate what he did not consider definitive. In general, I feel that there is too much time spent by scholars on variants and pre- and post-texts in relation to the amount of work that needs to be done on definitive texts. What the French call "avant-texte" has a legitimate value only as a supportive document for verification of chronology, or for psychological factors that may be demonstrated in them; none of these considerations apply to the esthetic and existential elements here scrutinized.

6. Translated by Donald Friedman.

A Crisis before "the Crisis": On Mallarmé's "Les Fenêtres"

Takeo Kawase

"Plus j'irai, plus je serai fidèle à ces sévères idées que m'a léguées mon grand maître Edgar Poe,"[1] Mallarmé wrote to Henri Cazalis on 7 January 1864. As these words indicate, Stéphane Mallarmé's veneration of Poe was absolute and was never shaken throughout his life. It was exactly for this reason that Mallarmé composed "Symphonie littéraire"—his poetic triptych, which is considered to have been completed by April of the same year[2]—with Gautier, Baudelaire, and Banville, excluding Poe. The poet of "The Raven" occupied an exceptional place.

In contrast, there is ambivalence in Mallarmé's stance toward Baudelaire—the poet often regarded as a decisive influence on Mallarmé along with Poe—to the extent that we hesitate to call young Mallarmé simply a "disciple de Baudelaire."[3] For example, while at the death of the author of *Les Fleurs du Mal*, Mallarmé wrote to Villiers de l'Isle-Adam, "J'ai bien peur de *commencer* . . . par où notre pauvre et sacré Baudelaire a fini"[4] (I am indeed afraid to begin—where our poor sacred Baudelaire left off). He had written, just a few months before, "Le livre de Dierx est un beau développement de Leconte de Lisle. S'en séparera-t-il comme moi de Baudelaire?"[5] (Dierx's book is a fine development of Leconte de Lisle. Will he part from him as I did from Baudelaire?). If there was a time, however temporary, when Mallarmé separated himself deliberately from Baudelaire, when was it and how did it come?

"When" is unmistakable. It was when "Les Fenêtres," one of the most important of Mallarmé's early texts, was written. But the question of what the "separation" meant to him has not been fully discussed. The reason for this inattention might be sought in the fact that the commentary on Mallarmé's poems has been concentrated, for more than a century, largely on his "difficult" poems written after the so-called "Crisis," and that his earlier poems, including "Les Fenêtres," have not been subjected to a serious reading due to their apparent simplicity. Even Georges Poulet's interpretation,[6] so far the most extensive, reveals its fragile foundation on which its original argument is based, because of his serious misreading of a variant, as will be indicated below.

What seems to be especially characteristic of Mallarmé's poetic quest in the first half of the 1860s is his highly conscious effort to locate his own poetry in relation to his forerunners. The "Symphonie littéraire," dedicated to the three "maîtres inaccessibles," is a representative text resulting from such an endeavor. We might easily dismiss it as no more than a trait of the poet's imitation period prior to his successful self-establishment. But we hesitate to do so because there was another poet whom Mallarmé mentioned regularly during this period, in addition to the famous established figure mentioned above. This poet, Emmanuel des Essarts, was an up-and-coming young writer, who came from Paris as a French teacher in October 1861 to the lycée in Sens from which Mallarmé had just graduated.

Des Essarts is known to have brought a flavor of the resplendent poetry scene of Paris to Mallarmé, who was writing poems in solitude while working as an apprentice at a register office in Sens. It was also des Essarts who introduced Mallarmé to his Paris friends—among others, to Cazalis—and took pains to get his earliest texts published in *Le Papillon* or *Le Sénonais*. But, above all, des Essarts's presence was important because Mallarmé found in this elder poet a "vivante antithèse" of himself.[7] Indeed, it was des Essarts to whom Mallarmé referred most frequently, yet always as a negative referent, in his musing on poetry in the period from 1862 to 1864. For example, in the letter to Cazalis quoted earlier, Mallarmé stressed how des Essarts's theories of literary composition were distant from the poetics of the "effet" that came down directly from Poe, and emphasized his point by saying "comme son âme enthousiasme [sic], ivre d'inspiration, reculerait d'horreur devant ma façon de travailler!"[8] (how his enthusiastic soul, drunk with inspiration, would recoil with horror before my way of working).

We might recall here that Mallarmé's first essay on poetry, published in *Le Papillon* (10 January 1862), was a review of des Essarts's first book of poetry, *Les Poésies parisiennes*. In this review, Mallarmé concisely defines des Essarts's purpose as "les sentiments de la vie parisienne pris au sérieux et vus à travers le prisme de la poésie, un idéal qui n'existe point par son propre rêve et soit le lyrisme de la réalité."[9] (The feelings of Parisian life taken seriously and seen through the prism of poetry, an ideal that does not wish by its own dream and is the lyricism of reality.) We must give credit for Poulet's acumen when he argues that if this statement is reversed into "un idéal qui *existe* par son propre rêve et qui ne soit *pas* le lyrisme de la réalité" (an ideal that exists by its own dream and is not the lyricism of reality), it would be exactly Mallarmé's purpose.[10] In any case, that Mallarmé had been highly conscious of des Essarts as a poet in striking contrast to himself since then is evidenced by his second review of *Les Poésies parisiennes,* published in *Le Sénonais* two months later. In it, Mallarmé characterizes des Essarts's poetry in comparison with that of Banville: "notre moderne Aristophane [i.e., Banville] qui décoche contre la Réalité la flèche d'or de son arc divin, l'Idéal, fait juste le contraire d'Em. des Essarts, lequel prend le Réel au sérieux et le lyrise"[11] (our modern Aristophane [i.e., Banville] who releases against Reality the golden arrow of his divine bow, the Ideal, does just the opposite of Em. des Essarts, who takes the Real seriously and lyrisizes it). Taking sides with Banville, here Mallarmé is launching a straightforward attack on des Essarts's poetic stance.

The error committed by the poet of *Les Poésies parisiennes* consists, according to Mallarmé, in "taking Reality too seriously"; as a result, the Ideal cannot take off from the ground and soar high in the sky. At the beginning of his career as a poet, Mallarmé thus imposed on himself the task of defining the relationship between Reality and the Ideal in poetry. It was a task this young author had to complete to find for his poetry the place of its own.

The next year, Mallarmé would be in London with Maria Gerhard and would work out the final answer to this assignment, yet by making use not of only des Essarts but also Baudelaire as a "negative referent."

On 3 June 1863, Mallarmé wrote to Cazalis the following:

Je trouve qu'Emmanuel se fait beaucoup de tort en se laissant aller à sa grande facilité: il commet trop aisément de ces sortes de pages brillantes et vides. Il confond trop l'Idéal avec le Réel. La sottise d'un poète moderne a été jusqu'à se désoler que «"l'Action ne fût pas la sœur du Rêve"»—Emmanuel est de ceux qui regrettent cela. Mon Dieu, s'il en était ainsi défloré et abaissé, où donc nous sauverions-nous, nous autres malheureux que la terre dégoûte et qui n'avons que le Rêve pour refuge. O mon Henri, abreuve-toi d'Idéal. Le bonheur d'ici-bas est ignoble—il faut avoir les mains bien calleuses pour le ramasser. Dire «"Je suis heureux!" c'est dire» "Je suis un lâche"«—et plus souvent» "Je suis un niais." Car il faut ne pas voir au-dessus de ce plafond de bonheur le ciel de l'Idéal, ou fermer les yeux exprès. J'ai fait sur ces idées un petit poème «"Les Fenêtres,"» je te l'envoie.[12]

[I find that Emmanuel hurts himself badly by letting himself go to his great facility; he commits too easily those kinds of brilliant and empty pages. He confuses too much the Ideal with the Real. The stupidity of a modern poet has gone so far as to be sorry that "Action wasn't the sister of Dream"—Emmanuel is among those who regret that. My God, if it was deflowered and lowered their way, where would we flee, we whom the earth disgusts and who have only Dream as a refuge. O my Henry, quench your thirst with the Ideal. The happiness of this world is ignoble—one must have very callous hands to pick it up. To say "I am happy!" is to say "I am a coward"—and more frequently "I am a ninny." For it must be that one doesn't see beyond the ceiling of happiness the sky of the Ideal, or close one's eyes on purpose. I have made a little poem on these ideas, "Les Fenêtres," I send it to you.]

The purpose of quoting this passage, the one almost always referred to in a discussion of "Les Fenêtres," is to reaffirm that this poem was written exactly from a disapproval of this "poète moderne," the author of "Le Reniement de saint Pierre," that is, Baudelaire.[13] In other words, placing Baudelaire with his "vivante antithèse"—des Essarts—Mallarmé here is making a desperate effort to refute his attitude.

> Las du triste hôpital et de l'encens fétide
> Qui monte en la blancheur banale des rideaux
> Vers le grand crucifix ennuyé du mur vide,
> Le moribond, parfois, redresse son vieux dos.[14]

> [Tired of the sad hospital and the fetid incense
> That rises in the banal whiteness of the curtains
> Toward the great bored crucifix of the empty wall,
> The dying man, at times, turns his old back.]

If that is the case, the "allegory" Mallarmé incorporated in this first stanza is self-evident. As commentators have already pointed out,[15] the scene of the hospital with the great cross is boldly taken from the third stanza of "Les Phares" ("Rembrandt, triste hôpital tout rempli de murmures, / Et d'un grand crucifix décoré seulement"[16] [Rembrandt, sad hospital full of murmurs, / And decorated only with a big crucifix]). Acknowledging this, however, let us say this "dying patient" weary in the hospital—in the modern world, that is—is none other than Baudelaire. And is this Christ, weary as well on the bare wall of the same hospital, not the remains of that Jesus crucified in "Le Reniement de saint Pierre," that "failed revolutionary" who tried to bring to earth the "Ideal" of the City of God in vain? Even on the linguistic level, it would not be a coincidence that the second line of this poem and that of Mallarmé's "Les Fenêtres" start with the same phrase ("Qui monte ... [vers]" [That climbs ... [toward]). And the "encens," which in "Correspondances" "[chante] les transports de l'esprit et des sens," ([sings] of the transports of the spirit and the senses), here gives off only repulsive odors and aggravates the weariness of the modern world.

Thus, of the ten stanzas with forty lines of "Les Fenêtres," the first twenty lines are insistently filled with borrowings from Baudelaire's literary world, most of whose elements are almost parodically twisted. The patient in the second and third stanzas, who is agonized by the fever and drags his feet toward the windows for the sunshine, also appears in "Réversibilité" with his unforgettable lips and the almost identical gestures ("les Fièvres, / Qui, le long des grands murs de l'hospice blafard, / Comme des exilés, s'en vont d'un pied traînard, / Cherchant le soleil rare et remuant les lèvres"),[17] (the Fevers, / which, along the great walls of the dreary hospice / Like exiles, go off with dragging foot / Seeing the rare sun and moving their lips). And the expression, "Comme un luxurieux dont la lèvre s'endort / A respirer la fleur d'une peau jeune," (As a lecher whose lip falls asleep / While breathing the flower of a young skin)[18] may strike us as a pastiche of Baudelairian vulgar eroticism. We should recall, in the first stanza of "Le Reniement de saint Pierre," God "falls asleep [s'endort]," hearing the mellifluous sound of blasphemous voices.

> Ivre, il vit, oubliant l'horreur des saintes huiles,
> Les tisanes, l'horloge, et le lit infligé,
> La toux. Et quand le soir saigne parmi les tuiles,
> Son œil, à l'horizon de lumière gorgé ...
>
> [Drunk, he lives, forgetting the horror of the holy oils,
> The tisanes, the clock, and the inflicted bed,
> The cough. And when the evening bleeds amid the roof-tiles,
> His eye, gorged with light on the horizon ...]

Moreover, one of Baudelaire's basic themes is faithfully repeated in this fourth stanza—that of forgetting the fear of death, time's pressure, and life's misery by the effect of the "intoxication" elicited by love, wine, or opium. The image of the "blood" the evening sun sheds might be taken from a line in "Harmonie du soir" ("Le soleil s'ést noyé dans son sang qui se fige"). And the magnificent sunset scene with the "galères d'or" on the crimson river is an unmistakable variation on the third part of "L'Invitation au voyage." Where Baudelaire writes "Vois sur ces canaux/Dormir ces vaisseaux,"[19] Mallarmé pens "Voit des galères d'or, [. . .] / Sur un fleuve de pourpre et de parfums dormir." What is witnessed here is not something on the level of literary "influence," nor is it "un beau développement" of the master's achievement in the disciple's hands. Mallarmé's purpose is an unmitigated caricature of Baudelaire's world of poetry.

> Ainsi, pris du dégoût de l'homme à l'âme dure
> Vautré dans le bonheur, où tous ses appétits
> Mangent, et qui s'entêtent à chercher cette ordure
> Pour l'offrir à la femme allaitant ses petits,
>
> Je fuis, je m'accroche à toutes les croisées
> D'où l'on tourne le dos à la vie, et, béni,
> Dans leur verre lavé d'éternelles rosées
> Que dore le matin chaste de l'Infini.
>
> [Thus, overwhelmed with disgust at the hard-souled man
> Sprawling in happiness, when all his appetites
> Eat, and who stubbornly seeks this filth
> To offer it to the wife suckling her babies,
>
> I flee, I cling to all the casements
> Whence one turns one's body on life, and, blessed,
> In their glass washed with eternal dew
> Gilded by the chaste morning of the Infinite.]

Is the second half of the poem, linked to the first by the hinge-like "Ainsi," no more than a decoding of the first half, a typological paraphrasing of the dilemma of Reality and the Ideal, with the "dying patient" replaced by the poet's "I (Je)," as most commentators have argued? Probably not. If so, then Mallarmé's elaborate "caricature" would totally lose its meaning. What is displayed here is not a "correspondence" but an "opposition." Unless we see Mallarmé refuting the negative "caricature" and trying to present a new poetic vision in a sharp contrast to it, we would never understand the real dynamism of the text of "Les Fenêtres."

Thus, the "man with a stubborn soul" who disgusts the poet is none other than the "dying patient," des Essarts/Baudelaire, who "takes Reality too seriously" and laments thoughtlessly that "the

Action is not Dream's sister." For Mallarmé, as Austin Gill rightly points out,[20] their blemish lies not in their acknowledgment of the conflict between the Ideal and Reality, but in their weakness of deploring it. Mallarmé has thus concluded that as long as the poet is bound by such mentality, poetry can never "escape" from the confine of Reality and that the Ideal to which it should aspire would never achieve its transcendent freedom.

The aspersion to this "man with a stubborn soul" prompts the poet to an eccentric act; he clings to the windows. The poet's gesture is obviously an imitation of Jesus, for the "croisée" here, as its shape indicates, is a kind of cross. However, while Jesus with deep "remorse" in "Le Reniement de saint Pierre" is confronted with mundane Reality, here the poet "turns his back to life." The gesture thus indicates a reversal of the Holy Cross. In like manner, the images in the first half of "Les Fenêtres" are reversed in the second half one by one. The Baudelairian sunset scene is turned into the "immaculate morning," and the "lukewarm windowpanes," defiled hideously by the "long bitter kiss" of the "dying patient," are now shining cooly, washed in the "eternal dews."

Yet the "reversal" even more decisively takes place in the eighth stanza:

> Je me mire et me vois Ange! Et je meurs et j'aime
> —Que la vitre soit l'Art, soit la Mysticité—
> A renaître, portant mon Rêve en diadème
> Au ciel antérieur où fleurit la Beauté!

> [I mirror myself and see myself as an Angel! And I die and love
> —Whether the pane be Art, or Mysticity—
> To be reborn, carrying my Dream as a diadem
> To the former sky where Beauty flowers!]

The poet clings to the windows not because he wishes to gloat on the outside scenery like the "dying patient." He does so, we might argue, to soar at a stretch to the clear heaven of the Ideal, maintaining the introvert posture of "self-crucifixion." The device that realizes this ascension is the play of the "mirror," which is precisely magical. This transparent partition that separates the Ideal from Reality not only returns the poet's image to his gaze as the exquisite mirror, but superimposes the image on the vast stretch of the blue sky in the background. And in that very moment, the poet finds himself transformed into an "angel" who lives in the sphere of the Ideal. But, at the same time, the poet is dead ("je meurs").

Poulet, noticing an earlier variant, "je songe," says that Mallarmé drastically changed the meaning of the whole poem by substituting "die" for "dream." The replacement of an inactive "reverie" by a spirited act of "death," he argues, created a possibility of transcending the Baudelairean dualism at last.[21] Presumably the critic of *Etudes sur le temps humain* sees in this revision the reflection of Mallarmé's "Crisis" ("heureusement, je suis parfaitement mort"[22] [fortunately, I am perfectly dead]), which was set off by his encounter with the "Nothingness" in the spring of 1866. However, the first appearance of the phrase "je meurs" was not in the first printed text of the poem, that is, *Le Parnasse contemporain* of May 1866, as Poulet assumes; it had appeared as it was in the four of the five earlier manuscripts, including the *Carnet de 1864* version, which is adopted in the present essay, as the more recent textual criticism has clarified.[23] In other words, since the "songe" is an exceptional variant and what was written in "Les Fenêtres" from the beginning was "meurs," Poulet's interpretation must be judged invalid.

As long as we follow the logic within the poem, there is no denying that this "death" is an inevitable result of the poet's "self-crucifixion" and that it exhibits a striking contrast to the phrase "Ivre, il vit (. . .)" of the first part of the fourth stanza. The poet declares to the "dying patient," who clings irresolutely to the life in Reality, that he will give up this worthless life on earth. For he is fully aware that this relinquishment is a necessary condition for achieving the real life in the realm of the Ideal. Mallarmé has thus reached his resolute conclusion on the question assigned to him at the start of his poetic career, namely, that of grasping the relationship between the Ideal and Reality in poetry. Poulet's comment that "Les Fenêtres" is "le premier où Mallarmé dépasse nettement le baudelairisme"[24] is correct, if not his interpretation of the poem.

Mallarmé could have concluded this poem as a tour de force of the "poem about composition," at the point where, by placing des Essarts/Baudelaire as a "negative referent," he acknowledged his own poetic stance and defined a new vision of poetry based on it. However, he continued to add two more stanzas with eight lines of unexpected development, as if to devastate this "conclusion" of his own will. This has turned "Les Fenêtres" into a "drama of composition" with a spectacular depth.

> Mais, hélas! Ici-bas est maître: sa hantise
> Vient m'écœurer parfois jusqu'en cet abri sûr
> Et le vomissement impur de la Bêtise
> Me force à me boucher le nez devant l'azur.
>
> [But, alas! This world is master: its haunting
> Comes to disgust me at times even in this sure shelter
> And the impure vomiting of Stupidity
> Forces me to hold my nose before the azure.]

The first tragic recognition here is that one who was born in this world cannot escape the insistent constraint of Reality, even if he "turns his back" to the "mundane world," determined that the Ideal is the realm where he should live. Even the "rêverie," his only "hiding place," is in fact always threatened by the invasion of Reality, for the unarmed poet has no other means of resistance but ignoring it, not "taking it seriously." Then another surprising event occurs here, one comparable with that eccentric gesture of "self-crucifixion": the unexpected vomiting of "la Bêtise." The poet now has to pinch his nose because of the stench of the vomit worse than that of the "fetid incense" in the "hospital" of the first stanza. Besides, it seems to have been thrown up to the "windowpanes." They are thus soiled twice in this poem, first by the "long bitter kiss" of the "dying patient," and second by this abrupt vomiting, even though they are once cleansed in the "eternal morning dews."

But what is this "Bêtise," personified and throwing up abominably? If, as the text indicates, what "nauseates [the poet]" is the disgust with Reality, which harrasses him in spite of his attempt to drive it away, then there is no one but the poet who is throwing up. The "Bêtise," therefore, is something in the poet. He is choked by the stench of the vomit welling up from his own mouth, and spoils the exquisite mirror of the "windowpanes." If so, then, why must his lucid mind aspiring to the Ideal join itself with the "Bêtise"?

The only possible reading, however bizarre it seems, is that the vomit the poet spews is a metaphor for language. In fact, the idea that language—the poet's "given" in actuality and his medium for expression—is for Art an element of "Bêtise" can be found in Mallarmé's 1862 essay on poetry, "Hérésies artistiques—L'Art pour tous."[25] In this essay, Mallarmé indicates that in contrast to other artistic genres, such as music and painting, poetry alone lacks "mystère," the "caractère nécessaire" that can never be sullied by "aucune pensée profanatrice"; poetry cannot but use language, mundane and common to all, as its medium of expression, for the very reason that "une langue immaculée," like the music score, was not invented to keep away the "bête" who has nothing to do with Art by nature. If this is the case, then the speech act itself could be an error in Art that should aspire to the Ideal. Indeed, this uncompromising recognition is articulated in the first movement, dedicated to Gautier, of "Symphonie littéraire" as the following:

> Maintenant qu'écrire? Qu'écrire, puisque je n'ai pas voulu l'ivresse, qui m'apparaît grossière et comme une injure à ma béatitude? . . . je ne saurais même louer ma lecture salvatrice, bien qu'à la vérité un grand hymne sorte de cet aveu, que sans elle j'eusse été incapable de garder un instant l'harmonie surnaturelle où je m'attarde: et quel autre adjuvant terrestre, violemment, par le choc du contraste ou par une excitation étrangère, ne détruirait pas un ineffable équilibre par lequel je me perds en la divinité? Donc je n'ai plus qu'à me taire,—non que je me plaise dans une extase voisine de la passivité, mais parce que la voix humaine est ici une erreur, comme le lac, sous l'immobile azur que ne tache pas même la blanche lune des matins d'été, se contente de la refléter avec une muette admiration que troublerait brutalement un murmure de ravissement.[26]

> [Now, what to write? What to write, since I didn't want drunkenness, which seems gross to me and like an insult to my beatitude? . . . I can't even praise my saving reading, although in truth a great truth emerges from that avowal, that without it I would have been incapable to keep for a moment the supernatural harmony in which I linger: and what other earthly aid, violently, by the shock of contrast or an alien stimulation, would not destroy an ineffable equilibrium through which I lose myself in divinity? So I have only to remain silent,—not that I am pleased to be in an ecstasy close to passivity, but because the human voice is an error here, as the lake, under the motionless azure that even the white moon of summer mornings doesn't tarnish, is content to reflect it with a mute admiration that a murmur of delight would brutally distrub.]

It is Mallarmé who desired the solemn, serene heights of the heavenly Ideal, where it is nothing but an error to utter a "human voice." And yet it is also Mallarmé who was determined to become a poet at the risk of all his life. Here is the tragic dilemma that faced Mallarmé in this period. If the poet's utterance is no more than a "bêtise" (folly) on earth and, as disgusting vomit, ruthlessly spoils the "windowpanes"—the Art of the "mystère" the poet entrusted with the hope of renaissance in the realm of the Ideal—

then there is nothing he can do as a poet. He has no choice but to "remain silent." What Mallarmé has glimpsed in the final phase of "Les Fenêtres" is therefore an aspect of the serious "crisis," the impossibility of poetic composition. Moreover, it is a premonition of the total collapse of that project for the new poetry that he has just defined.

> Est-il moyen, mon Dieu qui savez l'amertume,
> D'enfoncer le cristal par le monstre insulté
> Et de m'enfuir, avec mes deux ailes sans plume,
> —Au risque de rouler pendant l'éternité?
>
> [Is there a means, my God who know bitterness,
> To smash through the crystal insulted by the monster
> And flee, with my two featherless wings,
> —At the risk of rolling throughout eternity?]

Note the poet, who has once found himself to be an "angel" through the magical work of the "windowpanes," has lost his "plume" (pen) here ("sans plume")—a sorrowful figure of the fallen angel who has lost the faculty of flight, or a sterile poet who no longer can write a line. Mallarmé's theme of "stérilité," which appears consistently in his early poems, would be nothing but an expression of the "crisis" in the poet facing the theoretical dead end of poetic impossibility, a crisis of different dimensions but no less serious than the metaphysical crisis that Mallarmé encountered in the late1860s.

It must be left for another occasion to demonstrate that the hidden theme of the whole of the *Carnet de 1864*—which "Les Fenêtres" opens as the "frontispiece"—is a development of this "crisis." However, it should be noted here at least that the resolution of abandoning poetry is enunciated in a poem with no title and placed at the end as "epilogue" in correspondence to "Les Fenêtres"; for in this poem beginning with "Las d'un amer repos"[27] the poet says, "Je veux délaisser l'Art vorace d'un pays / Cruel."[28] This was the tough conclusion Mallarmé gave to his own poetic youth, when he completed the *Carnet* as a small book of poems in the summer of 1864. Indeed, Mallarmé virtually put an end to the composition of his early verses in April 1864,[29] and since then would turn to an attempt at a new genre, that is, prose poems. And it is well known that the composition of the drama, "Hérodiade," begun in October of the same year, would beckon another "crisis" to the poet.

Finally, let us note the fact that the image of the broken "windowpanes" in the last stanza of "Les Fenêtres" is, as Austin Gill points out,[30] borrowed from Baudelaire's prose poem, "Le Mauvais Vitrier." The "I" who gets angry with the lack of the "vitres magiques," which would "make life look beautiful," is a poet who "takes Reality seriously." Intoxicated with his own madness, this poet thus continues to cry hysterically, "La vie en beau! la vie en beau!" (A beautiful life, a beautiful life!) in spite of a foreboding sense of "l'éternité de la damnation" in the crashing of the panes of glass on the back of the glazier like "un palais de cristal crevé par la foudre." In contrast, the poet of "Les Fenêtres," no less resolved to "roll for eternity," cannot but acknowledge that the destruction of "the crystal insulted by the monster" would lead to no liberation nor pleasure. For he is well aware that the very act of destruction means the annihilation of his own Ideal and the renunciation of poetic composition.

Whether or not it was a prank of ironic Fate, in early April of 1864, the manuscript of "Les Fenêtres," before it was published in *Le Parnasse contemporain,* was recited by des Essarts in the salon of Madame Le Josne—Cazalis's cousin—in the presence of Baudelaire.[31] The great master, in the last phase of his life, is said to have listened attentively but made no remark that deserved to be called a comment. Des Essarts, who probably could not understand the profound meaning of this poem, reports the scene of the reading in his letter to Mallarmé dated 7 April: "Baudelaire les a écoutés sans désapprobation ce qui est un très grand signe de faveur. S'il ne les avait pas goûtés, il m'eût interrompu"[32] (Baudelaire listened to them without disapproval, which is a very great sign of favor. If he hadn't liked them, he would have interrupted me). However, the name of the younger poet must have been deeply inscribed in the heart of the author of *Les Fleurs du Mal,* with totally different implications from des Essarts's conjecture.

Soon after the reading, as if running away from debt collectors, Baudelaire left Paris to stay in Brussels, Belgium. In March the following year, Cazalis picked up a rumor from somewhere and wrote to Mallarmé, "Il paraît que ton Dieu, Baudelaire, te hait."[33] Indeed, in the letter to Madame Aupick of 5 March 1866, just ten days before he fell from his fatal illness at the Eglise Saint-Loup in Namur, Baudelaire wrote the following, bewildered to find that there seemed to exist "l'école Baudelaire": "Il y a du talent chez ces jeunes gens; mais que de folies! quelles exagérations et quelle infatuation de jeunesse! Depuis quelques années je surprenais, ça et là, des imitations et des tendances qui m'alarmaient"[34] (There is talent in these young men; but what follies! What exaggerations and what an infatuation of youth! For several years I have come upon, here and there, imitations and tendencies that alarmed me).

Even though the immediate topic here is Verlaine's panegyric for *Les Fleurs du Mal* in *L'Art*, it is highly probable that the poet of "Les Fenêtres" was on his mind even at this time. For the name of Mallarmé is unmistakably read in the expression, "des imitations et des tendances qui m'alarmaient."

Translated by Akitoshi Nagahata

Notes

1. Stéphane Mallarmé, *Correspondance complète, 1864—1871*, followed by *Lettres sur la poésie 1872-1898*, ed. Bertrand Marchal (Paris: Gallimard-Folio, 1995), 161. (Hereafter cited as *CC*.)
2. Published in *L'Artiste*, 1 February 1865.
3. Cf. Lloyd James Austin, "Mallarmé disciple de Baudelaire: 'Le Parnasse contemporain,'" *Revue d'histoire littéraire de la France* (April-June 1967): 437–49.
4. *CC*, 367; 24 September 1867.
5. *CC*, 346; 14 May 1867, addressed to Cazalis.
6. Georges Poulet, *Etudes sur le temps humain: La Distance intérieure* (Paris: Plon, 1952), 2:304–6.
7. *CC*, 113; 11 April 1864, addressed to Albert Collignon.
8. *CC*, 161.
9. Stéphane Mallarmé, *Oeuvres complètes*, ed. Henri Mondor and G. Jean-Aubry (Paris: Gallimard-Pléiade, 1945), 249. (Hereafter cited as *OC*.)
10. Poulet, 298.
11. *OC*, 255.
12. *CC*, 143–44.
13. The lines in question from "Le Reniement de saint Pierre," which is included in the "Révolte" section of *Les Fleurs du Mal*, read: "Certes, je sortirai, quant à moi, satisfait / D'un monde où l'action n'est pas la sœur du rêve" (Certainly, I will leave, for my part, satisfied / A world where action is not the sister of dream).
14. Henri Mondor, *Autres précisions sur Mallarmé et inédits* (Paris: Gallimard, 1961), 43. Since the original manuscript sent to Cazalis is unfortunately lost, I have used the version included in the so-called Carnet de 1864, which is closer to the original manuscript, instead of the definitive text, which shows the traces of revision after "the Crisis."
15. Baudelaire's prose poem, "Anywhere out of the World," which begins with "Cette vie est un hôpital où chaque malade est possédé du désir de changer de lit," was published in September 1867, after the publication of "Les Fenêtres."
16. Charles Baudelaire, *Oeuvres complètes*, ed. Claude Pichois (Paris: Gallimard-Pléiade, 1975), 1:13.

17. Ibid., 44. In addition, there is such correspondence on the linguisitic level as "le long des murs" / "le long des grands murs" or "Se traîne et va" / "s'en vont d'un pied traînard" (along the wall / along the great wall or Drags himself and goes / goes off with dragging foot).

18. This obviously unnatural Baudelairianism was revised into a purely Mallarméan diction, "Telle, jeune, elle alla respirer son trésor, / Une peau virginale et de jadis!" (This, young, it was going to breathe in its treasure, / A skin virginal and of yore!) in the first printed text and after.

19. Baudelaire, 53–54.

20. Austin Gill, "Mallarmé on Baudelaire," in *Currents of Thought in French Literature: Essays in Memory of G. T. Clapton* (Oxford: Oxford University Press, 1965), 100.

21. Poulet, 53–54.

22. *CC*, 342; 14 May 1867, addressed to Cazalis.

23. "Les Fenêtres: historique du poème, 1863–1893," in Carl Paul Barbier, ed., *Documents Stéphane Mallarmé V* (Paris: Nizet, 1976), 437–74.

24. Poulet, 305.

25. Published in *L'Artiste*, 15 September 1862; *OC*, 257–60.

26. *OC*, 262.

27. Mondor, 54. The intended correspondence to the beginning of "Les Fenêtres" ("Las du triste hôpital") would be unmistakable.

28. "Art," of course, is the object of the poet's aspiration imaged in the "windowpanes" in "Les Fenêtres," and "vorace" also appears in the first line of the third stanza ("Et sa bouche, fiévreuse et d'azur bleu vorace"). Thus, the "cruel country" here is the "blue sky," namely, the Ideal.

29. The only exception is "Brise marine" composed presumably in 1865.

30. Gill, 101.

31. See Cazalis's letter to Mallarmé, written in early April in 1864 (Carl Paul Barbier, ed., *Documents Stéphane Mallarmé VI* [Paris: Nizet, 1977], 195).

32. Ibid., 196.

33. Ibid., 258.

34. Baudelaire, *Correspondance II (mars 1860—mars 1866)*, ed. Claude Pichois with Jean Ziegler (Paris: Gallimard, 1976), 625.

III
On Translating Mallarmé

Mallarmé and Critic-Friendly Translators
Judd D. Hubert

In their renditions of masterpieces, such as the poems of Mallarmé, English and American translators tend to fall back on the sort of literary discourse and modes of expression to which their favorite anglophone writers had accustomed them. They undertake their translations with what William Empson, I believe, defined as a "taste in the head." Scott Moncrieff, whose translation of *A la recherche du temps perdu,* even in its unrevised form, deserves high praise, never could rid himself of attitudes and tastes prevalent in the English novels of his day, for instance, those of Arnold Bennett, tales that Proust's fiction had relegated to the past. Indeed, *Remembrance of Things Past* substitutes from the very beginning a realistic and psychological bias for Proust's far more mystical approach. For this reason, Scott Moncrieff's translation displays an air of familiarity bound to appeal to contemporary anglophone readers. His radical change of title reveals an attitude typical of many translators. By putting Shakespeare on his side, he felt no doubt that he could more safely deal with a disturbing alien genius even though, by so doing, he failed to convey the ideas of effort and discovery emphasized in the original.

Perhaps even the best translators can hardly avoid transforming foreign texts into conforming additions to their own literary heritage. The aristocratic poets of the Pléiade actually triumphed over Greek and Italian poets in the very act of adapting them to their own militant program. Ronsard expressed most aptly this thirst for conquest: "Je pillay Thebe, et saccageay la Pouille."[1] Although most translators and adaptors since then have shown apprehension and humility rather than arrogance in fulfilling their tasks, particularly if they happened to choose hermetic poems for target practice, their renditions of foreign masterpieces function nevertheless as relatively innocent appropriations.

Translators, of course, see themselves not as thieves or parasites, in the sense that Michel Serres gives this term,[2] but as benefactors of their compatriots as well as of the author whose readership and reputation they purport to increase. But whether innocent or guilty, translators inevitably suffer, in their capacity as creative writers, from a lack of immediacy. They automatically transform themselves into observers, into critics. For that reason, translations have much in common with critical interpretations and paraphrases of the original texts or even with mimetic book illustration. Two major French modernists have translated *Hamlet*. Although André Gide's version might not hold the stage, it provides a metaphorically reliable translation of the tragedy, pedagogically useful to French readers,[3] while Bonnefoy's equally faithful translation shows outstanding performative qualities.[4] Whereas the former often relies on paraphrase, the latter functions as a suitably dramatic and poetic vehicle.

Because they can hardly avoid interpretation and paraphrase, translators unwittingly provide unexpected help to critics and scholars in search of meanings. This holds true in particular for hermetic poetry, which relies far more heavily than other writings on ambiguity, paradox, and other forms of polyvalence. Faced with a pun, translators, whether they notice it or not, will inevitably short-change the original. By looking for such imbalances in verbal exchanges, the critic stands a fairly good chance of noticing hidden aspects of the original poem. It so happens that the exercise of comparing the two may allow readers to suspend for the time being their own interpretations and thus prevent them from taking the poem's meaning for granted.

Here I will attempt to compare Mallarmé's famous sonnet: "Ses purs ongles très haut dédiant leur onyx" to two poetic renditions, one by Arthur Ellis dating back to 1927[5] and the other, far more recent, by Henry Weinfield.[6] I should add that critical comments accompany and, to a certain extent, sustain both these renditions. I shall make critical use of these two translations rather than evaluate their merits.

> Ses purs ongles très haut dédiant leur onyx,
> L'Angoisse, ce minuit, soutient, lampadophore,
> Maint rêve vespéral brûlé par le Phénix
> Que ne recueille pas de cinéraire amphore
>
> Sur les crédences, au salon vide: nul ptyx
> Aboli bibelot d'inanité sonore,
> (Car le Maître est allé puiser des pleurs au Styx
> Avec ce seul objet dont le Néant s'honore).

MALLARMÉ AND CRITIC-FRIENDLY TRANSLATORS

Mais proche la croisée au nord vacante, un or
Agonise selon peut-être le décor
Des licornes ruant du feu contre une nixe,

Elle, défunte nue en le miroir, encor
Que, dans l'oubli fermé par le cadre, se fixe
De scintillations sitôt le septuor.
(Mallarmé)

[Her pure nails on high displaying their onyx,
The lampbearer, Anguish, at midnight sustains
The vesperal dreams that are burnt by the PhŒnix
And which no funeral amphora contains

On the credenzas in the empty room: no ptyx,
Abolished shell whose resonance remains
(For the Master has gone to draw tears from the Styx
With this sole object that Nothingness attains).

But in the vacant North, adjacent to the window panes,
A dying shaft of gold illumines as it wanes
A nix sheathed in sparks that a unicorn kicks.

Though she in oblivions that the mirror frames
Lies nude and defunct, there rains
The scintillations of the one-and-six.)
(Translated by Henry Weinfield)

[Her hands to heav'n outstretching their pure sardonyx,
Anguish upholds, as cresset-torch of midnight's gloom,
This eve's so many dreams their PhŒnix did consume
To ashes, that enurns no cinerary pyx

Through all this chamber's emptiness!—there is no ptyx,
Annull'd is every bauble of words' empty boom
(For with this only trophy worth Destruction's doom
The Master is away, drawing tear's flow from Styx).

But nigh the northward casement of the poet's room
A tortur'd gleam its imag'd struggle doth illume
Of unicorns that pelt with fire a water-nix—

She dead and naked in the mirror's quenching womb,
Whose Lethè-waves at once Heav'n's living lights inhume,
To rigid stare the Pleiads' leaping fires transfix.]
(Translated by Arthur Ellis)

In Weinfield's translation, the first line imposes a major change on the sonnet without seriously modifing its conceptual meaning. But some of us might wonder whether conceptual meanings in poetry matter all that much. Weinfield has replaced "dédiant" by "displaying." As Robert Greer Cohn has shown (140),[7] we should hardly take "dédiant" for granted. The word "displaying" eludes among other meanings the religious connotation of consecration, while eliminating poetic self-designation—you can dedicate a poem—in favor of the unilateral designation of the nails as nails, for, etymologically, "onyx" brings us right back to "ongles." Mallarmé, who probably took very seriously the etymologies provided in Littré's remarkable dictionary, proceeds here in much the same manner as in *Un Coup de Dés jamais n'abolira le hasard*, where "hasard," thanks to its Arabic etymology, repeats "un coup de dés," thus deliberately producing an evocative tautology. The etymology of "dédiant" programs a major development in the sonnet, for the Latin word "dicare," a dressed-up offshoot of "dicere," refers to the solemn and heightened enunciation of ritualistic words. It thus relates to "lampadophore"—a Greek torch-bearer in a religious ceremony—"vespéral" in the liturgical sense of evensong, and perhaps even to "crédences," indicative of faith and, more important still, referring to a liturgical console on which the priest could place altar-cruets. As etymologists regard "dire" and "dedicate," because of their diegetic functions, as closely related to "digit"— "doigt," "dédiant" redoubles, so to speak, the presence of fingers, of nails whereas "displaying" involves little more than a theatrical unfolding—a gesture.

In all probability, Weinfield had no better choice than to render "lampadophore" by "lampbearer," thus obscuring, but without completely eliminating, the word's relevant etymology. In any case, "lampbearer" emphasizes the materiality of the object, underplaying at the same time possible evocations of light emanating from the stars, from the Big Dipper, or from the moon. As a result, Anguish's upward thrust appears to fall short whereas "l'Angoisse" reaches for the stars. Incidentally, "le Maître" descends all the way down to the Styx. Thus, the antithetical relationship between the closed in "salon" and the constellated sky manifests itseif throughout the poem.

In translating "maint rêve vespéral" by "those vesperal dreams," Weinfield has emphasized plurality at the expense of discriminating choice. In any case, "dreams" hardly conveys the same connotations as "rêve," traditionally associated with poetry. In the seventeenth century, a time when the French temporarily held poets in low esteem, they condescendingly referred to them as "rêveurs." But however debased, "rêve" differs, for instance, from the American dream, so often synonymous with property. The term "rêve" in the singular reinforces self-designation to such an extent that we can identify "maint rêve vespéral" with the sonnet itself as well as with whatever creative works the persona failed to produce. For similar reasons, "contains" hardly does justice to "recueille," a far more active verb bringing to mind a "recueil de poèmes." As a result, "cinéraire amphore" acquires some of the characteristics of a book, unfortunately consisting of empty pages. Moreover, "cinéraire" shows greater concreteness and liveliness than the abstract and definitive "funeral," a word more closely associated with "urn" than with "amphora," a container of wine rather than ashes.

Weinfield felt compelled to add an explanatory corollary to "ptyx" by helpfully identifying it as a marine shell, which may very well have consigned to memory the sound of the sea, whereas Mallarmé leaves the reader in a state of suggestive perplexity. Moreover, the confrontation between the descriptive "abolished shell whose resonance remains" and "aboli bibelot d'inanité sonore" suggests that the translator has bypassed the persona's esthetic rejection, for "inanité" compounds the ideas of emptiness and meaningless futility, the conceptual equivalent of doggerel. A conch shell may very well represent the reduction of a poetic voice to inanity—a *reductio ad absurdum* fully countered and reversed by the sonnet itself. Esthetics plays a part by means of etymology, for "bibelot"—"bauble"—derives from a childish reiteration of "bel" in the same way that "bonbon" owes its existence to a repetition of "bon." Though expressing verbal futility, the line paradoxically captures a beauty all its own, resulting perhaps from the coincidence of onomatopeia and deprivation.

Unfortunately, English lacks a suitable equivalent for "puiser." Because "draws tears" or even "wells up tears" fails to express the connotations of depth and narrowness inherent in the French word, the translator had to forego the perpendicular tension so intensely evoked in the quatrains. Weinfield redefines "ptyx" as "The sole object that Nothingness attains." In so doing, he unwittingly attracts attention to the reflexive verb "s'honore," personifying even more clearly "le Néant." Nothingness appears to take pride in possessing the "ptyx" as though the void had found a kindred soul or perhaps a worthy offspring, or even, in a quite different register, a vapid "légion d'honneur." In that case, we might see "le Néant" as an ironic mirror image of "le Maître." I must admit that I would not have unearthed this perhaps wrongheaded suggestiveness in the second quatrain without the translator's unintentional help.

In the first tercet, Weinfield attributes vacancy to the north rather than to the window panes without radically changing the meaning of the sonnet. However, the reductive "window panes" hardly produce the same effect as "croisée," not only because the latter evokes a cross and an "X," but because it brings to mind a crossing, an encounter, suggested at various moments throughout the sonnet. Of course, the meeting will never take place and, by the same token, the Master, neither Mallarmé nor his persona, will remain forever absent. Indeed, "vacante" indicates emptiness in the sense of unoccupied, as in an empty house. Moreover, Weinfield appears to have deliberately shunned the very idea of an encounter, for he has translated "un or agonise" by "a dying shaft of gold illumines." While "agonise," no less than "dying," entails a definitive ending, it conveys in addition the notion of struggle—the coming to grips of two opposing, if unequal, forces. Because the term originally had the same meaning as "angoisse," it leads us back to the opening lines of the poem. In any case, the translation reveals, by what it leaves out, the dynamic qualities present everywhere in this sonnet, which paradoxically records the static encounter of an empty room and a nocturnal sky. Moreover, Weinfield has managed to conjure away "décor," suggesting a theatrical performance. After all, "agon," the origin of "agonie," refers to a dramatic confrontation between the chief characters in a Greek tragedy and, in the present instance, to the erotic battle between fired-up unicorns and a water nymph as well as to the unequal struggle between a flickering light and darkness. Because the poem has moved agonistically from a fiery to a watery element, we can regard the aggression of the unicorns against the Nixie as recapitulating the passage from ashes to tears.

Although Weinfield recaptures the watery element in the second tercet: "there rains the scintillations"—pouring out no doubt from the Big Dipper—his choice of "the one-and-six" as a translation of "septuor" and, inevitably, of "frames" for "cadre" adds grist to my mill. Though numbers, as Cohn has proved (144–45), play a major role in this sonnet and other texts by Mallarmé, Weinfield may have gone too far in selecting his final rhyme even though "one-and-six" inevitably equals seven. In so doing, he has discarded the musical implications of "septuor," which brings this particularly alliterative text to a resounding closure. Moreover, "septuor" harks back to, and amplifies, the music conveyed by such terms as "vespéral" and "sonore." Taken either as a noun or a verb, "frame" hardly differs in connotation from "cadre." Both in French and in English, the word can evoke the idea of painting, thus adding a third artistic dimension. But unlike "frames," "cadre" has the advantage of introducing, by etymology, still another number: four, particularly relevant because it brings to mind the four corners of that essential letter "X" and the Big Dipper's division into a four-star container and a three-star handle. It would appear that a translation no less than a critical commentary could entail drastic reductions.

I shall have far less to say about Arthur Ellis's translation because Weinfield has provided me with more than enough material. Ellis starts out with a "taste in the head" quite different from Weinfield's insofar as he shows a particular fondness for the sort of verse practiced by Spenser and adopted by most poets until the modernists took over. In any case, he gives a Spenserian ring, familiar to English readers, to the sonnet—a ring to which Mallarmé, an anglicist, might not have objected.

Although Ellis does not impose a metaphorical ceiling on Anguish's upward mobility, he avoids the evocative redundancy of onyx and nails. The imaginative "cresset-torch" replaces the ritualistic Greek torch-bearers and "eve" reduces "vespéral" to a moment in time. Although the translator moves out of the "salon" its most suggestive piece of furniture, "les crédences," he makes up for it by bringing in a "pyx," a container of the Eucharist rather than of ashes. Thus, "cinerary Pyx" provides an oxymoron quite suitable to Mallarmé's sonnet. The translator comes close to the original in "Annull'd is every bauble of words' empty boom" for he takes into account poetic self-designation. He also emphasizes the confrontation of fire and water in "water-nix," "quenching," "Lethè-waves," "pelt with fire," and "leaping fires." Although Ellis has brought out many of the hidden elements in the sonnet, he, too, comes up against that ever-present obstacle: the reflexive verb. Somehow, the impersonal "se fixe" becomes somebody's "stare," undoubtedly not that of the Master.

By substituting "tortured gleam" for "un or agonise," Ellis brings out an aspect of the poem I had completely missed. I had indeed taken "gold" too much for granted by reducing it to a mere color or gleam. Its glaring absence suggests that it may have a symbolic meaning derived from alchemy and directed toward poetry. Indeed, every poet aspires to transform lead into gold. In the sonnet, "un or agonise" has much in common with the struggle of the imprisoned swan of "Le vierge, le vivace et le bel aujourd'hui."

Thus, among other occurrences, "Ses purs ongles" recounts the tragic agony and final disappearance of a poem, of a "rêve." The word "tortur'd" retains from "agonise" the sense of suffering. The knowing translator spells out later in the line the idea of struggle. But "tortur'd" also has an unfortunate implication: that of twisting and contorting, hence evocative of a spiral, hardly a feature of Mallarmé's poetry. Since Octavio Paz (in this volume) by insisting on the conch shell has elicited a breathing spiral—"Espiral espirada de inanidad sonora"—from "Aboli bibelot d'inanité sonore," I wonder to what extent such interpolations lend themselves to critical interpretations of the sonnet. Painters have traditionally represented the Styx, and real rivers, as rolling along in curves, thus bringing to mind a spiral while a conch shell, within and without, undoubtedly assumes the requisite shape. These two examples, as far-fetched as the Stygian waters, minimally justify the interpolations. Nonetheless, "espiral espirada," by its lively if hardly meaningful alliteration, wittily conforms to Mallarmé's expression of poetic nothingness.

Although critics do not really require translators to interpret hermetic poetry, translations may serve a useful pedagogical purpose for anglophone students of French literature. They will learn at the very least that by reading major works only in translation they will remain at an insuperable remove from the original texts and confined as a result to their own literature. Poets, however, have found an alternative to direct translation: writing a poem in their own language that somehow incorporates the essential creativity of an admired foreign text. In his "Aristotle to Phyllis," John Hollander has captured the essence of Mallarmé's sonnet, "Brise marine," in the very act of composing his own poem. But it would take another paper to show how admirably he has succeeded in this enterprise.

Notes

1. *Les Odes,* "A sa Lyre," Livre I, XXII.
2. Michel Serres, *Le Parasite* (Paris: Grasset, 1980).
3. William Shakespeare, *Hamlet,* trans. André Gide (New York: Pantheon Books, 1945).
4. William Shakespeare, *Hamlet,* trans. Yves Bonnefoy (Paris: Club Français du Livre, 1957).
5. Stéphane Mallarmé, *Mallarmé in English Verse,* trans. Arthur Ellis (Folcroft, Penn.: Folcroft Library Editions, 1927).
6. Stéphane Mallarmé, *Collected Poems,* trans. and commentary by Henry Weinfield (Berkeley and Los Angeles: University of California Press, 1994).
7. Robert Greer Cohn, *Toward the Poems of Mallarmé* (Berkeley and Los Angeles: University of California Press, 1965).

Mallarmé's Humility: "Quelle soie aux baumes de temps..."

Kenneth Fields

My task here is simple, or ought to be. Compared with discussing Mallarmé as Mallarmé, or Mallarmé in Italy, Spain, or Germany, or even translations, plural, of Mallarmé, I will discuss only my adaptation of a single poem, the late sonnet beginning "Quelle soie aux baumes de temps." Although I will look briefly at some moments in the poem, I want to talk about what kind of poem I take this sonnet to be and why I incorporated it into the larger conception or structure of my book, *The Odysseus Manuscripts*, a series of poems I drew from *The Odyssey*, a book I hope will authorize my brief but wandering argument.[1]

As long as I have made my simple task more complex, I want to go a bit further and tell you something of my relation to the intimidating Chimaera of Mallarmé. Before coming to Stanford as a graduate student, I had struggled with Mallarmé as a forbidding presence, and, although I was not among that small group who, as Valéry puts it, found in the work "the secret home of *that which cannot bear not to understand*," I knew something of what Mallarmé's disciple meant by "the brilliance of those pure crystalline systems, polished as they were from every angle" that, according to Jackson Mathews, "struck the terror of perfection in him."[2] I had come to Stanford to study with the poet Yvor Winters, a man of great kindness and generosity, who likewise struck the terror of perfection in me. And it is not too much to say that Winters's poetic was formed out of a long, continuing dialogue with Mallarmé, though that is another story.

Robert Greer Cohn has written of Winters's misprisions of Mallarmé. I only wish to point out that the trenchancy of Winters's pronouncements may seem at odds with his admiring fascination with The Master. In his midtwenties, Winters wrote a beautiful translation of "Soupir," and Mallarmé is the first writer he quotes in his Stanford Ph.D. dissertation, which later became *Primitiv-*

ism and Decadence.³ Truth to say, Winters may have loved Mallarmé because he gave rise to Valéry. I know that I read Mallarmé through Valéry's eyes and later through those of R. G. Cohn and others.

In those early days, I was drawn to the vigil sonnets, those evocative empty rooms, one of them illumined by a reflected constellation. More than thirty years ago, at work on my first book of poems, *The Other Walker*,⁴ I tried my hand at a tribute to Mallarmé. As I was finishing these remarks, I found myself making several small revisions to get it closer to its subject after all those years. At that time I was drawn to the dictum, "paint not the thing, but the effect that it produces,"⁵ and I wanted to create an empty room filled by the powerful absence of a great figure—hence, perhaps, its appropriateness to our business this weekend. I called it "On a Theme by Mallarmé," but today I call it, simply, "The Master." I am certain that I had two masters in mind:

> Defined by the vacant room
> The empty teacup rims
> With light; the pale bouquet
> Of faintly scented flowers
> Spreads color through the air.
> Held by the gilded edge
> Of thick rococo scrolls,
> With deft ancestral poise
> The master stares. The dim
> Reality of air,
> Fixed in that mobile gaze,
> No more than what it is,
> Settles, dense with repose.

Shortly afterward, I began teaching a course comparing French Symbolist poets with some Americans, and I especially looked forward to teaching Mallarmé, because for a week or two I felt as if I had entered into another universe, full of odd feeling and the charm of occult procedures I could almost guess at. (Solomon Feferman told me later that mathematicians were often among Mallarmé's amateurs.) I was taken by what Walter Conrad Arensberg called the haunting "duplicities" of language in *L'Après-midi d'un Faune*⁶ and elsewhere, and came to suspect that this alleged "poet of refusals" did not leave the world of passion and full air behind him in his later poems.

So I came back periodically to Mallarmé, always hoping to find something I could translate, and I went on writing my own poems, including a sequence, *Anemographia*,[7] named after a Greek trope for describing the wind, a convenient figure for describing what could be seen only in its effects.

Nearly twenty years ago, I felt the shock of another master when I reread *The Odyssey* and, bowled over this time by its power, drew amused stares from my friends when I began telling them that *The Odyssey* was a great poem. "We know it's a great poem," they told me. "No, I mean it's really a great poem." I began to wonder, as some of Mallarmé's circle must have wondered, how anyone could have written any poems after this one. I wanted to respond to Homer, but I was not a Greek scholar. Then I fell upon the writers of the Homeric Hymns, whose names have not survived, who were called simply "The Sons of Homer" and were content to take a small piece of the epic for their material—their strategy was humility, the lesser engaging the greater. I began to see my way.

My friend, Elroy Bundy, the Pindar scholar, introduced me to the classical *topos* the *recusatio*, a rhetorical device by which the poet declines (or sometimes pretends to decline) a public, often a military or political subject in favor of a more personal one, as, for example when Horace says, You may wonder, Agrippa, why I haven't written about your glory and Caesar's; well, you know me—I can only write about battles of virgins in my own light-headed way. The mode is used with varying degrees of irony, as I have shown elsewhere, sometimes accomplishing the task that seems to be refused, as when Horace argues that he cannot write in Pindar's style, then sets about to give an example of it. It is related to the humility *topos* and to the retirement poem. Examples may be found frequently in Homer, as in Telemachos's speeches to the suitors; and in fact, the entire *Odyssey* may be seen as a long retirement poem—from the tragic glories of war, through fantasy, to the pleasures of home and old age. The lesser chosen over the greater may turn out to be the greatest privilege of all.[8]

In an ambitious if grudging review of my book in *Salmagundi*, Terrence Diggory notes a reference to Mallarmé in my dedication, but finds only "mallarmesque syllabic fog," with nothing of Mallarmé, he thinks, something he seems to blame mysteriously on the influence of Winters.[9] In fact, I read the review, taking perverse pleasure in knowing that Mallarmé was solidly in *The Odysseus Manuscripts*, not spread out ambiguously through the book, as Diggory seems to assume, but in a single poem, a reasonably direct translation of "Quelle soie," which I called "Retirement."

Perverse, too, was my indirect way of citing, since I dedicated my book to people I had quoted, and I hoped Mallarmé would be visible to some readers. Again, Sappho: "Someone I tell you will remember us."[10]

While I was writing these poems, I had also found my poem from Mallarmé, though I did not think of including it in my book until I was nearly finished. Gradually it occurred me that it was indeed a species of retirement poem, a *recusatio* that seemed to pay the compliment of preferring a woman in her bedroom to the triumphal military glory outside, preferring the lesser to the greater, a choice of poetic significance even before Sappho.[11] I decided to have Odysseus speak the poem, a princely lover now reunited with his wife, both of them wanting to stay inside for a while, enjoying the cunningly made bed, where they may introduce each other into their private histories.

R. G. Cohn's commentary on the poem is definitive. Mallarmé compares the fluid hair and torso of his lover with the silks inside on the walls, embroidered with the fabulous Chimaera and to the undulating flags parading by outside, while the princely lover stifles the cry of glory in the "considérable touffe" of her hair. I push the phrase a little ("considerable thick bush") to bring out something I think is in the poem. Wallace Fowlie strangely finds the poem "passionless," partly because he may not be noticing that the refusal includes the subject that the poet claims to decline, and partly because he believes that Mallarmé, "timid and overcome, seems only able to hide his face in the tresses." As he says of another poem, "What was the real experience is for ever absent from such a sonnet as 'Victorieusement fui.'" But we have surely exhausted impotence as a theme to pursue in Mallarmé, for the poem describes a completed sexual act.[12]

In the notes to his ambitious translation, the *Collected Poems*, Henry Weinfield acknowledges R. G. Cohn's sexual reading of the poem—"morsure" and "mort sûre" and a series of other puns. Weinfield concludes, with a quaint finickiness, that "The 'tuft' of line 12," which is Cohn's reading, "would seem to point to a type of hair that does not sit on the head." Further, Mallarmé is displaying "an ambivalence to pubic glory as well as to the public." And he renders the great line, "Dans la considérable touffe" (In the considerable brake), a line of pubic ambivalence, to be sure, but not, I think, Mallarmé's.

To make a point (and to give Odysseus and Penelope something for their trouble), I have perhaps overemphasized "la considérable touffe" as "bush," setting the lesser hair against the greater, an alleged lesser sexual practice against a greater—though it may be that the lesser is the greater, after all. I was thinking of the lines describing the nymphs at the beginning of *L'Après-midi:* "Si clair, / Leur incarnat léger, qu'il voltige dans l'air / Assoupi de sommeils touffus." The slumbers are tufted and leafy because of the glade they are in, but tufted here also connotes bushy, shaggy, the faun's fur, and the hair, and the hair of the nymphs. Later the Faun decides that his crime was to have divided the disheveled tuft of kisses that the gods kept so well mingled, separating the nymphs, attempting to hide his ardent smile under the happy folds ("les replis heureux") of one, while trying to hold the other down with "un doigt simple," which, as Arensberg wryly remarks, "was not, perhaps, so simple as he says . . . ."

Here, with Mallarméan flourish, is Mallarméan humility:

> Quelle soie aux baumes de temps
> Où la Chimère s'exténue
> Vaut la torse et native nue
> Que, hors de ton miroir, tu tends!
>
> Les trous de drapeaux méditants
> S'exaltent dans notre avenue:
> Moi, j'ai ta chevelure nue
> Pour enfouir mes yeux contents.
>
> Non! La bouche ne sera sûre
> De rien goûter à sa morsure,
> S'il ne fait, ton princier amant,
>
> Dans la considérable touffe
> Expirer, comme un diamant,
> Le cri des Gloires qu'il étouffe.

And, at long last, my translation:

> *Retirement*
>
> What silk, embalmed by the breath of time,
> The Chimaera wearing away, is worth
> This twisted, native, naked cloud
> That from your glass your brush draws forth.
>
> The holes of those meditative flags
> Exalt in our streets outside, in sighs:

> I have your naked, cloudy hair
> Burying my bright, contented eyes.
>
> No, his mouth will not excite
> The taste of anything in its bite
> If he does not—your princely lover—
>
> In this considerable, thick bush
> Expire—like a diamond under cover—
> The glorious cry he tries to hush.

Now if this poem is a poem of humility, it is a magnificent, triumphant humility. When one thinks of Mallarmé's dealings with his friends, humility is an appropriate term, and certainly he confronts le Vide or l'Azure with a tormented humility. But what are we to think of the man so absolute that he forbade the use of the word et cetera in his presence and, with a single glittering sentence, gave rise, for better or worse, to modern theoretical entrepreneurship?[13] If Mallarmé exemplifies humility, then it must be qualified by terms like *fierce* or *intransigent*.

In theological discussions, it might be difficult to find an oxymoronic construction that united humility and pride in a positive sense. But in a poem like "Quelle soie aux baumes de temps," such things are possible. Perhaps this is what Winters meant, at the beginning of *Primitivism and Decadence,* when he spoke of Mallarmé's conviction "that the poetic line be a new word, not found in any dictionary, and partaking of the nature of incantation (that is, having the power to materialize, or perhaps it would be more accurate to say, *being,* a new experience)."

I conclude with a coda. Valéry's essay, "The Necessity of Poetry," begins by naming some poets who wrote in French and became French poets of their own wills, an idea that would have appealed to Mallarmé—D'Annunzio, an Italian; Van Lerberghe, Maeterlinck, and Verhaeren, Flemings; Jean Moréas, a Greek; and the Americans Stuart Merrill and Francis Vielé-Griffin, "who recently died at Bergerac" in 1937.[14] Valéry states that Vielé-Griffin, an acolyte of Mallarmé, "was born in the United States. His father, a general in the Northern army during the war of Secession, was at the siege of Charleston at the moment of his son's birth." He came to France at an early age, and made himself into a French poet, "of his own will." "In commemoration and salute to [Vielé-Griffin's] noble memory," Valéry quotes the poem Vielé-Griffin composed to commemorate the death of the Master:

Thrène

Si l'on te disait: "Maître!
Le jour se lève;
Voici une aube encore, la même pâle;
Maître, j'ai ouvert la fenêtre,
L'aurore s'en vient encor du seuil oriental,
Un jour va naître!"
Je croirais t'entendre dire: "Je rêve."

Si l'on te disait: "Maître, nous sommes là,
Vivants et forts,
Comme ce soir d'hier, devant ta porte;
Nous sommes venus en riant, nous sommes là,
Guettant le sourire et l'étreinte forte,"
On nous répondrait: "Le Maître est mort."

Des fleurs de ma terasse,
Des fleurs comme au feuillet d'un livre.
Des fleurs, pourquoi?
Voici un peu de nous, la chanson basse
Qui tourne et tombe,
Comme ces feuilles-ci tombent et tournoient,
Voici la honte et la colère de vivre
Et de parler des mots—contre ta tombe.

Winters made his version of "Thrène" at about the same time that he was translating other nineteenth-century French poets, including Baudelaire, Rimbaud, Verlaine, Corbière, Heredia, and Mallarmé:

Threnody for Stéphane Mallarmé
from the nineteenth-century French

If one said to you: Master!
Day again!
Here is the dawn once more, the same and pale;
Master, I have left the window clear,
The dawn comes in across the eastern sill,
A day is here!
Then I should think to hear you say: I dream.

If one said to you: Master, we are here,
Alive and hale,
As we were here last evening at your door,
We have come in laughing, and once more

Await the strong embrace and the old look,
Then they would answer us: the Master's dead.

The flowers of my terrace,
Flowers as if between the leaves of a book,
Ah, why the flowers?
Here is some part of us, with this low song of ours
That turns and falls
As these leaves fall and turn—
Here are the shame and anger that it is to live
And say these words—against your tomb.

Notes

1. Kenneth Fields, *The Odysseus Manuscripts* (Chicago: Elpenor Books, 1981), 42.

2. Paul Valéry, "Letter about Mallarmé," tr. Malcolm Cowley, *Leonardo Poe Mallarmé* (Princeton, N.J.: Princeton University Press, 1972), Bollingen Series 45, *The Collected Works of Paul Valéry*, ed. Jackson Mathews, 8: 245–46, 247–48. Jackon Mathews, "A Note on Valéry," in *Monsieur Teste* by Paul Valéry (New York, Toronto, London: McGraw-Hill, 1964), vi.

3. Yvor Winters, *In Defense of Reason* (Denver: Alan Swallow, 1947), 18. For Winters's translations of French poets, including Mallarmé and Vielé-Griffin, see *The Poetry of Yvor Winters* (Manchester: Carcanet Press, 1978).

4. Kenneth Fields, *The Other Walker* (Georgetown, Calif.: Talisman Press, 1971), 24.

5. Mallarmé's letter to Henri Cazalis, October or November 1864, quoted in *Mallarmé*, The Penguin Poets, ed. and trans. Anthony Hartley (Baltimore: Penguin Books, 1965), ix.

6. Walter Conrad Arensberg, *Idols* (Boston and New York: Houghton Mifflin; Cambridge: Riverside Press, 1916), 63–68, 78–81.

7. Kenneth Fields, *Anemographia: A Treatise on the Wind* (Berkeley: Hit and Run Press, 1984). Very rare; first published in *Sequoia: Stanford Literary Magazine* 27, no. 3 (Autumn 1983): 32–38.

8. Kenneth Fields, "Your Humble Servant," *Sequoia* 29, no. 3 (Autumn 1985): 34–64. Looking at Mallarmé's work in terms of this trope gives sharper focus and wider application to the tag, "poet of refusals," and surely shows that he gains, rather than loses, by his characteristic spiritual position.

9. Terrence Diggory, "Elpenor Among the Shades," *Salmagundi,* no. 57 (Summer 1982): 159–71. Given the subject of my essay, I feel some qualms about finding fault with such a thoroughgoing reading of my work, but Diggory seems to get it backward in the first paragraph, when he takes Elpenor's request, on behalf of all the lost sailors, that Odysseus "make [his] living mind our cenotaph" a "threat." He remarks that Eliot, by way of contrast, preferred a living mind to a cenotaph. If I must generalize, I intend my book to show that Odysseus and Athene and I share that preference. Mallarmé, too.

10. *The Poems of J. V. Cunningham* (Athens: Swallow Press, Ohio University Press, 1997), 105–7. The line I quote is a fragment. Cunningham's unmatched translations of Sappho's two great odes, "Bright-throned, undying Aphrodite" and

"He is, I should say, on a level / With deity" are in the mode I am describing in Mallarmé.

11. Jim Powell, tr., *Sappho: A Garland* (New York: Farrar Straus Giroux, 1993), 28. See the ode beginning, "Some say thronging calvary, some say foot soldiers, / others call a fleet the most beautiful of / sights the dark earth offers, but I say it's what-/ ever you love best."

12. Robert Greer Cohn, *Toward the Poems of Mallarmé*, expanded ed. (Berkeley, Los Angeles, London: University of California Press, 1980), 218–22; Wallace Fowlie, *Mallarmé* (Chicago and London: University of Chicago Press, Phoenix Books, 1962), 38–39, 48; Stéphane Mallarmé, *Collected Poems*, tr. and commentary by Henry Weinfield (Berkeley, Los Angeles, London: University of California Press, 1994), 81, 236–37.

13. Paul Valéry, "Et cetera. Et cetera," *Cahier* 10:105, included in *Leonardo Poe Mallarmé*, 377. The famous sentence, followed by Hartley's translation: "L'oeuvre pure implique la disparition élocutoire du poëte, qui cède l'initiative aux mots, par le heurt de leur inégalité mobilisés; ils s'allument de reflets réciproques comme une virtuelle traînée de feux sur des pierreries, remplaçant la respiration perceptible en l'ancien souffle lyrique ou la direction personnelle enthousiaste de la phrase" (The pure work implies the elocutory disappearance of the poet who abandons the initiative to words mobilized by the shock of their inequality; they light one another up with mutual reflections like a virtual trail of fire upon precious stones, replacing the breathing perceptible in the old lyrical blast or the enthusiastic personal direction of the phrase).

14. Denise Folliot, trans., "The Necessity of Poetry," in *The Art of Poetry* (New York: Vintage Books, 1961), Bollingen Series 45, *The Collected Works of Paul Valéry* 7:216–18.

Scratching the Adamant
Walter Martin

Once upon a time, when I was a freshman at Stanford University, I found, to my dismay, as the one and only comment on the very first essay I wrote, the following admonishment: "Beware of *pronunciamentos!*" Even after I had looked up the word in the dictionary, it took me some time to digest that pithy criticism. But apparently I never learned my lesson, for here I am, thirty-five years later, standing on the same spot, about to make the same elementary error, for I intend not only to read you a pair of sonnets in translation—and what is a translation if not a pronouncement?—but also to make *pronunciamentos* galore, beginning now.

"I am not unaware, of course, that there are many readers who take persistent pleasure in deprecating everything and that they will vent their spleen on this work too," says Saint Jerome, patron of translators. "It is difficult when you are following another man's footsteps, to keep from going astray somewhere.... If I translate word for word, the result is ludicrous; if I am forced to change the words or rearrange them, it will look as though I had failed in my duty as a translator." This is where the trouble starts, in the too-well-worn equation of translation with treason.

The ideal translator is not a traitor, but an arbitrator, bent on reconciling the conflicting claims of two languages, both competing for the reader's undivided attention. He is in the business of settling differences by give-and-take, by trade-off, by compromise—a go-between, the one who must make the ever-more-delicate decisions upon which the life of the text that he holds in his hands depends.

"Let it be granted at once," says the critic, "that it cannot be done." And, indeed, there are so many good reasons why the translation of poetry should not be attempted, and so many reasonable explanations why the attempt is bound to fail, that it is a wonder anyone still tries. Those who persist are like hummingbirds, who have to be told time and again that flying backward is impossible.

Whether we think of it, as Mallarmé did, as a calque, or direct tracing, or as Baudelaire liked to, as a matter of decipherment, the translation of poetry is unavoidably love's labors lost, labors not of equivalence but of approximation. To kick a dead horse until it gets to its feet and gallops away is the task of the translator. Why pretend otherwise? How to bring the poet back to life is a long-standing conundrum, unsolved since Jerome's day, unlikely to be solved in ours, and without solution, perhaps—which is why we keep trying.

Anyone foolhardy enough to address a distinguished group of Mallarmé scholars—above all, anyone foolish enough to offer them English versions of poems they will all know by heart in French—will be as bemused as I am by one particular sentence in the lecture that Mallarmé delivered at Oxford and Cambridge, a century ago, namely: "Now then, what better amusement can we find for the next few minutes than the comedy of errors and misunderstanding?"

This is not the place to look into the perplexed relationship between the dying Baudelaire and the living Mallarmé. Every poet wants to be the last of his line, the last link of that ancient chain coming down to us from Homer. The author of *Les Fleurs du Mal* alienated the affections of the would-be apprentices, the *fervents de Baudelaire*, refusing to acknowledge the good will of the young, as his good will had been refused by Hugo and Sainte-Beuve, those literary demigods to whom, throughout his career, he had tried in vain to attach himself.

In a letter to his mother, Baudelaire, alarmed by these younger poets anxious to become him, to displace him, writes: "I know of nothing more compromising than imitators and I like nothing so well as being left alone. But it isn't possible and it seems that there exists a school of Baudelaire." The question becomes whether imitation really is the sincerest form of flattery or the most insidious kind of encroachment. His advice to these upstarts, thrown like a bone to a pack of pups is this: If you want to be the poet I am, *stay at home, meditate, and scribble on a lot of paper.*

The Tomb of Charles Baudelaire

[W. B. Yeats, at the start of a reading, says: "It gave me the devil of a lot of trouble to get this thing into verse, and I WILL NOT read it as if it were prose."]

> Out of a dismal sewer's slobbering mouth
> Spill rubies mixed with nauseating filth

> Up from the catacombs Anubis comes
> Whose jackal jaws gnash wildly with the flames
>
> Or if the foul wick's twisted in the gas
> That wipes out who knows what disgrace
> Endured as deathless sex by lurid light
> Fleeing beneath the streetlamps through the night
>
> What votive wreaths could hallow cities where
> Evening never dwells as well as his own Shade
> Reposed in vain against the stone of Baudelaire
>
> Absent within her trembling veil and made
> To be inspired with every breath
> A poisonous muse beside us to the death.

What wouldn't we give, now, to have had the opportunity to be in that Oxford audience on 1 March 1894, when the Taylorian Lecture on "La Musique et les Lettres" was read by the distinguished French poet? The lecture went well, and is worth a brief divagation that sheds a little light upon the lecturer. His host, the regius professor of Christ Church, York Powell, comments: "[Mr. Mallarmé] was delightful and we are thick as thieves . . . a charming man; beautiful manner and speech."

Mallarmé, on his side, writes home:

> M. *Powell* is a fine person. He took perfect care of me. Last night there was a big dinner in my honor. It was marvelous, except for the champagne, the sherry, and the water which don't agree with me at all. I have just now had dinner with [my friend] Payne: I drank my first beer and liked it a lot. . . . But, Lord! the lecture! If I had only known! Only two or three professors in the audience, a few students, and all the rest were ladies. I can't really complain, though; they were all scrupulously polite, they applauded for a decent length of time, perhaps a little artificially, when it was all over. I am the one who is in the wrong: I never should have served up a dish of tough æsthetics like that; I could have just chatted with almost no preparation at all.

At one point in that famous lecture Mallarmé says this: "For verse is everything, from the moment we take pen in hand. As long as there is cadence, there will be style and versification. That is why the careful prose of discriminating writers—ornamental prose—can always be thought of as *broken verse*."

Hearing, which one member of the audience, himself an English master—*the* English master of ornamental prose, or *broken verse*—would have pricked up his ears and taken a mental note, while twiddling his extravagant moustache. How odd, and how appropriate, that Walter Pater should have been in that gathering, himself a forefather of modernism, the man who had done more than anyone else to introduce recent French culture into England and formerly as much a champion of Baudelaire the critic as Mallarmé once had been of the poetry of Baudelaire.

In his recent book on Pater, Dennis Donoghue recalls the occasion:

> Powell assumed that Pater would be pleased to meet Mallarmé, not only a great poet but an artist in prose. Perhaps he was pleased, but he did not converse with Mallarmé on the relation between music and literature or upon any other topic ... Mallarmé taught English in a lycée; Pater was deeply versed in French; but neither would venture on the language of the other master. While Powell's voice was heard in alternate tongues, they regarded each other in silence, and were satisfied.

Poets passing in the night. Hard not to find a poignancy in that propinquity. There is a fascination attached to the meeting of minds, but also to those that come close, yet just miss meeting: Heine, living and dying in Baudelaire's Paris for thirty-six years, and yet, for reasons I find hard to fathom, despite having at least two friends in common—Nerval and Gautier—never colliding with one another. Gerard Manley Hopkins, sitting in a café on a week-long holiday in Paris, could have struck up a conversation with M. Baudelaire—a conjunction I amuse myself trying to imagine, another chapter in the yet-to-be-written literary history of what might have been.

As it happened, Mallarmé never met his much-admired elder either, except by proxy. We know that at a dinner party in April 1864, two friends of Mallarmé read *Les Fenêtres* and *L'Azur* to Baudelaire, who listened very attentively, but said nothing. This reaction was relayed to the twenty-two-year-old poet as a sign that Baudelaire had listened "without disapproval," which, in fact, was to be interpreted as "a very strong indication of approval"—to put the best possible face on what must have been a sharp and disenchanting shock.

In that same month, Mallarmé finished the first draft of his *Literary Symphony,* a piece of "ornamental prose" that is, in one of its three movements, a heartfelt homage to Baudelaire: *"Come winter, when my lethargy has worn me out, I dive delightedly into the treasured pages of* Les Fleurs du Mal. *No sooner have I opened my Baudelaire than I am drawn into a stunning landscape that strikes my eyes as if created by some marvellous opiate.*" But one cannot remain an acolyte to a poisonous muse forever. The younger poet was beginning to be illuminated by his own light.

Is it coincidence, then, that Mallarmé's horrible year in Tournon in 1866–67 was the year of Baudelaire's collapse and silent agony and death? "I am completely dead," at that time Mallarmé confesses to a friend.

On 24 January 1867, in *Le Figaro,* one H. de Sandemoy writes an article deploring the influence of Baudelaire on young writers. On 14 May, Mallarmé announces to his friend Cazalis that he has "freed himself from the influence of Baudelaire." Nevertheless, after the death of the older man, on 31 August of that year, Mallarmé agrees to be the president of his memorial committee, and the result was the Tombeau that you have heard.

Let the last word on this subject be Robert Greer Cohn's: "'The Tomb of Charles Baudelaire' . . . express[es] succinctly his attitude toward the cloacal, luridly morbid, and stagily diabolical aspects of his great ancestor's aesthetic. Not that Mallarmé didn't appreciate Baudelaire for what he was, but he couldn't stop there and still be worthy of him" (*Toward the Poems of Mallarmé*).

One does not need to be Dryden to see that translation comes down to a "scrupulous anxiety over niceties." Isaac Stern, in a master class, comments:

> Casual notes? There are no casual notes! Personally, I don't think Mallarmé went far enough when he told Degas that poetry was written with words and not ideas. What he should have said is that poetry is made with syllables, tiny elements of sound, none of which is expendable. There are no casual syllables in poetry or its translation, any more than there are casual notes in a Brahms sonata, or casual brushstrokes in a painting by Degas. It is the translator's business to treat what seem like trivial things as if they were crucial, because they are.

The result is more complicated in the case of Mallarmé, of course.

C. F. MacIntyre, with the confidence of Cassandra, made this prediction back in 1957: "[Mallarmé] has had a profound effect on poetry since his time, but it is impossible to believe that people in 1998, the anniversary of his death, will spend much time in unraveling his abracadabras." This shows you what translators know, and how much our theories are to be trusted. To paraphrase Marianne Moore:

> Baudelaire writes a poetry that cats and dogs can read; by and large, his words mean what they say and nothing more. Well, cats and dogs

will never make heads or tails of Mallarmé. That much I know. To name an object, he tells us, is to do away with three-quarters of the enjoyment of the poem, which is derived from the satisfaction of guessing little by little: to suggest it, to evoke it—that's what charms the imagination.

This brings me to my second poem, and if it seems to your critical ear—as it does to my own—less of a strict "translation" than something we might call *bémolisé*, or Mallarmé in a minor key, so be it. As William Caxton said centuries ago: "I have but folowed my copye in Frenshe as nygh as me is possyble."

> *Toute l'âme résumée . . .*
>
> Our concentrated souls
> When carefully exhaled
> Form perfect aureoles
> With each new halo veiled
>
> In smoky artifice
> For good cigars burn best
> If after each long kiss
> We lay their ash to rest
>
> Likewise with lyric trash
> All clap-trap should be shunned
> Reality's dead ash
> Leaves verses moribund
>
> Your strophes should evoke
> While going up in smoke.

The host of those Tuesday evenings in the rue de Rome smoked like a chimney. An eyewitness reports: "To see him stand by the fireplace rolling a cigarette, talking in a low voice, half to himself, half to his visitors, was to see a man free from conventional bondage. This little room was the one place in Paris where the soul could manifest itself in freedom. Here was a man, living very near the borders of actual want, exercising a power which no millionaire could claim."

Roger Shattuck, distinguished critic of Proust, translator of Jarry and Daumal, of Valéry and Apollinaire, author of the unforgettable *The Banquet Years,* and of a new book titled *Forbidden*

Knowledge, needs no introduction to this public. He sends it his greetings in the form of a translation of (appropriately) "Salut":

Cheers

Mere froth, these virgin verses
Cut like glass to hold the void
Where mermaids gambol to avoid
The drowning scenes my eye rehearses.

We set our sails, my motley friends,
I standing on the wintry poop
To watch young poets on the prow usurp
The pomp this thundering night portends;

Tipsy upon a tossing deck
Yet fearless of pitch I now elect
To make this stern free-standing toast

Solitude, or reef, or star
To lines our empty sheets disbar
From sounding at this gay repast.

What is a translator? Who grows up to become a member of this anchoritic order, each in his own desert, with his own lion? A translator is that person who, when given the time-honored injunction of every parent, "Go look it up in the dictionary!"—did. And does.

In closing, and before I transmit one final *jeu d'esprit* from Roger Shattuck, I am going to reveal the magicians' secret: I am going to tell you *how to translate Mallarmé*. First, arrange on one side of your desk the seven hulking volumes of the Robert, or the five of the big Littré, or both, and on the other, the twenty-one volumes of the *OED*. Then, in between the two, like a referee in a boxing match, prop up your dog-eared copy of *Toward the Poems of Mallarmé*, pour yourself a large cup of coffee, and let the two contenders battle it out. That's really all there is to it.

Anyone can do it.

But very few, having done it, will believe that they have scratched the surface of Mallarmé, that "poetical or rhetorical name for the embodiment of surpassing hardness; that which is impregnable to any application of force."

Macaronics for Mallarmé
[To be recited with a thick French accent.]

I.
Degas:
Mallarmé, cher maître,
please help me do better.
Ideas fill my bonnet,
yet I find no sonnet.

Mallarmé:
Pauvre Degas,
ideas—ha! ha!
A sonnet grows
only from mots.

II.
Poets deplore
the dark of jour
and mock the sweet
lightness of nuit.

III.
Poor Mallarmé
had lots to say.
He never quite
left the page white.

Note

Walter Martin's translation of *Les Fleurs du Mal* is forthcoming from Carcanet Press in Manchester, England.

IV
On the Poet's Influence

"Le Livre" of Mallarmé and James Joyce's *Ulysses*

William Carpenter

For more than three decades, Mallarmé projected a Great Work. He originally wrote of it as a book, but from about 1885 onward, he also contemplated its performance as a drama or public ritual. The final fruit of his meditations, however, was neither a drama nor a Mass nor a book, but the poem *Un Coup de Dés jamais n'abolira le hasard*.[1] Although the poet spoke modestly of this miracle of concision as merely an "état,"[2] it realized his cosmological intentions, as Robert Greer Cohn has demonstrated. In this essay, celebrating Mallarmé's life and art, I propose to credit Mallarmé with furnishing the design and inspiration for another culminating work of the modern era, James Joyce's *Ulysses*.

Taking Mallarmé's formulations broadly, anyone mad enough to attempt a literary microcosm of the universe would be striving toward the Mallarméan book. Mallarmé described his ideal book as embodying "au monde, sa loi—bible comme la simule les nations"[3] (the law of the world—bible as simulated by the nations). To attempt such a book was to enter "un immense concours pour le texte véridique" (367). The Hebrew Bible is Mallarmé's model, with its fusion of cosmology, law, and prophecy; he also alludes to a Greek inspiration when he calls the book "l'explication orphique de la Terre" (665). Looking beyond the boundaries of my own scholarship, Mallarmé's predecessors, in conceiving the Book as microcosm or blueprint of the universe, seem first to be the allegorists who devised esoteric, bibliolatrous interpretations of the Bible (and of Homer and Virgil); second, Dante, who single-handedly drafted such a blueprint, demonstrating an unprecedented freedom in rewriting the Book in the face of his august authorities; and third, Dante's successors who self-consciously adopted the role of poet as prophet and composer of revelation. Dante's successors would include Milton, Blake, and Wordsworth, among the English, perhaps Hugo in France. Careful to give full play to both head and heart, Mallarmé followed his prophetic antecedents at a scrupulous distance. Joyce did the same, assuming Mallarmé's cosmological purpose, as well as that of Dante and Blake, in a critical and comic mode.[4] American poets such as Pound, Williams, and Olson have followed Joyce on his bibliolatrous way, and have thus sought to realize the Mallarméan Book.

Early in his career, Mallarmé expressed his sense of the sacred quality of poetry in his essay "Hérésies artistiques" and in poems describing the poet as accursed and divine (257).[5] Neither the poems nor the essay indicated that a lifelong revelatory vocation was to follow. The calling to the Great Work forced itself on Mallarmé in the course of a painful and drawn-out personal crisis, the resolution of which Guy Michaud relates to Mallarmé's discovery of Hegel.[6] In 1866, Mallarmé wrote to his friend Thodore Aubanel, "J'ai jeté les fondements d'un oeuvre magnifique.... Il me faut vingt ans pour lesquels je vais me cloîtrer en moi"[7] (I have laid the foundations of a magnificent work.... I need twenty years to cloister myself in myself). A few days later he wrote in explanation:

J'ai voulu te dire simplement que je venais de jeter le plan de mon oeuvre entier, après avoir trouvé la clef de moi-même, clef de voûte, ou centre, si tu veux ... je prévois qu'il me faudra vingt ans pour les cinq livres dont se composera l'oeuvre.[8]

[I simply wanted to tell you that I've just laid the plan for my entire work, after having found the key to myself, the keystone or center, if you will... I foresee that I will need twenty years for the five books that will compose the work.]

At this point "l'oeuvre" meant only the projected ensemble of the poet's production over the course of his career. As the crisis continued, however, and continued to resolve itself in the image of a comprehensive literary expression, the poet increasingly conceived of his "oeuvre" as a single "work." In 1867, the poet wrote to Henri Cazalis,

Fragile comme est mon apparition terrestre, je ne puis subir que les développements absolument nécessaires pour que l'univers retrouve, en ce moi, son identité. Ainsi je viens, l'heure de la Synthèse, de délimiter l'oeuvre qui sera l'image de ce développement.... Trois poèmes en vers, dont *Hérodiade* est l'Ouverture ... Et quatre poèmes en prose, sur la conception spirituelle du Néant. Il me faut dix ans: les aurai-je?⁹

[Fragile as my terrestrial apparition is, I can only undergo the developments absolutely necessary for the universe to find its identity in this ego. Thus I have just, at the hour of Synthesis, delimited the work that will be the image of this development.... Three poems in verse, of which *Hérodiade* is the overture.... And four poems in prose, on the spiritual conception of Nothingness. I'll need ten years: will I have them?]

Thus, Mallarmé began sketching his life's work as a comprehensive and universal spiritual itinerary. Twenty years later, he described his vision of a still unrealized Great Work to Verlaine:

... j'ai toujours rêvé et tenté autre chose, avec une patience d'alchimiste, prêt à y sacrifier toute vanité et toute satisfaction, comme on brûlait jadis son mobilier et les poutres de son toit, pour alimenter le fourneau du Grand Oeuvre. Quoi? c'est difficile à dire: un livre, tout bonnement, en maints tomes, un livre qui soit un livre, architectural et prémédité, et non un recueil des inspirations, fussent-elles merveilleuses.... J'irai plus loin, je dirai: le Livre, persuadé qu'au fond il n'y en a qu'un, tenté à son insu par quiconque a écrit, même les Génies. L'explication orphique de la Terre, qui est le seul devoir du poète et le jeu littéraire par excellence: car le rythme même du livre, alors impersonnel et vivant, jusque dans sa pagination, se juxtapose aux équations de ce rêve, ou Ode. (662–63)¹⁰

[I've always dreamt and attempted something else, with the patience of an alchemist, ready to sacrifice all vanity and satisfaction as one used to burn his furniture and roofbeams to feed the furnace of the Great Work. What? It's difficult to say: a book, plainly, in multiple volumes, a book that would be a book, architectural and premeditated, and not a collection of chance inspirations, however marvelous.... I will go further and say, the Book, persuaded that at bottom there is only one, unwittingly attempted by whoever has written, even the geniuses. The orphic explanation of the Earth, which is the sole duty of the poet and the literary game par excellence: for the very rhythm of the book, living and impersonal down to its pagination, is juxtaposed with the equations of this dream, or Ode.]

The spiritual crisis of Mallarmé's youth gave way to meditations on art and society. The mature Mallarmé thought long on the life of his time, which he had come to regard as an "interregnum" of spiritual anarchy. In his critical writings, he examined contemporary culture and found a hunger that church and state could no longer feed. "Quelque royauté environnée de prestige militaire, suffisant naguères publiquement, a cessé: et l'orthodoxie de nos élans secrets, qui se perpétue, remise au clergé, souffre d'étiolement" (395) (A royalty surrounded by military prestige, publicly sufficient until recently, has ended: and the orthodoxy of our secret drives, which continues, entrusted to the clergy, suffers from etiolation). Like Nietzsche, he concluded that the common ground of European civilization had evaporated. There was no longer a reality, no longer a present.

> "Unique fois au monde," he wrote, "il n'est pas de Présent, non—un présent n'existe pas. . . . Faute que se déclare la foule, faute—de tout. Mal informé celui qui se crierait son propre contemporain, désertant, usurpant, avec impudence égale, quand du passé cessa et que tarde un futur ou les deux se remêlent perplexement en vue de masquer l'écart." (372)

> [For once in the world, there is no Present, no—a present does not exist. . . . Failing a declaration by the crowd, failing all. Ill-informed he who would herald himself as his own contemporary, deserting, usurping, with equal impudence, when the past has ended and a future lags or the two mix confusedly to mask the gap.]

This lack of a common reality drew him toward a public venue for the Great Work, which would fill the vacuum of efficacious communal representation. His thinking along these lines appears in his essay on Wagner, where he speaks of an ideal theatrical experience as a "Sacre d'un des actes de la Civilisation," which would serve to unveil "la Fable . . . inscrite sur la page des Cieux et dont l'Histoire même n'est que l'interprétation" (544–45) (the Fable . . . inscribed on the page of the skies and of which History itself is only an interpretation). The hero of this universal fable would be an impersonal, universal figure, a "Type sans dénomination préalable" (545) (type without prior denomination). The action would be essentially the mise en scène itself, in which "l'Homme, puis son authentique séjour terrestre, changent une réciprocité de preuves" (545) (man, then his authentic terrestrial sojourn, exchanges a reciprocity of proofs).

Mallarmé offered the results of his long efforts in *Un Coup de Dés*, published in the journal *Cosmopolis* in 1897. Robert Greer Cohn has explained the many ways in which this poem embodied Mallarmé's plan for the Book, from the dialectical itinerary of the Master, rooted in *Hérodiade* and *Igitur,* to the cosmic and cosmogonic Tetragrammaton and "tétralogie de l'An" (393) (tetralogy of the year), created by the typography, to a multitude of etymological and graphic details, to the contemplation of the mystery of human/divine creation. My task is not to persuade the reader that *Un Coup de Dés* is "Le Livre," but that a writer of another generation, in another country, writing in another language, adopted Mallarmé's program for the Book and gave it shape in what is probably our century's most notorious literary work.

When James Joyce was a teenager in Dublin in the 1890s, the Irish literary scene was dominated by Yeats and Wilde. Both admired Mallarmé intensely and both had been guests at his Tuesday evenings. A friend of Yeats's, Arthur Symons, wrote *The Symbolist Movement in Literature,* in which he described, anthologized, and translated the poetry and prose of Mallarmé and others.[11] Yeats promoted this book and quoted Symons's quotations of Mallarmé in an 1898 essay.[12] Because the essay preceded the publication of Symons's book, it may have been Joyce's first exposure to Mallarmé. The passage quotes *Crise de vers,* Mallarmé's 1886 essay on contemporary developments in poetry:

> Mr. Symons has written lately on Mallarmé's method, and has quoted him as saying that we should "abolish the pretension, aesthetically an error, despite its dominion over almost all the masterpieces, to enclose within the subtle paper other than for example the horror of the forest or the silent thunder in the leaves, not the intense dense wood of the trees."

Joyce wrote the passage into his notebook and took it to heart.[13]

Joyce's progressive mastery of Mallarmé's "suggestive method" is a story in itself. David Hayman's *Joyce et Mallarmé* shows how Joyce put the "suggestive method" to work from *Dubliners* to *Finnegans Wake*. Following Mallarmé, Joyce became a psychologist of reading, refining his writing in accord with his and Mallarmé's analysis of how printed words present themselves to the reader.[14] As interesting as the suggestive method is, we will discuss it no further. It has no special relationship to the concept of the Book, except that its engagement of the reader's associative and analogical faculties permits the practitioner to conjure up a universe from a Book or a Book from a few choice words.

In *Ulysses,* Joyce depicted his young artist as having assimilated Mallarmé, and this is half my argument for *Ulysses* being an attempt at the Mallarméan Book. It is acknowledged that when Joyce incorporates the words or ideas of other writers, "the quotation most obviously relevant to the situation" is studiously omitted.[15] Joyce does not cite *Un Coup de Dés* in *Ulysses* or passages relating to Mallarmé's attempt to write "le texte véridique." Instead, he shows Stephen Dedalus applying the imagery of *L'Après-midi d'un Faune* and *Hérodiade* to his own memories and perceptions. He also shows Stephen as the most knowledgeable student of Mallarmé among his contemporaries. By indirection, Joyce shows himself a serious student of Mallarmé and leaves us to draw what inferences we may from this and other evidence.[16]

As *Ulysses* opens, Stephen Dedalus has recently returned from Paris, where he has acquired a profounder understanding of Mallarmé than that shown by his fashionable elders. He has also recently lost his mother. All his thoughts and feelings are colored by this loss, and his story on 16 June 1904 is one of coming to terms with her ghost. He thinks of himself as Hamlet, and it is on the subject of Hamlet, one dear to Mallarmé,[17] that Stephen shows his superior knowledge of Mallarmé.

In the chapter known as "Scylla and Charybdis," Stephen is attempting to navigate between the whirlpool of esoteric idealism, associated here with John Eglinton and "A.E.," historical figures of the Celtic Twilight movement, and the rocks of a cynical materialism, personified by Stephen's treacherous friend Buck Mulligan. In earlier chapters, we have seen Stephen developing a theory of art based on the hard facts of life, perceptible by eye and ear, not on the "formless spiritual essences" favored by A.E. Stephen has proceeded from the "applied Aquinas" he developed in *A Portrait* to applied Aristotle, whom he champions against the theosophists' Plato. The chapter opens Stephen in the midst of a conversation about *Hamlet* at the National Library. A.E. declares sententiously that "France has produced the finest flower of corruption in Mallarmé but the desirable life is revealed only to the poor of heart."[18] The assistant librarian, who takes the role of frivolous aesthete, displays another shade of ignorance:

> Mallarmé, don't you know, he said, has written those wonderful prose poems Stephen McKenna used to read to me in Paris. The one about *Hamlet*. He says: *il se promène, lisant au livre de lui-même*, don't you know, *reading the book of himself*. He describes *Hamlet* given in a French town, don't you know, a provincial town. They advertised it. His free hand graciously wrote tiny signs in air.
>
> *Hamlet*
> *ou*
> *Le Distrait*
> *Pièce de Shakespeare*

He repeated to John Eglinton's newgathered frown:

—*Pièce de Shakespeare,* don't you know. It's so French. The French point of view.[19]

From Stephen's point of view, the man is making a fool of himself. Of course, he cannot be held responsible for not knowing that Stephen knows inside out the text he is describing. But he may be held responsible, first, for plagiarizing Mallarmé's perception of the playbill as expressing "un goût joliment français," and, second, for having drawn only a piquant flavor of national character from Mallarmé's analysis of *Hamlet*. The assistant librarian is not a discerning reader. Stephen comments on this by translating to himself another phrase from the same note: "Sumptuous and stagnant exaggeration of murder" (1564).[20]

Stephen knows that Mallarmé is not a "flower of corruption" and that he is not "distressingly shortsighted on some matters" as the assistant librarian alleges the French people to be. He knows that Mallarmé has a firm grip on Shakespeare's tragic vision and on the message of *Hamlet* for the modern poet. The vision is one of the destructive isolation of intellectual man, which is the high cost of doubt, of war against "le néant," and thus of truth. The lesson is that the dramatic form is moving toward the expression of this vision in the form of a "Monologue ou drame avec soi, futur" (1564) (monologue, or future drama with the self). Indeed, "Man Thinking" (cf. Emerson) is Mallarmé's persona from *Hérodiade* and *L'Après-midi d'un Faune* to *Un Coup de Dés*.

Because Joyce considered the "interior monologue" to be a signal achievement of *Ulysses*, and widely advertised his debt in that regard to Edouard Dujardin, the young symbolist and associate of Mallarmé's who published *Les Lauriers sont coupés* in 1887, it is not too much to see in Joyce's quotation of this passage an allusion to the narrative technique of *Ulysses* and a justification of the technique. The fact that such a justification appears in conjunction with an unsentimental appraisal of the cost of spiritual life—which is Stephen's and Mallarmé's reading of *Hamlet* —suggests that Joyce is enlisting Mallarmé as an ally both for Stephen and for himself. Stephen's theory of *Hamlet,* which follows the passage quoted above, is applied *Igitur,* for Stephen imagines the living artist depicting himself in the work of art as a ghost addressing his living son. It is a clever theory, reflecting Stephen's sense of betrayal and persecution at the hands of comrades like Mulligan, Lynch, and Cranly, but is curiously at odds with Stephen's own experience of being haunted and admonished by the ghost of May Dedalus.

The confrontation in the library shows us the young artist in the course of testing his possessions. Stephen argues for an art born of the artist's whole life, instead of a one-sidedly intellectual or speculative art. He makes Shakespeare his protagonist for such an art, but it is a Shakespeare interpreted through the lens of Mallarmé and a Mallarméan sense of modernity—a haunted, solitary Shakespeare, who in his solitude leads the way to a modern individualism both in the form and content of artistic expression. The "Monologue" is the future mode of drama to Mallarmé because individualism is the mode of human experience in modern civilization. In its first several chapters, *Ulysses* establishes monologue as the mode of experience of his modern individuals, Stephen and Bloom, though the book as a whole is at least superficially a chorus of the individuals and languages that Joyce uses to fill out his encyclopedic vision.

Stephen's encounter at the library is evidence of the significance of Mallarmé for Joyce. It is also evidence that Joyce knew Mallarmé's critical writings, in which Mallarmé diagnosed contemporary culture and prescribed his poetry of the future. *Finnegans Wake* furnishes fuller evidence of Joyce's familiarity with Mallarmé's poetry and his esteem for it (*Culpo di Dido!* Joyce exclaims). But none of this tells us that *Ulysses* is an attempt at the Mallarméan "Livre" instead of, for example, a transposition of the *Odyssey* to 1904 Dublin, or an Irish *Don Quixote,* or an Irish *Gargantua and Pantagruel.* Indeed, to the unassisted eye, *Ulysses* resembles each of those works more closely than it does the eleven-page free-verse meditation on poetry and truth, *Un Coup de Dés.*[21] In addition to Stephen's "Mallarméism," and the fact that Joyce took the foundation of his technique from Mallarmé's "suggestive method" as elucidated by David Hayman, I rely on circumstantial evidence that Joyce followed Mallarmé's prescriptions for the Book down to the letter.

First, the architecture. Mallarmé wrote in his 1885 letter to Verlaine that the Book must be "architectural et prémédité," that its "rythme même" must "se juxtaposer aux équations de ce rêve, ou Ode" (663) (its very rhythm [must] juxtapose itself to the equations of this dream or Ode). Describing "L'Oeuvre" in "Crise de vers," he wrote of a "symétrie . . . qui, de la situation des vers en la pièce se lie à l'authenticité de la pièce dans le volume" (367) (a symmetry which, from the situation of verses in the piece is linked to the authenticity of the piece in the volume). In *Le Livre, instrument spirituel,* Mallarmé wrote that the structure of a book should be such that every motif should have its own significant position on the page (380). In addition, the Book must be organized from the highest level to the lowest, for the very letters of the alphabet are its most significant units. "Le livre, expansion totale de la lettre, doit d'elle tirer, directement, une mobilité et spacieux, par correspondances, instituer un jeu, on ne sait, qui confirme la fiction" (380) (The book, total expansion of the letter, must draw from it, directly, a mobility and, spacious, by correspondences, institute a game, who knows, which confirms the fiction). Each letter of the alphabet corresponds to "une attitude de Mystère" (375). In a note gathered in the *Oeuvres complètes,* he spoke of the twenty-four letters as a "spirituel zodiaque" that had "sa doctrine propre, abstraite, ésoterique comme quelque théologie" (850) (its own doctrine, abstract, esoteric like some theology). In *Les Mots anglais,* he analyzed the import of individual letters in detail, and R. G. Cohn has shown the great extent to which the poet applied his researches in his own writing.[22] In Mallarmé's view, the author of the Book should give a meaningful role to these skilled and experienced actors of the written language, which embody the fundamental, hieroglyphic mystery of language and contribute to the complex significance of words and verses.

Joyce followed Mallarméan architectural principles. He sought to order *Ulysses* to an extraordinary degree, as reflected in the tables he passed to favored critics. According to these tables, each "episode" of *Ulysses* (i.e., chapter) corresponds to an hour of the day (Bloom remembers "The Dance of the Hours"), an organ of the human body, an art, a "technic," and a symbol. (This is in addition to the Homeric correspondences.) Although fifteen organs do not add up to a body any more than eighteen hours make a day, the intent is clearly comprehensive, encyclopedic, and allegorical. The book is a man, the one day is all days, the one city is all cities, with the constitutive arts of civilization represented. The city is a man and vice-versa. Joyce's correspondences between hours, arts, and organs may have a closer apparent kinship to Renaissance astrology than to Mallarmé's more generalized correspondences between man and the seasons, but both authors structure their "books" as microcosms of the universe of analogy with its hierarchy of correspondences.[23]

Joyce lampoons the cult of letters in the symbolist and decadent world as one of Stephen's youthful follies. "Books you were going to write with letters for titles. Have you read his F? O yes, but I prefer Q. Yes, but W is wonderful. O yes, W."[24] Joyce nonetheless analyzes the sounds of letters in the "Sirens" episode (chap. 11), in which he focuses the reader's ear on the phonetic dimension of language. He thus sculpts the "ear" of Ulysses at the same time as illustrating the art of "music" under the symbol of "barmaids" and through the technic of "fuga per canonem."[25] An extended account of Joyce's use of letters is beyond the scope of this essay, but his use of "U" has caught my eye and ear. It has the shape of a vessel or bottom, and at moments seems to embody Bloom's most intense desires. When Bloom begins to sink into a whirlpool of grief and desire, as he thinks of feminine things and Molly's assignation with Blazes Boylan, Joyce writes his thoughts thus: "Perfume of embraces all him assailed. With hungered breath obscurely, he mutely craved to adore."[26] U's abound in this rush of lust, though their effect is inseparable from other peculiarities of Joyce's prose-poetry, especially the regulation of stresses. Still, the long U's, which narrow the lips, seem to constrict the mouth and oral cavity into a thin pipeline, through which the breath carries feeling from the heart. Again, when Bloom and Stephen step outside to view the Dantean, Mallarméan firmament above 7 Eccles Street, what they observe is couched in U's: "The heaventree of stars hung with humid, nightblue fruit."[27] Though we laugh at Stephen's W and his O, Joyce revered the letters in much the way Mallarmé did, as mysterious incarnations of sound, shape, and primordial meaning. His, and Mallarmé's, attention to the hieroglyphic quality of written language is akin to Pound's study of Chinese characters and Charles Olson's study of ancient Mayan.[28]

Other circumstances: Mallarmé frequently wrote that the hero of the new art should be a "Type." Joyce's creation of Leopold Bloom, a partly converted half-Jew of mixed Irish and Hungarian descent, points toward a kind of universality, at least within the European world. In *Un Coup de Dés*, Mallarmé presented "Le Maître" as the Type, a master mariner struggling against the elements. Mallarmé thus adopted the line of literary and historical heroes that includes Odysseus, Aeneas, St. Paul, Sinbad, Columbus, Magellan, Da Gama, Captain Cook, and Coleridge's Ancient Mariner. Although Bloom is nothing if not a landsman, Joyce, too, adopts the Homeric mariner type and comically reinforces it with references to pantomime Sinbads.

The modern mariner is a scientist, a Galileo as well as a Sinbad. Mallarmé's Maître seeks a "unique number" from the abyss of sea and sky that surrounds him, while Bloom plucks a continuous stream of scientific inferences from his observations of the perceptible world. As *Un Coup de Dés* culminates in an appraisal of a constellation "selon telle obliquité par telle déclivité de feux" (477) (according to such and such obliquity by such and such declivity of lights). *Ulysses* culminates in what Joyce called the "mathematical catechism" and contemplation of "the huge earthball slowly surely and evenly round and round spinning" through its "four cardinal points."[29] Though quoted from a letter, the image echoes the final image of *Un Coup de Dés*, in which "une constellation" is described as "veillant doutant roulant brillant et méditant avant de s'arrêter à quelque point dernier qui le sacre" (477) (watching doubting rolling shining and meditating before stopping at some final point which sanctifies it).

The Type is a martyr as well as a mariner. He exemplifies the human condition, doomed to failure and pain and betting everything on a dubious possibility of redemption. The redemption of Bloom, as of Le Maître, is to possess and transmit the highest good. The mariner goes down, but maybe he has sighted or identified or created a constellation. Bloom suffers ridicule and betrayal, but maybe he has been able to pass on his magnanimity to Stephen Dedalus.

Both heroes, Bloom and Le Maître, suffer the human condition acutely in the loss of a son. In *Un Coup de Dés*, the master bears a "cadavre par le bras," described as "son ombre puérile caressée et polie et rendu et lavée / assouplie par le vague" (464) (his boyish shade caressed and polished and rendered and laved/softened by the wave). Leopold Bloom carries with him the memory of his son, Rudy, named for his father, Rudolf. Rudy died in infancy, and persists in Leopold's memory as "a fairy boy of eleven, a changeling, kidnapped, dressed in an Eton suit with glass shoes and a little bronze helmet, holding a book in his hand. He reads from right to left inaudibly, smiling, kissing the page. . . . A white lambkin peeps out of his waistcoat pocket."[30] Rudy embodies every hope for Bloom, from social advancement, to the continuity of generations, to the coming of Messiah. Loss of the son also suggests a loss of self, especially to a male. For both Joyce and Mallarmé, loss of hope, which leaves behind a sublimate of hope, figures largely in the portrait of the universal hero. Joyce likely knew that Mallarmé, like Bloom, had lost a son but kept a daughter.

In addition to the lost son, both authors depict the adolescent hero as Hamlet. Stephen dons his "Hamlet hat" and wears black far too long for the taste of the worldly Mulligan. Stephen identifies with Hamlet's burden of grief and persecution, even with his haunting by a deceased parent, suffering fearful visions of his dying and decomposing mother. He is introspective and philosophical as well as melancholy. Mallarmé's Maître, in his own mind or on the screen of the page, becomes a Hamlet figure before the end, wearing the shadowing plume Mallarmé associated with Hamlet. The image is of adolescent man maddened, rebellious, and haunted by the lost Ophelia whom Mallarmé saw as a figure of Hamlet's indestructible inner purity of soul, "joyau intact sous le désastre" (302) (jewel intact beneath the disaster). The drowning mariner is also haunted by the "faux manoir," the mock manor of an ancestral castle or utopia that in the end is no more than a painted backdrop for the drama of struggle and despair.

Ophelia indeed appears in *Un Coup de Dés* as a half-glimpsed siren, "une stature mignonne ténébreuse" (470), who surfaces just long enough to slap the foot of the disappearing castle with her tail. The "joyau intact" of the essay on *Hamlet* has become an amphibious creature, a lasting temptation, who may have some association with the "ultérieur démon immorial" that has drawn the mariner to his doom. The suicidal soul has grown gills. The Ophelia of *Ulysses* has a less certain future. Stephen encounters his sister Dilly at a bookstall and fears she will drag him down with her. "She is drowning. Agenbite. Save her. Agenbite. All against us. She will drown me with her, eyes and hair. Lank coils of seaweed hair around me, my heart, my soul. Salt green death."[31] Bloom's daughter Millie is another Ophelia, barely glimpsed as she begins her own life as a woman.

Mallarmé and Joyce both unite their male heroes to feminine figures of the natural world. For Le Maître, the figure is "la mer." On the brink of catastrophe, as his destiny flashes before our eyes, the poem reflects his "Fiançailles" with the sea, which gave birth to the son-number that the mariner now holds in his hand. "Folie" is the verdict on that distant consummation which was a blind, early step on the way to this "conjonction suprême avec la probabilité" (464). Molly Bloom, instead of the sea, is the "huge earthball turning," the master image of the final episode of *Ulysses*. Bloom's recurring thoughts of their life together do not suggest that their marriage was pure folly, but something mad and blind nonetheless emerges from his, and Molly's, memories of their courtship. If anything, this madness is the dominion of Aphrodite in the hearts of the young, which Joyce sets up at the close of *Ulysses* as the archetype of the life force that "zieht uns hinan" (pulls us onward) even to such unsensual fulfilments as Bloom's good citizenship and Stephen's poetic ambition (cf. the role of Aphrodite in Pound's *Cantos*). Bloom as mariner and Le Maître share this conjunction with the feminine in their past. Joyce and Mallarmé share a vision of the role of the feminine as the womb or matrix of male achievement, but Joyce does not carry the metaphorical possibilities as far in *Ulysses* as he later did in *Finnegans Wake*. He does not make Molly Bloom an embodiment of the Dublin that Bloom-Ulysses navigates, while he insistently depicts Anna Livia as the river on which HCE builds Dublin.

The more essential point about the dramatis personae of *Un Coup de Dés* and *Ulysses* (and *Finnegans Wake*) is that both works present a matrix of family at the core of the self and of the self's inner and outer experience. The matrix of family is divided in one direction between male and female, in the other by youth and age. It is the beginning of the self, and it is the sea the self traverses, and the transcendence sought by the hero is a sublimation of the desires that arise in the matrix (son becomes number becomes stars).

Two last coincidences bear mention. First, in one of his rare sorties into criticism of the contemporary novel, Mallarmé wraps up his discussion, characteristically, by finding the form inferior to the public poem of the future. What did he discern to be the proper subject matter for this future art form? "... c'est l'éternel retour de l'exilé, coeur gonflé d'espoir, au sol par lui quitté mais changé ingrat, maintenant quelconque au point qu'il en doive partir cette fois volontairement, où! enveloppant d'un coup d'oeil les illusions suggérées à sa jeunesse par le salut du lieu natal" (345) (it's the eternal return of the exile, heart swelling with hope, to the soil left by him but become ungrateful, now indifferent to the point that he must leave this time voluntarily, whither! enveloping with a glance the illusions suggested to his youth by the safety of the native place.)

The scholar of Mallarmé learned that the proper subject for the Great Work that would transcend the modern novel was the story of Ulysses. The second coincidence is similar. When Yeats, writing in 1898, predicted the application of Mallarmé's suggestive method to longer works, he had this to say:

> ... I think we will not cease to write long poems, but rather that we will write them more and more as our new belief makes the world plastic under our hands again. I think that we will learn again how to describe at great length an old man wandering among enchanted islands, his return home at last, his slow-gathering vengeance, a flitting shape of a goddess, and a flight of arrows, and yet to make all of these things "take light from mutual reflection, like an actual trail of fire over precious stones," the signature or symbol of a mood of the divine imagination as imponderable as "the horror of the forest or the silent thunder in the leaves." (378)

Joyce's *Ulysses* is a mock-epic, tongue-in-cheek realization of Yeats's prophecy, but it is a realization nonetheless, and the sense of art as the presentation of the "divine imagination" is not incompatible with Joyce's, and Mallarmé's, critical and anthropological "purification" of literature in search of its supreme expression in the Book.

Joyce aspired to be the rightful heir to Mallarmé's ambition to write "the book as world." He incorporated Mallarmé's literary and aesthetic theories and adopted his sense of uncompromising vocation. *Ulysses* embodies this integrity of vocation on every page, and in its architecture as a whole embodies the encyclopedic ambition to recreate "des relations entre tout" (378). The fact that *Ulysses* consists of a thousand times as many words as *Un Coup de Dés,* and that its minute depiction of material life in 1904 Dublin is utterly alien to Mallarmé's practical aesthetics, does not alter the fact that it expresses a life lived by the Mallarméan formula, "tout est fait pour aboutir à un beau livre" (all is made to end in a beautiful book).

Unlike Mallarmé, Joyce actually tried to write the Book a second time. *Finnegans Wake,* published in 1939, is patently the Mallarméan "Livre," with its impersonal hero, its circular, fourfold seasonal movement through the four Viconian ages, its supranational English, its indefinition of time and space, its fusion of the law of the world with the law of the mind, and its universalizing themes of hesitation, creation, persecution, and survival. With its historical and anthropological themes, it more clearly seeks to express "au monde, sa loi," and with its incorporation of sacred writing, seeks the status of a "bible comme la simulent les nations." R. G. Cohn developed this idea in his *L'Oeuvre de Mallarmé*. My purpose in this essay has been to show that in 1914, when he began *Ulysses,* Joyce was already aiming at the Mallarméan "texte véridique."

Notes

1. See Robert Greer Cohn, *L'Oeuvre de Mallarmé:* Un Coup de Dés (Paris: Librairie Les Lettres, 1951).

2. Stéphane Mallarmé, *Oeuvres complètes* (Paris: Gallimard-Pléiade, 1945), 456. (Unless otherwise indicated, subsequent references indicated within parentheses in the text.)

3. "Crise de vers," *OC,* 367.

4. See Marilyn French, *The Book As World: James Joyce's* Ulysses (Cambridge: Harvard University Press, 1976). French's excellent interpretation of *Ulysses* lays stress on Joyce's debt to Dante, but does not mention Mallarmé.

5. See "Contre un poëte parisien," *OC*, 20, or "Le Guignon," *OC*, 28.
6. Guy Michaud, *Mallarmé,* tr. Marie Collins and Bertha Humez (New York: New York University Press, 1965), 52–53.
7. Stéphane Mallarmé, *Correspondance, 1862–1871,* ed. Henri Mondor and Lloyd James Austin (Paris: Gallimard, 1959), 222, letter dated 16 July 1866. (Hereafter cited as *Corr.*)
8. *Corr.,* 224–25, letter dated 28 July 866.
9. *Corr.,* 242.
10. "Autobiographie," OC, 661.
11. Arthur Symons, *The Symbolist Movement in Literature* (London: Heinemann, 1899).
12. William Yeats, "The Autumn of the Body," in *Essays and Introductions* (New York: Collier Books, 1968), 193.
13. David Hayman, *Joyce et Mallarmé* (Paris: Les Lettres Modernes, 1956), 1:28.
14. Marshall McLuhan early recognized Joyce's debt to Mallarmé for a poetics of print: "Joyce, Mallarmé and the Press," *Sewanee Review* 62 (1954): 38–55. Charles Olson's theory of "composition by field" is a direct descendant of the ideas Mallarmé set out in his preface to *Un Coup de Dés*.
15. James S. Atherton, *Books at the Wake* (Carbondale: Southern Illinois University Press, 1974), 50.
16. In *A Portrait of the Artist as a Young Man,* Joyce depicts Stephen Dedalus earnestly, explaining his theory of genres, in which drama holds the highest place because "the artist, like the God of the creation, remains within or behind or beyond or above his handiwork, invisible, refined out of existence, paring his nails." This echoes *Crise de Vers,* where Mallarmé wrote that "the pure work implies the elocutionary disappearance of the poet." The passage rather shows Stephen fighting the same battles Mallarmé fought, for the liberty of art, than adopting Mallarmé's aesthetics.
17. *Hérodiade* and *Igitur* correlate closely with the Hamletic situation in which the hero, assailed by thoughts and ghosts, hesitates to act. Mallarmé also wrote a critical essay quoted in *Ulysses* as discussed below.
18. James Joyce, *Ulysses* (New York: Vintage Books, 1986), 153.
19. Joyce, 153–54.
20. The note appeared in the *Revue blanche* in 1896 and in the bibliography of *Divagations* in 1897.
21. At the Mallarmé Festival, John Felstiner remarked that *Ulysses* was many books. This is no doubt true, and does not exclude the hypothesis that Joyce adopted Mallarmé's sacred, microcosmic, and encyclopedic view of what his Book should be.
22. See Robert Greer Cohn, *L'Oeuvre de Mallarmé* and *Toward the Poems of Mallarmé* (Berkeley: University of California Press, 1980), 265–80.
23. Just as crucially, Joyce's encyclopedia of Dublin culture permits Joyce to perform the same kind of peripatetic urban anthropology that Mallarmé conducts in his critical writings. Stephen and Bloom, isolated Hamlets and students of the world they confront, examine contemporary attitudes, beliefs, and institutions in a continuous search for truth, beauty, and goodness. In this, they contrast starkly with many of their fellow citizens, who sacrifice their intelligence for easy applause, their aesthetic sense for current fashion, or their morality for the approbation of the group. If anything, Stephen and Bloom's individualistic sincerity in

seeking the highest human goods is Joyce's prescription for a world where "il n'est pas de Présent."

24. Joyce, 34.

25. See Stuart Gilbert, *James Joyce's Ulysses* (New York: Vintage Books, 1955), 211.

26. Joyce, 138.

27. Joyce, 573. Joyce was undoubtedly familiar with Rimbaud's U: "U vert . . . U, cycles, vibrements divins des mers virides, / Paix des pâtis semés d'animaux, paix des rides/ Que l'alchimie imprime aux grands fronts studieux." He may have agreed with the marine element of Rimbaud's U.

28. Perhaps Joyce shows a hieroglyphic mood when he places a giant S, a giant M, and a giant P on the opening pages of *Ulysses*'s three sections. The snakelike S for the sly sad son's introductory chapters? The mighty M for Bloom the Man, or for maternal Bloom who feeds Molly and their cat before setting out to shop and earn the daily bread? The pushy, paternal P for Bloom's homecoming, his protection of Stephen, his revenge and his demand for breakfast in bed? Or for Penelope? Professor Gabler's corrected edition drops these page-sized letters, so I am uncertain whether Joyce ordered them in the first instance.

29. Letter to Frank Budgen, 16 August 1921, in Richard Ellmann, ed., *Selected Letters of James Joyce* (New York: Viking, 1975), 285.

30. Joyce, 497.

31. Joyce, 200.

"Here we go round the prickly pear" or "Your song, what does it know?" Celan vis-à-vis Mallarmé

JOHN FELSTINER

PAUL Celan's name was first paired with that of Stéphane Mallarmé in an early review of Celan's début volume *Mohn und Gedächtnis* (1952), the collection that introduced a Jewish survivor-poet to German readers. In the respected monthly *Merkur*, Hans Egon Holthusen, an influential poet and critic, welcomed a talent that "translates certain principles of modern French lyric into the German language.... Here one sees language kindled not by an object confronting it, but by itself."[1] The book in question, it should be remembered, centered on Celan's relentless unappeasable "Todesfuge" (Deathfugue):

> Black milk of daybreak we drink it at evening
> we drink it at midday and morning we drink it at night
> we drink and we drink
> we shovel a grave in the air . . .[2]

Yet, Holthusen noted "unqualified arbitrary lyric fancy," "self-inspired, purely lexical configurations," "not meaning but form," "absolutely musical effects," "Mallarmé ... Mallarmé ... Mallarmé." This German critic saw Celan's gruesome theme (with its litany of "hounds" and "iron rod" and "shot made of lead") "escaping history's bloody chamber of horrors to rise into the ether of pure poetry."

Purity, after a "Thousand Year Reich" and its "Final Solution" had abused the German language, Celan certainly sought in his poetry. But already in 1954 he felt the implacable cadences of "Deathfugue," grounded as they were in exile and genocide, being aestheticized, absorbed by the Bundesrepublik's postwar efforts at *Vergangenheitsbewältigung* (overcoming the past). He felt constrained to steel his verse against such appropriation. "Sprich auch du" (speak you too), he wrote right after the *Merkur* review in a kind of manifesto to himself, "Wahr spricht, wer Schatten spricht" (Give your say this meaning too: / give it the shadow. / . . . Speaks true who speaks shadow).

Given Mallarmé's revolutionary banishment of the real world from his poetry, and given the facile designation of his work as *poésie pure* by proponents of *poésie engagée,* the idea that Paul Celan might translate Mallarmé comes fraught with interest.

By 1953, Celan, living in Paris, had translated Yvan Goll, Aimé Césaire, and André Breton, and was beginning a long affiliation with Guillaume Apollinaire. Later in the 1950s, he translated Baudelaire, Nerval, Rimbaud, Éluard, Desnos, Artaud, and Char, as well as Shakespeare, Marvell, Dickinson, Frost, and Marianne Moore. Meanwhile, from Russian, the language imbibed during two Soviet occupations of his hometown Czernowitz, Celan translated Blok, Esenin, and, above all, Osip Mandelshtam (1891–1938). It was with Mandelshtam, who perished in Siberian exile as a poet and as a Jew, that in 1958 Celan had what he then began calling a *Begegnung,* an "encounter" that verged on blood brotherhood.

Another signal encounter, though far removed from the affinity Celan felt for Mandelshtam, occurred around that time with the poetry of Paul Valéry. He made a full version of *La Jeune Parque* (The Young Fate), over five hundred rhymed German alexandrines that mainly adhere to the French. But in his rendering—or rending—of the opening verse, Celan declares his independence from the poem that Valéry called an "exercise," "perfectly useless and released from time."[3]

> Qui pleure là, sinon le vent simple, à cette heure / Seule
>
> [Who weeps there, if not the simple wind, at this hour / Alone]
>
> Wer, so der Wind nicht, er nur, weint hier, zur Stunde, die / allein ist
>
> [Who, if not the wind, it only, weeps here, at this hour, which / is alone]
>
> (4:114)

Celan's hatchetlike caesuras yield six segments as against Valéry's three—an act of doubling whereby difference in translation becomes defiance.

Facing poets he esteemed absolutely, such as Mandelshtam and Shakespeare, along with Apollinaire and Dickinson, Celan appears anything but cowed, compliant. In fact, he translated them with a penetrating idiosyncrasy amounting to possession. Mallarmé's remarkable renditions of Poe come to mind, and his own line opening "Le Tombeau d'Edgar Poe"—"Tel qu'en Lui-même enfin l'éternité le change" (Such as into himself at last eternity transforms him) might be paraphrased to point up the transmutative effect, the originative hold, that strong translators have on their chosen poet: "Tel qu'en Soi-même enfin le traducteur le change."

The encounter, the confronting, that poses Celan vis-à-vis Mallarmé involves bottomless questions of literary representation, and especially questions about postwar European lyric. Because Celan's German mother tongue suddenly turned brutally into the murderers' tongue, he took on the task of writing poems that might themselves purge this same language by their strange newness. Mallarmé's recognition of Poe for purifying common speech, "donner un sens plus pur aux mots de la tribu," applies to Celan a century later with unpredictable force.

Although Celan translated only one brief lyric by Mallarmé, sometime during 1958 that single point of tangency touches off many recognitions. For in 1958, he was seeking, as he said in his Bremen speech that year, "to orient myself, to find out where I was and where I was meant to go, to sketch out reality for myself" (3:186). This speech, Celan's first major statement on poetry and all the more critical for being spoken to German listeners, focuses on language as the only thing "amid the losses" that was "not lost" to him: "But it had to pass through its own answerlessnesses, pass through frightful muting, pass through the thousand darknesses of deathbringing speech." And he stressed, perhaps with Mallarmé in mind, that "a poem is not timeless. Certainly it lays claim to infinity, it seeks to reach through time—through it, not above and beyond it."

Later in 1958 Celan wrote to a critic, "Es geht mir nicht um Wohllaut, es geht mir um Wahrheit" (My concern is not euphony, it's truth).[4] And that same year, in a Paris bookshop's almanac, he began an outspoken paragraph this way: "The German lyric is moving, I believe, along other paths than the French" (1:167). Granted, Celan was speaking of postwar poetry, but he ends up distinguishing himself partially from Mallarmé. "With the most dismal things in its memory, and dubiousness all around it," Celan says, German poetic language "has grown more sober, more factual, it mistrusts 'Beauty,' it attempts to be true." Recalling to mind those "most frightful things" that must now constrain postwar poetry, Celan goes on: "It does not transfigure, does not 'poetize' ... it is never language itself, mere language at work, but always an I speaking from a particular angle of inclination, its own existence ... reality must be sought and won."

Those constraints, emerging from loss, exile, and mass death, show up tellingly in Celan's poetry of the late 1950s. "Snowfall, thicker and thicker," he begins a poem called "Homecoming" (1955), where "the sleigh track of what's lost" conveys "an I slid into muteness" back to the Ukrainian winter in which his parents perished (1:156). Celan's phrase, "ichter und dichter" (thicker and thicker), could also be "denser and denser," as it plays on *Dichter* (poet), suggesting a poetry now chillingly, fatally concentrated to snow.

Another poem, from New Year's 1958, goes back to "Round graves" within a landscape of primal geologic space and time:

> Lavas, basalts, worldheart-
> red-heated stone.
> Wellspring tuff,
> where light grew for us, before
> breath.

(1:184)

Like tuff itself, a rock formed by consolidated volcanic ash, the German here compacts, hardens, seeking the historically least corrupted, most primal state of language, even "before breath."

In view of such stringency, Paul Celan chose to translate one of Stéphane Mallarmé's two rondels, a lyric form with thirteen lines but only two rhyme sounds, the first two lines recurring in the middle and line one at the end:

Si tu veux nous nous aimerons	Willst du's, solls die Liebe sein,
Avec tes lèvres sans le dire	Du, dein Mund, wir sagens nicht,
Cette rose ne l'interromps	Schenkst der Rose Schweigen ein,
Qu'à verser un silence pire	Bittrer, so du's unterbrichst.
Jamais de chants ne lancent prompts	Lieder, willig, schicken kein
Le scintillement du sourire	Lächeln, sprühen uns kein Licht,
Si tu veux nous nous aimerons	Willst du's, solls die Liebe sein,
Avec tes lèvres sans le dire	Du, dein Mund, wir sagens nicht.
Muet muet entre les ronds	Stumm-und-stumm, hier zwischenein,
Sylphe dans le pourpre d'empire	Sylphe, purpurn, kaiserlich,
Un baiser flambant se déchire	Flammt ein Kuss, schon teilt er sich

Jusqu'aux pointes des ailerons
Si tu veux nous nous aimerons.

Flügelspitzen flackern, fein,
Willst du's, solls die Liebe sein.

(4:817)

[If you wish we'll love each other
With your lips without saying it
This rose do not break into it
Only to pour out worse silence

Never do songs release right off
The scintillation of a smile
If you wish we'll love each other
With your lips without saying it

Mute and mute between the rondures
Sylph in purple imperial
A flaming kiss will rend itself
Out to its utmost pinion points
If you wish we'll love each other]

[If you wish, it shall be love,
You, your mouth, we'll say it not,
Pour out silence for the rose,
Bitterer, if you break in.

Songs, all willing, yield up no
Smiling, sparkle us no light,
If you wish, it shall be love,
You, your mojth, we'll say it not.

Mute-and-mute, here in between,
Sylph, purple, imperial,
Flames a kiss, now splits itself,
Pinion points, flickering, fine,
If you wish, it shall be love.]

Whatever else transpires here, Celan concentrates Mallarmé's already restrained eight-syllable line into seven syllables. It seems fitting to keep that difference in literal English versions of the French and German poems.

But what really is the relation between those English versions, when my version of Celan's German "Rondel" in fact constitutes a reversion or retroversion? Genetically speaking, Celan's German translation of Mallarmé stands in the same relation to the French original as does my English translation of Mallarmé. They are siblings. Thus, a further translation of Celan's German occurs in the next generation. At the same time, for the American reader, the two English versions provide a heuristic vis-à-vis. It all becomes rather complex. Perhaps these two rondels and their (hélas!) unrhymed kin form most interestingly a sort of circle, another rondel, testing the metamorphic possibilities of poetry in translation. Of course, it is always the French that resounds against silence, and the German that strongly refracts that sound.

Even while slightly curtailing Mallarmé's verses, Celan repeatedly interrupts them (as if defying the Master's "Cette rose ne l'interromps"). Where there was only one mark of punctuation in the French, a stop at the end, the German version enters 28 commas and periods—signs of essential rupture, of fluency lost. And in place of perfect rhymes, Celan devises a triple slant rhyme: "nicht" / "brichst" / "sich." What's more, Mallarmé's refrain rhymes on "aimerons" and "dire," on love and speaking, but Celan introduces "sein" and "nicht," being and nothingness —

quite another emphasis. And whereas "nous nous aimerons" has the speakers swearing love, "wir sagens nicht" gives to that "we" the task of not speaking.

Translating poets that mattered for him, Celan often came on or came up with words that carried extra charge within his own German lexical economy—in this rondel: "mouth," "say," "not," "rose," "silence," "bitter," "song," "light," "mute." With Shakespeare, for instance, he kept lifelong contact, translating the sonnets in his youth, then in the ghetto and in labor camps. On the Bard's four hundredth anniversary in 1964, he published a collection under the title (from sonnet 1) *Die Rose Schönheit soll nicht sterben* (The rose [of] beauty must not die). Roses, for Shakespeare an emblem of fading youth and perishable beauty, take on for Celan the unprecedented mortality of "that which happened" between 1939 and 1945, as he put it in his Bremen speech. Thus, a key poem, "Psalm," centers on "die Nichts-, die / Niemandsrose" (1:225) (the Nothing-, the / No One's-Rose).

With Mallarmé, then, it is not surprising to see a kind of spasm in the German version when "rose" occurs in French. If the rondel suggests a kiss between lovers—"Cette rose ne l'interromps / Qu'à verser un silence pire"—Celan in some way exacerbates the issue: "Schenkst der Rose Schweigen ein, / Bittrer..."). The pouring of silence stays close to the original rondel, but when you would have thought that Mallarmé's "pire" was bad enough, Celan's "Bittrer" lends extra stress. Likewise in stanza two: "Jamais de chants ne lancent prompts / Le scintillement du sourire." In Celan's German, "scintillation" and "smile" get disjoined, so that his "songs" —poetry being all that was left him, his only raison d'être—not only "yield up no smiling," they also "sparkle us no light" after the thousand darknesses of deathbringing speech.

Celan's opting to engage with Mallarmé in a rondel, a richly harmonious form, implies already that the question of music will be at stake. His prosody in stanza two even overcharges the case, with its fourfold alliteration "Lieder ... Lächeln ... Licht ... Liebe" (and later another, more uncalled-for: "Flammt ... Flügelspitzen ... flackern ... fein"). What most exposes a skew in translation, though, is the simple yet elusive verse beginning the last stanza: "Muet muet entre les ronds" (mute mute between the rounds). Possibly it figures a quietness between the lips of a kiss, mirrored by Mallarmé's doubled "Muet muet" and the mouth-rounded open "o" in "ronds." For a moment here, at the songlike heart of this poem, a small miracle occurs as form and substance speak in one breath: the rondel voices rondure.

Nothing songlike, however, mates the German to the French:

Muet muet entre les ronds   Stumm-und-stumm, hier zwischenein,

[Mute and mute between   [Mute-and-mute, here in between,]
  the rondures]

In February 1958 Celan began a long, musically shaped successor to "Deathfugue" entitled "Stretto," whose verse leads with graphic literality toward "that which happened." At one point we hear:

> Came came.
> Came a word, came,
> came through the night,
> would lighten, would lighten.
>
> Ashes.
>
> Ashes, Ashes.
> Night.
> Night-and-Night.

(1:199)

Like "Nacht-und-Nacht," "Stumm-und-stumm" in Celan's "Rondel" forms a strange locution —not fluent, not euphonious, challenging a key word by forcing it chock-a-block against itself. During the war, his 1958 Bremen speech claims, language had to "furchtbares Verstummen" (pass through frightful muting).

It is as if Celan could not hear "muet" as Mallarmé uttered it, but only in the echo hamber of his own mind. Just around the time he translated "Rondel," he also did a strong version of Marvell's "To His Coy Mistress" —except that Celan made his own title "An seine stumme Geliebte" (To his mute mistress). The French have a saying that strong translations are *les belles infidèles*, beautiful and ipso facto unfaithful. Apart from its invidious assumption, that formula does not hold for Celan, whose most idiosyncratic renderings become faithful in their fashion. An early lyric of his says as much, though in the context of an I-Thou love relation: "Ich bin du, wenn ich ich bin" (2:33) (Faithless only am I true. / I am you, when I am I). German even has a term for translation that "makes it new" (in Pound's sense): *Umdichtung,* where *um-*

indicates a poem that goes "round about" the original or does it "over again" or "in another way." T.S. Eliot, for instance, hearing a hollowness in the repetition and circularity of Mallarmé's central line "Muet muet entre les ronds," might have made it: "Here we go round the prickly pear" —with eight syllables just like the French.

Besides his version of "Rondel," which appeared in the Insel Almanach for 1959, Celan addressed Mallarmé on only one other occasion. His 1960 "Meridian" speech distinguishes *Kunst* (art) from *Dichtung* (poetry): Is the point "to enlarge art"? Celan asks. "No. But with art go into your very selfmost straits. And set yourself free" (3:200). Given that distinction, Celan asks elsewhere in his speech: "May we, as happens in many places now, proceed from Art as from something already given, something we unconditionally assume, should we, to put it quite concretely, above all— let's say—be thinking Mallarmé through to the end?" (3:193). More an open than an obviously rhetorical question, thinking Mallarmé through to the end would still, for Celan, probably lead to a vanishing point rather than to a setting free of poetry via its selfmost straits. After the "Meridian" speech, Celan told a friend who had translated all those Valéry alexandrines "so as to earn the right to say something *against art*" (gegen die Kunst), and the emphasis is Celan's.[5]

Paul Celan did once think Mallarmé through to the end by way of a 1964 lyric, "Keine Sandkunst mehr":

> No more sand art, no sand book, no masters.
> Nothing on the dice. How many
> mutes?
>
> Seventeen.
>
> Your question—your answer.
> Your song, what does it know?
>
> Deepinsnow,
>
>   Eepinnow,
>   E—i—o.
>
>   (2:39)

Even before taking in the words here, we might see their disposition on a white page —the isolated "mutes"? that is, the staggered ending —as a visual echo of Mallarmé's typography in *Un Coup de Dés*. Then, right away that word *Kunst* (used for the first time by Celan in a poem)—or rather, "No more" *Kunst* —sets this lyric athwart a tradition. No art, no book, no masters, and "Nothing on the dice": These negations reject any aestheticism for a desert people whose seed was to multiply "as the sand of the sea" but instead ran out in the hourglass.

"Your song, what does it know?" Celan's question turns in midpoem from the *Maître* Mallarmé toward himself: "Dein Gesang, was weiss er?" And not sand now but snow packs the terrain, stifling breath itself:

> Tiefimschnee,
>   Iefimnee,
>   I—i—e.

While Rimbaud's *voyelles* reveal their *naissances latentes* (latent births), Celan's almost die out. They do indeed die out if translated into Hebrew, which has no vowel letters. What does this song know? Only that after "The Final Solution to the Jewish Question," words verge on silence within the Jews' founding and their sometimes saving language.

Celan vis-à-vis Mallarmé: They may well remain akin in the sense of a reality to be sought only in —or through —the language of poems, disjunct from familiar utterance. But between their facing pages fall "the thousand darknesses of deathbringing speech."

Notes

1. Hans Egon Holthusen, "Fünf junge Lyriker," *Merkur* 8, no. 74 (spring 1954): 378–90.
2. Paul Celan, *Gesammelte Werke,* ed. Beda Allemann and Stefan Reichert, with Rolf Bücher (Frankfurt: Suhrkamp Verlag, 1983), 1:41. This five–volume edition is hereafter referred to in parentheses in the text by volume and page number. All translations from Celan and other sources are mine.
3. Leonard Moore Olschner, *Der feste Buchstab: Erläuterungen zu Paul Celans Gedichtübertragungen* (Göttingen: Vandenhoeck and Ruprecht, 1985), 183.
4. Letter to Jean Firges, 2 December 1958, in Firges, "Sprache und Sein in der Dichtung Paul Celans," *Muttersprache* 72, no. 9 (1962): 266.
5. Otto Pöggeler, *Spur des Worts: Zur Lyrik Paul Celans* (Freiburg: K. Alber, 1986), 121. Gerhart Baumann, *Erinnerungen an Paul Celan* (Frankfurt: Suhrkamp Verlag, 1986), 85, quotes Celan towards the end of his life as saying: "Mallarmé —das ist auch ein Fetish!" (Mallarmé —that too is a fetish!)

Mallarmé and Germany
Gerald Gillespie

THIS selective glimpse concerns German poetic modernism.[1] The bilingual poet Yvan Goll has provided us a valuable statement that clearly dates the apogee of the Mallarméan example as occurring at the juncture when Expressionism was overlapping with and displacing Symbolism in German arts and letters. Written under the shadow of the ending First World War and published in 1919 in Kasimir Edschmid's pro-Expressionist series *Tribüne der Kunst und Zeit* (Tribune of Art and the Times), Goll's three-part essay "Die drei guten Geister Frankreichs" (France's Three Good Spirits) extols Diderot's seminal role at the boundary of Romanticism, and Cézanne and Mallarmé as pathbreaking renewers who pushed beyond the achievements of Romanticism and the nineteenth century.[2] A measure of Goll's atunement to modernism is that in Switzerland, during the war, he founded the Rhein Verlag, which published the first German translation of Joyce's *Ulysses*. Readers can consult William Carpenter's remarks on affinities between Mallarmé and Joyce for a better understanding of this symptomatic linkage.[3] It exceeds my scope here to detail what Goll understood in 1919 by his own view of Expressionism as a modern approach that should benefit from the recovery of the insights of Novalis and Hölderlin, and should mean "Heute wie zur Romantik: Kniefall vor dem Unfaßbaren, Auflösung des Ich, weil es durch wissenschaftliche Erkenntnis zu konkret und zu irdisch geworden" (46) (today as in Romanticism genuflection before the ungraspable, the dissolution of the ego, because it has become too concrete and earthly through scientific cognition). More pertinent here is his dictum that Mallarmé is "der Cézanne der Dichtung" (the Cézanne of poetry), and that "Das Wort wurde seine Urmaterie, der Keim seiner Welten" (the word became his primal material, the embryo of his worlds), and "Das Wort wurde zur eigenen Persönlichkeit erhoben, mit eigenem Gesetz ausgestattet" (66–67) (was elevated to its own personality, outfitted with its own laws).

This reference to Cézanne will instantly bring to mind the great cosmopolitan Cézanne-idolator Rainer Maria Rilke, who stated his yearning to write poems the way the Provençal master painted. And indeed Rilke has left us fine renditions of Mallarmé's "Autre Éventail de Mademoiselle Mallarmé" and of "Tombeau: Anniversaire—Janvier 1897,"[4] honoring Verlaine, both German versions being published at the very start of the twenties soon after Goll's tribute.[5] But there is no evidence of devotion to Mallarmé on the part of the younger Rilke during his considerable sojourns in Paris. What is striking, rather, is the keen instinct drawing the mature Rilke to poems that contain the key Mallarméan term "pli" ("Falte" in German, cognate with English "fold"). As we can plainly see from *Die Aufzeichnungen des Malte Laurids Brigge* (The Notebooks of Malte Laurids Brigge), Rilke's 1910 novel set in turn-of-the-century Paris, as well as from innumerable other sources, he was so thoroughly steeped in the French poetic tradition and in contemporary currents of French arts and letters that he absorbed the major lessons of the Mallarméan turn through multiple channels by a general osmosis. Paul Valéry, with five complete poems done into German by Rilke in the twenties, obviously plays a proportionately bigger role in the foreground as a post-Mallarméan force for the author of the *Sonette an Orpheus* (Sonnets to Orpheus) and the *Duineser Elegien* (Duino Elegies).[6] Perhaps, having reached our own fin-de-siècle, we finally can accept francophile Rilke's own view of himself not as a German or a Praguer, but as a good European who wrote primarily in German. Rilke was gifted linguistically and turned his hand to translation on a number of occasions, reaching across to Italian, English, and even Danish and Swedish. During his lifetime, he occasionally wrote poems in other languages, including Russian; in his latter, years he wrote hundreds of poems in French. Thus, it is not illegitimate to think of him as a foreign cousin with his own profile, yet bearing some unmistakable Mallarméan familial traits.

Betokening a new stage of breakthrough, the decade of Rilke's brilliant final flowering also saw the first significant wave of critical commentaries on Mallarmé by German scholars, such as Franz Rauhut, Franz Nobiling, and Walter Naumann.[7] In *The Fictions of the Poet: From Mallarmé to the Post-Symbolist Mode*, Anna Balakian draws incentives for the interpretation of specific Rilkean poems from the longer range pattern of the German poet's development. Placing Rilke (chap. 5) in a comparative context alongside Valéry (chap. 4), Yeats (chap. 6), Stevens (chap. 7), and Guillén (chap. 8), she argues persuasively that the fact it took a generation for his Mallarméan traits to mature and that Valéry served as a catalyst and filter in no way detracts from the deeper affinity to Mallarmé, most evident in the *Sonnets* and the *Elegies*.[8] In addition to Rilke's break from Romantic and Parnassian roots in his turn toward the world of things and the image around the time of his association with Rodin, Balakian sees a second, intermittent but progressive, turn from the "image" (Bild) to the "figure" (Figur). "Figure" is caught in suggestive motion, in such guises as the dancer, rider, acrobat, or blossoming tree, and through mythic embodiments of transformation and movement between realms like Orpheus, archetype of the poet. Art becomes the famous "double realm" (Doppelbereich) where inner spaces can exist because, and in the way, language enacts them. Over the past two decades, a scholarly consensus has clearly formed on the affinity of Rilke's sense of the game or play of language to Mallarmé's.[9]

Curiously, Stefan George, the major pioneer who introduced Mallarmé to the leading poetic spirits of Germany at the turn of the century, despite many affinities, extensive sharing of vocabulary traits and motifs, and a personal relationship, emits a tonality that today may no longer resonate as being proximate to the admired French master in the degree that Rilke sometimes appears to be. This judgment says nothing, however, about the individual merits of these three distinct, independent talents. Nine years senior to Rilke, George, too, occasionally composed in other languages and was an avid, excellent translator—really more productive than Rilke if we consider that he took on no less than Shakespeare's sonnets, Dante's *La Divina Commedia,* Baudelaire's *Les Fleurs du Mal,* and many dozens of poems deriving from Danish, Dutch, English, French, Italian, Norwegian, Polish, and Spanish.[10] George's acquaintance with Flemish as well as French Symbolists was outstanding, and francophone Symbolist critics reciprocated his interest with notices of his efforts, beginning with the new Parisian review *L'Ermitage,* which carried translations by Albert Saint-Paul of two of George's poems from *Hymnen* (Hymns), "Métamorphoses" (Verwandlungen), and "Rivage" (Strand), as early as 1891. When a committee comprising Leconte de Lisle, Heredia, Sully Prudhomme, Verhaeren, Huysmans, and other luminaries was formed under Mallarmé to erect a monument to Baudelaire, George was the sole German invited as a member.[11]

Verlaine, with a score of published German versions by George's hand, outweighs both Rimbaud with three and Mallarmé with four, purely by count. But if we take a look at which Mallarméan works the young George transcribed for himself—a list including "Apparition," "Sainte," "Surgi de la croupe," "Prose pour Des Esseintes," *L'Après-Midi d'un Faune, Hérodiade,* and "Hommage à Wagner"—we are struck by his sure judgment and range. It was George's temperamental gift to be a preceptor. His energy and will acting as a catalyst in the modernization of German poetry in the Symbolist direction opposed to Naturalism, more than any specific poems, brought him closer in spirit to Mallarmé at a crucial moment for German poetic culture. George's programmatic statements in *Blätter für die Kunst* (Folio for Art), the magazine he started in 1892,[12] make it clear why he sought out Mallarmé during his Paris sojourn in 1889 and why the French master kept in touch with him by letter during the nineties. In a letter of 1897 to George, aglow with respect for him as "Meister," the junior Rilke, who had attended a George reading in Berlin, averred his allegiance to the goals expressed in *Blätter für die Kunst*.[13] In Rilke's Nachlaß from the same period are two poems dedicated to George and the new poetic ethos.[14] Volume five of the first series of *Blätter für die Kunst* carried George's cogent panegyric study of Mallarmé in 1893 and some samples of verses from *Hérodiade* and the *Après-Midi d'un Faune*. Most important for its impact on the modernist threshold was George's tangible representation of newer models beginning with his own verses from *Algabal* in volume one of *Blätter* in 1892. George was then still under the strong influence of Baudelaire, the first batch of whose *Fleurs du Mal* in translation he had issued in a limited handwritten edition in 1891. Volume two of *Blätter* also carried translations by George of Mallarmé's "Brise marine" and "Frisson d'hiver," as well as of Verlaine, Moréas, and Régnier.

Without derogation from the German "Seebrise" of 1892 (Mallarmé's "Brise marine"), I would emphasize the cardinal importance of George's return to the prose-poem in "Winterschauer" (Mallarmé's "Frisson d'hiver") as a means to repristinate native poetic roots. George could not have failed to recognize that German Romanticism had exhibited powerful experimental impulses in the creation of poems in prose, but that this initiative had passed to Baudelaire and Mallarmé in the second half of the nineteenth century and the prose-poem had evolved into a supple vehicle of modern sensibility in their hands. He greatly admired Mallarmé's *Hérodiade* and eventually published his own recreative rendition or "Umdichtung" (poetic recasting) based on it.[15] This attention that George called to French and Belgian Symbolist poet-playwrights, above all Mallarmé, and the example of the monologues of his own character Algabal and a selection from his own play *Manuel,* reinforced the inspiration of another early George admirer, the young Hugo von Hofmannsthal. Hofmannsthal published *Der Tor und der Tod* (Death and the Fool), one of the most important German lyrical dramas in the Symbolist vein, in 1893, and he appeared in volume three of *Blätter* in the same year with a dramatic idyll in a Böcklin setting. After relations with George ceased in 1906, a broader public was to enjoy further fruits of Symbolist dramatic expression through Hofmannsthal's collaboration as librettist with Richard Strauss. On the significance of Mallarmé for the theater, I refer you to the essay by Charles Lyons in this volume.[16] I would like to underscore how clearly the new direction emerges also as a programmatic matter in George's magazine, for example, in Carl August Klein's essay "Das Theatralische" (The Theatrical) in series one, volume four, which in 1893 firmly asserts that the lyrical element will rule the coming epoch and, until the theater public and institutions are transformed, plays of genius will have to remain closet pieces for reading.

There is another kind of relationship that deserves mention although it is more difficult to trace or describe, and that is the heritage Mallarmé bequeathed to Europe by way of specific whole works that through their themes and spirit influenced chains of artists in a general sharing until a work's substance, in effect, became built into literature at large as a kind of second nature. My favorite example is a special moment in Thomas Mann's *Der Zauberberg* (The Magic Mountain) of 1924 when Hans Castorp has entered the dangerous seventh stage and year of his hermetic-alchemical education. Pent-up feelings and saturnine melancholy pose a grave threat to his survival as an ominous storm gathers over Europe. In a gesture that we may rightly associate with those high modernists such as Mallarmé and Joyce, who create in full awareness of death and nothingness, Mann has Hans listen to the human spirit as it emerges from the mysterious contemporary nowhere, out of the grammaphone as if from a coffin. In the subchapter "Fülle des Wohllauts" (Fullness of Harmony), Hans communes with his own accrued insights in a vocabulary that consists of entire works of art, principally operas. In thinking with these "words"—Gérard Genette would call them hypertexts—he arrives at affirmation in the pit of despair. The main progression, which I foreshorten here, leads us from Offenbach's *Orphée* and *Gaîté Parisienne* by way of Mozart's *Don Giovanni* and Puccini's *La Bohème,* to Hans's deep response to Verdi's *Aida,* a play and music that affirms human love and life's heroicism from the tomb; and then we reach the recaptitulative juxtaposition of Bizet's *Carmen* and Gounod's *Faust*.

Mann composes the suite of these directly cited compositions in narrative terms, but with constant cross-reference among the arts, including painting, as if he is engaged in a long Proustian orchestration in which the complex response of the modern mind to entire works provides the materials of motivic bridging and development. By this late juncture in the novel, we have grounds for being confident that some deepest human truth binds the fluctuating levels in the special poetic register here to the many other registers which, as Hans has discovered in his voracious studies and maturing oberservations, comprise the awesome repertory of culture. The "musical" logic of this suite in the prose narrative would fail were it not for the presence of Mallarmé's *L'Après-Midi d'un Faune* at a crucial point. Mallarmé's work appears as a redemptive satyr-piece to assuage the terror present alongside the heroism in the meditating character's (and outer ironic narrator's) appreciation of *Aida,* and this interlude allows humane, conscious, and moral reentry into the Bizet (*Carmen*) and Gounod (*Faust*) themes and our approach to the mysterious death-allurement of the "Lindenbaum" song without surrender to the abyss.

By a magical hermetic act, Mann reappropriates the Mallarméan text out of the interior of Debussy's orchestral *Prélude* of 1892 which, so the narrator's mediating voice attests, has "von konzentriertem Zauber war" (a concentrated power of enchantment). "Ein Idyll, aber ein raffiniertes Idyll, gemalt und gestaltet mit dem zugleich sparsamen und entwickelten Mitteln neuester Kunst" (this "idyll," yet *raffiné*, shaped and turned with all the subtlety and economy of the most modern art) has the power to set "die Seele in Traum zu spinnen" (his spirit a-dreaming).[17] But this is now, despite everything, and out of inner need, a lighter dream than that of the earlier "Schnee" (Snow) subchapter, which was also unleashed by musical memories. Imaginatively, as narrated by indirection in the third person, Hans becomes the faun whose gazing at the nymphs we otherwise already know through the first-person voice of a consciousness that asks, in Mallarmé's poem, "Aimais-je un rêve?" Mann has already prepared the connection through Hans's earlier profound experience of affirmation in arriving at his notion of "ein Traumgedicht vom Menschen" (the dream poem of humanity) and resisting the appeal of death in the snow.[18] Fleetingly, as the faun, Hans gets to play those ancient pipes and to participate "für einen flüchtigen Augenblick, dessen wonnevoll-vollkommenes Genügen aber die Ewigkeit in sich trug. Der junge Faun war sehr glücklich auf seiner Sommerwiese" (in a single fugitive moment that yet held all eternity in its consummate bliss. The young faun was joyous on his summer meadow).[19] I cannot find any direct testimony from the artistic kleptomaniac Mann that he actually studied Mallarmé's text intensively or reread it around the time of writing this passage, but we have reason to suspect so because of several points of thematic convergence, including the complex framing of the vision.

What is striking about this page-long interlude in a crisis that Mann poses by translating psychohistorical forces into the orchestral and operatic terms of European culture in the throes of modernism is that the faun motifs appear suddenly in the narrative flux much as, historically, that breathtaking, luminous vision came to us in the late nineteenth century in Mallarmé's text. Mann is plumbing the intertangled questions of the meaning of Europe's passage through so-called decadence, the opening of an abyss with World War I, and the purpose of contemporary artistic consciousness in the face of this trauma. But he celebrates the survival of the Edenic memory. No matter how perplexed the human spirit may have grown in the fin-de-siècle, art remains a liberating gift of humanity. While George strives for the strong, clean qualities of repristinated language and image that we admire in Mallarmé, here, in the post-Symbolist twenties, Mann again grasps for that fundamental Edenic vision, the site of an innocence regained despite everything, even by a mind that sees itself in the mirror.

This is a nurturing insight that flashes in Mallarmé's poetry as surely as the "glaive sûr" of "L'Azur" pierces the bereft poet's heart and mind. The Edenic memory gives answer in the midst of the loss of trust in the flesh and under the burden of having read all the books. We can easily draw up a list of correspondences between Mallarméan and Mannian themes, which can seem to be negative, or at least ambivalent. One example must suffice here: The idea that the Western mind and art amount to a self-poisoning, but ambiguously, because they are a kind of daring inoculation by truth. We hear this in Mallarmé's sonnet, which celebrates the "shadow" of Baudelaire; we imbibe his poetry as "un poison tutélaire / Toujours à respirer si nous en périssons" (a tutelary poison / To be breathed over and over again even if we perish from it). I would suggest that there is much to be gained in devoting more attention to such thematic fundamentals as the rescue of faith from the abyss, and the spiritual pleasure in the final innocence of our origins, despite our exile from Eden.

Notes

1. The broader story is recounted in Enid Lowry Duthie, *L'Influence du symbolisme français dans le renouveau poétique de l'Allemagne: Les "Blätter für die Kunst" de 1892 à 1900* (1933; reprint, Geneva: Slatkine, 1974).
2. Iwan [Yvan] Goll, "Die drei guten Geister Frankreichs," *Tribüne der Kunst*, V (1919; reprint, Nendeln Liechtenstein: Kraus Reprint, 1973). Unless otherwise noted, all translations are mine.
3. William Carpenter, *Death and Marriage: Structural Metaphors for the Work of Art in Joyce and Mallarmé* (New York and London: Garland, 1988).
4. Citations in French follow the Pléiade edition: Stéphane Mallarmé, *Oeuvres complètes*, ed. Henri Mondor and G. Jean-Aubry (Paris: Gallimard-Pléiade, 1945).
5. Rainer Maria Rilke, *Ausgewählte Werke*, ed. Ruth Sieber-Rilke, Carl Sieber, and Ernst Zinn, vol. 2: *Prosa und Übertragungen* (Leipzig: Insel-Verlag, 1938), 359–60.
6. A still invaluable outline of the gathering influence of French poetry on Rilke, a process that lasted well past the first major moment of George's example in Germany, is Kurt Wais, "German Poets in the Proximity of Baudelaire and the Symbolists," in *The Symbolist Movement in the Literature of European Languages*, ed. Anna Balakian (Budapest: Akadémiai Kiadó, 1982), 145–56. This second volume in the series, A Comparative History of Literatures in European Languages, sponsored by the International Comparative Literature Association, remains the indispensable global reference work.
7. E.g., Rauhut's *Das Romantische und Musikalische in der Lyrik Stéphane Mallarmés* (Marburg, 1926); and Naumann's pioneering *Der Sprachgebrauch Mallarmés* (Marburg, 1936). Cf. the account of reception in Lloyd James Austin, "Presence and Poetry of Stéphane Mallarmé: International Reputation and Intellectual Impact," in *The Symbolist Movement*, 43–63.
8. Anna Balakian, *The Fiction of the Poet: From Mallarmé to the Post-Symbolist Mode* (Princeton, N.J.: Princeton University Press, 1992).
9. For example, Ursula Franklin, "Mallarmé's Living Metaphor: Valéry's Athikté and Rilke's 'Spanish Dancer,'" in *Pre-Text/Text/Context*, ed. Robert L. Mitchell (Columbus: Ohio State University Press, 1980); and Anita Rosenblithe, "Moving Space: Mallarmé's 'jeux circonvolontoires' in Rilke's *Sonette an Orpheus*," *Comparative Literature Studies* 33 (1996): 141–60.
10. Stefan George, *Gesamtausgabe der Werke, endgültige Fassung*, 18 vols. (Berlin: Georg Bondi, 1927–34), vols. 15 and 16, *Zeitgenössische Dichter: Übertragungen*, gather his renditions of European contemporaries.
11. A useful chronicle and documentation of this relationship is given in the exhibition volume, *Stefan George und der Symbolismus: Eine Austellung der Württembergischen Landesbibliothek Stuttgart*, ed. Werner Paul Sohnle (Stuttgart: Württembergischen Landesbibliothek, 1983).
12. *Blätter für die Kunst*, begründet von Stefan George, herausgeben von Carl August Klein (1892–1919; reprint, Düsseldorf and Munich: Verlag Helmut Küpper vormals Georg Bondi, 1967). For an indexed treatment of the principles

and contents, see Karlhans Kluncker, *Blätter für die Kunst: Zeitschrift der Dichterschule Stefan Georges* (Frankfurt am Main: Vittorio Klostermann, 1974).

13. Sohnle, 24.

14. Having the appearance of fragments of two sonnets, these products of the Berlin-Wilmersdorf period 1897–98 bear the title "An Stephan George," in Rainer Maria Rilke, *Sämmtliche Werke,* ed. Ernst Zinn et al. (Leipzig: Insel-Verlag, 1963), 3:596–97.

15. *Gesamt-Ausgabe,* 16:37–44.

16. Also consult the section "Connection with Symbolist Drama" (458–63) in Gerald Gillespie, "The Past Is Prologue: The Romantic Heritage in Dramatic Literature," in *Romantic Drama,* ed. Gerald Gillespie (Amsterdam and Philadelphia: John Benjamins, 1994); 429–64; as well as *The Symbolist Movement,* passim.

17. *Zauberberg,* 683; Thomas Mann, *The Magic Mountain,* trans. H. T. Lowe-Porter (New York: Modern Library, 1952), 645–46.

18. *Zauberberg,* 523; *Magic Mountain,* 496.

19. *Zauberberg,* 684; *Magic Mountain,* 646.

Mallarmé's Hispanic Heirs
Michael P. Predmore

In the early 1920s, the distinguished Mexican scholar, poet, and essayist, Alfonso Reyes, is living and working in Madrid, and he provides us with an anecdotal report on a most unusual ceremony.[1] Inspired by the announcement that members of the "Societé Mallarmé" in Paris plan to meet in Valvins on 14 October 1923, to commemorate the twenty-fifth anniversary of the death of Mallarmé, Reyes conceives of the idea of doing something similar right there in Madrid. He sends out an anonymous note to each of twelve different people, proposing that a meeting take place at exactly 11:00 A.M. on 14 October, at the gate of the Botanical Gardens, just south of the Prado Museum, overlooking the Book Fair, to observe five minutes of silence in memory of Mallarmé. The remarkable thing is that nine of these twelve people invited, without knowing either the author of the invitation or the names of the others invited, showed up at the gate of the Botanical Gardens at exactly 11:00 A.M. and solemnly observed those five minutes of silence in honor of Mallarmé, according to plan. This distinguished group of intellectuals, poets, and critics included the leading poet of the day, Juan Ramón Jiménez,[2] the most prestigious philosopher, José Ortega y Gasset; and the most influential art critic and cultural historian of his day, Eugenio d'Ors. A report of this tribute to Mallarmé, plus testimonials by each of the participants, was published the very next month in Spain's most eminent intellectual journal of that era, the *Revista de Occidente*, directed by Ortega y Gasset. This event even received a favorable review in the French press, in the *Mercure de France* (1 February 1924) and *Le Journal littéraire* (5 July 1924), though one French journalist struck a lighter note when he expressed astonishment that any group of Spanish intellectuals could maintain a silence for as long as five minutes! At any rate, it is fair to say, I think, that the influence and prestige of Mallarmé reaches its peak in the Spanish-speaking world toward the end of the second decade and on into the third decade of the twentieth century.

I would like to establish now the context in which we might better understand how an eminent Mexican scholar and poet organized for his Spanish colleagues in Madrid an event celebrating the importance and the spirit of the great French master. I would like then to report to you briefly on what we might call the external history of the presence and influence of Mallarmé in the Spanish-speaking world, and, finally, suggest with the aid of two examples something of the enduring legacy of Mallarmé in the development of twentieth-century Spanish lyric poetry.

In the Renaissance of Hispanic lyric poetry that takes place at the turn of the last century, all would acknowledge the decisive influence of nineteenth-century French poetry through the successive stages of its development—Romanticism, Parnassianism, and Symbolism. All would equally acknowledge the exceptional importance of the great Nicaraguan poet, Rubén Darío, leader of the poetic movement of Latin American modernism, which extends approximately from the publication of his foundational work of *Azul* in 1888 to his death in 1916. No other poet of his time had Darío's capacity for assimilation and imaginative transformation of the great achievements of nineteenth-century French poetry. Most of his life was spent in the capitals of Spanish American countries and in Europe, on diplomatic missions and as a newspaper correspondent, primarily for the Argentine newspaper *La Nación* in Buenos Aires. He made countless trips across the Atlantic, and had significant periods of residence in Central America, Santiago, Chile, Buenos Aires, Paris, and Madrid. Through his brilliant poetry and literary criticism, and his constant traveling as consul and correspondent, he conveyed the message of a new poetic movement to all the capitals of the Spanish world. When he visited Spain for the second time in 1899, he formed personal friendships with and made a lasting impression on the most talented and inspired members of the new generation: Ramón del Valle-Inclán, Antonio and Manuel Machado, and Juan Ramón Jiménez. Rubén Darío was the great catalyst of a literary revolution—symbolist and modernist in character—that affected the entire Spanish-speaking world.

It can be seen, therefore, that any account of Mallarmé and Spain must also include Mallarmé and Spanish America. And just as Darío served as mentor to a younger generation of Peninsular Spanish poets, so Juan Ramón Jiménez, perhaps the greatest of that younger generation, served as mentor, in turn, to successive generations of both Spanish and Latin American poets who followed him. Indeed, a striking characteristic of this poetic movement as it evolved into the twentieth century was the sense of community and common cause that developed between the poets of Spain and Spanish America. The leading figures shared a special commitment to poetry and, as the century advanced, a deep commitment to a political cause that brought so many of the very best Latin American poets to Spain, in solidarity with the very best of the Spanish poets, in defense of democracy and of the Second Spanish Republic. Any account of the history of lyric poetry in the Hispanic world during the first four decades of the twentieth century must see the developments on both sides of the Atlantic as parts of an interrelated whole.

The influence and reception of Mallarmé in the Spanish-speaking world has not been a matter of serious or sustained study. Very little is known and very little written on the subject. What we can say is that knowledge of Mallarmé in Spain and in Latin America in the 1880s and 1890s was very limited and fragmentary, and his influence was clearly secondary to that of Verlaine and his followers.[3] Both the early Darío of the 1880s and 1890s and the early Juan Ramón Jiménez, from 1900 to 1912, acknowledge their preferences for Verlaine. Nonetheless, in October of 1898, one month after the death of Mallarmé, Rubén Darío wrote an article entitled "Stéphane Mallarmé" for the literary journal, *El Mercurio de América*, in Buenos Aires. It is an impressive lyrical homage as well as a remarkably well-informed commentary on many of the poems and some of the prose, revealing that the Nicaraguan poet by this time had read carefully and well much of the work of the French master.

From this point on, we can begin to document and assess the interest in Mallarmé's work among Hispanic poets and writers. The best source of information, and as far as I know, the only source, is provided in a little book entitled *Mallarmé entre nosotros* (Mallarmé among Us) by Alfonso Reyes. Reyes is himself a first-rate poet, a dedicated and superb translator of the poems of Mallarmé, and a lifelong devotee of the work of the French master. There are several things to be noted in Reyes's book. He provides us with a very useful bibliography of translations of Mallarmé's poems into Spanish that began to appear in the year of his death in 1898 and continued at least until 1945. The bibliography lists some twenty-five Latin American and Spanish poets and critics whose translations appear in leading journals of the time located in Madrid, Buenos Aires, Mexico, Barcelona, and Paris, with an occasional translation appearing in Bogotá, Colombia, Havana, Cuba, and San José, Costa Rica. What we can conclude from

Reyes's bibliography is that there was a small, but significant and sustained interest in Mallarmé for over a forty-year period, cultivated, at least, by some of the leading Hispanic poets and critics of the time.

With respect to the specific poems translated, one notes in Reyes's bibliography the predominance, as might be expected, of the earlier, more accessible poems of Mallarmé: "Apparition," "Les Fenêtres," "Brise marine," "Soupir," as well as special efforts directed toward the longer, more important poems of *Hérodiade* and *L'Après-midi d'un Faune*. Most noteworthy of all is the translation of *Un Coup de Dés* by the brilliant Spanish scholar, critic, and poet, Rafael Cansinos-Assens. He published his translation in 1919 in one of the most important avant-garde journals of the day, entitled *Cervantes*. A particular interest and importance attaches itself to this translation in tracing the influence of Mallarmé on the great Peruvian poet, César Vallejo, as the critic Xavier Abril has done. Abril argues vigorously that the hermetic construction of Vallejo's most original and most enigmatic work of poetry, *Trilce*, in terms of its symbols, syntax, and typographical disposition of words on the printed page, owes a great deal to the aesthetics of *Un Coup de Dés*.[4] Because Vallejo did not know French at the time he was writing *Trilce* between 1918 and 1922, he depended entirely upon Cansinos's translation of Mallarmé's masterpiece.

With respect to the influence and prestige of Mallarmé in Spain during these years, we have, first of all, the authoritative testimony of Cansinos-Assens, who, in the preface to his translation of *Un Coup de Dés*, in 1919, traces to the inspiration and intention of Mallarmé the latest avant-garde currents of poetry in Spain. Cansinos notes, particularly, the influence of Mallarmé on "el creacionismo" and upon its founder, the prominent Chilean poet, Vicente Huidobro, and he states quite emphatically "we are witnessing right now the posthumous flowering of Mallarméan intentions."[5] There is also, as we have seen, the silent but eloquent testimony of that select group of participants in the five minutes of silence for Mallarmé in 1923. In the brief report of this event, published in the *Revista de Occidente* one month later, solemn respect is paid to the great significance of Mallarmé's poetry and to the power of his influence on literature not only in France, but everywhere, particularly in Germany, England, and Spain.[6] Finally, we have the testimony of one of the most influential voices of his time, José Ortega y Gasset. In his famous collection of essays on aesthetics, entitled *La deshumanización del arte* (The Dehumanization of Art) and published in 1925, he devotes several pages to

Mallarmé and concludes "all the new poetry now advances in the direction pointed to by Mallarmé."[7] And in support of Ortega, we should mention that two outstanding representatives of the "new poetry" inspired by the example of Mallarmé are the eminent Spanish poet Jorge Guillén and the Mexican poet and Nobel Laureate, Octavio Paz. Both Guillén and Paz, in their own poetry, in their translations, and in their personal correspondence, reflect the influence of the French master.[8]

I would like to provide now two examples of what Henri Peyre is suggesting in his *What Is Symbolism?* when he wisely observes, with reference to the great Spanish poets at the beginning of the twentieth century, "Nowhere else did the example of French symbolist poetry act with more discretion and, at the same time, in greater depth."[9] Nowhere is this discretion and this depth more clearly evident than in the "new poetry" of Antonio Machado and Juan Ramón Jiménez, Machado in his masterpiece of *Soledades, galerías y otros poemas* (Solitudes, Galleries, and Other Poems) of 1907, and Jiménez in his epoch-making work of 1917, *Diario de un poeta reciéncasado* (Diary of a Newly-Wed Poet). Together these two poets, in these two works, assimilate the most enduring part of French symbolism, initiate a new mode of poetic composition in Spanish letters, and set the course for the development of twentieth-century Spanish lyric poetry. Let us examine their work briefly in the light of Mallarmé.

Antonio Machado, in his famous lecture in 1931 to the Real Academia Española, shows himself well aware of a brilliant tradition of European lyric poetry—from English and German romanticism, through French symbolism, on into the twentieth century.[10] He expresses the highest regard for French symbolism, particularly its penetrating exploration of the subconscious and "the subterranean city of its dreams." Though Machado does not mention Mallarmé by name on this occasion, he does at other times in his critical and philosophical prose, when he reflects on the nature of lyric poetry.[11] He clearly accepts and assimilates in his poetics the dictum of Mallarmé, "Paint not the thing, but the effect it produces," as well as Mallarmé's aesthetic of suggestion, and his special and profound use of the symbol to evoke and to reveal little by little a state of mind or a state of soul, all of which involves or eventually leads to private associations of images, of memory, of experiences, or of dreams.

Let us consider now the section "Del camino" (Of the Road), composed of eighteen intricately interrelated poems, which constitute the nucleus of themes, images, and emotions elaborated throughout the ninety-six poems of Machado's *Soledades*. From the very first poem, "Preludio" (Prelude), we note how a sense of prayer and religious yearning pervades this section. It is here where the figure of the traveler on the road is definitely established and in terms that clearly indicate a spiritual quest. From the very beginning, a strange and supernatural atmosphere seems to pervade these poems. There are rivers to cross, subterranean passages to negotiate, unscaled mountains in the distance, special signs from the sky, as well as gardens and fountains and peaceful landscapes of repose. There is also a strange undercurrent of anxiety and fear in the mind of the traveler, complicated by a vein of irony, mockery, and irreverence—an undercurrent of feeling that is disruptive and that detracts from the seriousness of purpose of the pilgrim. One notes the recurring presence of a voice offstage, a recurring perception that interrupts the scene to mock, to ridicule, and to despair of the conduct and aspirations of the pilgrim.

The mystery of all this begins to be clarified, and can only begin to be clarified, I think, in the last poem, Poem XXXVII, of this section of eighteen interrelated poems. It is here where we acquire full awareness of the strictly mental character of the traveler's quest. Poem XXXVII describes and summarizes, in dialogue form, the essential drama of the preceding seventeen poems. I quote to you about half the poem in translation:

> Oh, tell me, friendly night, old love,
> who brings me the puppet stage of my dreams
> always empty and forlorn, and
> with only my ghost inside,
> my poor sad shadow
> on the high plain and under a fiery sun,
> or dreaming bitter dreams
> in the voices of all mysteries,
> tell me, if you know, old love, tell me
> whether the tears I shed are my own.
> The night answered me:
> To me you never revealed your secret.
> I never knew, my love,
> whether you were that ghost of your dream,
> nor did I ever find out whether his voice was yours,
> or the voice of a grotesque buffoon.
> . . . .
> peer into the souls when they weep
> and listen to their deep prayer,
> humble and lonely,

> the prayer you call true psalm:
> but in the soul's deep vaults
> I do not know whether the lament is voice or echo.
>
> In order to listen to your complaint from your lips,
> I sought you out in your dream,
> and there I saw you wandering
> in a cloudy maze of mirrors.[12]

"My poor sad shadow" describes exactly the figure of the traveler and his environment in many of the preceding poems. Yet, these images are seen to be called forth by the "puppet stage" of his dreams. It becomes clear, finally, that we are meant to recognize that the adventure of the traveler-pilgrim along the roads of life amidst the desolate and deserted landscapes is strictly a projection of dream and memory images. The quest in *Soledades* is strictly a drama of the mind and a projection of the mind. The special symbolism of the dream images and the mirror images tells us that this is above all the poetry of self-contemplation. The poet looks deep within himself and sees there, reflected upon the mirrors of his inner dream world, images of himself and of aspects of self from the present and the past. This is the significance of the mournful dialogue with the "friendly night," which is really a dialogue with self.

This is no ordinary dialogue, then. It is an "intimate monologue" in which the various voices of a split personality break the silence of the solitary wanderer. There are two personalities in *Soledades* competing for supremacy over the psychic constitution of the self. The ideals and goals of the pilgrim are under constant attack, in the language of Machado, by the "metaphysical faith" of the militant solipsist. It is the genius of Machado to have created a symbolic mode of expression adequate to the demands of a consciousness at war with itself. The powerful and contradictory emotions of a divided personality are converted into objects for aesthetic contemplation by the symbolism of aspects of the Christian allegory and by the symbolism of the language of dreams. *Soledades* thus presents a drama of the mind, a modern psychic projection of an ancient quest for lost origins, in which the twentieth-century "hero" suffers defeat and participates in parodying that defeat—an achievement that is directly and profoundly within the symbolist aesthetics of Mallarmé. One thinks immediately of the "hauntingly, self-probing" adventure of *Igitur*, so profoundly illuminated by Robert Greer Cohn.[13] Clearly within this tradition, Machado has produced the first masterpiece of twentieth-century Spanish lyric poetry.

Let us turn now to the Nobel Laureate, Juan Ramón Jiménez, and observe how he assimilates what Machado has begun and develops much further a poetic language and a poetic mode of composition that initiates a brilliant new period of creativity in modern Hispanic poetry. Of Jiménez's indebtedness to French symbolism, we have his own abundant testimony, scattered throughout his critical prose and in two different volumes of recorded conversations over a thirty-year period. The influence of Verlaine on the first period of his poetic creativity from 1900 to 1915 has been often noted. The more important influence of Mallarmé has gone virtually unstudied, despite tantalizing evidence that should encourage further investigation. We know from the poet's own testimony and Professor Gicovate's authoritative study that Jiménez was carefully reading and preparing translations of Mallarmé's poems around 1917 and after, which was precisely the period of his greatest creativity.[14] We learn from a published conversation with his friend Juan Guerrero Ruiz in 1931 that Jiménez reserved one special bookshelf of his personal library for what he called "la poesía mejor universal" (the best universal poetry), and the shelf contained Shakespeare, the Bible, the Greeks, and Mallarmé.[15] Finally, we may recall that Jiménez gave a course at the University of Puerto Rico at Río Piedras in 1953 on the subject of "Modernism and Lyric Poetry in the Hispanic World." The notes to this course have been published in a volume of over three-hundred pages, and they reveal a detailed attention to Mallarmé and to his stature as a master among the leading poets of his time.[16]

In the light of these repeated acknowledgments of Mallarmé's importance, let us reflect finally on Jiménez's masterpiece of 1917, *Diario*. The *Diario* was written in 1916 between January and July on the occasion of the poet's trip from Spain to the United States to marry his fiancée Zenobia Camprubí. The book is divided into six parts and records, in both verse and prose, the poet's day-to-day impressions, thoughts, and feelings as he travels from Madrid, to his native town of Moguer in the province of Huelva, to Cádiz, and then on by boat across the Atlantic to New York, and back again. The physical journey thus follows the round of a completed cycle. And the genius of Jiménez has been to transform this intimate narrative into perhaps the most intricately complex and densely symbolic work in modern Spanish poetry.

Though Jiménez's poetry does not possess perhaps the metaphysical depth of Mallarmé's greatest work, nor the immense complexity of the Mallarméan cycle, so precisely and so richly described by Robert Greer Cohn in his pioneering study of *Un Coup de Dés*,[17] there are, it seems to me, striking parallels between Mallarmé's *Igitur* and Jiménez's *Diario*. In fact, R. G. Cohn's description of *Igitur* applies very well to aspects of the archetypal pattern elaborated in the *Diario*. We may paraphrase slightly his words to say that at the core of both works (*Igitur* and the *Diario*,) there is a spiritual adventure, a descent into the dark womb of the unconscious, eternal night, and reemergence, rebirth to a vision of light and truth.[18] This crisis of being and personality involves an adventure of self-discovery and, in the case of both poets, reflects the parallel maturation of the artist. Indeed, in the case of Jiménez, the profound existential struggle for self-definition and wholeness involves an equally intense and successful struggle to forge a new poetic language capable of probing more deeply than any previous Spanish poet the workings of the human mind. Not only does a new mode of poetic composition achieve full artistic maturity in the *Diario*, but a new age of poetry writing is born in Spanish literature.

Jiménez himself has pointed to the historic importance of his work in a recorded conversation with the eminent critic, Ricardo Gullón, when he observes in November 1953: "Con el *Diario* empieza el simbolismo moderno en la poesía española" (Modern symbolism begins in Spanish poetry with the *Diary*).[19] Earlier we have argued that the eighteen interrelated poems of the section "Del Camino" in Machado's *Soledades* constitute the construction of the first symbolic system in twentieth-century Spanish lyric poetry. What, then, is the difference between Machado's achievement in 1907 and the claims Jiménez makes for his work in 1917? The answer is, I believe, that Machado works primarily, though not exclusively, within an inherited literary language and a well-known traditional symbolism. The beginnings of a symbolic mode of composition and a dreamlike quest for self-definition and self-discovery that we can identify in those eighteen poems of the early *Soledades* develop in Jiménez in the immensely more complex creation of a vast mental universe and the forging of a private semantic system, elaborated throughout the 217 interrelated poems of the *Diario*.

The key poem of the *Diario* is found at the end of part 4, in Poem 191, entitled "Todo" (Everything). It is addressed to the sea and to love, in the midst of a series of seven poems, all written on

19 July. This is the climactic point of much careful and elaborate development, and testifies dramatically to the hermetic nature of the *Diario*'s poetic world:

> True, yes, yes; the two of you have finally cured
> my insanity.
>
> The world, open and limpid, with you,
> has shown me the palm
> of its hand that earlier it kept hidden
> for so long from my wide-open
> eyes, so wide-open
> that they were blind!
>
> You, sea, and you, love, both mine,
> as the earth and the sky were earlier!
> Now everything is mine, everthing! I mean,
>   nothing is now mine, nothing![20]

This poem tells us triumphantly a certain number of things: that the poetic personality's insanity has been cured by the sea and by love, that the world has revealed itself to him in a way he had never experienced before, that the sea and love have become in the poet's experience what the land and the sky were earlier, and that the poet's possession of "everything" is corrected and described now as "nothing." Not only is the meaning of all this obscure, there is no basis within the poem itself for arriving at an intelligible interpretation. It is only after many readings of the entire work, seen as an intricately interrelated whole, that we discover the essential drama of the traveler. Like the hero of *Igitur*, the protagonist here is at the crucial crossroads between childhood and maturity, caught in a crisis of personal growth and development. The essential inner conflict of the *Diario* is the painful struggle between the child's attachment to the familiar boundaries of his early existence (the fledgling's reluctance to leave its nest) and the pull toward love, emotional maturity, and independence. During the course of this profound inner journey, the hero recapitulates the archetypal pattern of biblical history, from Genesis to Revelation, from the fall from innocence and the loss of Eden, to resurrection and the conquest of new territory, after experiencing an Apocalypse of the the mind, in which "the first heaven and the first earth" (the land and sky of his childhood) "were passed away" and replaced by "a new heaven and a new earth" constituted by love and the sea and a new world of adult experience.[21] The entire drama is conveyed through structures of polarity, through clusters and constellations of recurrent imagery, similar to the mode of poetic composition, characteristic of Mallarmé, so beautifully illuminated by Professor Cohn in his essential work on the French master.

Beginning with Antonio Machado and then in much more fully developed form in Juan Ramón Jiménez, a profound and special use of poetic language, a symbolic mode of composition, a drama of self-discovery, a mythopoetic vision built on clusters and constellations of recurrent imagery, that taken together crystallize into a single poetic universe, these are the essential elements that take root in twentieth-century Spanish lyric poetry. These are the elements that constitute the profound legacy of Mallarmé to his Spanish counterparts, and they, in turn, to the following generation of extraordinary poets: Lorca, Alberti, Guillén, Salinas, Cernuda, and Aleixandre. Surely something like this is what Ortega y Gasset had in mind when he observed that "all the new poetry advances in the direction pointed to by Mallarmé," and what Henri Peyre was thinking of when he comments on the depth of the influence of French symbolist poetry on two of the greatest of Hispanic poets, Darío and Machado. French symbolist poetry and Mallarmé surely constitute part of the essential context for understanding Jiménez's claim that "modern symbolism begins in Spanish poetry" with his *Diario*.

Within a brilliant tradition of European lyric poetry, Mallarmé constitutes a key link in a chain of continuity that extends from Blake and Shelley, to Baudelaire and Yeats, to García Lorca and Pablo Neruda.[22] And it is the profound legacy of Mallarmé that crossed the frontier into Spain, assimilated, transformed, and enriched in the masterpieces of Machado and Jiménez, that led to the remarkable flowering of Spanish lyric poetry during the first three decades of the twentieth century and endured in some of its greatest poets—Jiménez, Guillén, and Aleixandre—right up through the middle of this century.

Notes

1. Alfonso Reyes, *Mallarmé entre nosotros* (Mexico: Tezontle, 1955), 9–20.
2. Though invited, Jiménez was indisposed and was unable to attend the ceremony. He paid his respects in writing in three different communications to Alfonso Reyes. See his *Cartas* (Madrid: Aguilar, 1962), 248–51.
3. Bernardo Gicovate, *Julio Herrera y Reissig and the Symbolists* (Berkeley: University California Press, 1957), 12.

4. Xavier Abril, "Dos Estudios: Vallejo y Mallarmé," *Cuadernos del Sur* (January 1960): 7–26.
5. Rafael Cansinos-Assens, "Un interesante poema de Mallarmé," nota preliminar y traducción, *Cervantes* (November 1919): 69.
6. Alfonso Reyes, "El silencio por Mallarmé," *Revista de Occidente* 2 (October-December 1923): 238–56.
7. José Ortega y Gasset, *La deshumanización del arte,* 8th ed. (Madrid: Revista de Occidente, 1964), 44.
8. Robert Greer Cohn kindly shared with me personal correspondence he received from both poets, which testify to their admiration for Mallarmé.
9. Henri Peyre, *What Is Symbolism?* trans. Emmett Parker (University: University of Alabama Press, 1980), 141.
10. Manuel Machado's project for a speech was prepared in 1931 but never delivered. See his *Obras: Poesía y prosa,* ed. Aurora de Albornoz and Guillermo de Torre (Buenos Aires: Losada, 1964), 842–53.
11. Ibid., 320, 325, 709, 822–23.
12. Ibid., 80–81.
13. Robert Greer Cohn, *Mallarmé:* Igitur (Berkeley: University of California Press, 1981), 1.
14. Juan Ramón Jiménez, *La corriente infinita* (Madrid: Agilar, 1961), 176; and Bernardo Giocovate, *La poesía de Juan Ramón Jiménez* (Barcelona: Ariel, 1973), 106–7.
15. Juan Guerrero Ruiz, *Juan Ramón de viva voz* (Madrid: Insula, 1961), 161.
16. Juan Ramón Jiménez, *El Modernismo: Notas de un curso (1953)* (Madrid: Aguilar, 1962), 217.
17. Robert Greer Cohn, *L'Oeuvre de Mallarmé: Un Coup de Dés* (Paris: Librairie Les Lettres, 1951).
18. Cohn, *Mallarmé:* Igitur, 2.
19. Ricardo Gullón, *Conversaciones con Juan Ramón* (Madrid: Taurus, 1958), 93.
20. The translation is mine. This poem is taken from Jiménez's *Diario,* contained in *Libros de poesía* (Madrid: Aguilar, 1959), 470.
21. See my "Imágenes apocalípticas en el *Diario* de Juan Ramón: La tradición simbólica de William Blake," *Revista de Letras* 23–24 (September-December 1974): 365–82.
22. My thanks to Jaime Concha for calling to my attention some splendid pages by Neruda devoted to Shakespeare, in which his poetry, as well as that of Góngora and Mallarmé, are evoked with supreme respect and admiration. See Neruda's "Shakespeare, Príncipe de la luz," in *Para nacer he nacido* (Barcelona: Seix-Barral, 1977), 176–80.

V
On an Affinity and an Indigestion

Leo Tolstoy, Mallarmé, and "The Sickness of Our Time"

ROMAN DOUBROVKINE

> The poetry of Mallarmé and others. We, not understanding it, boldly state that it is nonsense, that it is poetry which has stumbled into a dead end.
> —L. TOLSTOY[1]

To this very day the reputation of Stéphane Mallarmé in Russian rests to a large extent on Tolstoy's strictures against the French poet in his important treatise, *What Is Art?* These strictures, in their turn, rest upon Tolstoy's own strongly felt personal opinions, but also on the vagaries of publication that include typographical errors, editing mistakes, and generally sloppy reproduction of Mallarmé's poems. If Mallarmé is to be read anew by Russian readers, this history of reception must be foregrounded and unraveled.

At the beginning of 1898, when *What Is Art?* was being finished, Mallarmé, a poet "considered [as Tolstoy ironically observed] the most significant of the young ones" (30:91), was drawing closer to the final, fifty-sixth year of his life.[2] Strange as it may seem, for some mysterious reason, in the eyes of "the great moralist," this "youth" was particularly linked with the talent of poets, or, more precisely, their lack of talent. This applied to the deceased as well. "You take in your hands a collection of poems by Baudelaire, Verlaine, Mallarmé, Moréas, and others, considered to be wonderful works of art, and the younger the authors, the less you understand," states one of the rough drafts of the treatise (30:365). In the treatise itself, Tolstoy continues to insist on the immaturity of the French symbolists: "There are, for example, poems of Mallarmé and Maeterlinck, which don't make any sense. In spite of this, or perhaps because of this, they are printed not only in tens of thousands of separate editions, but also in collections of the best works of young poets" (30:100).[3] Here Tolstoy unwittingly makes two mistakes: Maeterlinck was thirty-six in 1898, and—as it is well known—the works of the symbolists, and in particular, Mallarmé, were issued in deliberately limited printings. Only a narrow circle of "initiated" readers was expected. Thus, for example, the luxurious edition of *L'Après-midi d'un Faune*, with frontispiece, illuminations, and vignettes by Edouard Manet, was issued in 1876 in an edition of 200 copies that remained, for the most part, unsold ten years later. The "facsimile" edition of *Les Poésies de Stéphane Mallarmé* (1887), printed from the manuscript by lithograph, with Félicien Rops's *ex libris,* came out in 47 copies, of which only 40 numbered copies were put on sale. Single poetic works were reprinted by the press only as a curiosity, and by no means for the sake of popularization. Of course, occasionally some of them ended up in widely available editions: thirteen poems were included in the volume *Album de vers et de prose* (1887–88) of the popular series *Poètes et prosateurs. Anthologie contemporaine des écrivains français et belges,* published in Brussels and Paris and selling for only a few centimes. Exceptions like this were rare.

Disdain for "trifles" characterizes the entire tenth chapter of Tolstoy's famed treatise, which is devoted to the condemnation of the French decadents. Even the few names of French poets mentioned in the text are not always correct. Remy de Gourmont is named in the first magazine version as "Reney"; Saint-Pol Roux was turned into two poets: "St. Paul" and "Roux le Magnifique." Lamartine lost his final vowel.[4] In subsequent editions, some errors were corrected, but new ones appeared instead. Neither Tolstoy nor his supporters considered these inaccuracies significant. "If it is possible to disagree with some details and some examples," wrote the famous painter Ilya Repin, having in mind something more, "then in general, the main posing of the question is so deep, so incapable of being refuted, that it even becomes pleasant, joy breaks through."[5]

Publication of the treatise in French translation triggered a storm of indignation in the literary circles of Paris. The outrage focused mainly on the ideological contents of the treatise, not the mistakes and typographical errors. "Il est bien évident, quand Tolstoï parle de la littérature française, il parle de ce qu'il ne connaît pas."[6] (It is obvious that Tolstoy does not know what he is talking about when he speaks of French literature) countered Joris-Karl Huysmans. Other critics responded even more harshly.[7]

It is not for us to judge how well Tolstoy knew contemporary French poetry. His relationship to poetry in general, and to French poetry in particular, was deeply subjective. "The French and the Russians write poetry well," he said on 26 February 1906 to his household doctor D. P. Makovitsky.[8] It is known that the only French poet of the nineteenth century he accepted was Béranger, and the only prose writers were Anatole France and Zola. Tolstoy's literary tastes were distinguished by consistency: the list of favorite writers compiled when he was in his teens remained practically unchanged for the rest of his life. As for his views on the national character of poetic schools, they always remained liberal. Thus, in a letter to Octave Mirbeau dated 12 October 1903 Tolstoy wrote:

> Je crois que chaque nationalité emploie différents moyens pour exprimer dans l'art l'idéal commun et que c'est à cause de cela que nous éprouvons une jouissance particulière à retrouver notre idéal exprimé d'une manière nouvelle et inattendue. L'art français m'a donné jadis ce sentiment de découverte, quand j'ai lu pour la première fois Alfred de Vigny, Stendhal, Victor Hugo et, surtout, Rousseau. Je crois que c'est à ce sentiment qu'il faut attribuer la trop grande importance que vous attachez aux écrits de Dostoïevsky et surtout aux miens.[9]

> [I believe that every nationality uses different means in order to express a common ideal in art. For this reason we feel a particular joy when we find our ideal expressed in a new or an unexpected way. In the past, French art gave me such feeling of discovery when I first read Alfred de Vigny, Stendhal, Victor Hugo and most of all Rousseau. I think that the exaggerated importance you give to Dostoyevsky's work, and even more so to mine, must also be attributed to such a feeling.]

While at work on the treatise, Tolstoy made use of extensive critical literature, selecting works close to him in spirit. The main source of his information is explicitly named in the tenth chapter of the treatise. It is the book by René Doumic with the characteristic title *Les Jeunes. Etudes et portraits* (1896) (The Young Ones). It is precisely this title that apparently led to the Russian writer's misunderstanding. "The Young Ones" was the name in France for a distinct group of poets who interpreted the lessons of the founders of symbolism in their own way. That is how René Ghil, discussing the *vers libre* and rhythmic uncertainty of Gustave Kahn in a Russian revue, characterizes the work of the "'Young Ones'— the careless adepts of this 'free verse.'"[10] Mallarmé also mentions the "Young Ones" more than once, juxtaposing them with the Parnassians, in his sensational answer to Jules Huret's "Enquête sur l'évolution littéraire" (Paris, 1891), the second starting point for Tolstoy's criticism.[11]

As for Doumic, he does write about the young ones, Henri de Régnier and Vielé-Griffin, in one of the chapters of his book dedicated to the new poetry and new poetics ("La poétique nouvelle"). However, he does not attribute them to the generation of Mallarmé and Verlaine. On the contrary, he emphasizes the succession of various schools of French poetry:

> M. de Régnier a ce don de l'expression imagée et chantante où on reconnaît le poète. Il a commencé par subir la discipline parnassienne, et il s'en souvient jusque dans son dernier recueil, où telle vision antique fait songer à quelque pastiche de Ronsard. Il a fréquenté chez Leconte de Lisle et, chez M. de Heredia avant de prendre M. Mallarmé pour maître et pour émule M. Vielé-Griffin; c'est chez lui qu'on voit le mieux la fusion des traditions d'hier avec les plus récentes influences.... On ne saurait non plus négliger M. Francis Vielé-Griffin. C'est lui qui est considéré dans son groupe comme le plus hardiment novateur et c'est à lui que revient la plus grande part d'influence.[12]

> [De Régnier has the gift of the picturesque melodious style by which we recognize a poet. In the beginning he was subjected to the discipline of the Parnassians and has kept it to his last poetic collection in which some antique visions remind one of a pastiche of Ronsard. He paid frequent visits to Leconte de Lisle and Heredia before he found his Master in Mallarmé and his follower in Vielé-Griffin. It is in his works that we find the best examples of the fusion of tradition of the past with the most modern influences. [...] Vielé-Griffin should not be overlooked either. He is considered as the boldest innovator in his group and enjoys the greatest influence.]

A little further down, Doumic writes about the withdrawal of the young poets from the poetics of François Coppée and Sully Prudhomme, and of their adherence to the ideas of Mallarmé and Verlaine.[13] Speaking about the nefarious influence of free verse he states indignantly: "Il serait temps aussi d'en finir avec cette fameuse 'théorie de l'obscurité' que la nouvelle école a élevée en effet à la hauteur d'un dogme"[14] (It is high time to give up this notorious "theory of obscurity" that the new school has raised to the level of a dogma). Like Tolstoy, Doumic does not like symbolist poetry, whether young or old, considering it devoid of meaning and pretentious. However, he is far from considering the poets of previous generations as young. Tolstoy, on the other hand, blends all ages and quotes Doumic's opinion about Henri de Régnier and Vielé-Griffin right after Mallarmé's answer to Jules Huret ("Nommer l'objet..."), and so on.

Tolstoy had a predecessor, the well-known populist Nikolay Mikhailovsky. However, he forgot Mikhailovsky's warning that the name "Young Ones" must be "understood, it seems, in some figurative sense."[15] In his analysis, Tolstoy confused several schools and movements that had developed in France over the course of half a century. He extended his conclusions about the epigones of symbolism to its best representatives and even its forerunners. There is nothing surprising in this, because an analogous misunderstanding can be observed at the turn of the century concerning Russian literature. For a long time, poetry continued to be called "*new*," despite the fact that, as one famous critic noted, "though still called 'new' in a terminology that has already managed to become out of date, these movements are without a doubt obsolete."[16]

What has been said does not mean that Tolstoy's interest in the French decadents was short-lived or circumstantial. There is evidence to suggest that he was familiar with Emile Zola's polemical statements, in *Vestnik Evropy* (European Herald) of February 1878, and with the surveys that appeared in the Russian press during the last decade of the nineteenth century.[17] The French critic André Beaunier, to whom Tolstoy showed the proofs of his study and read several pages from it aloud, relates:

> Très consciencieusement, pour se mettre au courant de ce qu'il y a de plus nouveau chez nous, Tolstoï a lu toutes les petites revues françaises, les plus inconnues, les plus saugrenues. Il les abomine, il n'a pas de mots assez durs pour les qualifier, mais il les croit significatives. C'est là, sans doute, le reproche qu'il faudra faire à son livre: il s'appuie sur des renseignements nombreux, mais recueillis un peu au hasard. Tolstoï attache trop d'importance à des écrivains qui n'en ont aucune et dont les oeuvres ne sont pas du tout les signes d'un état d'esprit général.[18]

> [In order to know all about the newest trends in France, Tolstoy very conscientiously reads all the small French magazines, even the most obscure and the most preposterous ones. He loathes them, he cannot find words harsh enough to describe them, but he still believes them to be significant. This is without doubt the aspect for which we shall have to reproach his book: it relies on ample but rather haphazard information. Tolstoy attaches too much importance to writers who are of no importance at all and whose works do not represent in any way the general state of mind.]

Later, responding to the publication of the treatise *What Is Art?* René Doumic also reproached Tolstoy for bringing in incidental examples—examples that mean nothing, because symbolist poetry belongs forever to the past.

> Quant aux décadents, non seulement la tendance qu'ils ont représentée est aujourd'hui défunte, leur école s'en étant allée où vont les vieilles lunes, mais jamais ils ne sont arrivés chez nous à se faire prendre au sérieux, et je crois bien qu'ils n'y ont pas tâché. C'est hors de chez nous qu'on s'est penché pieusement sur leurs élucubrations, et que, faute d'une connaissance suffisante de notre langue et de notre tour d'esprit, on n'y a pas aperçu la part de mystification.[19]

[As for the Decadents, not only is the tendency they once represented dead today, but their school has disappeared into thin air; nor have they ever succeeded in being taken seriously in this country and I believe they have never even tried. It is beyond our borders that people have piously poured over the fruits of their futile toils and for lack of knowledge of our language and of our mind, have failed to notice a large amount of mystification.]

One should not suspect Doumic of trying to attack Tolstoy, however. A careful reading of his essay shows him to be quite loyal to Tolstoy. A little further down we read:

> Ces réserves faites, et nous y avons assez insisté pour qu'on puisse apprécier dans quelle mesure nous acceptons les idées de Tolstoï, il n'est que temps d'indiquer combien de questions s'éclairent d'un jour nouveau, quand on les envisage du point de vue où se place l'écrivain russe. Car si l'art est un langage, comme on ne parle que pour être entendu, c'est donc que l'art ne doit pas s'adresser aux seuls initiés et devenir le privilège d'une élite. C'est ici le grand péril qui menace l'art moderne, et Tolstoï, en le dénonçant avec tant d'âpreté, répond aux préoccupations de tous ceux qui réfléchissent.[20]

[Having expressed all these reservations and done it in such a way as to make clear to what extent we accept Tolstoy's ideas, it is high time to point out how many questions are cast in a new light if they are examined from the standpoint of the Russian writer. For if art is a language and we speak only in order to be understood, then art should not be addressed only to the initiated and become the privilege of the élite. Here lies the great danger that threatens modern art, and when Tolstoy denounces it with such sharpness, he responds to the concern of all thinking people.]

Concern over the fate of art preoccupied Tolstoy constantly, and naturally it was reflected in the character of his discussions with various cultural figures, some of them French. A visitor to Yasnaya

Polyana bears witness to one such episode. Henry Lapauze, journalist, economist, and, later, prominent art critic, visited Tolstoy on the evening of 22 May 1896. At some point during the meeting, the conversation turned to French poetry:

> Quelqu'un passe à Tolstoï une revue russe, cette fois. Tiens, me dit-il, rendez-moi le service de lire tout haut le sonnet que voici. J'aimerais bien savoir ce que l'auteur a voulu dire. Il y a de belles rimes, *"attentatoire et territoire . . .,"* mais je n'ai rien compris.—Mais c'est une des poésies les plus célèbres de Stéphane Mallarmé!—Soit, poursuit Tolstoï. En comprenez-vous au moins le sens? Moi pas. Et pas un point, pas une virgule?[21]

> [Somebody hands over a magazine to Tolstoy, this time a Russian one. Well, he says, do me a favor, read out loud this sonnet here. I would very much like to know what the author wanted to say. There are beautiful rhymes, "attentatoire et territoire . . .," but I have not understood a thing.—But, this is one of the most famous poems by Stéphane Mallarmé.—It may well be, continues Tolstoy. But do you understand its meaning at least? As for me, I do not. And not even a full stop, not a comma.]

Having included the above passage in his book, Henry Lapauze quoted Mallarmé's sonnet "M'introduire dans ton histoire . . ." and added the following opinion by Tolstoy: "Pas même le point final. C'est horrible. Ah! la littérature française peut se flatter d'avoir pour l'instant un joli lot de *nébuleuses*" (Not even a final full stop. It is horrible. Ah, French literature can boast of a lot of *vapor* right now).

The "Russian magazine" ("une revue russe") that Tolstoy showed to his French guest was, without a doubt, the fifth issue of *Severnyi vestnik* (Northern Herald) of 1896 with the article "Poetry of Decay," signed with the initials L. K. The author of this article, Konstantin L'dov (1862–1937),[22] was a second-rate Russian poet, who, a year later, published the collection *Lyric Poems* (St. Petersburg, 1897), labeled, in turn, "decadent."[23] The fact that L'dov's article appeared in *Severnyi vestnik,* a publication that prided itself on its reputation for expressing "new trends," says much about the true position of the magazine. Its position was essentially hostile to the modern trends imported from France. After similar articles, there were clear reasons why another, far more talented author, Fyodor Sologub, broke with the journal. In a letter to the editor, Sologub complained that *Severnyi vestnik* had "its own separate views" on art and did not concern itself with "such fundamentally non-serious matters as the seeking out of new beauty after foreign models."[24]

The editorial secretary, and regular contributor to *Severnyi vestnik,* Konstantin L'dov, proclaimed his task to be the separation of native-born decadence from true (read French) "poetry of decay." He even coined the phrase "pseudo-symbolists," characterizing in this manner Russian poets who published, in his words, "collections of monstrous rehashings of innovative foreign poetry."

Unlike Verlaine and Maeterlinck, who are linked to the "poetry of decay" "only by incidental, non-essential features of their talents," Mallarmé (L'dov's article stated) "is consciously and exclusively a singer of decadence." This is a poet, "gifted with an artistic talent, that is expressed brilliantly, however, only in his prose translations of the poems of Edgar Allan Poe."

This faint praise was followed by a number of stereotypical accusations, characteristic of those times, such as premeditated pretentiousness ("rhythmic trickery and somersaults"); melodious nonsense; "decay and loneliness" expressed "in simple, and upon careful examination, rather trite, sentimental-melodic forms"; "disenchantment and apathy with respect to phenomena in the external world"; and aesthetic ugliness and haughtiness. The conclusion of the article is passionate: "Not touching upon the spiritual, truly vital interests of humanity, the 'poetry of decay' is characterized by a superficial protest against generally-accepted forms of art. Insignificant in its aims and influence, it is the embodiment of the extreme tendencies of a period of transition."

As a poet, L'dov felt an urgent need, not so much to discourse on poetry, as to give his foreign colleague the possibility of expressing himself. He therefore spent the better half of his article on translations of three prose poems—"La Plainte d'automne," "Frisson d'hiver," and "Le Phénomène futur"—carried out, in spite of his grumbling about them, with great concern and zeal for the foreign text. However, L'dov did not dare translate "M'introduire dans ton histoire...," and instead printed it in the original, accompanied by the following words: "The poems of Mallarmé, abounding in sonorous and beautiful individual lines, are as a whole practically incomprehensible. In order to obscure meaning, the poet doesn't overlook even marks of punctuation, which have for him a meaning that differs widely from the commonly accepted one." Tolstoy's position, as we see, coincided with the position of this critic, who hid behind a pseudonym.[25]

Tolstoy's comments on Mallarmé's verse reported by Lapauze in a Paris newspaper marked the beginning of a remote conflict between Tolstoy and Mallarmé; it would last until the poet's death. It is interesting that the French symbolist, whose popularity within a small circle scarcely compared with the worldwide glory of the great novelist, met the attacks without irritation, as if hoping that he would someday be understood and valued.

On 22 June 1896, in *Gaulois,* the same newspaper where the story about Lapauze's visit to Yasnaya Polyana was printed, Mallarmé, having read "avec un vif intérêt, l'article de M. Lapauze; et les appréciations de Tolstoï")[26] (with the greatest of interest the article of Mr. Lapauze and the judgments of Tolstoy), answered the Russian author's accusations in a letter to the editor under the rubric "Echo of Paris":

> Les appréciations de Tolstoï, relativement à l'écriture présente, Monsieur, me semblent celles-là même qu'il faut accepter de lui, génie ample et simple, direct dans l'expression de l'idée; ce n'est pas fortuitement que le grand écrivain a, m'informe-t-on, appris le Français dans Stendhal. L'étranger doit connaître notre langue par ses grands traits typiques extérieurs, chez les classiques et leur descendance; mais voyez-vous que nous nous occupons à renforcer ce langage absolu, au lieu de faire à nos risques et périls des expériences individuelles, en tentant, s'il est possible, de les authentiquer?[27]

> [Tolstoy's opinions about modern writing seem to me to be the very ones one must accept from such an ample and simple genius, so direct in the expression of ideas; it was not by chance that the great writer (as I am informed) learned French in Stendhal. A foreigner must value our language by its major and typical outward features found in the works of the classics and their descendants; but as for us, may we be seen as strengthening this absolute language instead of undertaking at our own risk individual experiments in an attempt to render them, when possible, authentic?]

Leaving aside the rich field of linguistic connotations, let us turn our attention to the quoted phrase "m'informe-t-on" (as I am informed). This phrase points to Mallarmé's interest in the Russian novel, which was then popular in France.[28] It also hints at his close acquaintance with it, primarily due to the activity of the literati of his close circle, with the future translators of the treatise, Ely Halpérine-Kaminsky[29] and Teodor de Wyzewa,[30] who would play such an important role two years later in the defense of Mallarmé's good name.

Attacking foreign symbolism, Tolstoy was aiming, without a doubt, at symbolism in his own country, which came into being before his very eyes over the course of the fifteen years that he worked on the treatise. Classifying new literary phenomena in early sketches on this subject, he writes in one of the rough drafts about works of art, which have received "the label decadent, which are not only indecent and not appealing to the majority, but are simply foul, silly, and do not appeal to anyone or rather cannot appeal to anyone, being completely incomprehensible, something that is recognized even by their authors" (30:321). Tolstoy mentions in this context "a pretty well-known Frenchman Mallarmé" as the author of poems "the sense of which he himself refuses to explain," and attacks the young Valery Briusov (not mentioning his name): "One writer in Moscow wrote an entire volume of complete nonsense (there is, for example, a poem of one line: 'Ah, cover your pale legs'), and, thus it remained undecided whether he is mystifying the public that purchases and reads, while complaining and laughing (several also defend him), or whether he is mentally ill" (30:321).

The "pathological"—in the sense of Max Nordau—interpretation of modernist literature was beginning to reveal its full fallacy at that time. Concerned with agonizing searches for the truth, Tolstoy crossed out from the final text of *What Is Art?* the slightest hints at such insinuations and softened many other accusations, including alcoholism, and being déclassé, and so on.[31]

The writer's view of the essence of symbolism gradually became a nonacceptance of works without a clearly expressed idea, which he considered, precisely because of this lack of an idea, as elitist and amoral. On 17 December 1895, in an interview on the symbolists in *Peterburgskii listok* (St. Petersburg leaflet), Tolstoy remarked:

> I call decadents those artists who, not having their own thoughts and not knowing what to say, strive to make an impression on the reader by contrasting a series of scenes or simply words, but the idea, which twines through all creative works like a red thread, they lack. Decadence is much stronger and more dangerous than we like to think. Our critics look upon the decadents with disdain and derision, but they themselves don't suspect that this tendency has already had an effect on all types and forms of literature. It is only necessary to separate cryptodecadents, i. e. secret ones from those who manifest themselves as such. The former hide the fact that they belong to this school, while the latter simply act.[32]

What Is Art? was the culmination of Tolstoy's thinking about the "new tendencies." According it the significance of a fundamental moral-artistic manifesto, Tolstoy decided not to publish the treatise in Russia, fearing (not without justification) serious distortions by the censors. His first idea was to publish it "in its true form" in England, as the foreword to the London edition, dated 28 March 1898, says.[33] The English translation was produced by Aylmer (Aleksei Frantsevich) Maude (1858–1938), who later published *The Life of Tolstoy* (London, 1910). He worked on the translation under the direct supervision of the author. Tolstoy was outraged when, before the appearance of chapters 10–14 in London, a French decadent journal, *Revue blanche,* published in no. 111 (15 January) and no. 113 (15 February) "an outrageous translation of two chapters, torn from the whole and stripped of any meaning."[34] The second part of this publication, bearing the title "Decadents," was accompanied by the following note: "Cet article forme le 10ᵉ chapitre du nouveau livre de Tolstoï: *Qu'est-ce que l'Art?* Il fait partie du second volume qui doit paraître, le 25 février, à Londres, 'Brotherhood Publishing Company,' 26, Paternoster Sq., et à Moscou"[35] (This article constitutes the 10th chapter of Tolstoy's new book *What Is Art?* It is part of the second volume, which is to be published on 25 February in London, by "Brotherhood Publishing Company," 26, Paternoster Sq., and in Moscow).

It is not possible to state with certainty how the manuscript of the treatise made its way to France. In a letter to Tolstoy of 10 March 1898, Maude tried to explain what had happened and justify himself: "I was saddened to learn of the appearance of chapter 10 in print in Paris. I knew nothing about this, until it had already been sent to *Revue blanche* and it was too late to stop the presses" (30:552).

Even after he gave the treatise to be translated in England, Tolstoy continued to make fundamental changes in it. This had an immediate effect on the French translation, which can be seen as one of the intermediate steps of his work, or the reflection of one of its versions.[36] "The changes in the 10th chapter," wrote Tolstoy to Maude, on 8 November 1897, about the sections that interest us, "consist of moving Mallarmé's prose, the first article from *Divagations* ['Le Phénomène futur'] and the poems of the 4 poets to the first appendix. The lines preceding Mallarmé's prose and the poems of the 4 poets are therefore changed. Several words about the poems are changed as well" (70:86).[37] In the first Russian publication of the treatise, which appeared in the *Voprosy filosofii i psikhologii* (Questions of philosophy and psychology), the "appendices" were omitted. Subsequently, in separate editions,

Tolstoy decided to omit appendices altogether. The English translation, however, adhered to the original plan.

Tolstoy gives, as one of the outrageous examples of the new poetry, Mallarmé's sonnet "A la nue accablante tu . . ." (first published in *Obole littéraire*, 15 March 1894, and a year later in the German literary miscellany *Pan*), putting it up for ridicule as a poem completely devoid of meaning.[38] The Russian writer's argument was aided, not insignificantly, by the fact that the sonnet appeared on the pages of *Revue blanche* with the ninth line distorted to the point of absurdity ("braves" instead of "baves"), an error that was repeated in some of the later French editions of the treatise.[39] The editor of the journal, Félix Fénéon, gripped by anxious forebodings, had asked Mallarmé for the manuscript so he could check the galley proofs, but his request, alas, came too late.[40]

Mallarmé's sonnet was preceded in the French version of Tolstoy's work by this passage:

Continuons maintenant à citer des exemples de ces poètes. Après Baudelaire et Verlaine, les plus estimés sont Mallarmé et Maeterlinck. N'ayant pas sous la main les poésies de ces deux écrivains, je prends mes exemples dans une superbe revue allemande qui contient quelques-unes de leurs productions, les meilleures, peut-être.[41]

[Let us now continue to quote examples of the works of these poets. After Baudelaire and Verlaine the most esteemed ones are Mallarmé and Maeterlinck. Not having at hand the poems of these two authors, I take my examples from a superb German journal that contains some of their poems, perhaps the very best.]

We will not attempt to answer the question to what degree these words are Tolstoy's, and to what degree they belong to his French translator, Tarrida del Marmol. Our study includes neither an examination of the textual criticism on the treatise, nor the history of its writing. Our aim is to illuminate the vicissitudes of the publication of the short poem of Stéphane Mallarmé, all of whose work was denigrated by Tolstoy on the basis of this one poem. We have reason to believe that *What Is Art?* played a primary role in the discrediting of Mallarmé in Russia, inasmuch as there were no educated Russians who would not have been familiar with it. At the beginning of the century, at a time of widespread knowledge of French, distortions of perception occurred primarily because of typographical errors. In the Soviet period, erroneous translations compounded typographical errors.

Two or three mentions of the name of the French symbolist and fourteen quoted lines would not seem worthy of the present discussion. A study of the critical literature about Tolstoy shows, however, that half a page of the treatise laid the foundation for the constant denunciation of Mallarmé's poetry in all later publications, connected with the heritage of the Russian writer. B. Engel'gardt wrote, for example, that "Maeterlinck, Mallarmé, Manet, and Van Gogh caused Tolstoy, as an artist, nothing but deep irritation, and their works seemed to him 'affectations and grimaces.'"[42] It is curious that even such apparently inoffensive remarks by an unbiased scholar helped create the environment of unfounded, but devastating, condemnation. The absence of any commentary in the academic editions of Tolstoy's work, which would contain objective critical statements about Mallarmé, reinforces the already distrustful attitude of the Russian reader to his poems.

Returning to the Paris publication of the tenth chapter of *What Is Art?* we notice that the editor of *La Revue blanche* denies all responsibility for discrepancies between the French translation and the Russian original, placing the blame for the distortions completely on the translator: "L'auteur nous apprend, au dernier moment, qu'il se propose d'introduire quelques menues modifications dans le texte de cette étude. Si elles étaient de quelque importance, nous les signalerions dans notre prochain numéro"[43] (The author informs us at the last moment that he has endeavored to introduce some minor modifications into the text of the present study. If the changes prove to be of any importance, we will point them out in our next issue).

The Berlin literary journal *Pan* ("une superbe revue allemande") mentioned by the French journal was indeed a luxurious publication: It was large and printed on expensive, heavy paper. The miscellany printed poetic works in the original and had as its mission the propagation of modern trends in art. The manuscript of Mallarmé's sonnet was reproduced in facsimile in the first issue of *Pan* of 1895. As the poet himself intended, the poem was placed in the center of a blank page. On the page to the left was "Poetry of Stéphane Mallarmé," an illustration by the Belgian artist Fernand Knopf.

It has been established that Tolstoy quoted Mallarmé's sonnet precisely from this publication. In a letter of 19 August 1897, he thanks Vladimir Vasil'evich Stasov (1824–1906), who was at that time the supervisor of the artistic section of the Imperial Public Library in St. Petersburg, for sending him books, and promises to look at the *Pan* (not yet received) and return it "intact" (70:121). On 29 October, Stasov asked him to return *Pan,* which was sent to St. Petersburg on 7 November, "by the very same post," according to the letter Tolstoy wrote in reply (70:183). At this stage of work on *What Is Art?* the sonnet "A la nue accablante tu ...," apparently did not capture the writer's attention. After a little while, he again turned to Stasov, this time with a request to copy out for him selections of Mallarmé and Maeterlinck. We find the French verses copied out by Stasov as an enclosure to his letter of 6 January 1898. The manner in which this letter is written is very curious for an understanding of the literary atmosphere of that time. A clear opponent of Decadence, Stasov himself, over the course of many years, had worked on the book *Razgrom* (The Rout), in which he had tried to "shake up, stir up, toss around everything that has been done in art to this day."[44] In the letter to Tolstoy that accompanies the copied texts, he refers to his ill health, which, nonetheless, cannot diminish the obvious zeal in his words:

> Yes, and though my head is spinning, and there is still some kind of filth inside, I still took and copied the unimaginable nonsense of *Mallarmé* and *Maeterlinck*. Though I am sick I vouch for the *complete accuracy* of this nonsense in my copy: not one dot is false. It is a little difficult for me to write today, but, then it is better to write than not to write. And you know, I myself was going to include these two monsters, *Mallarmé* and *Maeterlinck* in my article which I began back in Moscow, about the exhibition "Decadent Posters" (international exhibition), which was here in December. This poetic delirium, as a matter of fact, relates to what I wanted to say about the decadent painters in this monstrous exhibition, about Paris, about Europe, about public tastes for art at this moment, and about the *pardon* (cursed!), which contemporary Europe continually grants to every kind of madness, every absurdity, every crime against sense and reason, as long as it is *"talented"* (Ah, these accursed false talents! They are accursed, dishonorable, and are destroying us all!).[45]

Vouching "for complete accuracy," Stasov was not mistaken. He deciphered Mallarmé's difficult handwriting and reproduced the sonnet "A la nue accablante tu..." and Maeterlinck's poems without changes. During the preparation of the treatise for printing in Russia, Tolstoy's assistants introduced their own arbitrary punctuation, and, to the errors which had crept into the publication of *Revue blanche,* they added yet another—totally absurd—typographical error in the second quatrain: "soir" instead of "sais."[46]

Considering the disorderly character of the preparation of the manuscript of the second part of the treatise,[47] these inaccuracies are not surprising. The foreign-language text was introduced as handwritten insertions in all four typewritten copies of the tenth chapter. Tolstoy entrusted V. Lazurskiy with the task of checking the foreign sources,[48] and the latter, most likely, merely glanced over these "trifles" while reading the proofs. More than that, the publishers of the treatise stripped the sonnet of its classical stanzaic form. To this day, it is printed in Russia without stanzaic divisions and with the most fantastic punctuation. The *Revue blanche* publishers, to their credit, rushed to correct the mistakes. In the issue following the first French publication of the extract from *What Is Art?* the editors apologized to Mallarmé and restored the sonnet to its proper form: "Nous rétablissons dans sa teneur le sonnet de M. Stéphane Mallarmé dont la seconde stance a été défiguré par une inexactitude grave"[49] (We are restoring in its strict form Stéphane Mallarmé's sonnet the second stanza of which was distorted by a serious inacuracy). However, the main blow had already been struck. One of Mallarmé's most complicated poems reached the reader, not only with a negative commentary, but with the key line disfigured, removing from the sonnet any linguistic logic whatsoever. In the English edition of the treatise, the poem was accompanied by the following footnote from the translator: "This sonnet seems too unintelligible for translation."[50]

Accusing the most prominent French poets of the nineteenth century of immorality, Tolstoy, in his "fanatical injustice" (the expression of André Suarès), listed as their first fault a striving toward deliberate incomprehensibility. At the level of content, the opacity of the texts quoted is quite varied. To a contemporary reader, accustomed to poetry of this type, the "elaborate" poems of, say, Verlaine ("Dans l'interminable . . ." and others) could even seem transparent. Mallarmé's poem "A la nue accablante tu . . ." is truly a hermetic work, extraordinarily interesting for our discussion, all the more for the Russian readers who have at their disposal four published Russian translations—one prose and three in verse—which allow for some very interesting conclusions.[51] Here, for obvious reasons, we will limit our analysis to the prose one.

To eliminate any further misunderstandings, we quote here the text of the sonnet based on the most authoritative French editions (we cannot help mentioning that even in one of the latest and most serious of them, *Oeuvres complètes*, the siren of the last line lost its feminine quality and became "un sirène"[52]):

> A la nue accablante tu
> Basse de basalte et de laves
> A même les échos esclaves
> Par une trompe sans vertu
>
> Quel sépulcral naufrage (tu
> Le sais, écume, mais y baves)
> Suprême une entre les épaves
> Abolit le mât dévêtu
>
> Ou cela que furibond faute
> De quelque perdition haute
> Tout l'abîme vain éployé
>
> Dans le si blanc cheveu qui traîne
> Avarement aura noyé
> Le flanc enfant d'une sirène

"This poem is not exceptional in its incomprehensibility," emphasized Tolstoy. "I have read several of Mallarmé's poems. They are all devoid of meaning" (30:101).

Tolstoy does not argue his point at all, because for him, any text of Mallarmé "has only to be quoted to be seen to be nonsense."[53] Today such an approach would hardly suffice. What is more, we have at our disposal a powerful scholarly apparatus for understanding the works of Mallarmé.

The sonnet "A la nue accablante tu..." is rightly considered by scholars to be a bundle of intellectual suggestion ("densité suggestive et intellectualisme")[54] connected to an eleven-page metaphor in the poem *Un Coup de Dés jamais n'abolira le hasard*. In spite of differences in understanding details (which spark arguments even today), all leading interpreters consider this poem, filled with maritime terminology, to be a sort of epilogue to the *Poésies* (1899), the prologue to which was the sonnet "Salut," issuing a call to the sea. Émilie Noulet shows that the contents of the poem are restored by a "straightening-up" of the syntax: "two quatrains form one winding, ornamental phrase, the violent movements of which are a graphic expression of the rocking of a boat. Following strict grammatical functions, it is possible to reestablish the following order for the utterance: Quel sépulcral naufrage... abolit le mât dévêtu..., naufrage, tu... par une trompe sans vertu... à la nue accablante."[55] And, further, about the tercets: "These two phrases blend into one tumultuous phrase, the subject of which is 'the whole abyss.'"[56]

Suzanne Bernard, in addition to the "dislocated" syntax, sees the source of the difficulty in the uncommon usage of the word "basse,"[57] strengthened by the oddity of the expression "A même les échos" (instead of "même aux échos") and a Latinized perception of the word "suprême" (suprema), which means here either "supreme" or "very last."

Today it is virtually impossible to say anything new about Mallarmé's poems. However, as far as we can judge, none of the scholars has so far drawn attention to the fact that the word "suprême" is connected by an internal rhyme with the phrase "A même" of the first stanza. Moreover, the position of "suprême" in the third line makes it parallel to "A même" above. The latter is, in its turn, parallel to the beginning of the sonnet "A la nue . . ." (similar to the parallelism of the repeated "jadis" in the poem "Sainte"). This double structure projects the horizontal plane of the sonnet which lacks a vertical plane. If we consider the quatrains in the categories of "high and low," then we will see that the first stanza describing the sky hovers over the "supreme" abyss of the second stanza representing the "top" of the sea-surface. This surface ("que la blancheur défend")[58] (that its whiteness protects) cannot be in any way penetrated by human sight. If we develop Robert Greer Cohn's remark that the word "accablante" contains several "flattening" *a*'s, then we can imagine the picture drawn by Mallarmé's sonnet as a thin line, uninterrupted either by the eruptions of lava, or the brass instruments of an orchestra, or by a mast aimed at the skies. The American scholar remarks that "*Basse* also means 'bank under water' which, together with the sense of 'low,' implies the murderous descent, reaching right down into the level of life, to the extent that cloud and water are mingled."[59] For our part, we would add that today, a hundred years after Mallarmé, this line can also mean the weakening oscillations of a cardiogram.

In the tercets, this vague sinuous line is emphasized by a childlike contour of a siren ("le flanc enfant"), an alternative victim of the silenced storm. Suzanne Bernard, who considers the first two stanzas on the whole relatively clear ("l'ensemble est relativement clair"),[60] sees the fundamental problem in the tercets, which present a series of unsolvable riddles, the most important of which is: How is it possible to drown a siren, an inhabitant of the sea by nature? The most she can do is drown herself of her own free will.[61]

We do not think that the siren, "an inhabitant of the sea by nature," went down to the sea-bottom. She must be lying on a volcanic bank under water thrown there by the storm which had failed to find a "*higher*" victim (italics mine). This "vertical" word in an entirely "horizontal" poem embodies Mallarmé's effect of presence/absence. The siren's hair floating on the flat surface of the sea emphasizes the silence of an unsung or a hushed song.

Or maybe there, faraway, we can distinguish the white torn sails of an abolished mast?[62]

The contemporary Russian reader who does not know any foreign languages must depend, in his dealings with such texts, on a translation by a qualified philologist. In Tolstoy's time, French excerpts in Russian works were given, as a rule, only in the original. This tradition was observed everywhere with reference to the tenth chapter of *What Is Art?* from the editions addressed to the more educated segments of the population right down to the popular supplement to the magazine *Chitatel* (Reader), which came out in 1898 as a separate pamphlet on low-quality paper. In the Soviet period, by contrast, the norm was to give a Russian translation of any foreign phrase. *What Is Art?* is an extremely unexpected exception: A translation of the French texts quoted by Tolstoy was not undertaken until 1951, and was completed only for the thirtieth volume of the anniversary *Polnoe sobranie sochinenii* (Complete Collected Works). In spite of the distortions in the original, the author of the translation (or, more precisely, word-for-word rendering), A. V. Zvenigorodsky, conscientiously attempted to figure out the subject of the sonnet and connect the divergent lines with a unifying content:[63]

> Under the pressing cloud the bass of lava and basalt grew silent, like servile echoes of a sounding trumpet.
> Such a funereal rocking of the boat (the evening grew silent, but the foam is still strong) destroys with the last piece of debris the mast without a sail!

Let us recall that modern scholars interpret the quatrains of the sonnet as the picture of the sea calmed after a storm. The reminiscence of a tragic shipwreck is being kept only by the foam floating on the surface. Bertrand Marchal writes:

> Tout le poème tourne autour d'une image centrale, celle de l'écume, qui sert aussi de point de départ à une double reconstruction imaginaire. Le poète, en effet, interroge une écume suspecte: bavant sur les hauts-fonds sinistres, sous un ciel orageux et bas, elle semble trahir un naufrage dont la mer garderait jalousement le secret. Mais rien,

sinon l'écume et le paysage trop sombre, n'avère ce naufrage, qu'il faut donc supposer total ("naufrage sépulcral"), pour qu'il ait ainsi, comme un crime parfait, abolit jusqu'au mât, cette épave suprême toujours dernière engloutie, plantée sur l'océan comme la croix d'un cimetière marin.[64]

[The whole poem revolves around a central image, that of foam, which also represents a point of departure for a double imaginative reconstruction. The poet, in fact, interrogates the suspect foam: drooling over sinister banks under water below stormy skies, the foam seems to betray a shipwreck whose secret is being jealously kept by the sea. But nothing except the foam and a gloomy scenery proves that the shipwreck has really taken place and, thus, must be considered as absolute ("a sepulchral shipwreck") since it is abolished, like a perfect crime, to the very mast, this supreme bit of floating wreckage, always the last to be swallowed, planted on the ocean like the cross of a seaside cemetery.]

By an evil irony of fate, this very image, crucial for understanding the poem, was destroyed by the errors in the Russian edition. It is not known whether the poem became "more opaque" because of the loss of the plural in the newly created epithet "braves" (instead of the verb "baver," which Mallarmé had in the second person singular). One thing is clear: The appearance of the noun "soir" instead of the verb "sais" moved the line in parentheses to the collection of meaningless words.[65] If it were not for this awkwardness, Zvenigorodsky might have succeeded in contrasting the "foam" of the second quatrain with the pale hair of the drowning siren in the concluding stanza. This not only would, without a doubt, have given some sense to the translation of the quatrains, but also to the internally structured rendering of the tercets: "Or this is nothing other than a violent need for some high perdition—the entire abyss, which, with carefully spread wings, dragging itself through the white manes, stingily drowns the maidenly belly of the siren."

Zvenigorodsky's interpretation may not enjoy the right to independent existence alongside scholarly interpretations; it nonetheless deserves respect for its unbiased attempt to synthesize the uncoordinated elements of meaning. To Tolstoy, this text seemed absurd, just as Baudelaire's "Duel" seemed absurd, though it has none of the grammatical difficulty of Mallarmé. For the contemporary reader, such ciphers ceased to be a limiting factor long ago.

A prominent ideologist of Russian formalism, Viktor Shklovsky, warned that "if we take Tolstoy's theoretical works and, in particular, 'The Introduction to the works of Guy de Maupassant' (1894) or 'What Is Art?' we will see that in these works a very interesting theory was created, in which, however, Tolstoy's own work does not fit at all."[66]

Mallarmé was certainly not the only poet whose works were the subject of derision by Tolstoy. Attacked, it seems, more than the others, Mallarmé was, nevertheless, much more keenly aware of the contradiction formulated by Shklovsky than all of his unsolicited defenders.

At the initiative of one of the first French translators of Tolstoy's treatise, E. Halpérine-Kaminsky, *La Grande Revue* printed, in a series of issues, the opinions of French writers about Tolstoy's treatise. In March 1899, several months after his death, Mallarmé's reply was published. Written in Valvins in June 1898, it was restrained and full of respect. Mallarmé had only an abridged translation of Tolstoy's book at that time. The definitive edition was sent to him by the translator later, as we can judge by the copy with the inscription from its donor that has been preserved in Mallarmé's library.

Upholding the high principles of art, the independence of creation, and freedom of religious views, Mallarmé cites, in his answer, the first publication of Halpérine-Kaminsky's *Le Rôle de l'art d'après Tolstoï*, a work that is based on quotations from the treatise, but that does not reproduce its text in full. The respectful tone, knowledgeability, and reserve of Mallarmé's reply are truly striking:

L'abrégé, quelquefois une paraphrase, par vous tiré d'un haut ouvrage sincère, où Tolstoï met en question l'existence même de l'Art, montre une fidélité clairvoyante: vous admettrez, cependant, que je ne juge pas sur des fragments lumineusement choisis et traduits, ou tant que je ne possède pas l'oeuvre intégrale, une méditation puissante qui prit quinze années. Je craindrais quelque interprétation erronée comme est la teneur, par exemple, qu'ici je lis d'un de mes poèmes. Omettant les morceaux où le Traité se spécialise, pour retenir les pages empreintes de désintéressement et de généralité, il me paraît que l'apôtre illustre assigne à l'Art, comme principe, telle qualité qui en soit plutôt la conséquence. L'Art, en effet, se trouve essentiellement *communicatif,* mais du fait, aussi, qu'*exclusif*—j'adopte les termes. Diffusion *à qui veut,* par suite d'un retrait, ou isolement, d'abord. A part quoi, l'instinct religieux reste un moyen offert à tous de se passer de l'Art, il le contient à l'état embryonnaire et l'Art n'émane, soi ou pur, que distrait de cette influence.[67]

[Your abridged version, sometimes a paraphrase, extracted from the sincere and lofty work in which Tolstoy questions the very existence of art shows a discerning fidelity. You must admit, though, that on the basis of fragments brilliantly selected and translated, and without the entire text, it would be wrong for me to judge a powerful meditation that has taken fifteen years. I fear an erroneous interpretation as, for example, is the case of one of my poems I can read here. Skipping some parts where the Treatise becomes too specialized and keeping to the pages stamped with impartiality and general ideas, I would think that the renowned apostle attributes to Art, as a principle, a quality that is rather its consequence. Art can, in fact, be mostly a means of *communication,* but it can also be a means of *exclusiveness*—I am borrowing your terms. Propagated *to those who want,* but first by way of withdrawal or isolation. Apart from that, the religious instinct remains a means offered to anyone who tries to do without Art; it contains Art in its embryonic state, and Art emanates as is or in its pure form only if detached from this influence.]

Again and again, we must emphasize that to analyze one or another of Mallarmé's statements about art in all its depth would require a separate work. We would also add that Mallarmé's position does not betray any ambiguity or weakness proper to his friends and defenders. The latter found themselves in a very delicate situation. Promulgators of Russian realist prose, they tried to present Tolstoy's treatise as an unfortunate mistake that in no case undermined the inherent value of the French poetry. As for Mallarmé, he did not surrender before Tolstoy's authority as did Halpérine-Kaminsky who limited his initial translation of *What Is Art?* to quotations, however numerous, or Teodor de Wyzewa who dared make direct omissions.

In the introduction to his version of the translation, apparently based on the English edition and appearing simultaneously with Halpérine-Kaminsky's version, Teodor de Wyzewa justifies some of the changes he made in the text of the treatise in this way:

"Aussi ai-je pris la liberté de supprimer, dans la traduction de ce livre, un passage où sont cités comme étant 'absolument incompréhensibles' deux poèmes en prose français, le 'Galant Tireur' de Baudelaire, et le 'Phénomène futur,' de M. Mallarmé"[68] (Therefore, in the translation of this book, I have taken the liberty to leave out a passage that quotes as being "absolutely incomprehensible" two French prose poems, the "Galant tireur" of Baudelaire and the "Phénomène futur" of Mallarmé).

Wyzewa quotes both mentioned poems and continues:

Que les sentiments exprimés par ces deux poèmes soient *mauvais,* au sens où l'estime le comte Tolstoï, qu'ils ne soient ni chrétiens ni universels, nous pouvons l'admettre, encore que les sentiments qu'exprime le *Phénomène futur* ne soient pas sensiblement éloignés d'être *tolstoïens,* en dépit de l'apparence contraire, et que jamais un poète n'ait flétri en plus nobles images l'action dégradante, abrutissante, anti-artistique de notre soi-disant civilisation. Mais certes ce ne sont point là des oeuvres absolument incompréhensibles.[69]

[Even if we admit that the feelings expressed by these two poems are *bad* in the sense that they are, in Tolstoy's view, neither Christian nor universal, we should also admit that the feelings expressed by the "Phénomène futur" are not far from being *Tolstoyan,* contrary to all appearances, and never has any poet stigmatized in more noble images the degrading, brutalizing, antiartistic influence of our so-called civilization. They are certainly not absolutely incomprehensible works.]

The art of Mallarmé and other leading symbolists was, in Tolstoy's understanding, evil, bad, and immoral because it did not answer the fundamental criteria of his conception.[70] "It is frightening to think," he exclaimed, "what would happen to humanity, if this kind of art had spread among the people" (30:173). In light of this, Wyzewa's remark about the "Tolstoyan" character of Mallarmé's poem is not as paradoxical as it might at first seem. Even today critics note elements of deep similarity between these two very different writers. Mallarmé is, according to R. G. Cohn, "closer to that secret Russian brother-under-the-skin than one might think: the haying scene in *Anna Karenina* provides a clue to the affinity."[71]

Quoting the prose poem "Conflict" (1895), the American scholar fundamentally refutes the notorious accusation that the essence of Mallarmé's art is an antidemocratic attitude.[72] In this we are quite far from the idea that this work, atypical for Mallarmé, "bears witness to the poet's dissatisfaction in the mid-90s with that position in which he had remained all his life,"[73] or expresses the poet's desire "to come closer to the proletariat,"[74] as the leading Soviet scholars insisted, even if we try to understand literally the line: "Le hasard, puisqu'il me rapproche, selon que je me fis, de prolétaires."[75] (chance, since it draws me near, according to my development, to proletarians) And yet, judging by Mallarmé's letters from the time of the Paris Commune, his social commitment was stronger than is commonly thought.[76] At that time, when the majority of French writers denounced the Communards with unbelievable cruelty, the poet, in April 1871, not only felt sorry for the victims ("je plains les victimes")[77], but openly sympathized with the rebels as well: "Il n'y a pas de mal que la politique veuille se passer de la Littérature et se régler à coups de fusil" (there is no harm in the wish of politics to do without literature and settle things through gunshots)"[78] In our opinion, both Tolstoy and Mallarmé reflected, although completely differently, the atmosphere of the "end of century" cultural crisis. Even with all his judgments about modern art, even with all his certainty that "all this decadence is complete lunacy,"[79] Tolstoy felt the strength of its attack and (it is unimportant for what reason) remained for many years an active reader of symbolist literature. "After the treatise was published," writes the memoirist on 14 February 1898, "Tolstoy continued to follow the decadents. He borrowed decadent books and magazines from Countess Sollogub, in order to 'smell how badly they smell.' Lev Polivanov, a well-known Moscow tutor, conveyed to Tolstoy, through his son Lev L'vovich, that he was struggling in vain with decadents, who were already dead and buried. Lev Nikolaevich, objecting to this, said that, on the contrary, it was necessary to pay more attention to the decadents because decadence is the sickness of our time, and must be taken seriously."[80]

Tolstoy was not mistaken. Mallarmé was the brilliant prophet of our "sick" century.

Translated from the Russian by Thomas Cunningham

Notes

The author expresses deep gratitude to Professor Wlad Godzich for his attentive reading of this article and his valuable suggestions.

1. *Dnevnik* (Diary) (28 May 1896) 53:96. All quotations are from the collection: L. N. Tolstoy, *Polnoe sobranie sochinenii* (Complete Works), ed. V. G. Chertkov, 90 vols. (Moscow, Leningrad: Goslitizdat, 1928–1958. Nendeln/ Liechtenstein Kraus Reprint, 1972.). Volume and page numbers are indicated in parentheses. The Russian text is translated by Thomas Cunningham, and the French quotations are translated by myself.

2. Five years before this, the poet and critic Platon Krasnov began his article "What Are Decadents?" with an analogous phrase: "In France there has recently appeared a new school of young writers. Its representatives are Maeterlinck, Moréas, Mallarmé, Péladan and others who attracted everybody's attention by their strange ways of life, but still more so by the contents and the form of their works" (Platon Krasnov, "Chto takoe dekadenty? Sochineniia Morisa Meterlinka i Stefana Mallarme" [What are decadents? Works of Maurice Maeterlinck and Stéphane Mallarmé], *Trud* [Labor], no. 9 [1893]: 628).

3. Shortly after Tolstoy, and clearly not without his influence, a doctor of psychiatry and literary critic, Nikolay Bazhenov, author of the book *Simvolisty i dekadenty. Psikhiatricheskii etiud* (Symbolists and Decadents: A Study in Psychiatry) (Moscow: T-vo tip. A.I. Mamontova, 1899) draws the following conclusion about Mallarmé's work: "Mallarmé, head of the young poets, although he is

now almost sixty, wrote very little. But what he did write, he wrote in such elaborate language, with such neologisms and archaisms and such wondrous-monstrous combinations of words and phrases, that he is, in most of his works, incomprehensible" (14–15).

4. *Voprosy filosofii i psikhologii* (Questions of Philosophy and Psychology) (1898), 1:31.

5. *I. E. Repin and L. Tolstoy* (Moscow: Iskusstvo, 1949), 1:16.

6. *La Grande Revue* (February 1899). Quoted in Thaïs Lindstrom, *Tolstoï en France (1886–1890)* (Paris: Institut d'études slaves de l'Université de Paris, 1952), 77.

7. Ibid., 76–82.

8. Quoted in *Literaturnoe Nasledstvo* (Literary Heritage) (Moscow: Izd. Akademii Nauk, 1937), 31–32: 981.

9. Quoted in Sophie Laffitte, "Tolstoï et les écrivains français," *Europe*, no. 379–80 (November–December 1960): 186, special edition dedicated to Tolstoy.

10. *Apollon*, no. 6 (March 1910): 14.

11. Tolstoy knew Jules Huret personally and quoted his "questionnaire" in the treatise; a copy of Huret's book with many of Tolstoy's notes is preserved in the library at Yasnaya Polyana.

12. René Doumic, *Les Jeunes. Etudes et portraits* (Paris: Perrin, 1896), 186–87.

13. Ibid., 189.

14. Ibid., 204.

15. N. K. Mikhailovskii, (Literature and Life) "Literatura i zhizn'", in (*Russian Thought*) (*Russkaia mysl'*) (1893), bk. 1, sec. 2, p. 150. "All this was very young," continued the critic:

> But since then, even the founders of the circle (hydropathes) had managed to grow up, and older people joined them (perhaps it is more precise to say that they joined the older ones). Now the most talented of them, and not only the most talented of them, but truly talented, Paul Verlaine is over fifty years old; Stéphane Mallarmé, unusually highly thought of by "his circle" is almost fifty; Moréas, also one of the eagles of this glorious flock is thirty-five. (150)

And further:

> Imagining that Mallarmé is one of the admitted leaders of symbolism, that they go to him for judgment, thirst for his advice, and expect from him great, "unheard of" works, one must think that his opinions and attitudes were shared by many decadents and symbolists. But why, in such a case, do these people call themselves "young"—"les jeunes?" We have already spoken about the distinguished age of several of them, including Mallarmé. As for youth of the soul, it is sufficiently difficult to discern in this attitude, characterized by the impotence of old age, toward the coming degeneration of the human race and to the dark precipice of the thousand-year work of mankind. (161)

16. S. A. Vengerov, ed., *Russkaia Literatura XX veka: 1890–1910* (Russian literature of the 20th Century) (Moscow: Izd. t-va Mir, 1914), 1:2.

17. In a series of sketches, "Lettres de Paris," Zola published an article "Nos poètes contemporains," in which, talking about the Parnassians, he says several words about Mallarmé:

> M. Mallarmé a été et est resté le poète le plus typique du groupe [parnassien]. C'est chez lui que toute la folie de la forme a éclaté. Poursuivi d'une préoccupation constante

dans le rythme et l'arrangement des mots, il a fini par perdre la conscience de la langue écrite. Ses pièces de vers ne contiennent que des mots mis côte à côte, non pour la clarté de la phrase, mais pour l'harmonie du morceau. L'esthétique de M. Mallarmé est de donner la sensation des idées avec des sons et des images. Ce n'est là, en somme, que la théorie des Parnassiens, mais poussée jusqu'à ce point où une cervelle se fêle.

[Mallarmé has remained the most typical representative of the (Parnassian) group. It is in his works that all the madness of form has burst out. Obsessed by a ceaseless concern for the rhythm and the order of words, he has ended up losing all awareness of the written language. His poems contain nothing but words placed side by side not for the sake of clarity of the sentence, but for the sake of harmony in the passage. The aesthetics of Mallarmé consist in giving the sensation of ideas with the help of sounds and images. It is, in short, the essence of the theory of the Parnassians, pushed however to the limit where the mind cracks.]

(In French first published in *La Voltaire* [1879]. In book form in Zola's *Les Documents littéraires. Etudes et portraits* [Paris: Charpentier, 1881]; quoted in the edition of 1891, p. 179).

18. André Beaunier, *Notes sur la Russie* (Paris: Tricon, 1901), 108.

19. René Doumic, "Les Idées du comte Tolstoï sur l'art," *Revue des deux mondes* (1 May 1898): 453.

20. Ibid.

21. Henry Lapauze, "Une Soirée chez Léon Tolstoï." Published first in the newspaper *Gaulois* on 12 June 1896. It was republished in the same year in the book *De Paris au Volga* (Paris: Flammarion, 1896), which was awarded the special prize by the French Academy. Quoted in Stéphane Mallarmé, *Correspondance [II–XI] (1871–1898)*, ed. Henri Mondor and Lloyd James Austin (Paris: Gallimard, 1965–85), 8: 175. (Hereafter cited as *Corr.*)

22. Real name: Vitol'd-Konstantin Rozenblum.

23. "For a good example of new symbolism, we may use the poem of a poet not unknown in the literary world, L'dov's 'Poplar'" (M. Stoliarov, *Etiudy o dekadentstve. Novoe veianie v sovremennoi literature* [Essays on Decadence: A New Trend in Modern Literature] [Khar'kov: Tip. Pechatnoe Delo, 1899], 42).

24. From a letter to L. Gurevich dated 25 March 1896. Quoted in P. V. Kupriianovskii, *Poety-simvolisty v zhurnale* Severnyi vestnik (Symbolist Poets in *The Northern Herald*), in *Russkaia sovetskaia poeziia i stikhovedenie* (Soviet Russian Poetry and Prosody) (Moscow: MOPI im. N. Krupskoy, 1969), 127–28.

25. In the remarks of both writers—L. Tolstoy and K. L'dov—there is no slander. The sonnet "M'introduire dans ton histoire . . ." truly was Mallarmé's first creation without periods and commas, about which the poet speaks frankly in a letter to Gustave Kahn from 9 June 1886: "vous remarquez l'absence de toute ponctuation, c'est à dessein" (*Corr.*, 3:37).

26. *Corr.*, 8:175.

27. Stéphane Mallarmé, *Oeuvres complètes*, ed. Henri Mondor and G. Jean-Aubry (Paris: Gallimard-Pléiade, 1945), 873. (Hereafter cited as *OC*.)

28. "The Russian novel from that period," remarked I. Annensky, "left a deep trace on the French novel, just as earlier Walter Scott had influenced it. And the French themselves (for example Lanson) admit that toward the end of the century in the sphere of the novel they created nothing to compare with the works of Tolstoy and Dostoevsky" (I. F. Annenskii, "Antichnyi mif v sovremennoi frantsuzskoi poezii" [Classical mythology in contemporary French poetry], *Hermes*, no. 7 [1908]: 179).

29. Il'ia Danilovich (Ely) Halpérine-Kaminsky (1858–1935) was the translator of Chekhov, Turgenev, and other Russian classics. Of Tolstoy's works he translated, among others, *Resurrection,* which was published with illustrations by L. O. Pasternak. He lived continually in France. He met Tolstoy personally in 1894, visited him in 1896 and 1898, and, in August 1902, settled not far from Tolstoy's estate. That fall he often visited Yasnaya Polyana. He compiled, translated, and commented Tolstoy's autobiographical notes and correspondence: *Tolstoï par Tolstoï: avant sa crise morale (1848–1879), autobiographie épistolaire* (Paris: Ambert, 1912). Tolstoy valued most highly Halpérine-Kaminsky's translations for conscientiousness and faithfulness to the original: "You always translate very accurately and diligently," he wrote in one of his letters (72:409).

30. Teodor de Wyzewa, a prominent symbolist critic, and a disciple of R. Wagner, was the author of the collection of essays *Nos Maîtres* (Paris: Perrin, 1895), one of the first books to admit Mallarmé's seminal influence on the development of French poetry. In 1896–1900, he published a series of books *Ecrivains étrangers* (Paris: Perrin), dedicated to Nietzsche, Whitman, Ibsen, Tennyson, Tolstoy, and Turgenev. He translated several artistic and critical works of Tolstoy, who thought highly of his work. Cf., for example, in a private letter: "Vizewa [*sic*] is a brilliant translator" (88:130).

31. In the abbreviated version of Tolstoy's article "O tom, chto nazyvaiut iskusstvom" (What Can Be Called Art) (1896), we read the following: "If there was another drunk sitting in the tavern with Verlaine, enraptured over his poems, that was enough. He served beauty, and his listeners, understanding that beauty valued him for it. Wagner, Mallarmé, Ibsen, Maeterlinck, and others were also satisfied in the same way" (30:265). It is noteworthy that the impression of the atmosphere of carousing of the early days of French decadence captivated Russian thinkers for many years to come. Cf. the statement of A. Bely of 1918: "Having taken symbolism in its academic, most narrow sense, we must bring it out of its poetic, original meaningless French circles, where the serious tasks of the fathers of 'symbolism' were mixed with the buffoonery of reformers, meeting in their cabarets; and having overthrown reality" (Andrey Bely, "O frantsuzskikh simvolistakh" [On the French Symbolists], *Russkaia literatura* [Russian Literature], no. 4 [1980], 172).

32. Quoted in *Briusovskie chteniia* (Readings on Briusov for 1963) (Yerevan: Ayastan, 1964), 274.

33. The first publication of the treatise in English was by "Brotherhood Publishing" as an "extra" to the newspaper *The New Order:* chapters 1–9 came out in January, chapters 10–14 in March, chapters 15–20 in May 1898. In July, *What Is Art?* appeared in a book form "embodying the Author's last alterations and revisions."

34. From Tolstoy's letter to V. G. Chertkov of 14 February 1898 (88:77).

35. *Revue blanche,* no. 113 (1898): 251 n.

36. After the publication of the Russian text of the treatise, Tolstoy bitterly complained about how the work was organized: "It is true that the mistake was made of premature printing," he admitted to his English translator in a letter of 20 March 1898. "This happened because I did not intend to publish in Russia and check the proofs. It required much additional work and is a great sin, which I will try to avoid in the future" (71:329–30).

37. The following note in Tolstoy's wife's journal dated 2 October 1897 applies to this variant: "Then Levochka gave me the 10th chapter of his article 'On Art,' and I inserted corrections from one copy to the other. It was difficult, straining,

mechanical work. I sat for three hours, and rejoiced that he was berating the decadents and exposing their deceit. He gives examples of the most meaningless poems of Mallarmé, Griffin, Verhaeren, Moréas, and others" (S. A. Tolstaia, *Dnevniki v dvukh tomakh* [Diary in 2 volumes] [Moscow: Khudozhestvennaya Literatura, 1978], 1:304–5).

38. About Mallarmé's prose, the first French publication of the treatise: "Quant à ses écrits en prose, tels que *Divagations,* il est impossible d'y comprendre quoi que ce soit" (As for his prose writings, such as *Divagations,* it is impossible to understand any of it) (*Revue blanche,* no. 113 [15 February 1898]: 259). What is said agrees with the text of the English edition, in which to this phrase is added another: "And that is evidently what the author intended" (*New Order Supplement,* no. 4 [1898]: 28).

39. Cf. the translations published almost simultaneously: Teodor de Wyzewa, *Comte Léon Tolstoï. Qu'est-ce que l'art?* (Paris: Perrin, 1898) ("A la nue accablante tu . . ." 110–11); henceforth the pages on which Mallarmé's sonnet is printed will be appear in parentheses and repeatedly: E. Halpérine-Kaminsky *Le Rôle de l'art d'après Tolstoï,* first in *Correspondant* (10 April 1898): 112, and then in book form (Paris: Imp. de Soye et fils, 1898), 31, the latter also translated: *Léon Tolstoï. Qu'est-ce que l'Art?* (Paris: Ollendorff, 1898), 154.

40. "Cher Monsieur Mallarmé, nous publions la traduction d'une extraordinaire étude de Tolstoï sur la poésie actuelle. Tolstoï cite votre poème 'A la nue accablante tu.' Voudriez-vous avoir l'obligeance insigne de nous en envoyer une copie, d'après laquelle nous corrigerons l'épreuve. Nous n'avons pas *Pan* et je ne sais pas par coeur ces vers" (*Corr.,* 10:102–3). (Dear Mr. Mallarmé, we are publishing the translation of an extraordinary study of Tolstoy on modern poetry. Tolstoy quotes your poem "A la nue accablante tu." We would be very much obliged to you if you could kindly send us a copy of it so that we may check the proofs. We do not have *Pan,* and I do not know your verses by heart.)

41. *Revue blanche,* no. 113 (1898): 259.

42. Quoted in *Literaturnoe Nasledstvo* (Literary Heritage) (1939) 37–38: 15.

43. *Revue blanche,* no. 113 (1898): 268 n. Tolstoy clearly was not satisfied with this, as his wrathful letters to *Journal des débats* and others testify.

44. Quoted in *Iubileinyi sbornik* (Lev Nikolayevich Tolstoy: Anniversary Volume) (Moscow-Leningrad: Gosizdat, 1928), 352.

45. First published in *Lev Tolstoi and V. V. Stasov* (Leningrad: Trudy Pushkinskogo doma Akademii Nauk, 1929), 214–15.

46. The publishers of Stasov's letters made entirely different errors than Tolstoy did: They arbitrarily placed periods and commas and replaced "Avarement" in the penultimate line with the incorrectly written "Assurément."

47. Cf. 30:564.

48. Cf. "K istorii traktata L. N. Tolstogo 'Chto takoe iskusstvo?'" (History of Tolstoy's *What Is Art?*) in V. Lazurskii, *Vospominaniia o L've Tolstom* (Recollections about Leo Tolstoy) (Moscow: Tip. Sablina, 1911).

49. *Revue blanche,* no. 114 (1 March 1898): 400.

50. Leon Tolstoy, *What Is Art?* Chapters 10–14, translated from the Russian by Aylmer Maude, *The New Order* Extra (March 1898): 28.

51. Poetic translations belong to Mark Talov (written not later than 1934, published in 1990), Ariadna Efron (1962), and the author of the present study (1995).

52. Stéphane Mallarmé, *Oeuvres complètes: Poésies,* ed. Carl Paul Barbier and Charles Gordon Millan (Paris: Flammarion, 1983), 1: 394.

53. H. W. Garrod, *Tolstoi's Theory of Art. Taylorian Lecture, 1935* (Oxford: Clarendon Press, 1935), 13.

54. Suzanne Bernard, *Mallarmé et la musique* (Paris: Nizet, 1959), 115.

55. Cf.: "les deux quatrains ne forment qu'une seule phrase sinueuse, arabesque dont les mouvement violents conviennent à la figuration de naufrage. En se tenant aux strictes fonctions grammaticales, on rétablit comme suit l'ordre des propositions: Quel sépulcral naufrage . . . abolit le mât dévêtu., naufrage, tu . . . par une trompe sans vertu . . . à la nue accablante" (Emilie Noulet, *L'Oeuvre poétique de Stéphane Mallarmé* [Bruxelles: Editions Jacques Antoine, 1974], 475).

56. "Les deux phrases ne forment qu'une seule phrase tumultueuse dont le sujet est 'Tout l'abîme'" (Ibid).

57. According to E. Noulet, "volcanic sandbar"; according to R. G. Cohn, an adjective for the word "cloud"; according to Guy Michaud and L. J. Austin, a musical term.

58. "Brise marine."

59. Robert Greer Cohn, *Toward the Poems of Mallarmé* (Berkeley and Los Angeles: University of California Press, 1965; 1980, expanded ed.), 230–31.

60. Bernard, 118.

61. Ibid. Another prominent authority on complex questions in Mallarmé's work, Charles Mauron, with whom Bernard disagrees on some points, considers the theme of the rocking of the boat of the first half of the sonnet to be juxtaposed to the "trivial" incident of the second half: "Les quatrains évoquent un sinistre naufrage, les tercets insinuent ironiquement: beaucoup de bruits pour rien" (Charles Mauron, *Introduction à la psychanalyse de Mallarmé* [Neuchâtel: La Baconnière, 1968], 139).

62. Like Mauron, Wallace Fowlie also sees a certain irony in the substitution of a fast and proud vessel by a child siren: "If it was not a ship that sank, might it have been a child siren drowned ironically because the ocean could find no lofty reason for its lashing fury" (Wallace Fowlie, *Mallarmé* [Chicago: University of Chicago Press, 1953], 217).

63. It is fortunate that Andrei Vladimirovich Zvenigorodsky (1878–1961) was a poet, a poet-decadent at that. He enjoyed influence among symbolists and released at the beginning of the century two collections of decadent poems—*Delirium tremens* (Moscow, 1906) and *Sub Jove frigido* (Moscow, 1909). In the fifties, Zvenigorodsky was remembered in Moscow editorial boards as an extraordinarily erudite conversationalist and an expert on literature.

64. Bertrand Marchal, *Lecture de Mallarmé* (Paris: Corti, 1985), 252–53.

65. In the early English editions of the treatise, every stanza of the sonnet was printed without commas and ended with a period. This denied the reader the possibility of linking the quatrains and tercets in one meaningful phrase. The word "baves" was not distorted; however, the second person form of the verb "to know" (sais) was transformed, as in the Russian editions, to "evening" (*soir*).

66. Viktor Shklovskii, *Lev Tolstoy* (Moscow: Molodaya Guardiya, 1963), 719.

67. *Corr.*, 10:221–22.

68. *Corr.*, 221.

69. Ibid.

70. "Bad art," explained the Russian writer to his English translator, "I call that which is accessible only to a select few, just as I call all art which is accessible only to exceptional people bad art" (from a letter to A. Maude [70:196]).

71. Robert Greer Cohn, *Mallarmé's Prose Poems* (Cambridge: Cambridge University Press, 1987), 122.

72. Tolstoy was convinced that in Russia, as in France, Mallarmé's poems, Maeterlinck's dramas, and the music of Wagner and Strauss could call up "in those unhappy and disfigured people, who hadn't the slightest understanding of the work of the true life of humanity, who are educated in depraved gymnasia, universities, academies, and conservatories, those feelings which these artists experienced, but for the laboring masses, living the true life of the people, they make no sense at all" (from an unfinished article, "O tom, chto nazyvaetsia iskusstvom" [What Can Be Called Art] [1896]. Quoted in *Literaturnoye Nasledstvo* [Literary Heritage] [Moscow: Izd. Akademii Nauk, 1939], 37–38: 75).

73. D. Oblomievskii, "Stéphane Mallarmé," in *Frantsuzskii simvolizm* (French Symbolism) (Moscow: Nauka, 1973), 246.

74. N. Balashov, "Symbolism: Mallarmé," in *Istoriia frantsuzskoi literatury* (History of French literature) (Moscow-Leningrad: Izd. Akademii Nauk, 1959), 3:367.

75. *OC*, 357.

76. In particular, see the letter to Cazalis of 9 April 1871, in Carl Paul Barbier, et al. eds., *Documents Stéphane Mallarmé 1–7* (Paris: Nizet, 1968–1980), 6:461.

77. Ibid., 466.

78. Ibid., 467.

79. Quoted in K. N. Lomunov, *Estetika L'va Tolstogo* (Aesthetics of Leo Tolstoy) (Moscow: Sovremennik, 1972), 346. Cf. also: K. N. Lomunov, "Tolstoy v bor'be protiv dekadentskogo iskusstva" ("Tolstoy in the Battle against Decadent Art" in *Lev Nikolayevich Tolstoy* [Moscow: Izd. Akademii Nauk, 1951]).

80. V. Lazurskii, 53.

Mallarmé and Basho

PATRICIA TERRY

MALLARMÉ and Basho, the earliest and best of haiku poets, are dissimilar in all but the one thing both regarded as central: their lofty aspiration for poetry. The nature of that aspiration corresponds to Robert Greer Cohn's definition of Mallarmé as "a poet of being," which touches the essential of Basho as well.

A poetry of being occurs at the intersection of the transient and its ground: the sea to which Le Maître succumbs, a river into which a woman dives, a rock and the sound of an insect, or, in another Basho poem:

> This summer grass
> remains
> of warriors' dreams.[1]

A poetry of being places itself in contrast to the poetry of Mallarmé's youth and of much of Basho's life, in which we hear the voice of an identifiable poet, separate from his subject. Yet the poetry of being is in its way the *most* personal—the encounter between a human awareness and the object of its perceptions. Words can only interrupt or refer to that encounter from which they themselves are absolutely excluded. So it is, for poetry, the most extreme aspiration: to bring into language what is, by definition, unsayable. Those who write of Basho often call his a Zen art, and not without justification. This is not usually said of Mallarmé, except when one calls his work a poetry of being.

Thanks to the familiar photograph, we know how Mallarmé appeared at nineteen years of age—a dandy, his eyes looking down on something, or everything. In Manet's wonderful portrait he is looking in the direction of his thoughts, away from what surrounds him. Mallarmé began to be the person Manet shows us not very long after that early photograph when he was in his midtwenties.

That must have been a most difficult time of his life. His painful but enjoyably dramatic inner debate on the subject of marriage was far behind him; now he was not only a husband but a father, already learning that babies, however amazing, are not amusing for a very long at a time: "Ma Geneviève est charmante à embrasser dix minutes, mais après?"[2] He was teaching English to disrespectful students who did not know his future and who probably would not have cared. His health was poor, he speaks of a threat to his lungs. He was sacrificing sleep for the sake of poems and rejecting every irrelevant grace for the sake of a concept of beauty. The empty paper protected by its whiteness would always, to say the least, prevent facility, but Mallarmé's concern was at first aesthetic, rather than a wrestling with the unsayable. The whiteness, or the silence, are simply more perfect than human words, the colors of life which, in Shelley's "Adonais," "stains the white radiance of Eternity." We always write, said Mallarmé, black on white, never like the stars against the dark.[3]

Less than a year after "Brise marine," as we learn from his letter to Henri Cazalis, the empty page turned into emptiness itself, "le Néant," as he called it, the realization that mind only imagines itself separate from matter. "Nous ne sommes que de vaines formes de la matière" (we are nothing but empty/meaningless manifestations of matter)—one hesitates about the translation of "vaine": not excluding vain.[4] Years later, the penultimate conclusion of *Un Coup de Dés* makes the experience behind that statement actually available to the reader: "Rien n'aura eu lieu que le lieu" (Nothing will have taken place but the place).

L'Azur had been the absolute, haunting, but *outside*. In the experience of Nothingness, there *is* no outside. This is the crucial difference between the exclamatory passages in early poems ("Vers toi j'accours O matière!") and his later work. *L'Azur* is still dualistic; the "I" is one thing and "matter" is another. Then, "en creusant le vers à ce point," in digging into, hollowing out, exploring the language of poetry *in all its depth,* something happened that destroyed his sense of identity, leaving in its place only despair, a dark night of the soul. When Mallarmé says that no one was reflected in his mirror, he means it literally: "Le néant auquel je suis arrivé": nothingness was his destination, the end of his journey, his death to himself.[5] But from that he emerged transformed, having discovered that the absence of personal identity is, in itself, the experience of being. Mallarmé knew, as he wrote to Cazalis, the secret all human beings possess and never find, unless they die: "Tout homme a un Secret en lui, beaucoup meurent sans l'avoir trouvé, et ne le trouveront parce que morts, il n'existera pas, ni eux. Je suis mort, et ressucité." (Every man has a secret in himself, many die without having found it, and won't discover it because, once they're dead, it won't exist, nor they. I am dead, and resuscitated.)[6]

The tradition Mallarmé evokes, directly, albeit retrospectively, is Buddhism: "Le Néant auquel je suis arrivé sans connaître le bouddhisme" (Nothingness that I came to without knowing Buddhism).[7] This would not, in itself, provide a connection with Basho, although Basho was Buddhist, except that central to Buddhism, particularly Zen, is what I take to be Mallarmé's understanding of the relationship between a poet and poetry. Mallarmé would have assumed that the Zen scholar D. T. Suzuki was speaking of poets when he refered to masters who, because they are at the crossing point of time and timelessness, become "instruments of communication in order that Nature may become conscious of itself."[8] This sounds Hegelian, but the evaluation of reason is quite opposed.

In 1867, Mallarmé wrote to Cazalis, "Je suis maintenant impersonnel et non plus le Stéphane que tu as connu,—mais une aptitude qu'a l'Universe spirituel à se voir et à se développer à travers ce qui fut moi" (I have become impersonal and am no longer the Stéphane you used to know. I am an ability of the spiritual universe to see itself and evolve through what used to be my self).[9] Here "through" has its strong physical sense. Dogen, who introduced Soto Zen to Japan in the thirteenth century, wrote something remarkably similar: "To carry yourself forward and experience myriad things is delusion. That myriad things come forth and experience themselves is awakening."[10] And the twentieth-century Zen master Shunryu Suzuki wrote: "When we forget ourselves, we actually are the true activity of ... reality itself."[11]

Of course, it is not only Buddhism that suggests the centrality of the experience of emptiness, or of transience. Meister Eckhart writes, "Things are all made from nothing; hence their true source is nothing."[12] In his superb biography of Celan, John Felstiner finds the same "paradox of emptiness and pure Being" expressed in the Jewish mystical tradition, as witness Gershom Scholem, "The Nothing is the Nothing of God, from which all true creation springs."[13]

Like Mallarmé, Basho participated in an established and fashionable literary tradition until it became inadequate for his needs. There are no letters from Basho explaining why he left the relatively comfortable life of a master poet (in a country where that could be quite lucrative) for a life of poverty and wandering. In his thirties, he studied Chinese poetry and Taoism, at one point had a teacher of Zen, and he practiced meditation. His poetry, which was rather flamboyant in style, became increasingly austere and deep. He traveled endlessly despite the danger to his health, and even at the risk of his life, because transience was the very substance of his poems.[14] The haiku form relates particularly well to Zen with its emphasis on direct perception, always recommending that we throw away the sutras. This is not to disdain the intellect, but to point out that it gets in the way of the here and now. Zen art, Basho's and Mallarmé's as well, aspires to give expression to what D. T. Suzuki defines as "consciousness caught at the very moment of rising from the unconscious. This moment is the absolute present, the crossing point of time and timelessness, of the conscious and unconscious."[15] It is also the experience of the unity of all things, or, as Mallarmé said, the "points de rencontre qui existent déjà dans le sein de la Beauté" (the intersections Beauty already enfolds).[16] This is the beauty that Mallarmé found in the wake of Nothingness. "L'Oeuvre," his true work, would be "l'hymne, harmonie et joie . . . des relations entre tout" (the hymn, harmony and joy . . . of the relationships among everything).[17]

"Awakening" was for Dogen, or Meister Eckhart, life itself, free of the illusions that had concealed it. Basho often thought he should devote himself entirely to religion, perhaps even enter a monastery, but the attraction of poetry was too great. His art itself, however, like Mallarmé's, entered the service of the impersonal vision. In Mallarmé's poetry after 1866, the "I" has not disappeared but changed. It is the poem's speaker, and not Stéphane Mallarmé.

Mallarmé imagined for poetry "a purity beyond what has ever been achieved, and which perhaps will never be achieved by anyone."[18] The nature of that purity, the disappearance of the self into Nothingness, into the Universe, into the very words of the poem, the "disparition élocutoire du poète," exposed him to nervous exhaustion and headaches so violent that even the most ordinary conversation became difficult to follow. He wrote to Villiers de l'Isle-Adam that he was afraid of beginning where Baudelaire came to end, Baudelaire having died insane a month before that letter was written (August 1867). Mallarmé's heroism, as I see it, is double: He did not allow his awareness of the risks to interfere with the project of writing poetry from the center, the empty center, of himself. And he never stopped being aware that not only do we inevitably write black on white, but, more important, from the vision of unity, of "relations entre tout," art is a separation (378).

Williams quotes Meister Eckhart in this same context: "Three things there are that hinder one from hearing the eternal Word: The first is corporeality, the second, number, and the third, time."[19] Mallarmé wrote to Théodore Aubanel about "la joie de contempler l'éternité et d'en jouir, vivant, en soi" (the joy of contemplating and delighting in the Eternal within the very moments of one's life).[20] This joy, he says, makes a mockery of the relative immortality available to the poet he might have been. Now his aspiration is to *write* "the eternal word," the orphic explanation of the world. He spent the rest of his life trying to find a poetic language powerful enough to abolish what he called chance, which is the order of language itself.

One tends to think of Zen art as spontaneous, instantaneous. Basho says as much: "Once one's mind achieves a state of concentration and the space between oneself and the object has disappeared, the essential nature of the object can be perceived. Then express it immediately. If one ponders it, it will vanish from the mind."[21] Anecdotes tell us how Basho spontaneously produced his most famous poem and even reached enlightenment in the process. The existence of revised versions, however, shows that the words to make the experience manifest were anything but immediately available, for him any more than for Mallarmé.

The "disappearance of the space between oneself and an object" means that one has become that object, and the object has become oneself. "La Nature existe," says Mallarmé, "on n'y ajoutera pas."[22] Almost everything we do gives us the impression of adding something—thoughts, judgments, emotions—to what exists. But even our purest encounters with objects in nature, when there is no separation between them and us, will be shaped by our own particular kind of attention. Nature itself, outside the range of our limited perceptions, is entirely unavailable to us. I think this is why Mallarmé speaks of "la notion pure" (368), the pure notion of an aspect of nature, as the subject of his work, somewhat in the English sense of having a notion of something.

"La notion pure" is usually understood as an abstract concept. This would be fair enough in regard to "je dis, une fleur," but to say "flower" is not at all the same as writing a poem. "Crise de vers" also speaks of transposing "un fait de la nature" (something that exists in nature) into words, which will evoke the "notion pure" that we had of it (368). This involves the other meaning of "notion," which has to do with intuitive, direct experience, and with Mallarmé's project for poetry, and Basho's "peindre non la chose mais l'effet qu'elle produit"[23] (to portray not the thing but the impression it makes on us)—not what the poet felt or thought about it, but its immediate effect, nondualistic and nonverbal.

Mallarme's approach is the opposite of "emotion recollected in tranquillity." His aim is to forget his own distracting personal reactions, "la gêne d'un proche ou concret rappel"[24] (the encumbrance of a close or too precise recollection), to find again—this time in words—the reality of the encounter. "Céder l'iniative aux mots" (366) (letting words take the initiative) does not mean to choose them at random as in a surrealist game. To achieve the poet's intention—"peindre l'effet"—is not within the scope of his intellect, but he does *have* an intention. The intersection of his mind and language will be like his ideal encounter with the aspect of nature involved: free from preconceptions and ideas. The "notion pure" is the source of the poem as well as its destination. "Thus" does not mean "like something," writes Dogen. "Thus" means "as it is."[25] And Basho's haiku:

> Whatever they compare it to
> is not
> the summer moon.

The relationship between immediacy of perception and transience is expressed in one of Basho's rare comments on poetry: "The basis of art is change in the universe. . . . Cherry blossoms whirl, leaves fall, and the wind flits them both along the ground. We cannot arrest with our eyes or our ears what lies in such things. Were we to gain mastery over them, we would find that the life of each thing had vanished without a trace."[26] The poet of being *does* gain mastery over the transient, not arresting but recreating it in words, witness Basho's:

> A dragonfly
> trying to subdue
> a grassblade

In Mallarmé's "Petit Air 1," the speaker shifts his gaze from the colors of the sunset as two simultaneous flashes of white catch his eye: a startled bird and the garment shed by his companion as she dives into the water, as her joy *becomes* the water:

| Mais langoureusement longe | But languidly floats by |
| Comme de blanc linge ôté | White as her slip flung overhead |

Tel fugace oiseau si plonge
Exultatrice à côté

A bird quick-winged if dives
Too close her exaltation

Dans l'onde toi devenue
Ta jubilation nue.

Within the water's curve now
Her naked jubilation.

"Petit Air II" centers on the bird and contains a stanza that Basho would surely have admired:

Voix étrangère au bosquet
ou par nul écho suivie,
l' oiseau qu'on ouït jamais
une autre fois en la vie.

A voice unknown to the woods,
or followed by no reply,
the birdsong never heard
an other time in life.

In contrast, we could consider Emily Dickenson's famous stanzas on the oriole. She perfectly elucidates the problem:

> The fashion of the ear
> Attireth that it hear
> In dun or fair

without considering that we do hear the birdsong *before* we make statements about it and *that* hearing *is* the birdsong for us.

Basho distinguishes between the cuckoo's song and the egocentric emotions he aspires to replace:

> Cure my loneliness,
> cuckoo,
> with your song of solitude.

The contrast reminds us of Mallarmé's cricket, in whose unique voice he heard the happiness of the Earth, which does not separate itself into mind and matter. In another haiku, silence and sound come together:

> Stillness—
> cicada voices
> seeping into the rocks.

In another, the voice itself is silence:

> Your voice,
> spider, your song
> through the autumn wind

Basho, like Mallarmé, felt the essential inadequacy of language, its failure to coincide with meaning. He says, "Language resides in untruth and ought to comport with truth. It is difficult to reside in truth and sport with untruth. These three elements do not exalt a humble person to heights. They put an exalted person in a low place." Nevertheless, reminding us of "donner un sens plus pur aux mots de la tribu," Basho continues, "The profit of haikai lies in making common speech right."[27]

Because the seventeen syllables of a haiku are segmented, creating an effect rather like the caesuras of classical French verse, it has been customary for translators to divide them into three lines. In Japanese, however, they are written in one line. They are like "le vers qui de plusieurs vocables refait un mot total, étranger à la langue et comme incantatoire" (368) (the line of verse which makes, out of several linguistic elements, a new and total word, foreign to the language, and like an incantation).

The most incantatory of poems is *L'Après-midi d'un Faune*. Mallarmé's Faun, who is himself an intersection with permanent myth, seeks to solidify a memory or identify a dream, in either case to perpetuate the objects of his desire. The nymphs are indeed perpetuated, but only as a trick of the light, a slight breeze in the sultry air—in the words that convey experience of these things. Even the years many of us have spent pondering difficult lines of this poem, extracting from it divergent scenarios, metaphysical erotics and erotic poetics, even our most absorbing analyses do not obscure what we experienced before we "understood" the poem at all: that the primary reality is indeed perpetual change, which, in itself, is both the transient and its ground. It is also the beautiful, "the splendor around us." The Faun's uncertainty, "amas de nuit ancienne," arising from the underlying abyss into the intricate network of his branching thoughts, gives way to the real branches of the woods.[28] But the woods, with their branches and leaves, are themselves unsubstantial, the light on them constantly shifting, glittering in the air, on the water, "les fleurs d'étincelles," the heaviness of noontime, the gold and ashes of the woods. "We cannot arrest with our eyes or our ears what lies in such things."

Of all Basho's haiku, of all the haiku ever written in Japan—which would be something like ten for every star in the sky—the most famous begins with the words "old pond." There are no articles in Japanese; no singular or plural, but the commentaries and translations usually assume the singular. A pond is the stillest kind of water; "old" in Japan would suggest venerable rather than untended or forgotten. The water would be dark; perhaps not much of it visible, silent.

An old pond.
a frog jumps-
water's sound

An irruption of life into nonlife, a passage of sound into stillness, a flash of energy now and nothing after. English has a choice between using "water" as the final word, with the *t* sound of "water," as in "oto," suggesting the brevity and distinctness of that happening. On the other hand, a more literal translation of "mizu no oto" (water's sound), seems to better suggest the unity that has occurred. Like the Faun's passage through his landscape, or the swimmer's dive into the water, the transient unites with the timeless, becomes its sound, or silence.

Notes

1. Translations in this essay are mine, unless otherwise noted. For texts of the Basho poems, see Makoto Ueda, *Basho and His Interpreters: Selected Hokku with Commentary* (Stanford: Stanford University Press, 1991). I am indebted to Dr. J. Mizoguchi for many illuminating suggestions.

2. Stéphane Mallarmé, *Correspondance,* ed. Henri Mondor and Lloyd James Austin (Paris: Gallimard, 1959), 1:151. Letter to Henri Cazalis, 1865. (Hereafter cited as *Corr.*)

3. Quoted by Thomas A. Williams, *Mallarmé and the Language of Mysticism* (Athens: University of Georgia Press, 1970), 36.

4. *Corr.*, 207.

5. *Loc. cit.*

6. *Corr.*, 222.

7. *Corr.*, 207.

8. William Barrett, ed., *Zen Buddhism: Selected Writings of D. T. Suzuki* (New York: Doubleday Anchor Books, 1956), 250.

9. *Corr.*, 242.

10. Kazuaki Tanahashi, ed., *Moon in a Dewdrop, Writing of Zen Master Dogen* (San Francisco: North Point Press, 1985), 69.

11. Shunryu Suzuki, *Zen Mind, Beginners's Mind* (New York and Tokyo: Weatherhill, 1982), 79.

12. Franz Pfeiffer, ed., *Meister Eckhart,* trans. C. de B. Evans (London: John M. Watkins, 1947), 50.

13. John Felstiner, *Paul Celan: Poet, Survivor, Jew* (New Haven and London: Yale University Press, 1995), 181, 183.

14. Makoto Ueda, *Matsuo Basho* (Tokyo, New York, San Francisco: Kodansha International, 1982), 20–35.

15. Barrett, 243.

16. *Corr.*, 225.

17. Stéphane Mallarmé, *Oeuvres complètes,* ed. Henri Mondor and G. Jean-Aubry (Paris: Gallimard-Pléiade, 1945), 378. (Subsequent page references indicated within parentheses.)

18. *Corr.*, 242.

19. *Corr.*, 82.
20. *Corr.*, 225.
21. Robert Hass, trans., *The Essential Haiku* (Hopewell: Ecco Press, 1994), 234.
22. Cited by Williams, 48.
23. *Corr.*, 137.
24. *Corr.*, 137.
25. Dogen, 129.
26. Hass, 233.
27. Hass, 235.
28. There is a poem by Dogen (214) that strangely seems to comment on this:

> *Viewing Peach Blossoms and Realizing the Way*
>
> In spring wind
> peach blossoms
> begin to come apart.
> Doubts do not grow
> branches and leaves.

VI
On the Whole

Mallarmé's Wake

ROBERT GREER COHN

AFTER a lifetime devoted to the study of Mallarmé, this essay contains just a few of my key thoughts and reflections, mostly from memory, which sum up my view of the poet and his work.

In *After Babel* (along with his *Real Presences* and *Heidegger*), George Steiner forthrightly gives Mallarmé the pivotal position in the formation of modern thought and literature, seeing Rilke as his only rival on the poetic front, Heidegger on the ideational one.

Like Julia Kristeva (who, in her *Revolution of Poetic Language*, pushes Lautréamont into the spotlight as well; but he comes later, as did Rimbaud), he singles out Mallarmé, starting with the "Sonnet allégorique de lui-même" (Sonnet allegorical of itself, 1868; published under the definitive title "Ses purs ongles" in 1887) as the pioneer who metamorphosed the use of language for our time, with a greater cultural impact than "World Wars I and II combined."

As he, Kristeva, and almost the entire French critical intelligentsia of our day see it, the master symbolist stretched the power of verbal expression beyond normal usage so far that he instituted a quantum leap, a whole new universe of modern literary reality.

Of course, this perspective did not wait for Steiner and his contemporaries. Mallarmé himself realized what he was doing and explained it in the demanding prose of *Divagations* (collected critical pieces, 1897) as well as in key passages of his poetry, such as "Prose (pour des Esseintes)." There was no lack of authoritative voices —notably, that of his prize pupil, Paul Valéry—to proclaim the unprecedented nature of the Mallarmé phenomenon: "Mallarmé the purest, the most intransigent, the hardest on himself of all those who have held a pen."

Proust, Claudel, and Gide were comparably impressed, with varying nuances according to their personal needs. The finest French critic of the early twentieth century, Albert Thibaudet, devoted his major work to him, and, from then on, it is hardly too much to say that no aspiring critic could avoid wrestling with that angel (Blanchot, Sartre, Poulet, Richard, Foucault, Barthes), who stood athwart their promising paths. For example, Blanchot, who occupies a position in the later century comparable to Thibaudet's, is unthinkable without the eminent ghost.

Arthur Symons, Edmund Gosse, James Huneker, Yeats, and T. S. Eliot first put us on, in the English-speaking world, to the groundbreaking events in Paris. Edmund Wilson, in *Axel's Castle* (1931), went further: He construed Mallarmé as the closest literary equivalent to Einstein, installing a whole new episteme, with practically all the major figures of modern writing—Proust, Valéry, Yeats, Eliot, Joyce, Gertrude Stein—as emanations of that *lux candida*, a hidden sun so dazzling as hardly to be contemplated, at least in his otherwise boldly venturous book, which has remained a classic, his central contribution (Wilson was, no doubt, our counterpart of Thibaudet). Saul Bellow recently, in *It All Adds Up*, recalls the decisive impact it had on his own cultural formation.

We must imagine those literary folks listening for the first time to Debussy's "Prélude à *L'Après-midi d'un Faune*" (Prelude to the Afternoon of a Faun), perhaps reading in the program the poem that inspired it as well as Nijinsky's ballet, vibrantly aware of the painterly impressionism influencing these intimately related arts. In airy openness, subtlety, exquisite French nuance of sensuality, the leap into modernity—like Nijinsky's onto the stage—is breathtaking.

In his time, Mallarmé's impact was limited to a "happy few," especially those privileged young people who came, in the waning years of the nineteenth century, to the *mardis* in his modest apartment on the rue de Rome, but that handful embraced practically everyone who was going to be anyone in the various twentieth-century arts. In addition to Proust, Claudel, Valéry, Gide, there were Debussy, Rodin, Whistler, Renoir, Monet, Pissarro, Gauguin, Vuillard, and Morisot. The greatest painter of the twentieth century, Matisse, was inspired by the *Poésies*—he illustrated them—to the culmination of his style. Subsequent figures in this lineage include Ravel (who set some of his poems); Picasso (who came to Paris partly because of him); the futurists, for example, Marinetti, who took off from his new free spatial structures in the *Coup de Dés* (Throw of the Dice); as did Apollinaire. Later came Faulkner, whose early poems bear the imprint of the "Faune," and poets proper such as Yeats, Eliot, Rilke, Stefan George, Ungaretti, Jorge Guillén. Toward the end of his life, Ezra Pound acknowledged, in a conversation with the de Campos brothers, that the *Coup de Dés* had worked on him, and he expressed his admiration for the "pure heart" of Mallarmé. Eventually there were Francis Ponge, for whom Mallarmé was *the* poet of "things," Pierre Boulez ("Improvisation sur Mallarmé"), Michel Butor, Yves Bonnefoy, Michel Deguy—sometimes singled out as the closest to Mallarmé in our era—Pierre Emmanuel, Nathalie Sarraute (who did a major essay on his originality versus Valéry's), and Robbe-Grillet who informed me personally of his debt, as did Guillén.

In the realm of theater, Haskell Block gives Mallarmé the key role—based on his essays in *Divagations*—as precursor of Lugné-Poe, Maeterlinck, Claudel, Yeats, Lorca, Hofmannstahl, Artaud, Strindberg, Ghelderode, and Samuel Beckett. Rosette Lamont added Ionesco to the lineup. Simply put, he went to the core of things, uncluttered the stage, deepened the sense of mystery and total meaning welling from the source of dramatic poetry.

Comparably, André Levinson saw him as the founder of modern ballet, based on essays on the dance in *Divagations*, where he plumps for a pure play of forms and a minimum of story.

Pierre Bernard gives him credit because of the revolutionary format of the *Coup de Dés,* for the main development of twentieth-century typography. Marshall McLuhan, in "Joyce, Mallarmé, and the Press," traces much of the breezy style of both *Ulysses* and *Finnegans Wake* to Mallarmé's observations on newspaper format. (According to Philippe Soupault, cited by David Hayman in his *Joyce et Mallarmé,* Joyce owned a copy of the *Coup de Dés.*) McLuhan, who urged his disciple Hugh Kenner to get in touch with me—we were studying at Yale—because of my first book on the late Masterwork, was comparably impressed and influenced by the explosive new freedom and coherence.

In America, beyond the mentioned great figures, Mallarmé's wake is more elusive: Wallace Stevens is occasionally referred to as "the Mallarmé of Hartford," and there is undoubtedly something to that. Kenneth Rexroth thought the *Coup de Dés* was the greatest poem ever written. Howard Nemerov and a few other poets dedicated poems to him. Wallace Fowlie paid homage through a major book. I know of Richard Wilbur's respect through personal correspondence and got secondhand information about the influence on Ben Jonson, the composer, and Robert Motherwell, the painter. To the extent that George Steiner is American, we can put him in the booster column, following Edmund Wilson, offsetting partial demurrals by Kenneth Burke and Yvor Winters. No doubt, the difficulty of Mallarmé, and his exceptional untranslatability made him a problematic figure here for the reading public at large, though in my experience our best cosmopolitan literary minds, including academic, now accord him a position rivaling that of Joyce or Proust. The plain-spokenness of our Whitman, Frost, and Williams tradition, Laforguian and Poundean understatement, minimalism later, led us in directions apart from complex "constellatory" symbolist networks of verbal "suggestion." Even T. S. Eliot, whose poetry, as Grover Smith demonstrated, is much marked by Mallarméan imagery—the Master shows up as part of the "familiar compound ghost" in "Burnt Norton" together with his "purify the dialect of the tribe"—kept some distance from him in the preface to Valéry's *Art of Poetry*, edging toward Laforgue.

But these cultural divergences, aggravated by the antielitist assaults since the late sixties, are familiar to literary history. We all recall the French view, expressed by Voltaire, that Shakespeare was a "barbarian," or that Brahms—up through World War II—was heavily Teutonic. *Et après!*

It is obvious that Mallarmé enjoys a worldwide status (notably in Japan, Spain, and Germany) comparable to few, and it is hard to think of anyone, including Pound (*vide The Pound Era,* by Hugh Kenner, who, like Edmund Wilson, compares Mallarmé to Einstein) who has a better claim as the founder of twentieth-century ideas and art: "Héros, mage, et tragédien ce petit homme . . . mérite de mourir au seuil de notre siècle: il l'annonce" (Sartre) (Hero, magus, and tragedian, this little man deserves to die at the threshold of our century; he announces it).

Like Keats, whom he is perhaps closest to of all writers (Mallarmé sketched out a supremely admiring fragment on him), he wrenched from an uncompromisingly tragic—yet humane and healthy—vision, a corresponding wisdom and joy. And as in Keats, and before him Plato, in Mallarmé the art and the philosophy are inseparable, especially in a major work such as the *Coup de Dés,* which sketched out his lifetime project comparable to Dante's or the one Keats outlines in "Sleep and Poetry." Because of its nearly impenetrable depths and elliptical complexities of expression, there are those, like Gardner Davies, who believe the "Poem" is a marginal venture, a sort of confession of failure in his hyperbolic aspiration. But important critics like Blanchot have come around to the view that the *Coup de Dés* was at very least a sketch—"un fragment d'exécuté," in the poet's own words—of the "Grand Oeuvre," as he called the aimed-at masterpiece, a last-ditch effort in his final years to offer a glimpse of what it would be like. That controversy is now largely over: For example, the latest editions of the *Petit Larousse* put it just that way, along with some recent anthologies and Gordon Millan's biography.

Blanchot, in various studies, saw Mallarmé as the counterpart of Hegel for leap of totalizing vision—the conception of one Great Work—at the opposite end of his century. Foucault, in *Les Mots et les choses,* paired him with Nietzsche as the creator of the twentieth-century mindset. Sartre agreed. Barthes said to an interviewer "All we do is repeat Mallarmé." The case for his seminal position in this respect (along with Heidegger, according to Steiner) would seem to be solid.

But Mallarmé is not easy to read and, more to the point, he is not a professional philosopher but rather a "thinker" in the Heideggerian sense. He usually plowed his theoretical insights back into his texts, or else they arose in them indistinguishably *ab ovo,* but in either event they are not usually visible as distinct entities. So we have to piece together his theoretical universe from various scattered sources for discursive purposes like the present one.

We are especially encouraged to do so, since the insights that seeped out over the years were powerful enough to elicit the sweeping comments just noted. So, let us have a look: Steiner was most impressed by the liberation of the sign from the referent and the complex new realm of expression that emerged from that. Indeed, but the point needs a major qualification: Mallarmé, in truth, never did ditch the referent. Even the famous text beginning: "Je dis: une fleur!" (I say: a flower!) ends with "la réminiscence de l'objet nommé baigne dans une neuve atmosphère" (the reminiscence of the named object bathes in a new atmosphere) (echoing Wordsworthian and Baudelairean aesthetic memory), and the referent of nature is constant in his poetry (his daughter insisted that was what he loved most).

Furthermore, a distinction beyond the Saussurian one of signifier, signified, referent is needed here; the referent also divides into two poles (Malraux, Ponge, and Hjelmslev concur on this point): ordinary and essential. Mallarmé seeks, for example, the shoey shoes, saturated with Being, that Van Gogh painted, according to Heidegger—not just any pair. Or his chairy chair, sunflowery sunflowers, comparable to Mallarmé's "sobbing" white lilies or "trop grand glaïeul" (too big gladiolus) whose calyx seems inseparable from the "gloire du long désir" (glory of the long desire) in our throats—the "gosier" where stars are lodged in "Aumône."

Thus, Jean-Pierre Richard visualizes Mallarmé as being "comme le Chardin de notre littérature" (sort of the Chardin of our literature); Ponge declares him to be the true poet of *things;* and Bachelard proclaims him the oneiric poet par excellence whose objects exude the real real, gorgeous or godawful, of dreams.

Hence, though it is true that Mallarmé did open expression, consonant with Saussure's later theoretical vision of the self-involvement of language, in a new emphasis on the sign and its proliferating virtualities, I agree with Kurt Mueller-Vollmer that Mallarmé is closer, ultimately, to the balanced position of Alexander von Humboldt for whom verbality occurs in marriages *between* sign and referent, fecundly.

Mallarmé's central epistemological contribution is polypolarity, based on paradox. For example, can a proposition be true and false simultaneously? If you say, as he would, "Yes and no," you are in a tetrapolar phase of polypolarity, that is, paradox squared.

Tetrapolarity is a prevailing pattern in him, for example, the "symphonic equation proper to the seasons," which, in "La Musique et les Lettres," announced the core structure of the Great Work to come (the *Coup de Dés* being a sketch of it, we noted).

Now, the four seasons can be seen statically as a cross: vertical summer-winter traversed by milder spring-autumn; spun out in time, we get summer-autumn-winter-spring as a wave-movement, the essence of rhythm, with a hint of eternal return underneath. Our subjacent concept of circular time, consonant with the original cross, is expressed on clock dials; the prevailing concept of linear time ("irreversible") is expressed on calendars. The wave-movement combines the two, at least virtually or suggestively, in a spiral, familiar to us as an archetypal cosmic pattern (galaxies; space-time vortices). All this is represented in the structure and imagery of the crowning Poem.

Another basic pattern is generated from the tension of bipolar paradox. Before reaching a fully tetrapolar stage, it can linger at the Hegelian phase of synthesis, as in thesis-antithesis-synthesis. This is likely to create somewhat "smug," self-deceptive "solutions" of predicaments, as Kierkegaard realized. Even if it does the Hegelian "double take" or leap (synthesis becoming a new thesis), the whole scheme moves on, repeatedly, in a one-sided way. As Kierkegaard did in "The Absolute Paradox" (from *Philosophical Fragments*) , but independently of him, Mallarmé saw, for example, that if the synthesis was a child (born, say, of thesis-mama, antithesis-papa), fusing and exalting the hopes of the two parents, it could die at birth or young, and would result in something worse than the loss of either parental aspiration: something we can call, philosophically, "antisynthesis."

The Tel Quellistes liked this notion: Kristeva, in her *La Révolution du langage poétique,* referred to it as the "Fourth Term" and claimed she found it in Hegel's *Logic,* but it is very fleeting and flimsy there: Hegel very deliberately opts for the triadic. Because she proclaims in the same book that "I follow Cohn's method closely," we have ample grounds for assigning the real credit to Mallarmé, who, as Jean Hyppolite agrees, along with Blanchot, made this decisive leap beyond Hegel. Incidentally, Derrida refers to antisynthesis in *La Dissémination* (where he also states his preference for my open approach over Jean-Pierre Richard's more limitedly Hegelian one), and promised a thorough discussion of it some day. This never happened, so far as I know. Curiously, in conversation, he avowed to me that he did not fully understand the concept, though he blushed with apparent pleasure when I explained it to him, exclaiming "C'est un univers!" (It's a universe!) His "clôture" (closure) and "différance" are rudimentary approximations to tetrapolarity, never explained in depth; the one-sided or unidimensional nature of his runaway "deconstruction" would indicate that, indeed, he never did fully understand the fresh and nimble thinking of Mallarmé.

When synthesis is cancelled by antisynthesis, we have a full tetrapolar situation, as in Kierkegaard's "absolute paradox," a crucifying four-polar dilemma. Kierkegaard at that point "leapt" (Camus's term) in the Instant of faith. We can invoke "quintessence" here, a fifth term, at the micro-macro (zero-infinite) central node. In his early discussion of Kierkegaard (*The Myth of Sisyphus*) , Camus rejected this resolution, staying loyal to the "absurd," but when this idea was put into agonizing question by World War II and the Holocaust, he leapt in his turn, in *The Rebel* (preface), from what he clearly identified as a four-polar dilemma, impulsively rejecting mass murder despite absurdist "logic," now correctly seen as arbitrary. Derrida muffed that point; Sartre never got that far in his reasoning.

In pure, free polypolarity, all the poles (and the zero-infinite node) are interchangeable, jump around. But more typically, in applications or prevailing patterns, we get the dimensionality and sometimes a certain limited interchangeability. In this sense, Mallarmé's world is parallel to music, where tone is produced geometrically—by multiplication or division (for example, of strings). And it has harmony as well as melody, which are interrelated by the same tonal laws (consciously, in twelve-tone systems). The *Coup de Dés,* as Mallarmé notes in the preface, is built that way, like a score. All our advanced French thought follows that lead: Jakobson's definition of poetry as projecting the vertical paradigmatic onto the horizontal axis of combination, the syntagmatic; Lacan's play between metaphoric (vertical) and metonymic (horizontal), or the similar play in "De l'instance de la lettre." Jakobson spoke to me personally of his fervent attachment to Mallarmé, going back to his fifteenth year. Lacan, his friend and tutee, is sometimes dubbed a combination of Freud and Mallarmé. There are parallel developments in his disciple Rosolato (*La Relation d'inconnu:* "l'oscillement" [The relation of unknown: oscillation]) and Edgar Morin.

This musicalization of his aesthetic, following a general nineteenth-century development in this respect (he too was influenced by the challenge and ambitious theorizing of Wagner), is a move toward totalization and organicity, fluidity and roundedness, allowing his creation to come closer to the Creation and its processes of expansion—"poésie éclatée" (exploded poetry)—and universal gravity (Mallarmé's words attract one another freely in a constellatory pattern, beyond flatly linear syntax) through spiral evolution of interrelated space and time and the successive crystallizations that give us the merciful specificities (such as fruit) of *things.*

The aesthetic of overall "effect" (or tone), derived from Poe, and "suggestion" (or connotation), which he found in Baudelaire and Hugo and romanticism generally, on the way to symbolism, as opposed to the hard-and-fast "sculptural" denotation favored by the Parnassians, all this tended to the one end of openness, complexity, and plenitude. Yet, unsurprisingly, in this resembling more his Parnassian friends (or Thomas Mann, or the later, classics-adoring, Camus), limits, form, and classical norms were equally a part of his vision and practice.

Applying polypolarity to his own oeuvre, one sees that he "touches all the bases," "boxes the compass." North-south, he is transcendental and fiercely erotic, "more civilized and primitive" (T. S. Eliot), sparklingly intellectual and wildly, volcanically spontaneous: romantic (or late romantic: symbolist). East-west, he noted that "Un vol d'aigle n'exclut pas un regard scrutant l'espace" (An eagle's flight doesn't exclude a look scrutinizing space). He was as coolly circumspect as Poe's C. Auguste Dupin, respectful of the forms and norms, healthily realistic. in another word, he was classic (Claudel thought that was his main type)—altogether a poet of life: "Ivre, il vit" (Drunk, he lives) ("Les Fenêtres") in a "profondeur de journée" (depth of day) ("Berthe Morisot"). Sartre called him an "existential" poet, which was his blinkered idea of class; that's not quite it.

Accordingly, his epistemology—which he presented theoretically only in sketches in posthumously published notebooks for "le Livre"—is, as Spinoza would say, "adequate" to life. Moreover, unlike Sartre, like Spinoza, Kierkegaard, and even Camus, he believed in an ultimate sacred: "You can't do without Eden."

In that micro-macro context, he is both wide open and closed, global and intimate, elusive and yet exquisitely present (like the hidden lady of "The White Nenuphar" or Keats's "unheard melodies"), beautiful and true, meaningful.

He never got stuck in the cold abstractions of one-sided intellect, any more than did his young friend, Proust, who clearly stated in *Contre Sainte-Beuve* his preference for intuition over reason, which he obviously honored but only in "second place." Or, as Steiner put it in refutation of Derrida and company, "Music means." Tone, one might add, is everything in these deciding moments.

"A throw of the dice will never abolish chance": this titular proposition of Mallarmé's "Poem" reminds us of our existential limitations, going back to the Fall. "The wind bloweth where it listeth," and we are utterly dependent to start with. Only a miracle could save us. The total meaning that we can only glimpse "way in" seems at other times to come from "way out," somewhere, "vers ... UNE CONSTELLATION." Our whole culture, in this sense, is a sort of row of telescopes, or radio-telescopes, scanning space-time for It. For Mallarmé, as for Ricoeur and many another thinker, however subtly, Judeo-Christianity provides a binding background to a lot of that telescopy, at least for us in the West, so it is not entirely fortuitous that he, like Camus, invoked St. John the Baptist—that pivotal figure par excellence—in some pithy late pages. Moreover, unlike Heidegger, he was a thoroughly decent human being, and it would be feckless to slight the Judeo-Christian elements in his upbringing, as in the case of Proust (his central heroine, with shades of Heine, is a Jewish princess).

But because, in his own terms, existence is a hit-and-miss affair, we get only so many miracles (as well as the reverse *coups*), such as being born, in helpful circumstances like his, loved, healthy, bright, and so on. And so it is with his epistemology, the closest I know of to being an "open sesame": you get hits only when life is good and ready. Still, over the years, an arresting list emerges. I will give only a few examples:

Starting with his philosophical (epistemological-metaphysical) base, he sketches out in his 'Poem" how the cosmos becomes from a Big Bang—the initial COUP of his text—and it evolves along the lines discussed above, for example, the generative tetrapolar structure governing the seasons, or any level of time such as four ages, four times of day, as well as space, for example, the four cardinal points. As with Einstein, to whom Edmund Wilson and Hugh Kenner compared him, space and time are in fluid relation, in what some black-hole theorists call "shearing motion."

This dimensional play is primordial and shows up everywhere in physics: James Clerk Maxwell describes the relation of magnetism and electricity as "transverse"—the term and the preoccupation are still very current. "Quadripolarity" has long been a familiar concept of electrical engineering. Further, a microorganism's movements across a lab slide are perpendicular. In our mathematics, cardinal and ordinal relate in the same pattern, going back to the Sumerians. Our number systems expand the way the cosmos does, with paradoxical events befuddling the hung-up linear schemes of systematic gamblers, when probabilistic continuity suddenly shifts to discontinuity. And, of course, our whole decimal system, depends on dimensionality as much as music does (Pythagoras and Plato were much taken with the original unity of this sublime pair).

The child, that supreme throw of the dice, as Mallarmé specifically puts it, emerges from that axial play in mitosis, cell-splitting, and so on. The family (this, too, is in his "Poem") is essentially a crystalline four-polar structure-parent-child polarity crossed by a gender polarity—and it holds up, we hope, for the same reasons as a chair, a house.

Political groups always have an internal left-right (perhaps reflecting ages) cognate to, and transversally reflecting, the overall left-right tension of parties. "Multipolarity" is now a familiar concept in international relations. Finally, our Founding Fathers gave us another blessedly crystalline structure in our Constitution. Whereas the French Revolution spawned a series of unidimensional fanaticisms based on a secular egalitarianism, "horizontal religion" as Camus called it—utopianism, communism, socialism, fascism—and the various fundamentalisms moved just as fanatically in a vertical direction, our framers gave us a sane and civilized (however ardent and inspired) axial balance between those two runaway extremes. Our executive, vertical, balances off our legislative, horizontal, with the Supreme Court at the contemplative originary nodal point between. The relation of representatives and constituent mass is homologously orthogonal.

Even in human typology there is something compelling to be said for four-square sorts like Harry Truman or Spencer Tracy. Camus deliberately built his Dr. Rieux in that mold. Likewise, in art, all one need mention is Fouquet, Leonardo, Rembrandt, l'Abbaye de Thoronet, and the Romanesque style generally, Matisse.

A list of important apparitions in world thought of tetrapolarity (with varying consciousness) would include Zen Buddhism (*I Ching*), the Hebrew tetragrammaton, Kabbalah and Rosicrucianism, the Christian cross, four Evangelists, and Thomism, Descartes's coordinate axes (influenced by Rosicrucianism), the four humors in Robert Burton and Renaissance thought generally, Jung's tetrad of temperaments, the "morris dance" of protagonists in Mann, Joyce (particularly *Finnegans Wake*), Iris Murdoch.

Mallarmé had heroically, sacrificially—as he outlines in "Sauvegarde" and finds in his favorite authors, who came into their own belatedly, posthumously—accepted personal obscurity. But he was also very human, and when he was invited to lecture at Oxford and Cambridge, in 1894, he was profoundly moved and clearly wanted to bring them something deeply revelatory. He spoke to them of the revolution going on in French letters, citing various of his contemporaries. As the pièce de résistance, he offered them a glimpse of the future Great Work which he pictured as being written by some possible genius. He invoked the previously cited "symphonic equation proper to the seasons" as its core structure, and noted the spirally overlapping cyclic pattern of human emotions (as in the four humors). This tetradic scheme, with fluid relations between nature and man, past and present (in memory)—or equivalents, for instance, present-future (in prevision)—and, dimensionally, time and space, is the core of his entire oeuvre, starting with a juvenile poem, "Tout passe" (All passes), where the rhythmic rise and fall of the sun, diurnally and seasonally, parallels the wave-movement succession of generations: the son rises as the father falls.

In the jottings called *Pour un tombeau d'Anatole*, the spiritual heir alluded to in the lecture is associated with his little boy who died at age nine, as a sort of reincarnation. This idea shows up also in the *Coup de Dés*, in the phantom shape of "son ombre puérile," the successor of the universalized father figure. There are closely analogous ideas in *Les Dieux antiques*, where the "double solar evolution" is seen to lie behind all myths: The rise, fall, and succession of heroes. *Igitur* portrays the natural-human ambiguity through four mutually reflecting walls of a mysterious meditation-chamber at a midnight of the mind; time and human succession also join in "the supreme Game."

The tetrapolar structure is the essence of the scheme of Drama Mallarmé sketched in jottings for "Le Livre," and of various other such schemes. It is the main focus of his aim, in "Catholicisme," to replace the old ritual, and draw on it: "la tétralogie de l'An" (the tetralogy of the year); in this regard, he invokes Greek drama and Wagner (with his tetralogy of operas), whom, in "Richard Wagner," he also planned to outdo in depth. All this induced the gifted scholar Suzanne Bernard, in *Mallarmé et la musique,* to agree fully on the central importance of the epistemological archetype in him. Michel Deguy, the leading poet—and president of the Collège international de philosophie—in a preface declared that it was *the* approach to the oeuvre. Hermann Broch, Giuseppe Ungaretti, and Philippe Sollers felt much the same way. Guy Michaud wrote, in his indispensable *Mallarmé* that the understanding of the poet had to be "entirely revised" in this sense. Jean Cassou, Jean Follain, Georges Poulet, Richard himself, Léon Cellier, and many other distinguished people of letters offered substantial approval.

In "Les Fenêtres," the two dimensions, of vertical space and horizontal time, that is, the life-death (rise-fall) and man-child polarities, are crystallized in the window, the "croisée" as he significantly also calls it. Windows are, accordingly, perhaps his most obsessive image ("symbol"): in "Hérodiade," "Une dentelle s'abolit," "Sainte," "Ses purs ongles" (A lace effaces itself, Saint, Her pure fingernails), and so on. To be sure, there are many other compelling reasons for the power of this image.

The extension of tetrapolarity to polypolarity brings about the pervasive image of the web, at the center of which (in an early letter) Mallarmé saw himself as a Sacred Spider. In "La Musique et les Lettres" he spoke of the future Work as embodying such a network of syntax, with "the ambiguity of some beautiful figures at the intersections." The spiderweb shows up in "Frisson d'hiver," associated appropriately with the "croisée," and also in *Igitur.* But, more importantly, the image exfoliates through a play of cognate images, in "universal analogy": text (from Latin "textus," woven), cloth, lace, sail, shroud, veil, and so forth, in his finest poems. Keats, incidentally, invoked "the wreath'd trellis of a working brain" as well as the web (Mallarmé, too, alludes to the trellis).

It will be noted that the cross-shape can take varying forms: the most familiar, as in our plus-sign, or Descartes's axes, can tilt, as it were, into the x-cross, which is familiar as the sign of multiplication. In this form, it shows up especially in the baroque period: notably in Sir Thomas Browne's "quincunx" and John Donne's "paradox" (implying fall crossing rise), with the letter x (also the sign of an unknown) suggestively involved. Mallarmé's hermetic poem, "Ses purs ongles," uses the x obsessively in his end-rhymes, echoed by the window-shape that is the central image ("croisée") along with a mirror ("cadre") and the Big Dipper, itself an enigmatic sphinxlike shape in the void; the four cross-patterned stars of the "bowl" seem mysteriously ticked off by the quatre, cinq, six, sept sounds in the last lines ("dans le cadre se fixe / De scintillations sitôt le septuor" [in the frame is fixed / of scintillations at once the septet]).

In *After Babel,* George Steiner singles out approvingly the interpretation of the sonnet by Octavio Paz, which shows no awareness of any of the foregoing. Paz sees the core structure of the two quatrains as the hollow spiral of a shell. Now, it is quite likely that the mysterious "ptyx" (a word Mallarmé thought he had invented for the ix, but it had been used by Hugo in "Le Satyre"; it meant "fold" or "shell" in Greek) refers to a derelict shell left on the mantelpiece of a departed "Maître," echoing the final hollow "bubble" of monument (including Mallarmé's) left behind at the demise of mankind in an Apocalypse, in the *Coup de Dés.* But nothing else in the sonnet or in Mallarmé altogether bears out the importance of the spiral shell-shape, which is more pertinent to the speculations of Valéry. The sense of "fold" (with cosmic, oceanic, and sexual valences), on the other hand, is extremely pertinent to Mallarmé (the "ptyx" was called a "vaisseau" in an earlier version). It is the universal archetype of trough-or womb-shape, paired with the eternal crest form, male, paradoxically inverting one into the other in all sorts of phenomena, beginning with a primordial rhythm, as in oceanic wave-movement, the pervasive scene of the "Poem," which ends like the sonnet with a vision of the Great Bear seen provisionally through the *cross* hairs of an astronomical fixing in space-time, "selon telle obliquité par telle déclivité" (according to a certain obliquity through a certain declivity), but really beyond that. The sonnet and the "Poem" need to be read together—they say much about each other—and with the rest of the oeuvre in mind, ideally. And the overall polypolar (paradoxical) play of Being-Nothingness, Being-Becoming (existence), high-low, mind-body, form-matter, light-darkness, life-death, motion-rest, past-present, hot-cold, male-female, and so on, all demonstrably involved in the run of his favorite symbols.

What is the use of an approach, such as a recent one, which denies the sexual undertones of Mallarmé, when another work, also recent, claims that everything in him is sexual! My own reading construes him as usually both, a poet of purity, transcendence, and Being and, simultaneously, a warmly (Sartre says "passionately") amorous and erotic one. Not just in a "summer" poem, like the *Faune*—that demigod with goat's legs, as inhibited as he is eager—but at every turn of *Hérodiade,* his "winter" poem, as well.

Absence makes the heart (etc.) grow fonder was never truer than in "le Nénuphar blanc," where violently sexual subliminal imagery gives pulsing life to a shimmery summer scene à la Monet, his intimate friend and admirer. Silence was never more golden than that of the unheard music in "Sainte," where the subjacent exquisite sensuality courses through the half-hidden images and subtle "musical" flow—in the letter-sounds, especially that enviable French "u" ("Sur le plumage instrumental / Musicienne du silence" [On the instrumental plumage / Lady musician of silence])—of unsurpassable infantile bliss: Marian, or Muse-given, mother milk, as in "Kubla Khan" or certain passages of Keats, Chateaubriand, Nietzsche, Verlaine, Rimbaud, and Celan.

The brimming, nourishing Mallarméan white page—the poet wanted his words to swim in its overwhelming presence—gives birth and melody to his meaning.

In "Don du Poëme," the ideal sky, *l'azur,* and the earthly bliss of mother milk are joined intimately, far in and far out. The father-poet, disappointed at his own nocturnal creation, turns to his sleeping wife (lying next to her infant girl) at naturally victorious dawn and apostrophizes her to "press her breast," musically and/or maternally to feed his poor little abortive poem that is "hungered" by the *air du vierge azur.*

In "Les Fenêtres," the images of lost "virginal" woman (his young mother died when he was five), her "treasure" breast, and this thirst for a transcendent substitute, the lactescent sky seen through, and as it were "frozen" and available in, the windowpane which the old-man figure pathetically mouths, are closely clustered:

> Et la bouche, fiévreuse et d'azur bleu vorace,
> Telle, jeune, elle alla respirer son trésor,
> Une peau virginale et de jadis! encrasse
> D'un long baiser amer les tièdes carreaux d'or.

[And the mouth, feverish and voracious for azure blue,
Such, young, it was going to breathe its treasure,
A skin, virginal and of yesteryear, dirties
With a long bitter kiss the warm golden panes.]

Here is the whole of "Don du Poëme" (Gift of the poem), followed by a loose translation:

Je t'apporte l'enfant d'une nuit d'Idumée!
Noire, à l'aile saignante et pâle, déplumée,
Par le verre brûlé d'aromates et d'or,
Par les carreaux glacés, hélas mornes encore
L'aurore se jeta sur la lampe angélique
Palmes! et quand elle a montré cette relique
A ce père essayant un sourire ennemi,
La solitude bleue et stérile a frémi.
O la berceuse, avec ta fille et l'innocence
De vos pieds froids, accueille une horrible naissance:
Et ta voix rappelant viole et clavecin,
Avec le doigt fané presseras-tu le sein
Par qui coule en blancheur sibylline la femme
Pour les lèvres que l'air du vierge azur affame?

[I bring you the child of a night of Idumea!
Black, with pale bleeding wing, unplumed,
Through the glass burned with aromatics and gold,
Through the icy panes, alas! still dreary
The dawn threw itself on the angelic lamp,
Palms! and when it showed this relic
To this father trying a hostile smile,
The blue and sterile solitude shivered.
O cradling-woman, with your daughter and the innocence
Of your cold feet, welcome a horrible birth:
And, your voice recalling viola and harpsichord,
With your faded finger will you press the breast
Through which woman flows in sybilline whiteness
For the lips that the air of the virgin azur famishes?)

The azure instilled the hunger of aspiration in his baby "bird" (with its feeble wings). Having failed as an artistic creator, Mallarmé turns to the natural creator, his wife, and asks her to feed his poem, with some pathetic irony. But those literal meanings are underpinned by more complex associations. The real and poetic hunger here is for the supremely sensuous Infinite after a night-long struggle, in shivery morning, as in Baudelaire's "Crépuscule du matin":

> l'âme, sous le poids du corps revêche et lourd,
> Imite les combats de la lampe et du jour.
> . . . .
> L'air est plein du frisson des choses qui s'enfuient,
> Et l'homme est las d'écrire et la femme d'aimer.
>
> [The soul, under the weight of the crabbed and heavy body
> Imitates the combats of the lamp and the day.
> . . . .
> The air is full of the shiver of fleeing things,
> And man is weary of writing and woman of loving.]

or:

> Quand chez les débauchés l'aube blanche et vermeille
> Entre en société de l'Idéal rongeur,
> Par l'opération d'un mystère vengeur
> Dans la brute assoupie un ange se réveille.
> (Baudelaire, "L'Aube spirituelle")
>
> [When in the debauched the white and vermillion dawn
> Enters together with the gnawing Ideal,
> Through the operation of a vengeful mystery
> In the sleepy brute an angel awakens.]
> (The spiritual dawn)

This most intimate thirst is for the original paradisial milk:

> Si tu me vois les yeux perdus au paradis,
> C'est quand je me souviens de ton lait bu jadis.
> (*Hérodiade*)
>
> [If you see me with eyes lost in paradise,
> It is when I remember your milk drunk long ago.]

Accordingly, it evokes the equally intimate beauty of music, which he associates in turn with the voice—What is more penetrating?—of a woman, his wife, who is at one with nature, innocent, asleep. Hunger and woman are one for the poet: *femme-affame;* and the wife-mother expands into something as eternal and ambiguous as the azure. The "virgin azur" is pure like her and, in one sense, by its ideality, brings a need for violent reversal toward the flesh—as in the Baudelaire lines, these extremes are very close in their poetry—and it subtly flows with its own milkiness, as in "Les Fenêtres" (quoted above) or Coleridge's "milk of paradise" and its nearby "damsel with a dulcimer" ("Kubla Khan").

This is the main sensibility of the piece, which is commented on at length in *Toward the Poems of Mallarmé*. Here I will add only a few notes.

The poem he was working on all night was *Hérodiade*, who was an Edomite (Idumean) princess, whence the place-name of the sonorous first line. The dawn rays (recalling Homer's "rosy-fingered") are associated with wings, reaching through the window mingled still with streaks of black night and cold morning air; the weak morning sun—like the poor poem—is an unfledged, "unplumed" bird, fallen prematurely from its nest, bleeding (its red rays) yet pale. The "glass burnt with aromatics and gold" is a reminiscence of his blonde oriental princess mingled with his oil-lamp and the dawn light coming through the window. *Palmes!* is the victory of the renewed Creation (with a further oriental touch), as opposed to his human failure, and because all the letters of *lampe* are in it, anagrammatically, the union of outdoors light and the indoors one (as in Baudelaire's "combat de la lampe et du jour") is consummated with masterful effect.

Mallarmé published a book, *Les Mots anglais*, in which he demonstrated the semiotic values of letters of the English alphabet. Because French and English are so close, and both are intimately in Mallarmé (he taught English for a living), it was like rolling off a log to show that his own poetry reflected these effects ("ronds abolis en d'autres ronds," for smoke-rings, and so forth). Valéry, in an essay, and Claudel, in a recorded interview, saw these effects—in sound and/or shape—as the main key to his poetics. Leading critics, for example, Guy Michaud and Jean-Pierre Richard, endorsed my findings in books on the poet. Curiously, another well-known commentator, Gérard Genette, in *Mimologiques*, documents such practice in dozens of figures starting with Plato (*Cratylus*), running through Hugo, Proust, and Claudel, but denies it in Mallarmé! I pointed out the grossness of this error in *Tel Quel* and received some heartening support. Genette lambasted me back in *Poétique*, condescendingly. Well, a subsequent article of mine demonstrated the parallel poetics in Richard Wilbur, almost letter for letter. Wilbur in a gallant postcard blessed the proceedings.

That kind of hard confirmation does not occur very often. The only comparable one in my own experience happened when

Mondor, although he knew I was working on the *Coup de Dés* using his collection of letters, gave the notebook of "Le Livre," directly bearing on the project, to a French scholar he knew, without informing me. When the scholar published the material, I trembled with fear as I cut the pages. Hallelujah! At every turn, the text verified my hard-won discoveries; whole sentences duplicated word for word ones I had made up to render the poet's meanings.

None of this, of course, will sway certain minds. Barbara Johnson, for example, in a much-reprinted essay, claims that Mallarmé uses the word "azur" as a deliberate cliché, in *L'Azur*. Subsequently, I queried, publicly, why, if this was so, was it one of his favorite words; he included it in poems such as *L'Après-midi d'un Faune*, written years later (Valéry found it equally indispensable for his masterly "Palme"). For a good ear and eye, the poetic reason is clear. So is the predictability of "deconstructive" readings like hers .

In a review many years ago, Edith Kern made convincing connections between the visions of Mallarmé and Heidegger, who was himself aware of his French predecessor and occasionally quotes him. One immediately sees the commonality of the search for pure Being, the paradoxical reverse (as in Plato's *Symposium*): earthiness, concreteness, Eros. Altogether, the bias for *poetic* wisdom, as in Hoelderlin.

Earlier I noted the connection between Heidegger's remarks on Van Gogh's "shoey shoes" (in "The Origin of the Work of Art")—implying an essential referent—and Mallarmé's comparable depth of imagery. An equally significant bond is tetrapolarity (as a phase of polypolarity). In "The Thing," Heidegger writes "earth and sky, divinities and mortals—being at one with one another of their own accord—belong together by way of the singleness of the united fourfold. Each of the four mirrors in its own way the presence of the others."

That is exactly what Mallarmé had noted in his sketch of Drama. He groups four terms, "Théatre," "Héros," "Idée," and "Hymne" around a node: "Drame ... Mystère." Obviously, Hero is to Theater (his earth-site, cosmically) as Idea is to the Hymn that embodies it. Mallarmé observes these relations and adds "cela forme un tout."

In Heidegger's formulation ("equation" as Mallarmé puts it), it is evident that a polarity of up-down is crossed by a polarity of nonpersonal (earth-sky) versus personal (divinity-mortal). In sum, a four-polar (tetrapolar) scheme in which one polarity reflects—is and is not—the other.

But Heidegger came to this insight very late in his own game and very long after Mallarmé's originary breakthrough, in the 1860s. And Heidegger's penetration reaches this peak only in this one text, whereas in Mallarmé it is widely disseminated throughout his oeuvre, from late adolescence on.

Like Tolstoy, who attacked him in print—Mallarmé replied very graciously, in an interview—they were really brothers under the skin, as is poignantly patent in "Confrontation" and "Conflit"—the French genius put life beyond any oeuvre, including his own. That, to me, is his true greatness. He said of Gauguin: "One doesn't have the right to abandon one's children, even to found a religion." What points up his difference from Heidegger in a very human way is his wistful offer (expressed in a conversation with his friend Thadée Natanson) to go pick up Dreyfus in his little sailboat.

Contributors

ANNA BALAKIAN was Professor Emerita of French and Comparative Literature (Chair), New York University and Director of the Symbolist Institute and author of numerous works on Symbolism, Surrealism, and world poetry. She died in late 1997.

WILLIAM CARPENTER's essay on Mallarmé won the annual Honors award (including publication) at Stanford University. He has a Ph.D. in Comparative Literature, Princeton University, and is the author of *Death and Marriage*, on Joyce and Mallarmé (Garland Publishers, New York, 1988). He is currently a lawyer practicing in San Francisco.

MARY ANN CAWS is Professor and Chair of Romance Languages and Comparative Literature, Graduate Center, City University of New York, and was former president of the Modern Language Association. She is the author of many works on Mallarmé, Char, Reverdy, Surrealism, modern art, and poetry.

ROBERT GREER COHN is Professor Emeritus of French, Stanford University, and the author of nine books on Mallarmé, one on Rimbaud, and various others. He is the Founding editor of Yale French Studies.

ALBERT COOK is Professor Emeritus of Comparative Literature, Brown University. He is the author of books on ancient Greek and Hebrew writers, Shakespeare, French classical drama, modern poetry and theater, the novel, history, and cultural history, as well as many books of poetry.

MICHEL DEGUY is a leading French poet of our time and author of many volumes of poetry and criticism. He has taught French literature and philosophy at various universities and was the former president of the Collège international de philosophie.

ROMAN DOUBROVKINE is the author of a volume of translations of Mallarmé, in Russian. A study of the poet's presence in Russia is forthcoming.

JOHN FELSTINER is Professor of English and Comparative Literature, Stanford University and the author of prize-winning books on Max Beerbohm, Neruda, and Celan.

KENNETH FIELDS is Professor of English, Stanford University, currently in the Creative Writing Program. He has published six volumes of poetry and numerous critical essays, and a novel is forthcoming.

GERALD GILLESPIE is Professor of German Studies and Comparative Literature, Stanford University and president of the International Association of Comparative Literature. He is the author of books on Tieck, German Baroque poetry, and Renaissance themes; and is the editor of a work on Romantic Drama and other comparatist compendiums. He has written wide-ranging essays on world literature, which have often been reprinted.

JUDD HUBERT is Professor Emeritus of French, University of California at Irvine. He has written books on Baudelaire, Racine, Molière, Corneille, and Shakespeare, as well as essays on Mallarmé.

TAKEO KAWASE is Assistant Professor of Literature, Waseda University, Japan. His essay was selected by the Mallarmé Circle of Japan for submission to this volume.

JULIA KRISTEVA is Professor and Director of the Ecole doctorale des Langues, Littératures et Civilisations, Paris VII (Diderot). She is the author of many works on linguistics, semiotics, literature, art, cultural history, and psychoanalysis. A practicing analyst, she has published two novels.

CHARLES LYONS is Professor of Drama and Comparative Literature and Chair of the Drama Department, Stanford University. He is the author of books on Shakespeare, Ibsen, Brecht, and Beckett, and has directed many plays.

WALTER MARTIN is the distinguished translator of Baudelaire (published at Carcanet) and proprietor of the well-known avant-garde bookstore, Chimaera, Palo Alto, California.

OCTAVIO PAZ is the Mexican Nobel Laureate of Literature and the author of many volumes of poetry, literary criticism, and cultural criticism.

MICHAEL PREDMORE is Professor of Spanish Language and Literature and former Chair at Stanford University. He has published extensively books and articles on Juan Ramon Jiménez.

ALBERT SONNENFELD is Professor of French and Chair of the Department of French and Italian, University of Southern California. He is the author of books on Corbière, French Catholic novelists, and major essays on Mallarmé

PATRICIA TERRY is Professor of French, University of California at San Diego. A Medievalist with a strong interest in the modern field as well as Japanese literature, she is the author, editor, or translator of various works, including one on Mallarmé in collaboration with Mary Anne Caws.